GÖBEKLI TEPE

GENESIS OF THE GODS

GÖBEKLI TEPE
GENESIS OF THE GODS

The Temple of the Watchers
and the Discovery of Eden

ANDREW COLLINS

Bear & Company
Rochester, Vermont • Toronto, Canada

Bear & Company
One Park Street
Rochester, Vermont 05767
www.BearandCompanyBooks.com

Bear & Company is a division of Inner Traditions International

Library of Congress Cataloging-in-Publication Data

Collins, Andrew, 1957–
  Göbekli Tepe: genesis of the gods : the Temple of the Watchers and the discovery of
Eden / Andrew Collins.
      pages cm
  Includes bibliographical references and index.
  ISBN 978-1-59143-142-8 (paperback) — ISBN 978-1-59143-835-9 (e-book)
  1. Göbekli Tepe Site (Turkey) 2. Excavations (Archaeology)—Turkey—Sanliurfa
Region. 3. Neolithic period—Turkey—Sanliurfa Region. 4. Sanliurfa Region (Turkey)—
Antiquities. 5. Sacred space—Turkey—Sanliurfa Region. 6. Eden. 7. Legends—Turkey—
Sanliurfa Region. 8. Sanliurfa Region (Turkey)—Description and travel. I. Title. II. Title:
Göbekli Tepe.
  DS156.G59C65 2014
  939.4'2—dc23
                                                                      2013046261

Printed and bound in the United States by Versa Press, Inc.

10 9 8 7 6 5 4

Text design by Priscilla H. Baker and layout by Virginia Scott Bowman
This book was typeset in Garamond Premier Pro and Gill Sans with Granjion, Garamond
Premier Pro, and Futura used as display typefaces

To send correspondence to the author of this book, mail a first-class letter to the author c/o
Inner Traditions • Bear & Company, One Park Street, Rochester, VT 05767, and we will
forward the communication, or contact the author directly at **www.andrewcollins.com**.

To Those Who Struggle for Freedom,

In the Garden of Eden,

Past and Present

And to the memory of

Filip Coppens

(1971–2012)

and

Colin Wilson

(1931–2013)

Friends and Genuine Seekers of the Truth

CONTENTS

Part Three
CATASTROPHOBIA

Part Four
CONTACT

Part Five
CONVERGENCE

Part Six
COMPLETION

ACKNOWLEDGMENTS

First, I would like to thank those who have been involved in providing visionary thoughts and information that helped inspire the creation of this current work. They include Richard Ward, David Southwell, Debbie Cartwright, Bernard G., Graham Phillips, and Catja de Lorenzo. I would also like to express my gratitude to Rodney and Joan Hale, for their indelible help in making sure my life continues; Storm Constantine and Jim Hibbert, for putting up with me in their home for over a month; Graham Hancock and Santha Faiia, for the wonderful introduction, and their precious time and help; and Greg and Lora Little, for their constant friendship and support.

In addition to this, I would like to thank Jonathan Bright, for his exchanges on the Greek language; Alberto Forgione, for the cover illustration; Idris Gurkin, for his friendship and kind help as a translator and guide in Turkey; Gülüzar and Hıdır Çelik, for their hospitality in Paradise; Catherine Hale, for her line editing and suggestions; Barbara Hand Clow, for the use of her brilliant term *catastrophobia;* J. L. Katzman of Aggsbach's Paleolithic Blog, for permission to use pictures; Suna Köse, for her invaluable help in finding me local contacts in eastern Turkey; Janet Morris, for her archive research into the more obscure topics under discussion here; Raffi Kojian, of the AniOnline forum, Gagik Avagyan, and Sunny Keshishian Ross, for their Armenian language translations and advice; Russell M. Hossain, for his wonderful 3-D sculpts; Professor Klaus Schmidt, for agreeing to answer my questions and permitting me to explore Göbekli Tepe; Dr. Harald Hauptmann, for his help regarding the excavations at Nevalı Çori; and Michael Tazzar, for his research discussions.

I would also like to extend a big thank-you to all the others who have helped me during the writing of this book, including Eileen Buchanan, Yvan Cartwright, Adam Crowl, Hakan Dalkus, Amadeus Diamond, Kelly Delaney Stacy, Adriano Forgione, Dawn Forgione, Stephen Gawtry, Richard D. Kingston, Peter Knight, Ian Lawton, Yuri Leitch, Chris Nemmo, Hugh Newman, Chris Ogilvie Herald, Khanna Omarkhali, Graham Phillips, Nigel Skinner-Simpson, Alby Stone, Geoff Stray, Alan Todd, Paul Weston and Rachel Blake, Leon and Lisa Flower, Pino Morelli and Roberta Formoso, Matt Kyd and Renny Djunaedi, Brent and Joan Raynes, Mark and Michelle Rosney, Buster and Abigail Todd, Bob Trubshaw and Judi Holliday, Caroline Wise and Michael Staley, Philippe and Domenique Ullens, John Wilding and Esther Smith, and staff at the Henge Shop, Avebury. Finally, I want to say a massive thank you to Olatundji Akpo-Sani, Kelly Bowen, Kevin Dougherty, Jon Graham, John Hays, Erica B. Robinson, Peri Swan, Jessie Wimett, Chanc VanWinkle Orzell and all the team at Inner Traditions/Bear & Company for being so patient with me over the past couple of years. It is very much appreciated.

NOTE ON DATING
SYSTEM USED

The long-held dating system of BC (before Christ) and AD (*anno Domini,* "in the year of the Lord") is used in preference to more modern forms, such as BCE (before the common era) and CE (of the common era). Occasionally BP (before the present) and KYA (thousand years ago) are used when expressing events of the past. All dates provided by the process of radiocarbon dating are recalibrated unless otherwise stated.

ILLUSTRATION CREDITS

Abbreviations

L = left-hand image

C = center image

R = right-hand image

Figure credits

Harald Hauptmann/Deutsches Archäologisches Institut, 1.2, 1.3, 1.4, 2.2R

Catherine Hale/Rodney Hale/Andrew Collins, 1.1

Rodney Hale/Andrew Collins, 1.5, 2.1, 3.1, 3.2L, 6.3, 7.1, 7.3, 8.1R and 8.1L, 8.2L,
9.4, 9.5, 10.4C, 10.5, 13.1, 19.1, 21.3R, 22.1, 23.1, 27.1, 27.2, 27.3, 28.1, 28.2,
33.3R, 36.1, 39.2

Michelle Rosney, 2.2L

Storm Constantine, 4.2, 9.3

Yuri Leitch, 6.1

Robert Braidwood/Halet Çambel/Univ. of Istanbul/Univ. of Chicago, 7.2

Greg Little, 8.3

Billie Walker John, 9.1, 32.1L, 37.3

Gaziantep Archaeological Museum, 10.2

J. L Katzman/www.aggsbach.de, 52B

Deutsche Archäologisches Institut, 52A & 52C

Russell M. Hossain, 26.1, 32.1R

Google Earth/DigitalGlobe 2013, 39.1

All other illustrations are from the author's collection and are thus copyright the
author of this work.

Color Plate Credits

Caroline Wise/Rodney Hale, Plate 25

J. L Katzman/www.aggsbach.de, Plate 25

Rodney Hale, Plate 26

All other plates are copyright the author.

INTRODUCTION

By Graham Hancock

The new millennium promised much—the rising of Atlantis, the Second Coming of Christ, and the discovery of the Hall of Records in Egypt. Yet those of a New Age persuasion who had waited patiently for this all-important date were to be sadly disappointed. Even so, an archaeological discovery brought to the world's attention for the first time in 2000[1] is now poised to make up for any sense of anticlimax that might have accompanied the millennial nonevent.

I speak of Göbekli Tepe, a megalithic complex of incredible beauty and importance located close to the ancient city of Şanlıurfa in southeast Turkey. Here, quietly, since 1995, a series of stone enclosures of immense sophistication, each containing T-shaped pillars up to 18 feet (5.5 meters) tall and weighing as much as 16.5 US tons (15 metric tonnes), is being uncovered on a mountain platform close to the western termination of the Anti-Taurus range.

Carved into the faces of the dozens of stone pillars and freestanding monoliths uncovered so far is a virtual menagerie of strange creatures that populated the world when these mysterious monuments were constructed between twelve thousand and ten thousand years ago. Foxes, wolves, lions, snakes, aurochs, hyena, ibex, and boars are seen alongside insects, arachnids, and various species of bird, including crane, vulture, flamingo, and a flightless bird with the likeness of a dodo.

The quality and style of Göbekli Tepe's strange carved art are at once breathtaking and mesmeric, a fact made even more incredible in the knowledge

1

that we are told the complex was built by simple hunter-gatherer communities that thrived in an age before the emergence of subsistence agriculture and animal husbandry.

NEOLITHIC REVOLUTION

Professor Klaus Schmidt, the forward-thinking German archaeologist in charge of excavations at Göbekli Tepe, now believes that the Neolithic revolution came about as a result of the creation of megalithic complexes of this kind across southeast Turkey, which forms part of what archaeologists refer to as the *triangle d'or,* or golden triangle. Schmidt proposes that the many hundreds of people involved in the construction and maintenance of the enclosures at Göbekli Tepe would quickly have depleted locally available food resources.

Add to this the thousands of "pilgrims" who would descend on the site for clan gatherings and other forms of ceremonial activity, and it is clear that another, more plentiful supply of food was required—one that could be provided year in year out, ad infinitum. Hence, subsistence agriculture rapidly emerged in the form of the domestication of wild species of wheat and rye. This required the hunter-gatherers of the region to become settled farmers and pastoralists living in more permanent environments, which gradually emerged as the first towns and villages of the Neolithic age.

Evidence of this transition from hunter-gatherer to settled farmer in southeast Turkey comes from the discovery by geneticists that sixty-eight modern strains of wheat derive from a form of wild wheat called einkorn that thrives to this day on the slopes of an extinct volcano named Karaca Dağ, which lies some 50 miles (80 kilometers) to the northeast of Göbekli Tepe.

All this was occurring in the Near East as much as two thousand years before the flowering of the first major city complexes at places such as Çatal Höyük and Aşıklı Höyük in what is today central Turkey. They emerged as part of the rapid expansion of the Neolithic revolution, which after embracing the Central Anatolian Plain very quickly reached Eastern Europe. The revolution moved southward also into the Levant, where forms of protoagriculture already existed, and eastward into Iran, Central Asia, and eventually India and Pakistan, home of the Indus Valley civilization. Schmidt is in no doubt that Göbekli Tepe was one of the key points of origin of the Neolithic revolution, meaning that for our present civilization at least this is where history begins.

GÖBEKLI TEPE
IN CONTEXT

Before going any further, it is important to place Göbekli Tepe in context with what is known about the emergence of the civilized world. Its earliest enclosures, which are by far the most sophisticated, existed as much as seven thousand years before the construction of Stonehenge in southern England, built around 3000 BC. Yet having said this, mounting evidence indicates that the Stonehenge we see today, with its familiar sarsen trilithons, Heel Stone alignment toward the midsummer sunrise, and bluestone horseshoe of standing stones, is simply the final phase of an evolution that began with the creation of a Mesolithic complex as early as 8000 BC. Who was responsible for this proto-Stonehenge thousands of years before the arrival on British shores of the first Neolithic farmers remains a mystery. Whatever the answer, the fact that this early date of construction coincides with the final abandonment of Göbekli Tepe must raise a few eyebrows and suggests there might have been a much greater communication network between prehistoric cultures than is currently accepted by scholars.

EGYPT'S FIRST TIME

Göbekli Tepe is also a full seven thousand years older than the conventional dates attributed to the construction of the Great Pyramid and its neighbors on Egypt's famous plateau at Giza. Even if we accept these monuments as the product of Egypt's pharaonic age, the evidence presented both by me and my colleague Robert Bauval in a number of our books suggests very strongly that much earlier structures must have existed in the Nile Valley during a mythical age referred to by the dynastic Egyptians as Zep Tepi, the First Time. It is a time when the gods themselves—Osiris, Isis, Seth, Horus, Thoth, and others—are said to have walked the earth.

An obvious marker of this age of the gods is the Great Sphinx, the leonine monument that sits on the eastern edge of the plateau at Giza—its gaze fixed toward the eastern horizon, where the sun rises at the time of the equinoxes.

During the mid-1990s convincing evidence was put forward by Boston geologist Dr. Robert Schoch and his colleague John Anthony West to suggest that the Sphinx is not the product of the Fourth Dynasty, when pharaohs such as Khufu, Khafre, and Menkaure built the surrounding pyramid complexes, but dates to a much earlier epoch of humankind. It might even be possible that this timeless monument was originally created to gaze at its celestial counterpart, the constellation of Leo, when that noble asterism last housed the equinoctial sun between the eleventh millennium BC and the ninth millennium BC.

Such a realization, if verified, would make the Sphinx pretty much contemporary with Göbekli Tepe, which lies at a distance of around 700 miles (1,100 kilometers) from Egypt's Nile Valley.

LION PILLAR BUILDING

It is therefore a matter of great interest that there are striking carvings of advancing lions on the inner faces of twin pillars in an east-west aligned enclosure at Göbekli Tepe dated to the ninth millennium BC. Called the "Lion Pillars Building," the structure's leonine pillars form a gateway at its eastern end, their advancing beasts appearing to rear out of the equinoctial horizon.

As Andrew Collins points out elsewhere,[2] there is every possibility that to the Göbekli builders this leonine art not only signified the blood-red might of the sun (like the lion-headed goddesses of ancient Egypt), but also the influence of the constellation of Leo, the celestial lion, as it rose in the predawn light of the spring equinox.

So the same inspiration behind the construction of the Great Sphinx might also have been present at Göbekli Tepe, leading us to ask whether there is a real connection between these two distant places. If so, was the emergence of high culture in both the Nile Valley and southeast Turkey related in some manner to the creation of proto-Stonehenge by an unknown culture that thrived during the very same epoch? Were all these sites, and many more besides, once connected in some unfathomable manner?

FORGOTTEN CIVILIZATION

In books such as *Fingerprints of the Gods* (1995), *Heaven's Mirror* (1998, authored with my wife, Santha Faiia), and the sequel to *Fingerprints of the Gods,* which I am writing for publication in 2015, I make the case for a global civilization, possessing immense technical sophistication and a profound understanding of our place in the cosmos, that thrived in an age before a terrible cataclysm brought the world to its knees soon after the end of the last ice age.

More than ever before, science is piecing together exactly what occurred during this global catastrophe, which is now firmly dated to ca. 10,900–10,800 BC. It is a moment in time known to paleoclimatologists as the Younger Dryas horizon, which defines the boundary between the Pleistocene geological epoch and the Holocene, which we still live in today.

It was a time also when the glaciers that had covered much of the Northern Hemisphere during the Ice Age began rapidly to readvance, for the Younger Dryas is the name given to a mini ice age that gripped the world for a period of around thirteen hundred years, from approximately 10,900 BC onward, and ended abruptly around the time the first major enclosures were under construction at Göbekli Tepe, ca. 9600–9500 BC.

It seems certain, now, that the cause of this worldwide catastrophe was a large comet that fragmented into thousands of pieces as it entered the upper atmosphere. Each fragment rained down on the earth, causing unimaginable detonations that pulverized vast swathes of land across the planet. Not only did this terrible cataclysm trigger the onset of the Younger Dryas mini ice age and with it the extinction of the Pleistocene megafauna, including the mammoth, mastodon, toxodon, great camel, and great sloth, but it also devastated the world's human population. The worst hit areas were on the American continent. Here the impact blasts, each one as powerful as a small atomic bomb, were more widespread than anywhere else.

CATASTROPHOBIA

Andrew, in this groundbreaking book, proposes that Göbekli Tepe was built as a response to the aftermath of this global cataclysm. The earliest enclosures were created, he postulates, by a hunter-gatherer populace still in fear of another comet impact, even though several hundred years had elapsed since the final reverberations of this catastrophic event.

Each structure, with its beautifully carved stones, was built with the specific purpose of preserving cosmic order through shamanic interactions with the unseen world. This was achieved using an idealized cosmology, envisaged as a sky pole, or umbilicus, linking earth and heaven. In this way the hunter-gatherers, under the instruction of a ruling elite, were able to maintain the status quo of the cosmos and prevent further attacks on the sky pole, the axis of heaven, from a cosmic trickster in the guise of a supernatural fox or wolf.

It was this absolute fear of another cosmic catastrophe, something that visionary writer Barbara Hand Clow refers to so aptly as *catastrophobia,* that caused the hunter-gatherers of southeast Turkey to suddenly start supersizing their cult buildings into the beautiful megalithic structures we see today.

It was also this obsession with preventing another cataclysm that was responsible, at least in part, for the collective amnesia that has allowed us to filter out and reject the existence of the proposed global civilization that thrived in the epoch immediately prior to the Younger Dryas Boundary impact event, as scientists call it today.

Yet some expression of the complex cosmology existing during this former golden age is almost certainly locked into the design, proportion, and carved art at Göbekli Tepe. It thus becomes a virtual Noah's ark in stone, bridging the gap between a former age of enlightenment and the emergence down on the Mesopotamia Plain of some of the oldest known civilizations of this current world age, most obviously those of Sumer, Akkad, Assyria, and Babylon.

ABODE OF THE GODS

The mythologies of these great civilizations speak clearly of wisdom bringers and creator gods responsible for the formation of the earliest towns, cities, canals, walled enclosures, and irrigation channels—and even of humankind. Named as the Anunnaki, these anthropomorphic, or humanlike, gods are said to have emerged from a primeval mound called Duku, situated on a cosmic mountain named Kharsag, beneath which was the world of mortal human beings.

Klaus Schmidt believes that Göbekli Tepe had a direct impact on the myths and legends regarding the Anunnaki, and that the site could be the role model for the original Duku mound. Indeed, he goes further, as Andrew points out in this book, by hinting at a connection between Göbekli Tepe and biblical traditions concerning the Garden of Eden, and perhaps even the very human angels of Hebrew mythological tradition known as the Watchers.

CULT OF THE VULTURE

A deep look at the description of the Watchers and their offspring, the Nephilim, in ancient Jewish texts such as the book of Enoch makes it clear that these mythical creatures were not incorporeal angels, but flesh and blood human beings with very distinct shamanistic qualities. They are occasionally said to wear dark, iridescent cloaks, or feather coats, and on occasion they take flight like birds, echoing the presence among the earliest proto-Neolithic communities of the Near East of a cult of death and rebirth focused on scavenger birds such as the vulture.

As Andrew points out, at Göbekli Tepe, as well as at the nine-thousand-year-old Neolithic city of Çatal Höyük in southern-central Turkey, there are abstract representations of vultures with articulated legs. Either they are shamans adorned as birds or bird spirits with anthropomorphic features.

Were these shamans of the early Neolithic age role models for the Watchers of Enochian tradition? Are the Watchers a vague memory of those behind the construction of proto-Neolithic complexes, amongst them Göbekli Tepe in southeast Turkey? Did the Watchers really introduce this current world age to forbidden knowledge carried over from a global civilization that once thrived in an antediluvian world?

FROM THE
ASHES OF ANGELS

These are questions we are only now beginning to ask for the first time. Yet they were asked as far back as 1996 by Andrew Collins in his groundbreaking book *From the Ashes of Angels*. What is more, there is little question that Andrew was one of the first writers to realize the greater significance of Göbekli Tepe, bringing it to the attention of the mysteries community as early as 2004. It is for this reason that his book *Göbekli Tepe: Genesis of the Gods* is such a masterwork, for it is the culmination of nearly twenty years of Andrew's original research into the origins of the Neolithic revolution and its relationship to Hebrew traditions concerning the location of the Garden of Eden and the human truth behind the Watchers of the book of Enoch.

In a testimonial written to accompany the publication of *From the Ashes of Angels,* I said that Andrew had "put important new facts before the public concerning the mysterious origins of human civilization." I stand by this statement and add only that with his vast knowledge of the subject under discussion, there is no one better suited to reveal Göbekli Tepe's place in history today.

Graham Hancock, born in Edinburgh, Scotland, is a British writer and journalist. His books, including *Fingerprints of the Gods, The Sign and The Seal,* and *Heaven's Mirror,* have sold more than five million copies worldwide and have been translated into twenty-seven languages. His public lectures, radio, and television appearances have allowed his ideas to reach a vast audience, identifying him as an unconventional thinker who raises controversial questions about humanity's past.

NOTES

1. Michael Zick, "Der älteste Tempel der Welt," *bild der wissenschaft* 8 (2000): 60–66.
2. Collins, Andrew, "Göbekli Tepe and the Rebirth of Sirius," 2013, www.andrew collins.com/page/articles/Gobekli_Sirius.htm (accessed January 13, 2014).

Also see the Notes and Bibliography of this book for further references related to the material in this introduction

PROLOGUE

IN QUEST OF ANGELS

September 16, 2013. Ever since kindergarten I have had a strange fascination with angels. Back then I was forced to endure Sunday school on a regular basis, and what I heard about Moses parting the Red Sea or Jesus feeding the five thousand with just a few loaves and fishes intrigued me. I loved hearing about miracles. Yet the lessons were always long and dreary. I wished only to be in the park, kicking about a soccer ball with my dad and brother.

Then one day my Sunday school teacher, a rather stern-faced woman, related how the Old Testament prophet Abraham received into his presence three angels. They sat with him beneath the shade of a tree, where they talked and ate food together.

I knew about angels, those with radiant bodies and beautiful wings, but what the teacher was implying seemed at odds with this ethereal view. Not only did angels seem to function in this world, but they could also be tangibly real. What's more, people could talk to them and perhaps even become their friends. This was an incredible revelation to me.

Abraham's meeting with the angels was not lingered on, causing me to raise my hand and ask: "Please miss, what are angels?" To which I was told: "They are messengers of God."

I needed to know more, so I asked the teacher to elaborate further. She just looked at me and said, slowly and decisively: "There is nothing to be explained—they are the angels of God."

9

For her, the existence of angels seemed arbitrary, so my curiosity bore no meaning or relevance. Yet clearly it mattered to me.

It was a moment in my life I shall never forget. Somehow it fired my interest in angels as corporeal creatures and was one of the reasons I was here in southeast Turkey, making my way through sun-baked, dusty streets looking for answers. All around me were market vendors plying their wares, stalls brimming with ripe melons, trays of tomatoes, and all manner of household goods sold at very competitive prices.

Amid the incessant din, I gazed up at an age-old stone archway, the only opening through a more or less intact wall of some considerable size. Beyond it, as far as the eye could see, were the ruins of an ancient city razed to the ground by the Mongol hoards in 1271. Known as Carrhae to the Romans, this sprawling Mesopotamian metropolis—a commercial center at the crossroads of several key trading routes—is better known by the name Harran.

All that remains of the ancient city today are a scattering of walls; a massive stone arch marking the entrance to the now-vanished Great Mosque; a ruined castle, built in the early Islamic period on the site of a pagan temple dedicated to the Mesopotamian moon god Sin; and a colossal stone structure, rising to a height of 110 feet (33 meters) and known locally as the Astronomical Tower. Although it too once formed part of the Great Mosque—or Paradise Mosque, as it was more correctly known—legend asserts that the Harranites, the inhabitants of Harran, were keen astronomers who used the tower's summit to observe and record the movement of the stars.

Although the Harranites acknowledged the faith of Islam following the Arab conquest, many belonged to an altogether different faith—one that came to be known as Sabaeanism. These curious people worshipped the sun, moon, and planets, which they honored in temples built specifically for this purpose. In addition to this, they saw the Pole Star, and the northern night sky in general, as the direction of the Primal Cause, of God himself, a fact celebrated each year in a grand festival known as the Mystery of the North. This fascination with the Pole Star was a belief shared by other religious sects of the region including the Ismaili Brethren of Purity, the Mandaeans of Iraq and Iran, and the angel-worshipping Yezidi, all of whom owe at least some part of their existence to the Sabaeans of Harran.

In addition to being star worshippers, the Harranites are said to have collated the sacred writings of Greco-Roman Egypt attributed to Hermes

Trismegistus, the Thrice Great Hermes. Following the destruction of Harran in the thirteenth century, this important corpus of religious literature known as the Hermetica was carried into Europe, where, some one and a half centuries later, it became the spiritual backbone to the Italian Renaissance and, with it, a revival of all things Egyptian.

Yet before even the Sabaeans flourished in Harran, the city was connected with the earliest events of the Bible. Here the prophet Abraham and his family stayed prior to their departure to Canaan, God's Promised Land. Local tradition asserts that the prophet hailed from the nearby city of Şanlıurfa, the original "Ur of the Chaldees." So strong is this belief that even today thousands of Kurdish Muslims arrive in the city, anciently known as Orfa, Orhay, or Edessa, in order to visit a cave shrine said to be the birthplace of the great prophet.

According to medieval belief, Abraham arrived at Harran and at once set about converting the local population to his monotheistic faith. Yet the Harranites claimed their teachings were older, having derived from Seth, the son of Adam, and Enoch, a later antediluvian patriarch. Some of the Harranites did convert to Abraham's faith and departed with him to Canaan. Those who did not are said to have remained in the neighborhood of Harran, declaring that "we acknowledge the religion of Seth, Idris (Enoch) and Noah."[1]

So much did the inhabitants of Harran honor Abraham's presence in the city that a temple was set up to him and his father, Terah, which apparently stood 2 parsangs (around 7 miles, or 11 kilometers) southeast of the city, close to the border with Syria.[2] Abraham was the perceived father of the Jewish people, and his descendants were responsible for bringing together the source material for the book of Genesis, the first book of the Old Testament, traditionally ascribed to Moses the Lawgiver.

Everywhere around Harran are sites associated with stories from the book of Genesis. On Cudi Dağ (Mount al-Judi), in the mountains to the east of Harran, Noah's ark is said to have made first landfall after the waters of the Great Flood receded. Here too Noah established his first post-Flood settlement, leaving his son Shem to continue his journey into the Eastern Taurus Mountains, where also Seth, the son of Adam, lived after his father and mother's expulsion from the Garden of Eden (see chapters 35 and 37). Even Harran itself, where Abraham dwelled with his family, had more ancient biblical connections, as tradition insists that Cainan, a grandson of Shem, founded the city. He was the originator of Chaldaism, the knowledge of the stars as practiced by the Sabaeans of Harran.[3]

More significantly, the book of Genesis records that the primordial Garden where Adam and Eve, the First Couple, existed in a state of innocence and bliss before the time of the Fall was located at the source of the four rivers of Paradise, two of which can easily be identified as the Tigris and Euphrates (see chapter 27). They take their rise in the mountains to the northeast of Harran. Here somewhere lies the original Garden of Eden, tended over by the angels of God, returning me to the pressing questions that had preoccupied my childhood: Who or what are angels? Where did they come from, and did they have some kind of earthly tangibility?

As I climbed Harran's giant occupational mound, which rises above the ruined city, and stared out toward the mesmeric Astronomical Tower, I felt I was getting closer to some real answers. For even as the first Bible stories were being played out across the region, Harran was already extremely old. Archaeological fieldwork has shown that its earliest inhabitants occupied the site as much as eight thousand years ago,[4] having arrived here from another occupational mound, located just 6 miles (10 kilometers) away, which dates back an incredible ten thousand years.[5]

Known as Tell Idris, the very name of this prehistoric mound reveals its association not just with the earliest events of the Bible but also with the angelic beings said to have guarded the Garden of Eden. For Idris is the Arabic name for the antediluvian patriarch Enoch, the great-grandfather of Noah. He is accredited with the authorship of one of the strangest and most mystifying religious texts ever written.

Called the book of Enoch, it recounts how Enoch, while resting in his bed one night, is approached by two strange beings of angelic appearance. Named Watchers (Hebrew *'îrîn*), they ask him to accompany them on a tour of the Seven Heavens, one of which includes the Garden of Righteousness, where the four rivers of Paradise take their rise, while another leads to the abode of the angels.

When in the Watchers' heavenly settlement, Enoch is shown a prison in which a whole group of these angelic beings are incarcerated. On asking what crime they have committed, the patriarch is informed that two hundred of their number disobeyed the laws of heaven by descending among mortal kind and taking wives for themselves. As a consequence, these women gave birth to giant offspring called Nephilim (a Hebrew word meaning "those who fell" or the "fallen ones").

More significantly, the book of Enoch relates how the rebel Watchers, who are described as extremely tall (like "trees"), with pale and ruddy skin, powerful eyes, white hair, and long, viper-like faces (see chapter 32), are said to have taught their mortal wives the arts and sciences of heaven. For this heinous crime they were rounded up and incarcerated.

Although these stories are understandably dismissed as allegorical fantasy by theologians and Bible scholars alike, there is an air about them that tells of a forgotten event in humanity's distant past—one connected integrally with Harran and the surrounding region, for it was here that the Neolithic revolution began.

On the upper reaches of the Euphrates and Tigris rivers, in the region that is today made up of eastern Turkey, northern Syria, northern Iraq, and northwest Iran, animal husbandry occurred for the first time, as did the domestication of wild cereals and the first metalworking and smelting. Here too some of the earliest baked and fired statuettes were produced, along with the construction of rectilinear and curvilinear buildings, some incorporating decorated standing stones and steles. With them came the first construction of terrazzo mortar floors, the first evidence for brewing beer, and perhaps even the first use of grapes to produce wine.

In the same region, as early as 8000 BC, diamond-hard stone drills were employed to pierce holes through large oval beads of carnelian and agate to produce beautiful necklaces, and green malachite powder was first used as a cosmetic to beautify the eyes.

Among the forbidden arts of heaven that the Watchers are said to have gifted mortal kind are the use of metals and metalworking, and the means for women to beautify themselves. They are also said to have provided the first polished mirrors, an interesting fact, as the earliest known mirrors, made of the black volcanic glass obsidian, were manufactured at early Neolithic sites in central Turkey, such as Çatal Höyük and Aşıklı Höyük.

Is it possible that some memory of the prime movers or driving elite behind this great transition in technology and innovation is recalled in the stories of the Watchers providing mortal kind with the rudiments of civilization? Is this what these human angels are—instigators of the Neolithic revolution?

Here at Harran are further clues to this baffling mystery. From the summit of its occupational mound the eye is drawn beyond the Astronomical Tower to the low ridge of mountains that dominates the northern horizon. Amid those peaks and in full sight of the Sabaean city is an archaeological site of incredible importance to world history.

Known as Göbekli Tepe, its existence, and the work currently being carried out there by a dedicated team of specialists, might one day help answer the pressing questions that have haunted me since childhood. Here, on a hilly ridge close to the southernmost limits of the Anti-Taurus Mountains, is the oldest acknowledged monumental architecture anywhere in the world. It takes the form of a series of circular and rectangular stone sanctuaries constructed as early as 9500 BC by an advanced group of hunter-gatherers who might well have been responsible for catalyzing the genesis of civilization in a manner echoing the very human-like activities of the Watchers in the book of Enoch.

Who were the builders of Göbekli Tepe, and what motivated them to construct such extraordinary monuments so soon after the end of the last ice age? What part of the ancient world did they come from, and what did they look like? Is it possible that a memory of their existence was preserved by the peoples of the region and later carried by the descendants of Abraham into the Holy Land, where it inspired the stories of angels trafficking with humankind preserved in religious texts such as the book of Enoch and book of Genesis?

Remarkably, an ancient Hebrew work known as the book of Jubilees, which also tells the story of the Watchers, relates how Cainan, the legendary founder of Harran, uncovered an inscription carved on a stone stela. When translated it was found to contain the antediluvian science of astrology as taught by the Watchers.[6] This knowledge went on to form the basis of the beliefs of the Chaldeans; that is, the pagans of Harran, whose progenitor is said to have been Cainan's father, Arphaxad, the son of Shem and grandson of Noah.[7] The name Arphaxad simply means "Ur of the Chaldees,"[8] taking us back to the site of Abraham's birthplace in nearby Şanlıurfa.

Was the stone stela found by Cainan and said to reveal the astrological knowledge of the Watchers a reference to the beautifully carved T-shaped pillars found at nearby Göbekli Tepe, some of which, as we see in part two of this book, seem to reflect a profound knowledge of the starry heavens during the epoch of their construction? Was this the true source of the Harranites' starry wisdom, adopted from their forerunners, who inhabited Tell Idris and other similar early Neolithic settlements on the Harran Plain as much as ten thousand years ago?

Further linking the Harran region with the Watchers is the belief that the city of Şanlıurfa, where a settlement site belonging to the same culture responsible for Göbekli Tepe was uncovered near Abraham's birthplace during the 1990s, was founded either by the patriarch Enoch[9] or by "Orhay son of Hewya," with *hewya* meaning "serpent."[10] Almost certainly, this serpentine founder of the city is an allusion to the Watchers, who are themselves occasionally described as Serpents (see chapter 34). Was it here, in Şanlıurfa, that Enoch met with the two Watchers who took him on a tour of the Seven Heavens, a mountainous realm that included the Garden of Righteousness?

What exactly was the Garden of Eden, where Adam and Eve are said to have lived in a state of perpetual bliss before the time of the Fall? Was this the true home of the Watchers of the book of Enoch? Could its discovery hold the key to understanding the origins behind humankind's contact with angels during some former age? Did it exist at Göbekli Tepe or somewhere else—in the mountains to the northeast, perhaps, where the four rivers of Paradise take their rise?

Only by understanding the mysteries of Göbekli Tepe would any real answers be forthcoming, and so it is here that our quest must begin, starting with its rediscovery in 1994 by a brilliant-minded German archaeologist, to whom we owe its existence today.

I will ask the reader to bear with me now as I switch from a first person to a third person narrative in order to determine who built Göbekli Tepe, and why. My personal quest is resumed in part four, when a powerful dream initiates a fresh search for the source of the terrestrial Paradise.

It is an intellectual adventure that will culminate not only in the discovery of Eden but also in the realization that the true meaning behind humanity's fall from grace, in the wake of the Neolithic revolution, is integrally bound up with the secret writings of Seth, the son of Adam. These forgotten books of Seth, glimpses of which can be found in Gnostic literature, tell us that in order to truly return to Paradise and partake of the immortality offered by the Tree of Life, we must first become like angels ourselves, as once we were in the Garden of Eden.

PART ONE

Construction

1

A LIFETIME'S WORK

One day in October 1994 Professor Klaus Schmidt, an archaeologist working with the German Archaeological Institute and the University of Heidelberg, made the trek out to a bleak limestone plateau, situated close to the southernmost limits of the Anti-Taurus Mountains, just 8 miles (13 kilometers) northeast of the Turkish city of Şanlıurfa. It was a decision that would change his life forever and alter the very way we perceive the rise of civilization in the ancient world.

Schmidt's intention was to inspect a large artificial mound composed of earth and rock debris, which sits on a mountain ridge that rises to a height of just under half a mile (780 meters) above sea level. Stretching away toward the south lay the Harran Plain, where the patriarch Abraham is said to have set out on his journey to the Promised Land some seven thousand years *after* the incredible events that gave rise to the almost alien world that awaited discovery here at Göbekli Tepe, the "hill of the navel."[1]

SITE V52/1

Schmidt knew that as early as 1963 a joint team from the universities of Istanbul and Chicago had visited the site and identified a number of "knolls," or rises, that cover an area of some 3.5 acres (1.44 hectares)—a figure extended to 22 acres (9 hectares) following a geomagnetic survey of the site in 2003.[2]

The 1963 expedition noted that immediately west of Göbekli Tepe's rounded summit prehistoric stone tools lay strewn across a wide area. They belonged to an age when the inhabitants of southeast Anatolia (modern-day Turkey) were making the transition from hunter-gatherers to settled pastoralists and farmers.

The survey team also recorded the presence at Göbekli Tepe (documented as site V52/1) of cut and dressed slabs of limestone bearing evidence of carved relief. Team member Peter Benedict, an anthropologist with the University of Chicago, concluded the fragments came from a lost Byzantine cemetery. It was a decision influenced perhaps by the fact that the local Kurdish community consider the *tepe* or *tell*—these being, respectively, the Turkish and Arabic words for a large artificial mound created by human occupation—as sacred, using it themselves as a cemetery for their dead. At its summit, modern graves lie within a walled enclosure clustered around a single fig-mulberry tree, a sight clearly visible to anyone approaching the mountain from the plain below.

SUBLIME SOPHISTICATION

Göbekli Tepe was not investigated further, with the entire matter being confined to a single report published in 1980.[3] Instead, the joint Istanbul-Chicago team concentrated their efforts on excavating an important early Neolithic site at Çayönü Tepesi, located 4 miles (6 kilometers) southwest of the town of Ergani, northwest of the city of Diyarbakır. Having thrived, in the main, between ca. 8630 BC and 6820 BC, Çayönü is noted for the discovery there of a series of rectangular buildings with distinctive "grill-plan" subfloors composed of low, parallel walls of stone, possibly to allow air to pass freely beneath the main flooring. Here too was found some of the earliest evidence for the use of copper, beaten into shape, not smelted, along with evidence of animal husbandry in the form of pig domestication and the earliest known use of linen fabric, a piece being found still wrapped around an antler.

The site's lead excavators, American archaeologist and anthropologist Robert J. Braidwood (1907–2003) and Turkish academic Dr. Halet Çambel, also came across other examples of advanced building design and technical achievement at Çayönü. In addition to the grill-plan floors, one structure, dubbed the Flagstone Building, was found to possess a floor of polished limestone slabs up to 6.5 feet

(2 meters) in length. Two tall stone pillars stood in the center of the room, with rows of orthostats (stone posts) set up against the interior walls.[4]

Another structure, known as the Terrazzo Building, bore a slightly different, although no less impressive, style of flooring. It consisted of a 16-inch (40 centimeter)-thick setting of terrazzo, a hard, polished surface made from burnt and crushed lime and clay, stained red with a substance called ochre. Into this, two parallel rows of white pebbles had been inserted to create a linear design of simple beauty. Orthostats again lined the interior walls, while a pair of standing stones, like those in the Flagstone Building, had been set up in the middle of the room.

Prior to the discovery of Çayönü, the use of orthostats had been found in just a few rare instances. For instance, at a proto-Neolithic site in northern Iraq named Qermez Dere, located on a south-facing mountain slope overlooking a vast desert expanse known as the Jezirah, stone pillars, their tops carved into the likeness of human shoulders and arms, were found to have stood at the center of two circular buildings with plaster floors. Both structures provided dates in the region of the early tenth millennium BC.[5]

SANGUINE DISCOVERIES

In one of the enclosures at Çayönü archaeologists discovered, both in the walls and beneath the floor, human skulls belonging to around seventy individuals. In one pit excavators came across large numbers of disarticulated human bones, most of them long bones, which, along with the skulls, suggested the presence of no less than 450 individuals. What fate had befallen them, and under what circumstances, remains unclear.

Unsurprisingly, this apparent mortuary structure, which had a round apse at its northern end, became known as the Skull Building, although it was what excavators found on an enormous cut and polished stone slab, 1.1 U.S. tons (about 1 metric tonne) in weight and set up like an altar table, that most disturbed them. On its surface were clear traces of blood from aurochs (an extinct species of wild cattle) *and* humans, in the form of crystals and hemoglobin.[6] Equally disturbing was the discovery next to the stone slab of a vicious-looking flint knife, like something out of an Aztec temple.

Some pressing questions arise regarding the presence of human blood inside Çayönü's cult buildings. Was it the result of human sacrifice or autosacrifice, personal blood-letting like that practiced in pre-Columbian times among Mesoamerican civilizations such as the Aztec and Maya? Perhaps the matter is best left alone until a much clearer picture emerges of what was really going on here. Yet whatever the answer, it would seem that, during the early Neolithic age, beauty, sophistication, and advances in technology and architectural design went hand in hand with dark, sanguine activities, just as they would thousands of years later among the peoples of Central and South America.

NEOLITHIZATION

For those who study the prehistory of the Near East, the transitional age between the hunter-gatherers of the late Paleolithic age and the later Neolithic farmers and herders is styled the Pre-Pottery Neolithic, a term devised by British archaeologist Dame Kathleen Kenyon (1906–1978) following her extensive excavations at Jericho in the 1950s. It is a term used much in this book, although in its formative stage this era is described as the proto-Neolithic period, while in Europe this same epoch is called the Mesolithic age (see figure 1.1 on p. 22).

The Pre-Pottery (i.e., preceramic) Neolithic age is split into two separate phases—A and B. The Pre-Pottery Neolithic A (PPNA) is generally seen to have occurred between ca. 9500 BC and 8500 BC, with the Pre-Pottery Neolithic B (PPNB) taking place between ca. 8700 BC and 6000 BC.[7] This marked the appearance of subsistence agriculture; that is, the domestication of plants and cereals, as well as the growing of crops on a large scale. Thereafter came the Pottery Neolithic, ca. 6400–4500 BC, when "neolithization" really began. It was an age not just of fired pottery but also of the rapid spread of agriculture from Western Asia into other parts of the ancient world, such as Europe, Central Asia, and the Indus Valley of India and Pakistan.

ARCHAEOLOGICAL MINEFIELD

Professor Klaus Schmidt was mainly concerned with the Pre-Pottery Neolithic on his first visit to Göbekli Tepe. He understood full well why the Joint Istanbul-Chicago Prehistoric Survey Team had focused their attentions on Çayönü instead of better investigating Göbekli Tepe, for, as he said himself: "Time was not ripe to recognize the real importance of this site . . . [so]

Years BC	Geological Period	Suggested Dates	Cultures	Suggested Dates	Zagros/Iraq	Suggested Dates	Anatolia	Suggested dates
19,000								
18,000	Last Glacial Maxim	18,500–17,000 BC	Middle Epi-Paleolithic	18,500–14,500 BC	Zarzian	18,000–11,000 BC		
17,000								
16,000								
15,000			Late Epi-Paleolithic	14,500–9500 BC				
14,000								
13,000			Natufian	12,500–9500 BC				
12,000	Allerød interstadial	12,600–10,600 BC					Abu Hureyra	11,340–5500 BC
11,000	Younger Dryas	10,900–9600 BC					Hallan Çemi	10,250–9600 BC
10,000	Holocene	9500 BC–present	Pre-Pottery Neolithic A	9500–8500 BC			Qermez Dere / Göbekli Tepe	10,050–9650 BC / 9500–8000 BC
9000							Çayönü	8800–7000 BC
8000			Pre-Pottery Neolithic B	8700–6000 BC			Nevalı Çori / Aşıklı Höyük	8500–7000 BC / 8000–7400 BC
7000			Pottery Neolithic	6400–4500 BC			Çatal Höyük	7500–5700 BC
6000					Halaf / Ubaid	6000–5000 BC		
5000			Chalcolithic	4500–3300 BC	Uruk	5000–4100 BC / 4100–2900 BC	Tell Arpachiyah	5200–4500 BC
4000								
3000			Bronze Age	3300–1200 BC	Sumer / Akkad / Assyria / Babylon	2900–1940 BC / 2334–2154 BC / 2300–605 BC / 1894–331 BC		
2000								
1000								

Figure 1.1. Chart showing dates of the Near Eastern cultures, civilizations, and paleoclimatological ages mentioned in this book.

Göbekli Tepe passed into oblivion, and it seems quite clear that no archaeologist returned to the site until the author's visit in 1994."[8]

Thankfully, Schmidt *did* make the decision to visit Göbekli Tepe and see for himself what the site had to offer, and it took him very little time to realize that beneath the huge artificial mound of reddish brown earth and compacted stone chippings, a Pre-Pottery Neolithic complex of immense significance awaited discovery.

Schmidt also realized that the carved stone fragments scattered about Göbekli Tepe were more than simply funerary slabs belonging to some lost Byzantine cemetery. They closely resembled pillars unearthed at another Pre-Pottery Neolithic site, named Nevalı Çori[9] (see figure 1.2), located on a hill slope overlooking a branch of the Euphrates River, halfway between Şanlıurfa and Diyarbakır, some 30 miles (48 kilometers) north-northeast of Göbekli

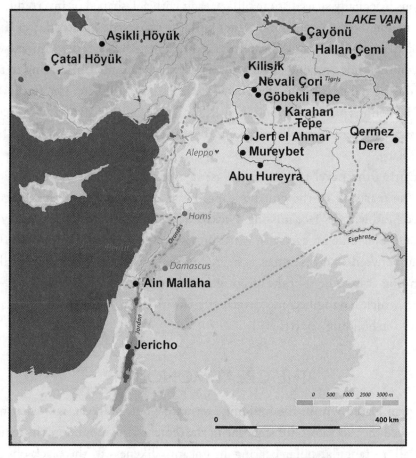

Figure 1.2. Map showing Pre-Pottery Neolithic sites
in southwest Asia mentioned in this book.

Tepe. He knew this because he had worked at the site under the auspices of fellow German archaeologist Dr. Harald Hauptmann from 1983 through to 1992, when the rising waters of the Euphrates submerged Nevalı Çori following the construction of the Atatürk Dam.

THE CULT BUILDING

Nevalı Çori was found to consist of a series of rectangular buildings clustered together to form a village settlement, which thrived between 8500 BC and 7600 BC; that is, from the end of the PPNA into the PPNB period. Among the structures uncovered by Hauptmann and his team was one much grander than the rest. Its rear wall backed up to the hill slope, while its interior walls, made of quarry stone, included a communal benchlike feature. This was divided into sections by equally spaced stone pillars, each with a T-shaped or inverted L-like termination. During one of its earliest building phases, designated Level II and dating to ca. 8400–8000 BC, twelve standing pillars had stood within its walls (two on each side and one in each corner), with the number increasing to thirteen during the next phase, designated Level III, ca. 8000 BC (see figure 1.3). Like its counterpart at Çayönü, Nevalı Çori's megalithic structure possessed a terrazzo floor of burnt lime cement, beneath which was a subfloor of huge stone slabs.

During the Level II building phase, a squared-off niche was constructed into the rear wall of the cult building. Here excavators found an elongated carved head with its face missing. Nicknamed the "skinhead," it is roughly life size and looks like an egg with ears. On its reverse is a highly unusual *sikha,* a long ponytail that resembles a wriggling snake with its head shaped like a mushroom cap. The "skinhead" originated, most probably, from a full-size statue, which having become detached from its body, had been hidden away within the building's north wall.

THE GREAT MONOLITH

The item placed within the building's terrazzo floor, however, was what most compelled the excavators, for standing in the center of the room were the remains of a tall, rectangular pillar bearing an uncanny likeness to the black obsidian monolith that appeared among the apelike creatures at the beginning of Stanley

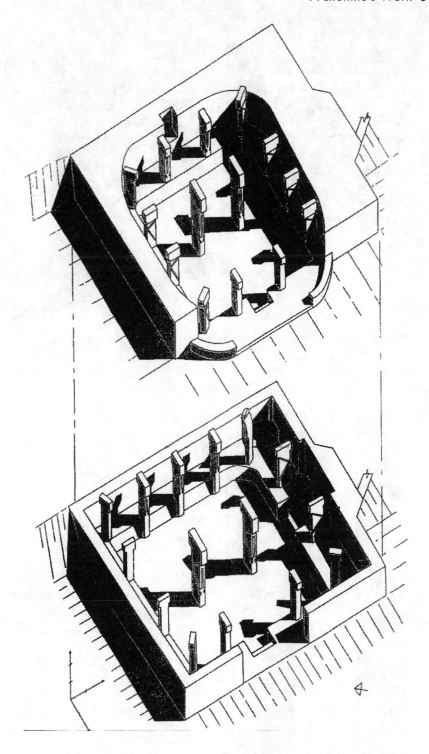

Figure 1.3. Nevalı Çori's cult building, showing cutaways
for Levels II and III, ca. 8400–8000 BC.

Figure 1.4. Nevalı Çori's cult building, showing the surviving central monolith still in situ.

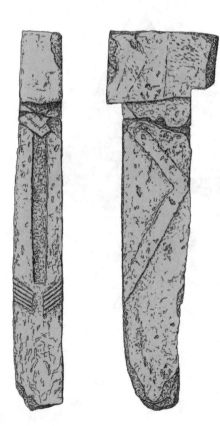

Figure 1.5. One of the stone pillars from Nevalı Çori. Note the stylized arms, hands, stole, and neck pendant.

Kubrick's movie adaptation of Arthur C. Clarke's *2001: A Space Odyssey* (figure 1.4).

The pillar, originally 10 feet (3 meters) high, had been carved to represent an abstract human form. In relief across its two widest faces were thin arms, bent at the elbow, with hands and fingers curling around to its front, narrow edge (see figure 1.5 schematic). Anthropomorphic shaping had previously been noted among the remains of the twelve to thirteen standing pillars that had been erected within the building's four walls, but that displayed on the central pillar was far more accomplished. Above the figure's hands were two parallel grooves, or chiseled vertical lines, clearly meant to represent the double hem of a woven garment, open to the waist, which some have seen as a scarflike stole, similar to that worn by a Catholic priest.

A broken fragment of the same pillar lay nearby. Its base matched the top of the standing remnant, although its upper end was so damaged that no semblance of the individual's head could be discerned. In spite of this, it was clear from the presence of the other stone pillars in the walls that this much larger monolith would once have had a T-shaped termination, creating a hammerlike head. As such, it constituted one of the world's oldest known 3-D representations of the human form.

A hole in the terrazzo floor close to the standing pillar showed that a second monolith must have stood parallel to it, although any trace of its presence had long since disappeared. Like the stone pillars in the walls, the twin pillars perhaps functioned as roof supports, although this is by no means certain. Twin sets of standing pillars had been found in the Flagstone Building and Terrazzo Building at Çayönü. Yet here it was the stone slabs' wider faces, and not one of their narrow sides, that had greeted the entrant approaching from the south.

A PERSONAL DIVINITY

So who or what did the twin pillars represent? Archaeologists at the time suggested they symbolized a "personal divinity."[10] This might have been so, but it did not explain why there were two monoliths side by side or why they faced out toward the cult building's southwesterly placed entrance (the building was found to be oriented almost exactly northeast to southwest). Perhaps the pillars were positioned to greet the entrant, like twin *genii loci* (spirits of the place) guarding the enclosure's inner sanctum. Very likely this presumed liminal, or sacred, area signified an otherworldly environment that existed beyond the mundane world. Indeed, it probably reflected the presence of a parallel realm, a supernatural world, accessible either in death or through the attainment of deathlike trances and other forms of altered states of consciousness, with the aim being to communicate with power animals, great ancestors, and mythical beings.[11]

EXPLORING GÖBEKLI TEPE

Klaus Schmidt had all this in mind as he examined the various carved fragments of "large-scale sculptures"[12] found scattered about Göbekli Tepe. Quickly, he realized that "the entire area had been used for the construction of megalithic architecture, not just a specific part of it."[13] He saw its function as ritual in nature.[14] Indeed, Göbekli Tepe's building structures would, he felt, reflect the same cultic influences as those at Çayönü and Nevalı Çori.

Having seen enough, Schmidt came to a frightening conclusion. If he did not turn around and walk away now, he would be there for the rest of his life. As fate would have it, he decided to stay and commit himself to excavating the site fully, and we can be thankful for Schmidt's decision, as it was afterward discovered that the entire hillside was about to become an open quarry to supply rock for the construction of the new Gaziantep to Mardin highway, a decision that was reversed only when the importance of the archaeological site became known.[15] So we can be pretty sure that without the intervention of this quick-thinking German archaeologist, the world might never have gazed upon the oldest stone temple in the world.

2

MONUMENTAL
ARCHITECTURE

U nder the joint auspices of the German Archaeological Institute and the
Archaeological Museum at Şanlıurfa, Dr. Klaus Schmidt started work
at Göbekli Tepe in 1995. Very soon his team, made up of undergraduates from
German and Turkish universities, as well as fifty local workers of Kurdish,
Turkish, and Arab ethnicity, began making remarkable discoveries. Beneath the
mound's topsoil his team came across stone pillars set vertically into the ground.
Each one was found to have a T-shaped head like those uncovered at Nevalı Çori.

Two principal structures were investigated between 1995 and 1997 at
Göbekli Tepe. One—uncovered immediately west of the solitary fig-mulberry
tree with its tiny walled cemetery of modern graves—was a rectangular enclosure that became known as the Lion Pillar Building because of the discovery at
its eastern end of twin pillars with carved reliefs of leaping lions on their inner
faces (see plate 17). The other was called the Snake Pillar Building.

SNAKE PILLAR BUILDING

The Snake Pillar Building was located beneath the southern slope of the occupational mound, some 50 feet (15 meters) lower in depth than the Lion Pillar

Building. Designated Enclosure A, it sits on the mountain's limestone bedrock, suggesting its extreme age. Excavators found it to contain five T-shaped pillars standing about an arm's length apart from one another. As at Nevalı Çori, they were set within quarry stone walls with stepped benches, a thin layer of clay mortar between each block.

Two pillars stood parallel to each other, with another two placed on the same alignment outside of them; a fifth, south of the central pillars, stood within the perimeter wall, one of its narrow edges facing toward the center of the room (a sixth pillar was found just outside the interior walls). The inner pair of stones acted as a gateway into a round apse containing a hemispherical stone bench, constructed at the rectangular structure's northwest end; a similar apse had previously been recorded in connection with Çayönü's Skull Building. As was the case with Nevalı Çori's cult building and Çayönü's Terrazzo Building, Enclosure A possessed a perfectly level terrazzo floor that covered the underlying bedrock.

Like the pillars in the Lion Temple Building, those in Enclosure A turned out to be revelations in prehistoric art. Pillar 1, the first to be exposed, bore on its front narrow face five slithering snakes, their heads pointing downward. One of the stone's wide surfaces displayed more snakes interwoven to form a mesh-like pattern of diamonds, collectively forming a snakeskin pattern (see figure 2.1).

Pillar 2 bore reliefs of an auroch, a leaping fox, and a wading bird, most likely a crane (see plate 4). At the top of the pillar's front narrow edge, just beneath the overhang of the hammer-shaped head, was a small bucranium (ox skull) in high relief. It faced outward toward the viewer, and its whereabouts on the figure made an interpretation easy. Anthropomorphic pillars found at Nevalı Çori had been found to possess a V-shaped relief, like a neck collar, in exactly the same place. In other words, the bucranium was, most likely, a carved pendant or emblem of office, worn around the "neck" of the figure.

CULT OF THE SNAKE

Pillars 3 and 4 were without relief, while Pillar 5 bore yet another representation of a snake. This strong presence of serpentine imagery on the carved stones at Göbekli Tepe begged the question of just what this creature might have symbolized to the peoples of the Pre-Pottery Neolithic age.

Universally, snakes are seen as symbols of supernatural power, divine energy,

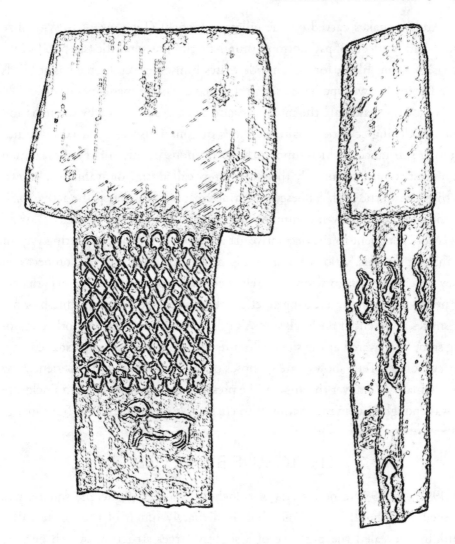

Figure 2.1. Snakes seen on Göbekli Tepe's Pillar 1 in Enclosure A.

otherworldly knowledge, male and female sexuality, and, because they shed their skin, metaphysical transformation. The snake also represents the active spirit of medicines, the reason it is today a universal symbol of the medical profession through its association with the cult of Asclepius, the Greek god of medicine and healing. Moreover, the snake is associated not just with beneficial medicines, but also with those that bring forth hallucinations and even death. In Christian legend, for instance, poison offered to John the Evangelist in a laced chalice of wine was made to slither away as a black snake moments before the apostle was about to drink it.

Are the snakes carved on the pillars at Göbekli Tepe meant to symbolize the visionary effects of psychotropic (mind-altering) or soporific (sleep-inducing) drugs? It seems likely, for as Schmidt writes himself, several large basalt bowls found at the site were perhaps used in the preparation of medicines or drugs.[1]

Visionary snakes are the most common creatures glimpsed by shamans and initiates during ecstatic or altered states of consciousness induced by mind-altering substances, which among the indigenous peoples of the Amazonian rainforest is most commonly the sacred brew called yagé or ayahuasca, known as the "vine of the soul."[2] These serpentine creatures are seen as the active spirit of the drug and can even communicate with the shaman or initiate.

More pertinent to the decorative art at Göbekli Tepe is that during yagé or ayahuasca sessions, visionary snakes appear in such profusion that on occasion they have been seen to wrap themselves enmass around either the experiencer or nearby houseposts,[3] creating an effect that cannot be unlike the mesh or net of snakes represented on Enclosure A's Pillar 1 and found also on other standing stones uncovered at the site (see figure 2.2). So is this what the snake imagery at Göbekli Tepe shows, rare glimpses of the visionary world experienced by the shaman? Whatever the answer, the presence of so many snakes in Enclosure A was enough to convince Schmidt to christen it the Snake Pillar Building.

ENCLOSURE B EXPOSED

In 1998 and 1999 a new series of trenches, 29.5 feet (9 meters) square, was opened at Göbekli Tepe. One, dug immediately north of the Snake Pillar Building, revealed the presence of a slightly larger structure, which became known as Enclosure B. This was found to be ovoid, measuring roughly 23 feet (7 meters) by 28.5 feet (8.7 meters), with no less than nine T-shaped pillars—seven placed within its temenos (that is, boundary) wall and two set parallel to each other in the center of a terrazzo floor—like those that had originally stood in Nevalı Çori's cult building. Schmidt remarked that it was like the "T-shapes," as he calls the anthropomorphic pillars, were gathered for "a meeting or dance."[4]

Pillar 6 displayed carved reliefs of a reptile and snake, while those set up in the center of the room (9 and 10) both bore T-shaped terminations and exquisitely carved leaping foxes on their inner faces. The creatures' animated stance made them appear as if they were jumping across the monolith, perhaps toward

Figure 2.2. Left, poison escapes from the chalice of wine about
to be drunk by John the Evangelist in the form of snakes, from a mosaic
on the wall of the church of Saint John the Evangelist, New Ferry,
Merseyside, England. Right, snakes on the front of Göbekli Tepe's Pillar
31 in Enclosure D. Do they represent the active spirit of medicines
and poisons, or do they refer more particularly to visionary experiences
induced through the use of psychoactive substances?

the entrant who would approach from the south, exactly in keeping with the
cult buildings at Çayönü, which also had entrances in the south.

NEW TEMPLES DISCOVERED

Work began around the same time on another structure of much greater
size, which became known as Enclosure C. Once again, T-shaped pillars
were soon exposed, and these too were set radially within stone walls containing the now familiar stone benches. One monolith, designated Pillar 12,
was found to bear a carved relief on its T-shaped head, the first to do so.

It showed five birds, either waders or a flightless species, amid a backdrop of V-shaped lines that were perhaps meant to represent water ripples. On the same pillar's shaft was a "threatening boar"[5] shown above a leaping fox. In front of the stone a portable sculpture of a boar was uncovered. Free-standing art of this kind, including carved human heads, are often found to be fragments of much larger pieces of sculpture, such as carved stone totem poles or life-size statues.

Soon after the discovery of Enclosure C, another massive building structure, Enclosure D, was uncovered immediately to its northwest. This would prove to be one of the oldest and most mysterious monuments ever uncovered in the ancient world. Both enclosures, C and D, are described in full within subsequent chapters.

DELIBERATE BURIAL

What started to become apparent to Schmidt's team, as it removed the vast amounts of fill that covered the various building structures beneath the tell at Göbekli Tepe, is that each one had been *deliberately* buried beneath an ever-expanding mound.[6] It was almost as if the idea of creating the bellylike tell, or tepe, was part of an original grand design, with each new enclosure playing some role in its greater purpose, a gradually evolving process that had taken some fifteen hundred years to complete. This ritual act of "killing," or decommissioning, each enclosure before the construction of a new one to take its place would seem to have occurred in stages until around 8000 BC, when the remaining structures were covered over and the site finally abandoned.[7]

For Schmidt and his team the burial of the enclosures was an immense bugbear, as it meant they were not easily able to determine the construction dates of the various monuments uncovered. Despite this problem, Schmidt was able to ascertain from the different types of flint tool found within the fill that the *earliest* phases of building activity uncovered at Göbekli Tepe belonged to the epoch known as Pre-Pottery Neolithic A, which began around 9500 BC.[8]

THE YOUNGER DRYAS MINI ICE AGE

It is a date that coincides pretty well with the culmination of a mini ice age, or prolonged cold spell, known as the Younger Dryas. This had enveloped much of the Northern Hemisphere for around thirteen hundred hundred years, ca. 10,900–9600 BC, bringing with it a pronounced dip in temperature as well as a sustained drought that severely altered the plant and animal life throughout what is known as the Fertile Crescent. This is the arclike region of verdant river valleys, steppes, and plains that stretches clockwise from Palestine and Israel, through the Levantine corridor of Lebanon, into the Middle Euphrates Basin of northern Syria, then across into what is known as Northern Mesopotamia, a region that embraces southeast Anatolia, before entering the Mesopotamian Plain, or what is today the country of Iraq.

The Younger Dryas period followed a two-thousand-year episode of global warming known as the Allerød interstadial. This in turn had brought to a close the last ice age proper, which had been with us for approximately ninety-five thousand years, reaching its last glacial maximum around twenty to twenty-two thousand years ago (an interstadial is a period when temperatures rise and glaciers go on the retreat).

With the cessation of the mini ice age, or big chill, ca. 9600 BC, the temperatures rose, bringing about a blossoming of new flora and fauna (in geological terms this point in history marks the transition from the Pleistocene age to the Holocene, which we are still in today). It was an ideal environment for new growth that led to the emergence of agriculture on the Middle Euphrates and farther south within the Levantine corridor. It was also around this time, Schmidt believes, that hunter-gatherers from across the region came together to create the extraordinary stone structures being uncovered today at Göbekli Tepe, which he is sure were not domestic in nature.

No evidence of fires, hearths, cooking areas, or any other signs of habitation have been found in or around the enclosures at Göbekli Tepe that might indicate the permanent presence here of a large community. Human remains *have* been found, plenty of them, although these are either retrieved from the fill covering the enclosures or are found concealed in walls or benches. Exactly what they are doing here remains unclear.

A LIFE OF BEER

One more anomaly at Göbekli Tepe is that the nearest water source is 3 miles (5 kilometers) away, meaning that any drinking water has to be carried to the site. This lack of a constant water supply seems illogical, especially given that the construction of the monuments would have required the presence of a labor force involving hundreds of workers and their families, all of whom would have needed to be fed on a daily basis. The only explanation is that the workers lived in settlements nearby and climbed the mountain with sufficient supplies to last them for the duration of their stay.

This said, there is a strong possibility that a form of beer made from wild wheat was on the menu at Göbekli Tepe. Large stone vats unearthed by Schmidt's team have been linked with beer production (see figure 2.3).[9] Whether the beer was brewed for reasons of necessity or for some ritual function remains to be seen, although as an intoxicating beverage it *is* likely to have possessed an otherworldly significance. The term *ale,* used today for beer, originally meant any kind of alcoholic drink made using wheat grain. The word could well derive from the Indo-European root *alu,* which has definite connotations of shifting realities and altered states of consciousness through its presence in key words such as *hallucinate* and *hallucination.*[10]

CUP MARKS FOR CARRION BIRDS

Another peculiar mystery at Göbekli Tepe is the presence on the exposed bedrock to the southwest of the main enclosures of large cuplike holes, up to 6 inches (15 centimeters) in width and depth (see figure 2.4). There are dozens of them everywhere. Similar cup marks are to be seen on top of some of the standing pillars, while clusters of them are found also at other Pre-Pottery Neolithic sites across the region.

On asking Klaus Schmidt what he thought these cup marks represented in September 2012, he shrugged his shoulders and said they are found everywhere, often in the company of carved rings marks, like those in Britain. Yet clearly they did once have a function, and the most obvious solution is that they were receptacles for something, either liquid—blood, beer, milk, or water perhaps—or, more likely, some type of food such as meat. Because they almost always seem to be carved in elevated positions, it appears possible that whatever they contained were offerings to carrion birds such as vultures, crows, or ravens, which might well have played some kind of symbolic function in the rituals taking place inside the sanctuaries (a large number of bones belonging to both the crow and raven have been found within the fill at Göbekli Tepe[11]).

Figure 2.3. Minor enclosure at Göbekli Tepe, dating to ca. 8500–8000 BC, showing a stone container thought to have held beer.

Figure 2.4. Examples of the incised cup marks found on exposed bedrock in the vicinity of Göbekli Tepe's Enclosure E.

Scavenger birds such as vultures play an important role in the Neolithic cult of the dead (see chapter 9), and so gaining their favor in a divinatory manner might well have been important to the success of a ritual. In other words, if the birds came down and took away the meat, it was a good omen, and if they didn't, then the opposite would be the case.

Interestingly enough, divination has been proposed as an explanation for the presence of similar cup marks found on exposed rock surfaces in the area of Mount Ararat in eastern Anatolia. Armenian prehistorians speculate that although the true purpose of the cup marks has now been lost, they were probably "used by oracles during fortune telling," a very credible explanation indeed, which sits well with their possible function at Göbekli Tepe.[12]

ENGINEERING CONUNDRUM

The standing pillars found in the various enclosures at Göbekli Tepe are regularly between 6.5 and 10 feet (2 and 3 meters) in size and are thought to weigh between 5.5 and 16.5 U.S. tons apiece (5 and 15 metric tonnes). Even more of an enigma is that sitting in a quarry a quarter of a mile (400 meters) away from the occupational mound is an unfinished T-shaped monolith some 22.9 feet (7 meters) in length and 9.8 feet (3 meters) broad, with an estimated weight of approximately 55 U.S. tons (50 metric tonnes).[13] As Schmidt asked back in 2001:

> How could the manpower be amassed at the mound to move such pillars? It seems obvious that only organized meetings of several groups of hunter-gatherers from the territories around Göbekli Tepe would be able to provide the capabilities for such an undertaking, meetings rooted in a ritual background.[14]

As Schmidt admits, the construction of huge megalithic architecture is not thought to have begun until many thousand years later at places such as Egypt and Stonehenge in England. Never before had the archaeological community conceived of such feats of monumental engineering going on even before the wide-scale appearance of agriculture. From the faunal (animal) remains retrieved from the fill covering Göbekli Tepe's occupational mound, it would seem that the main food source was wild game such as gazelles, red deer, wild boar, aurochs, and wild sheep,[15] supplemented with copious amounts of almonds and pistachios.

NEOLITHIC REVOLUTION

In Schmidt's opinion: "Hunter-gatherers living at Göbekli Tepe for an extended time would have caused a serious over-exploitation of the local natural resources."[16] For him the coming together of so many people led to the domestication of wild species of cereals and other plants in order to feed those present both here and at other similar sites across southeast Anatolia, causing what Australian archaeologist and philologist V. Gordon Childe (1892–1957) long ago christened the Neolithic revolution.

Yet Childe saw it the other way around—the rapid spread of agriculture at the beginning of the Neolithic, and the more settled lifestyle it brought with it—gave people time to invent new technologies and to think about the mysteries of life, leading to the construction of the first temples, an act that led to the creation of cities and civilizations. Now we know Childe was wrong. It was the temples that came first, with agriculture created in their wake to satisfy the needs of so many people engaged in the construction and maintenance of such mammoth building projects.

THE ORIGINS OF AGRICULTURE

Such a theory makes sense of another puzzling enigma that prehistorians are still trying to fully understand. Genetic research into the origins of cereal production has determined that no less than sixty-eight modern strains of wheat, used by us today to make bread, beer, pasta, and other products, can be traced back to a variety of wild einkorn that grows on the slopes of Karaca Dağ (pronounced *ka-rag-a dar*), a volcanic mountain just 50 miles (80 kilometers) northeast of Göbekli Tepe.[17] This means that wheat might well have been domesticated for the first time only a short distance away from the site of humanity's earliest known example of monumental architecture.

Over an extensive period of time einkorn was gradually domesticated through selective cultivation to create a much stronger variety whereby the kernels remained on the plants, instead of falling to the ground. This enabled a higher wheat yield through the heads being able to ripen better before harvesting took place.

Was it possible that the domestication of wheat occurred in southeast Anatolia in response to the sheer need to feed so many groups of hunter-gatherers either laboring away on site or visiting Göbekli Tepe as part of some huge socio-magical gathering? "Their idea, to meet again and again at a specific place," Schmidt argues, "seems to be a basic factor of the origins of neolithization."[18] Here then, really, is where the revolution began—the revolution in becoming Neolithic, in becoming farmers tilling the fields, herding animals, and living more communal lifestyles. It was a turning point in human existence that quite literally paved the way for the rise of civilization, which had its beginnings in what was happening at Göbekli Tepe some 11,500 years ago.

3

FROZEN IN STONE

A large number of the T-shaped pillars seen in the various enclosures at Göbekli Tepe show beautiful carvings of strange, eerie, and often terrifying creatures of the natural world. Those most frequently represented are, in order, snakes, leaping foxes, wild boars, and cranes. Others seen include aurochs, gazelles, lions, wild sheep, lizards, scorpions, spiders, and ants (with at least one bear and a hyena identified as well). Various species of bird are also found, including flamingos, vultures, ibises, and flightless birds. In addition to this, excavators have found a number of 3-D statues that include boars, aurochs, and at least three teeth-bearing predators, most likely wolves. These can be seen today in Şanlıurfa's museum of archaeology.

Too many species are represented by the carved art to easily assess what exactly they all mean or why there are so many creatures portrayed together, and perhaps this is a clue to their greater purpose. It is almost as if they constitute a snapshot of the abundance of life that existed when the monuments were constructed shortly after the end of the last Ice Age. Yet for the most part these are not friendly creatures by any stretch of the imagination: they bite, gore, claw, sting, tear apart, and generally kill whatever gets in their way. They are not the kind of animals you would want to be locked inside a claustrophobic room with, without any means of escape.

None of the animals shown on the stone pillars at Göbekli Tepe are nice

41

cuddly creatures, even though some of them, such as the auroch, wild boar, wild sheep, and even the wolf, would afterward become domesticated. Clearly, this was meant to be the case, suggesting that someone, an entrant or initiate, finding him- or herself inside an enclosure, would immediately be presented with a terrifying visual spectacle illuminated either by natural light or by torches of some kind. It was an assault on the senses that would have induced not a state of peace and calmness, but one of fear and alertness, something that must have been all too familiar to the hunter-gatherer, whose whole life was centered around the struggle for survival on a day-to-day basis.

Yet such mental assaults were perhaps not simply for focusing the mind on the dangers of the hunt, especially as by this time people were beginning to settle into more communal lifestyles away from the immediate concerns of the chase. There was clearly something else going on here, something that plunges us into the realm of deep-seated, instinctual psychological states.

For example, when we look at the magnificent accomplishment of the Paleolithic artists that entered the deepest caves of northern Spain and southern France to execute their work toward the end of the last ice age, ca. 30,000–9500 BC, a sense of immense beauty and tranquility is conveyed. This is in complete contrast to the overall sense of fear and anxiety that exudes from the more chilling art of Göbekli Tepe. This, simply from its manner of execution, has more in common with the visual art of the pre-Columbian civilizations of Central and South America than it does the majestic cave paintings of southwest Europe. It is an impression that only deepens the more we examine the various enclosures at Göbekli Tepe.

ENCLOSURE C

Of all the structures so far uncovered at Göbekli Tepe, by far the most complex is Enclosure C, which, like Enclosure B, is ovoid in appearance, being roughly 75 feet (23 meters) by 60 feet (18 meters) in size. It consists of two concentric walls of stone (the inner one being built after the structure's original construction[1]), each containing various pillars, most of them T-shaped.

At the center of the enclosure two enormous twin monoliths once stood. Only their stumps remain in situ, with a large fragment of the western monolith (Pillar 37) being reerected in 2009 under the leadership of German architect and engineering consultant Eduard Knoll. Similar to the central pillars in Enclosure B, a leaping fox appears on its inner face, the animal's gaze once again directed southward. Estimates suggest that originally Enclosure C's twin pillars would have stood around 16 feet (5 meters) in height. Yet unlike those of Enclosure B, these examples have not been set within a terrazzo floor. Instead, they are slotted into rectangular grooves cut into raised, steplike pedestals sculpted out of the bedrock.

A large area of smoothed bedrock, elliptical in shape, complete with a pair of rock-cut pedestals that also contain rectangular slots, had earlier been found on level ground 160 yards (146 meters) west-southwest of Göbekli Tepe's main group of structures. Yet here, in what has become known as Enclosure E, or the *Felsentempel* (German for "rock temple"), no clear evidence of any standing pillars or surrounding structure survives today. This said, it is clear that Enclosure E is of the same general age as Enclosure C.

Adjacent to Enclosure C's western central monolith is one of the most remarkable T-shaped stones discovered so far at the site. Running down the front narrow edge of Pillar 27 is a 3-D predator, a famished quadruped, with a long bushy tail and emaciated body. Its snarling jaws, complete with carved lines signifying whiskers, reveal a mouth full of razor-sharp teeth. That such a feat of artistic expression was carried out eleven thousand years ago by simple hunter-gatherers seems almost alien, although achieve it they did. As to the identity of this predator, Schmidt believes it is a feline, a lion most probably. Yet the shape of its body, the large incised teeth, and the long bushy tail make a case for its being a canine of some description.

A DOUBLE RING OF STONES

The exact number of standing pillars Enclosure C's outer ring once possessed is now lost, with just eight remaining in place. Its inner ring probably contained twelve T-shaped pillars, with eleven surviving today. The area between the two concentric walls into which the stones were set created a circular walkway, although there was no direct means of access from here into the central enclosure where the twin monoliths were located. So how might entry have been achieved? The answer is that either a porthole stone once existed within the wall of the inner ring (several such stones, some decorated with carved figures, have been found at the site), or the entrant had to quite literally climb inside, perhaps using ropes or a ladder. This is suggested by the presence of a steplike feature on the south side of the enclosure between two pillars, forming what appears to be an entranceway of some kind (see plate 7).

Another possibility is that there was once an overhead entry point within a covered roof. Certainly, there are angled slots and grooves on the upper surfaces of some of the stones making up Enclosure C's inner circle, which could easily have been cut to help support an overhead structure. Yet whether a roof of this sort was an original feature or one added at some later point remains unclear. Archaeologist Ted Banning of the University of Toronto has proposed that the T-shaped pillars at Göbekli Tepe were primarily roof supports and the enclosures themselves domestic houses,[2] a view not shared by Schmidt and his colleagues.

THE DROMOS

Enclosure C's circular walkway, between the outer and inner temenos walls, was entered from the south through a north-south-aligned stone passage measuring 25 feet (7.5 meters) in length. Schmidt calls it the *dromos,* after an ancient Greek word meaning *avenue* or *entranceway,* because of its likeness to the passageways attached to the beehive-shaped *tholoi* tombs of Mycenaean Greece.

At the southern end of the dromos a curious U-shaped stone portal, or inverse arch, was set up as an entranceway. The upright terminations of its two "arms" were carved into the likeness of strange, crouching quadrupeds that face outward; that is, away from each other. The identity of these twin guardians, only one of which remains roughly in situ today, is another puzzle (see plate 8). Schmidt calls this U-shaped doorway the "Lion's Gate,"[3] perhaps because of the twin lions carved in stone above the Lion's Gate entrance at the Mycenaean city of Mycenae in southern Greece.

Beyond the U-shaped entrance to the dromos, Schmidt's team has uncovered a stone stairway of eight steps constructed to navigate a noticeable dip or "depression" in the bedrock (see figure 3.1).[4] It is an incredible feat of ingenuity and constitutes one of the oldest staircases to be found anywhere in the world. Its presence here at Göbekli Tepe confirms both that an ascent was required to enter the enclosure and that the south was the direction of approach for the visitor.

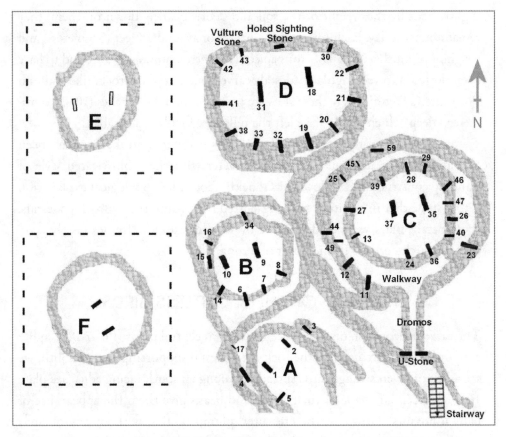

Figure 3.1. Plan of Göbekli Tepe showing the main enclosures uncovered so far.

ENCLOSURE D

Abutting Enclosure C to the northwest is Enclosure D, the most accomplished of all the structures at Göbekli Tepe. Once again it is ovoid, measuring approximately 60 feet (18 meters) by 47.5 feet (14.5 meters), and would originally have contained a ring of twelve T-shaped pillars (just eleven remain today). Its length-to-breath ratio is almost exactly 5:4, which, strangely enough, is identical to that of Enclosure B *and* Enclosure C, something that is unlikely to be coincidence. (The ovoid outline in the bedrock of the now vanished Enclosure E, located slightly west of the main group of structures, suggests that it too possessed a 5:4 size ratio.) It is a realization we return to in chapter 5.

Two enormous twin monoliths stand at the center of Enclosure D. Although slightly bent by the weight of the soil and debris bearing down on them, they remain intact today. Each one—with a height of around 18 feet (5.5 meters) and weighing as much as 16.5 U.S. tons apiece (15 metric tonnes)—was found to have been slotted into rectangular pedestals carved out of the bedrock, like those in Enclosure C. Yet bizarrely these slots are no more than 4–6 inches (10–15 centimeters) deep, which would have left the pillars particularly unstable.

Such a decision to erect the pillars in this manner is unlikely to have been a design fault, as it seems so out of character with the sophisticated style of building construction employed at Göbekli Tepe. The only logical explanation is to assume that in addition to being slotted firmly into the bedrock pedestals, the central pillars were held in place by wooden support frames (as they are today), which perhaps formed part of a roof.

MYSTERY OF THE FLIGHTLESS BIRDS

The carved decoration on Enclosure D's eastern central pillar (Pillar 18) is quite extraordinary. Starting with the rock-cut pedestal supporting the monolith, we see a line of seven strange birds spread out along its south-facing edge (see plate 16). The peculiar shape of their heads and beaks give them the appearance of baby dinosaurs! However, the creatures' plump bodies, without any obvious wings, reveal them to be flightless birds that sit on their haunches, their legs stretched out in front of them. So what species do they represent? An examination of known flightless birds from the past right down to the present day suggests they could be dodos (see figure 3.2).*

No other bird type known to have existed in the tenth millennium BC even comes close to matching what we see at Göbekli Tepe, and to ignore this conclusion would be to miss an opportunity to better understand the geographical world of the Göbekli builders. This is not to say they visited the island of Mauritius in the Indian Ocean, where the dodo was hunted to extinction by the first Europeans to reach the island, only that somewhere on their travels the Göbekli builders might have encountered a similar bird that is today extinct.

As to why birds of this type are represented at Göbekli Tepe we can only speculate. Perhaps the fact that they are flightless is the clue. Since they can't fly away, they are rooted to the ground, just like the bedrock pedestals on

---

*I would like to thank Richard Ward for his suggestion that the birds represent dodos.

Figure 3.2. Left, seated dodo bird and, right, two of the seven flightless birds seen on the pedestal of Göbekli Tepe's Pillar 18 in Enclosure D.

which they're carved, implying therefore that the birds symbolize permanence and a point of foundation.

LATER PHASES OF BUILDING ACTIVITY

Various smaller enclosures and cell-like rooms, uncovered to the north and west of the main group of buildings at Göbekli Tepe, were found to have been constructed during a slightly later building phase, ca. 9000–8000 BC. This seems certain, since they are positioned as much as 50 feet (15 meters) higher than the other enclosures constructed on the bedrock below. In other words, these much younger structures were built long after the older structures had been buried (at least in part) below the gradually emerging tell. Like their forerunners, these rooms contain T-shaped pillars, communal benches, and stone-lined walls, invariably rectangular in design. Yet in size and quality they are often greatly inferior. In some cases, they are the size of bathrooms, with their stones no more than 3.2 to 5 feet (1 to 1.5 meters) in height. Some of the pillars are T-shaped, with clearly carved anthropomorphic features like their predecessors, while others are left unadorned. Clearly the later Göbekli builders were downsizing in architectural style and artistic design, while at the same time retaining some elements of the earlier enclosures.

Around 8000 BC the remaining structures at Göbekli Tepe were covered with fill and abandoned completely, this unique style of architecture continuing only at a handful of other Pre-Pottery Neolithic sites in the region, including Çayönü and Nevalı Çori, which we have already explored; Hamzan Tepe,[5] Sefer Tepe,[6] and Taşlı Tepe,[7] all near Şanlıurfa; and Karahan Tepe.[8] This last mentioned site, set within the Tektek Mountains some 40 miles (64 kilometers) east of Şanlıurfa, has yet to be fully excavated, even though in size it could easily match that of Göbekli Tepe (it was investigated by the present author in 2004, who noted carved stone fragments, exposed heads of T-shaped pillars, a stone row, and countless flint tools scattered across a very wide area indeed). At a place named Kilisik, close to the town of Adıyaman, around 53 miles (85 kilometers) north of Nevalı Çori, a mini T-shaped figure in the form of a small stone statue was found in 1965,[9] leading prehistorians to consider that another early Neolithic site awaits discovery here (see chapter 10 for more on this remarkable statue). At a place named Kilisik, a village close to the Kahta river in Adıyaman province, in the foothills of the Anti-Taurus Mountains, some 46.5 miles (75 kilometers) north-northwest of Göbekli Tepe, a mini T-shaped figure in the form of a small stone statue was found in 1965,[9] leading prehistorians to consider that another early Neolithic site awaits discovery here (see chapter 10 for more on this remarkable stature).

TRIANGLE D'OR

All of these sites, where T-shaped pillars and portable statues have been found, lie within a very small area no more than 150 miles (240 kilometers) in diameter, with its center close to Karaca Dağ, where the genetic origins of modern wheat have been traced to a variety of wild einkorn growing on its lower slopes. This area of southeast Anatolia, where neolithization began, has been christened the *triangle d'or,* the "golden triangle," due to the key role it played in kick-starting the Neolithic revolution.[10]

It is a grand title, the *triangle d'or,* but it does seem to express the sheer genius of inspiration that led to the emergence of sites such as Göbekli Tepe, with their unique architecture, which seems almost alien to the modern world. Yet where did this genius of inspiration come from? Dr. Mehrdad R. Izady, professor of Near East studies at New York University, wrote in 1992 (two years before Klaus Schmidt first visited Göbekli Tepe) that at the beginning of the Neolithic age the peoples of southeast Anatolia "went through an unexplained stage of accelerated technological evolution, prompted by yet uncertain forces."[11] What exactly were these as "yet uncertain forces"? Were they material or divine? Were they human or something else altogether? All we can say is that something quite extraordinary happened in the *triangle d'or* some twelve thousand years ago, and the key to understanding this mystery might well await discovery among the T-shaped pillars and carved art of Göbekli Tepe.

To date, seven major structures (Enclosures A, B, C, D, E, and F, as well as the Lion Pillar Building) have been explored at Göbekli Tepe. Yet the geomagnetic survey undertaken in 2003 suggests that this constitutes just a small fraction of what lies buried beneath the occupational mound (Schmidt estimates there might be as many as fifteen more enclosures still to be uncovered, providing a total of some 200 standing pillars[12]). As can be imagined, with two digging campaigns a year (April to May and September to November), Klaus Schmidt's multinational team is constantly discovering new structures and monuments.

Very gradually our fragmented picture of what went on here as much as twelve thousand years ago will slowly take shape. Trying to unravel its mysteries too soon is rife with problems, although simply stepping aside and allowing the archaeological evidence to speak for itself is to miss an opportunity to get inside the minds of the Göbekli builders and truly know what motivated them to give up their hunter-gatherer lifestyle to create monumental architecture on a scale never before seen in the world. Why exactly did they do this? Why create the earliest known megalithic monuments anywhere in the world? One possible clue is the strange carved symbolism on the stones that includes quite specific glyphs or ideograms, which, as we see next, might well reveal the Göbekli builders' fascination with the heavens.

4
STRANGE GLYPHS
AND IDEOGRAMS

The eastern central pillar (Pillar 18) in Göbekli Tepe's Enclosure D sports a wide belt on which are a sequence of abstract glyphs, or ideograms, which are likely to have had some symbolic meaning to the Pre-Pottery Neolithic world of the tenth millennium BC. One, looking like a thin letter C, is seen sometimes turned toward the left and at other times toward the right. Another glyph, resembling the letter H, is found both in an upright position and rotated 90 degrees (see figure 4.1 and plates 11 and 13). It appears in the same sequence as the C-shaped glyphs, and both seem to work in concert with each other.

On the "front" of the T-shape's belt the H symbol appears no less than five times, two upright and three on their side. In addition to these glyphs is another, slightly larger ideogram that appears in the position of the figure's belt buckle, below which a fox-pelt loincloth appears in high relief (both are explored in chapter 12).

THE H GLYPH

How might we interpret these strange ideograms in use among the Göbekli builders so soon after the end of the last Ice Age? Let's start with the H glyph.

Figure 4.1. Mid-section of Göbekli Tepe's Pillar 18 in Enclosure D showing the figure's wide belt decorated with C- and H-shaped glyphs.

Searching the archives of prehistoric symbolism throws up very little. They could be shields made of animal hide, as examples in prehistoric art do occasionally resemble the letter H. Yet if so, why do they appear so many times on the same pillar? Also apparent is that the H character resembles two letter Ts joined stem to stem. It is an association that might not be without meaning, especially in view of the general appearance of the T-shaped pillars at Göbekli Tepe and the presence of the twin monoliths at the center of the enclosures. If so, then what might this mirrored double T actually represent?

Is it possible that the H glyph conveys the connection between two perfectly mirrored worlds, states, or existences linked by a conceived bridge or tunnel, represented by the crossbar between the two "columns"? If this is the case, it really does not matter whether the glyph is depicted upright or rotated 90 degrees; the meaning would always be the same.

SHAMANIC POT STANDS

Some idea of how indigenous cultures have portrayed the relationship between the two worlds, and the transition between the two, can be found in the design of ritual pot stands used by the Desana shamans of Colombia. Taking the shape of an hourglass, that is, two cones point to point, they are made from spiraling canes bound together in such a manner as to leave a central hole connecting the two cones, which, when looked at from either end, have the appearance of a hole-like entrance through a spiraling vortex or whirlpool (see figure 4.2). Yet "when seen in profile, as an hourglass, the object can be interpreted as a cosmic model, the two cones connected by a circular 'door', an image that leads to others such as 'birth', 'rebirth', the passage from one 'dimension' (*turí*) to another while under the influence of a narcotic, and to similar shamanistic images. . . . In sum, the hourglass shape contains a great amount of shamanistic imagery concerned with cosmic structures and with transformative processes."[1]

These are the words of anthropologist Gerardo Reichel-Dolmatoff (1912–1994), who conducted an extensive study of the beliefs and practices of shamanic-based cultures of the Amazon rainforest. He saw the hourglass-shaped pot stand of the Desana as symbolic of the connection between the two worlds, the hole created between the two cones being the point of entrance and exit between the two dimensions of existence. This bears out the interpretation of Göbekli Tepe's H glyph as being a mirrored symbol of movement between two worlds, whether across space or time. If so, then it is likely that the accompanying C glyph also has some kind of transformative role. It would not be unreasonable to see the twin C shape as the slim crescents of the old and new moon, which when shown together, face to face, signify the transition period between one lunar cycle and the next.

Figure 4.2. Desana shaman's ritual pot stand from the side and looking down through its hollow interior (after Gerardo Reichel-Dolmatoff).

AUSTRALIAN ABORIGINAL ART

Another possible interpretation of the C-shaped glyph can be found among the symbolic art of the aboriginal peoples of Australia. Here the C-shape ideogram depicts a bird's-eye view of a seated man or woman, the arms of the symbol representing those of the individual.[2] When two Cs are shown together, face to face, this denotes two people sitting opposite each other.[3] Occasionally there will be a bar shown between them, signifying a small, benchlike mound constructed for special ceremonies and said to symbolize a mound of creation associated with a primeval snake.[4]

A photograph in British anthropologist Sir Walter Baldwin Spencer's book *Across Australia* (1912) of a Worgaia medicine man from Central Australia, who was himself "a great maker of medicine men,"[5] shows the double C ideogram, with a bar in between, painted on his chest. It is nearly *identical* to one that appears on the chest of a T-shaped pillar at Göbekli Tepe (see figure 4.3 on p. 54),[6] the only difference being that here the horizontal line forms the connecting bar of the H symbol earlier described.

EMBLEMS OF OFFICE

Like other major pillars at Göbekli Tepe, Enclosure D's central monoliths have carved symbols upon their "neck," just below their T-shaped heads. On

Figure 4.3. Left, double C and H symbol on the chest of Pillar 28 in Göbekli Tepe's Enclosure C. Right, Worgaia medicine man from Central Australia with the same symbol on his body.

the eastern pillar two are seen, the uppermost being the same H-shaped glyph found on the belt. This particular example is upright with a small, hollowed-out oval shape within its crossbar (here the symbol looks like two matchstick men holding hands, which lends credence to the idea that the C-ideogram might sometimes mean a seated man or woman, just as it does in Australian aboriginal art). Immediately beneath the H shape is a well-defined, horizontal crescent, its horns turned upward. Cupped within its concave form is a wide-banded circle with a deeply incised hole at its center. A thin, V-shaped "collar" or "chain" is visible either side of the two glyphs (see figure 4.4 on p. 56), making it clear that these symbols are emblems of office worn around the neck, perhaps denoting the individual's status or identity.

Confirming the use of collars or chains by the elite of the Pre-Pottery Neolithic is a life-size statue of a man, 5 feet 9 inches (1.8 meters) in height, found at Şanlıurfa, just 8 miles (13 kilometers) from Göbekli Tepe (see plate 23). Located today in the city's archaeological museum, the figure was discovered in 1993 on Yeni Yol Street in Balıklıgöl, the oldest part of the city, where a Pre-Pottery Neolithic A settlement was investigated in 1997.[7] It is here also in Balıklıgöl that the prophet Abraham is said to have been born within a cave shrine renowned throughout the Muslim world as an important place of pilgrimage. The statue, which has black obsidian disks for eyes, a prominent nose, arms that end in hands clasped over the genitalia, and a conelike lower half where the legs should be, dates to around 9000 BC. The fact that it also sports a double V-shaped collar in high relief is evidence that the neck emblems on the T-shaped pillars at Göbekli Tepe are most likely pendants or medallions attached to a chain or collar of office.

THE EYE AND THE CRESCENT

Although it is conceivable that the crescent on the neck of the eastern central pillar in Enclosure D signifies the moon, the carved circle with the hole in its center is more difficult to understand (see figure 4.4 on p. 56). Perhaps it is a representation of an eye, as similar circles with hollow middles act as eyes on the 3-D carving of the snarling predator seen on the front face of Enclosure C's Pillar 27. The likeness is too close for this to be simply coincidence. So if the circle *is* an eye, then the slim crescent that cups it must form the lower eyelid.

In ancient Egypt the eye was the symbol of the sun god Re (or Ra), while the title Eye of Re was given to various leonine goddesses including Sekhmet, Tefnut, and Bastet, showing the clear relationship between the sun and the all-seeing eye.

THE WESTERN CENTRAL PILLAR

Enclosure D's other central pillar (Pillar 31), positioned to the west of the one just described, also sports a belt and buckle, although in this instance both are almost featureless (other than a small bovine scratched into the belt on its eastern side). Like its neighbor, the T-shape sports a fox-pelt loincloth, while around its "neck" is a small bucranium, or ox head, worn as a pendant or emblem of office. French prehistorian Jacques Cauvin saw the bull in early Neolithic symbolism as representative of male domination over nature.[8] This

Figure 4.4. H, eye, and crescent symbol together on the neck of the eastern central pillar (Pillar 18) in Göbekli Tepe's Enclosure D.

might well be so. Yet if the combined circle and crescent symbol on the neck of the eastern pillar does represent the sun, then there has to be a distinct possibility that the bucranium on its western neighbor represents the moon, the twin pillars displaying some kind of dual, solar-lunar polarity.

That bucrania perhaps symbolized the crescent moon in the Upper Paleolithic is shown by the Venus of Laussel, a carved stone relief of a naked full-bodied woman, 17.5 inches (45 centimeters) in height and carved into a block of limestone. Dating to ca. 27,000–20,000 BC, she was discovered in 1911 at the entrance to a rock shelter at Laussel in the Dordogne region of southwestern France. In her right hand she holds a bison's horn on which are inscribed thirteen vertical notches, interpreted by some prehistorians as symbolizing the thirteen-month lunar cycle.

Should these speculations prove valid, it implies that some of the glyphs displayed on the T-shaped pillars at Göbekli Tepe have distinct spatial, temporal, and celestial values. The C and H ideograms, along with the eye symbol and bucranium, all suggest as much. So are the anthropomorphic pillars personifications of higher intelligences—some kind of *divine company* that reflects these otherworldly influences? We now begin to explore the true function of Göbekli Tepe's quite extraordinary monumental architecture.

PART TWO

Cosmos

5

GATEWAY TO HEAVEN

I t is impossible today to assess the exact number of stones in each of the main enclosures uncovered at Göbekli Tepe. There were certainly twelve stones in Enclosure D's main circle. Eight remain in Enclosure C's outer wall and eleven within its inner ring, with the likelihood of a twelfth having once existed. Seven are known from Enclosure B (not counting the two central pillars), while Enclosure A is so different in style that guessing its original design becomes difficult. Enclosure F is so small, and from such a later date, that it is unlikely to have been built with the exact same motivations as its predecessors; ditto the Lion Pillar Building on the summit of the mound.

Having said this, it does appear that a twelvefold division of stones did once exist in Enclosures C and D, arguably Göbekli Tepe's oldest and most accomplished structures uncovered so far, while twelve T-shaped pillars are known to have existed in the walls of Nevalı Çori's Level II cult building, the number increasing to thirteen during its next building phase, Level III, ca. 8000 BC. (The level system runs from the oldest layer, Level I, ca. 8500 BC, to the most recent occupational layers, Levels III–V, ca. 8000–7600 BC.)

That the earliest enclosures at Göbekli Tepe might originally have had twelve T-shaped pillars within their elliptical walls raises the question of whether this number had any significance to the hunter-gatherers who created these strange structures over eleven thousand years ago. Was it simply by chance that twelve stones were chosen for the purpose, or might there be some deeper meaning behind the use of this myth-laden number?

A CLOCKWISE MOTION

A clue to this mystery lies in the fact that at least half of the standing pillars in Enclosures C and D have reliefs both on their shafts *and* on their T-shaped "heads." Yet the head decoration appears only on the right-hand "faces" of the figures, *never on their left sides.*[1] If these facial carvings had to be viewed in any kind of order or sequence, then it implies the entrant would have had to perambulate the enclosures in a clockwise motion. Doing so in a counterclockwise direction would have meant not being able to see any of the cranial reliefs.

Of course, this could all just be coincidence or a simple case of design preference on the part of the Göbekli builders. However, a preferred navigation of the sacred enclosures in a clockwise fashion, along with the possible celestial nature of the glyphs on key pillars in Enclosures C and D, does hint at some kind of synchronization with the motion of the celestial bodies—the sun, moon, and planets—which all rise in the east and move around to the south before setting in the west.

This clockwise, or *sunwise,* movement is seen in the shadow cast by a vertical pole or sundial gnomon. For this reason, the hands of the first analog clocks were set to move "with the sun"; that is, *clockwise,* and not counterclockwise, or *anticlockwise,* something that was seen as against the natural order of the universe.

THE SUN'S PATH

These realizations invoke compelling thoughts. The ecliptic, the sun's course through the heavens, is divided into twelve divisions, or "months," a consensus reached long ago based on the placement along its circular course of twelve key constellations, which each rise with the sun across one complete calendar year. Each remains visible in this role for a period of around thirty days, or one month, before giving way to the next constellation in line, the whole process occurring twelve times in all before the first constellation returns to the predawn sky.

These zodiacal constellations provide us with a twelvefold division both of the solar year and the vault of heaven, with the combined twelve 30-degree sections making up a 360-degree circle. Thus in this manner both time and space are intrinsically bound together in recurring cycles, which through the passage of the seasons and the movement of the planets control the destiny of humankind, this being the root of astrology.

The problem here is that the creation of the zodiac, along with the twelvefold division of the ecliptic and the establishment of the zodiacal houses, is thought to have taken place only around three thousand years ago, with all its different elements coming together finally in the Greek zodiac, which evolved into its current form during the first millennium BC. Despite this, a twelvefold division of the heavens *did* exist before this time. For example, as early as 2400 BC the Indus Valley civilization divided the celestial horizon into twelve parts.[2] Excavations at Lothal in India between 1955 and 1960 revealed knowledge among the inhabitants of an eight- and twelvefold division of the horizon and sky. They utilized a thick, ringlike instrument made of shell, which divided the horizon into 360 degrees—all this coming some fifteen hundred years before the Greeks "invented" the zodiac.[3]

COSMIC HARMONY

The twelvefold division of the enclosures at Göbekli Tepe suggests a basic knowledge of cosmic geography in the design and layout of its monumental architecture. If correct, then the apparent 5:4 size ratio of Enclosures B, C, D, and E, which are all ovoid, suggests not only a basic understanding of cosmic harmony and proportion but also an interest in the interaction between different time cycles, most obviously those relating to the earth's eccentricity, its axial tilt, and the precession of the earth's orbit against the starry background (see chapter 7 for more on the Göbekli builders' apparent interest in precession). Although many of these cosmic notions were not fully recognized until fairly recent times, there is some hint that they were known at least in principle during the age of Pythagoras and Plato.[4]

So the next most obvious question would be to ask whether the carved art at Göbekli Tepe confirms its builders' interest in a twelvefold division of the night sky. The answer, unfortunately, is frustratingly disappointing, for although certain zoomorphs found carved on the T-shape pillars *do* resemble the signs of the zodiac (such as scorpions, rams, goats, bulls, birds, and lions), there are too many other creatures featured to make any realistic comparisons with existing zodiac forms.

Despite such drawbacks, some kind of astronomical or celestial motivation behind the construction of the various enclosures at Göbekli Tepe cannot be ruled out. If this is the case, then the T-shaped pillars found within the walls of its sacred enclosures might well act as symbolic markers representing the twelvefold segmentation of the heavens and the twelvefold division of the year. Yet what does this tell us about the true function of these monuments?

CENTER OF THE WORLD

With the rings of T-shaped stones acting as the divisional markers of a symbolic clock face, the main enclosures' pivotal axis would have been their twin central pillars. In cosmological terms these constitute the site's *axis mundi,* or "axis of the earth," a concept familiar to shamanic societies worldwide. This was a symbolic axis or world pillar—symbolized usually by a rope, pole, or tree trunk and often associated with a "world mountain" or "cosmic mountain"— seen to link the center of the earth with the rotation of the starry canopy via the celestial pole and marked in the night sky by the Pole Star. Each different tribe, culture, or territory had its own axis mundi, while shamanic cultures often had movable axis mundi represented by poles erected for this express purpose. Indeed, an axis mundi would often be the pole inside a communal tent, the smoke hole at the top of the structure acting as the entrance to a sky world thought to exist beyond the physical world.

The concept of an axis mundi is most easily understood through its place in Greek cosmological architecture, for here it was marked permanently by an *omphalos,* a word meaning "navel." These were bullet-shaped or conical stones of varying sizes set up in the inner sanctums of chief sanctuaries to signify the center of the physical world (very much like the *Shiva-lingam* of Hindu tradition, a navel-like stone set up in a temple's most holy place, usually a darkened crypt immediately beneath the main building).

According to Greek mythology the site of the original omphalos was determined when the sky god Zeus let fly two eagles, one from either "end" of the earth. Where they came together would be the absolute center of the world, which, in the version of the story handed down to us, turns out to be Delphi (omphali existed in other Greek kingdoms as well). Here the omphalos was said to allow direct access to the realm of the gods, a fact borne out by its supposed placement in the temple's *adyton,* or Pythia, where a priestess, known as the Oracle, would deliver prophecies after breathing vapors rising from a chasm in the rock.

Although the origin of the term *omphalos* has been lost, it is very likely linked to the idea that it was connected to the so-called cosmic axis, or turning point of the heavens, by an invisible umbilical cord. This was a concept based on the belief that the earth, as the offspring of the greater universe, was nourished in a fetal state within some kind of cosmic womb, seen in terms of the starry vault of heaven.

PLACE OF THE PLACENTA

Is it possible that the elliptical shape of the large enclosures at Göbekli Tepe, with their 5:4 size ratios, symbolizes the womb chamber, within which is the ovoid placenta that nourishes a prenatal child during pregnancy via the umbilical cord? Completing the picture would have been the site's occupational mound, constructed around the enclosures to represent a belly swollen by pregnancy. It is a theme expressed, of course, in the name Göbekli Tepe, which, as we saw in chapter 1, means in Turkish "navel-like (*göbekli*) hill (*tepe*)."

There is no way of knowing exactly when Göbekli Tepe gained its current name, although the chances are it replaced an earlier one meaning exactly the same thing, a process that might have been going on since the site's final abandonment around 8000 BC. Evidence of this comes from the fact that the Kurdish name for the tell, which local people see even today as sacred, is Gire Navoke, which means "hill (*gire*) of the swollen belly (*navoke*)," with an emphasis on fertilization and pregnancy (Armenians, who formerly occupied eastern Turkey when it was part of Armenia Major, call Göbekli Tepe *Portasar,* meaning the "hill of the navel." However, no historical evidence exists to show that this name was used prior to news of the site's discovery in the year 2000.)

Possibly significant in this respect is that in the language of the Sumerians, who thrived on the Mesopotamia Plain from ca. 2900 BC to 1940 BC, the word for *placenta, úš,* is more or less identical to that used for *blood* and *death* (*úš*), as well as the word for *base* or *foundation place* (*úš*), as in a place to set up the central pole for a tent.[5] Such a term might easily have applied to Göbekli

Tepe, where the "pole" in question was represented by the enclosures' twin central pillars.

In various indigenous cultures and civilizations the placenta was, and still is, considered a very sacred object, the disposal of which was of great importance not just to the future of the postnatal child, but also to the well-being of the family. Among the Acholi tribe of Uganda and the Sudan, for instance, placentas are buried in a spirit house made of stone at the center of a lineage shrine known as the *abila*.[6] In Eastern Asia, Japan in particular, the placenta is buried with great dignity, often beneath a tree (another symbol of the sky pole). The site is thereafter venerated as a sacred place, with the placentas of emperors becoming the subject of annual festivals relating to the fecundity of the land and the prosperity of the people.[7]

TEMPLE OF THE TWINS

Placentas, when featured in ancient myth and ritual, are often associated with the theme of twins, a matter that may well have some bearing on the presence of the twin pillars at the center of the enclosures at Göbekli Tepe. For example, among the Baganda tribe of Uganda the placenta and umbilical cord of the king are considered the source of his "twin" (*mulongo*), which is seen as the ghost or spirit of the placenta.[8] During the monarch's life it is kept under constant watch in a specially built Temple of the Twin, and at the first sight of the lunar crescent each month it is brought into the king's presence for a special ceremony. Once the ceremony is complete, the "twin" is "exposed in the doorway of the temple for the moon to shine upon it, and also anointed with butter."[9] This exposure to the light of the moon takes place also on a second night, before the "twin" is hidden away for another month.

After the king's death the "twin," that is, the placenta and umbilical cord, is buried in the temple, along with his jaw, which thereafter functions as a point of communication with the dead monarch's spirit, the relics being brought out on special occasions for oracular purposes.[10] At the same time a new Temple of the Twin is created for the next king, with the whole process being repeated (rather like the periodic construction of new enclosures at Göbekli Tepe).

Even in ancient Egypt the placenta formed the twin of the king, quite literally the seat of his soul double or alter ego. As in Baganda tradition, it was retained and carefully protected throughout his life and, following his death, was most probably buried in a special room, where it served as his *ka,* or double. To the ancient Egyptians the royal placenta was seen as a divinity in its own right, its cult attested as early as the late Predynastic period, ca. 3250–3050 BC.[11]

More disturbingly, it is reported that in addition to placing placentas in the abila cult shrine, the Acholi tribe of Africa is said to have buried alive twins placed in jars at the same spot.[12] Whatever the reality of this macabre act, it further emphasizes the connection between twins and the placenta, which derives in the main from the primordial belief that when a child is born, his twin, symbolized by the placenta, is the one who dies, and thus becomes a spirit double of the living person. In this knowledge, it was considered that during pregnancy the womb *always* contains twins, each with his or her own soul and destiny.

The association between twins and the placenta is expressed also in the creation myth of the Dogon of Mali, in West Africa, where a double placenta forms inside the cosmic egg of Amma, the creator god, each one attached to a pair of twins.[13] A Dogon pictogram showing the double placenta inside Amma's egg closely resembles the elliptical appearance of the sanctuaries at Göbekli Tepe (see figure 5.1). More incredibly, vertical strokes drawn to represent the two sets of twins inside the egg eerily echo the placement and orientation of the twin pillars at the center of the enclosures.

TWIN PORTALS TO THE SKY WORLD

This information makes it highly likely that similar themes might have featured among the beliefs and practices of the Göbekli builders. If so, then the twin sets of pillars in the various enclosures at Göbekli Tepe could well signify human twins, either twins that exist in the womb during pregnancy or twins that are seen to have reentered some kind of symbolic womb in death (something that every entrant might have been seen to do when he or she entered the enclosures for shamanic purposes). Indeed, if the central pillars do symbolize twins, one representing the human soul, the other signifying the soul double, or ghost, then this practice might be related to a belief expressed by the Karo Batak peoples of Sumatra, which asserts that of the twin souls, a person's *true* soul is that of the placenta, which was probably seen as "the seat of the transferable soul."[14] In other words, in order to enter and navigate the spirit world, shamans or initiates had first to transfer the consciousness from their physical body to that of their twin; namely, the placenta soul. Thus the twin central

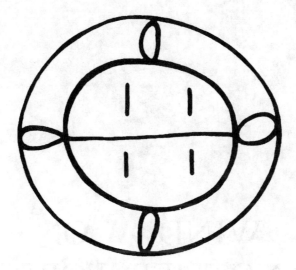

Figure 5.1. Dogon pictogram showing the two sets of twins
inside the double placenta within Amma's egg.
Note how the vertical lines, representing the twins, eerily echo
the twin central pillars in the enclosures at Göbekli Tepe.

pillars at Göbekli Tepe might have enforced a similar belief in the minds of entrants standing between them.

Allied to this belief is the fact that the twin pillars at Göbekli Tepe most probably signified portals or gateways; that is, entranceways into the conceived axis mundi that would have transferred you instantly to the sky world (hollows in tree trunks are often seen to serve this function among shamanic-based societies). An instantaneous dimension shift of this sort would have been achieved through the use of one or more shamanic processes, including ecstatic dancing, ritual drumming, long-term sensory deprivation, and, of course, the ingestion of psychotropic or soporific substances (something suggested at Göbekli Tepe, as we have seen, through the profusion of snakes in its carved art and also by the presence of large basalt bowls used perhaps in the preparation of drugs and medicine). All of these methods would have enabled the mind to, quite literally, jump between worlds without any kind of delay involving regular space or time.

So where exactly was the sky world of the shaman during the age of Göbekli Tepe? In an attempt to answer this question, we must examine the deepest, most profound, cave art of Ice Age Europe.

6

WINDOW ON ANOTHER WORLD

I f the hermetic axiom of "as above, so below" were to be applied to the construction of Göbekli Tepe in the tenth millennium BC, then it would suggest that ritual activity taking place within its enclosures was reflected in some manner in the heavens, and vice versa. Going beyond the imagined portal created by the twin pillars standing at the center of the structures is likely to have projected the shaman or initiate into some part of the night sky, but where exactly?

Some idea might be gleaned from the Ice Age cave artists of the late Paleolithic age. Although much of the beautiful imagery seen in the caves suggests a clear interface between the physical world and the perceived supernatural realms existing beyond human consciousness, certain painted panels are now thought to convey abstract celestial themes as well.[1] Three examples can be cited in this respect, and in each case the panels or friezes are positioned in the direction of the area of sky where the relevant stars were to be seen during the epoch in question.

THE LASCAUX SHAFT SCENE

The first example is the famous Shaft Scene from Lascaux Caves near Montignac in France's Dordogne region. Located in a pit 16 feet (4.9 meters) deep, which could only be accessed using a rope (the remains of which have been found), the scene is composed of a set of images that have mystified paleontologists since the chance discovery of the cave complex by four teenagers in 1940.

From right to left, the painted fresco—which is approximately ten feet (three meters) across—shows a wounded bison, a birdman, a bird on a pole, and a rhinoceros (see figure 6.1 on p. 70, although the rhino is not shown here). Black loops drawn beneath the bison's belly indicate the release of its entrails, perhaps by the barbed spear seen cutting across its body at an acute angle. Either that or it has been gored by the rhinoceros, which appears to be walking away from the scene. Facing the bison is a male human figure, who either has the head of a bird or wears a bird mask. He leans backward in a most awkward position and has an erect penis, a stance that could indicate he is a bird shaman experiencing an ecstatic trance state (the ingestion of psychotropic substances often causes male erection).

Confirming the significance of the figure's avian features is the presence just below his feet of a bird on a pole, its head and beak resembling those of the birdman. Off to the left is the rhinoceros, whose role is debatable; he could have gored the bison, or he might simply be associated with the birdman's blatant display of virility (rhino horn, being phallic in appearance, is valued in some cultures as an aphrodisiac). Next to the creature's upraised tail are six black dots drawn in pairs, the meaning of which is unclear.

The panel's awkward positioning at the bottom of a deep shaft, along with the fact that it shows the only human figure in the entire cave complex, indicates that it held some special significance to the Upper Paleolithic peoples who entered Lascaux and decorated its corridors and halls with a whole menagerie of Ice Age animals.

THE SUMMER TRIANGLE

Many scholars have attempted to understand Lascaux's Shaft Scene, although no consensus regarding its meaning has ever been reached. However, in 2000

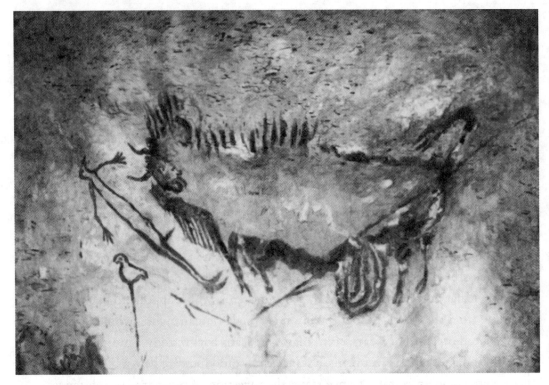

Figure 6.1. The Shaft Scene inside the pit at Lascaux in southern France. Solutrean period, ca. 16,500–15,000 BC.

German scholar Dr. Michael Rappenglück of the University of Munich came up with a truly inspired interpretation of the painted panel. He argues that the entire scene is an abstract map of an area of sky featuring a group of three bright stars known collectively as the Summer Triangle, these being Altair in Aquila, Vega in Lyra, and Deneb, the brightest star in the constellation of Cygnus, the celestial bird or swan, known also as the Northern Cross.[2] At the time the Shaft Scene was created, ca. 16,500–15,000 BC, Deneb acted as the Pole Star, as it was the closest star to the celestial pole, the turning point of the heavens.

Today Polaris, a star in the constellation of Ursa Minor, the Little Bear, marks the position of the celestial pole in the northern night sky. Yet over time, the Pole Star changes due to the effects of precession—the slow wobble of the earth across a cycle of approximately twenty-six thousand years. During the pyramid age, Thuban, a minor star in the constellation of Draco, the celestial dragon, held the position of Pole Star. Going back further, Vega in Lyra was Pole Star from around 13,000 BC to 11,000 BC. Before that the pole had been marked by Delta Cygni, one of the wing stars of Cygnus. It gained the role from its neighbor Deneb, which was Pole Star from around 16,500 BC until ca. 14,500 BC.

That Deneb was Pole Star when the Shaft Scene was created makes sense of its connection with the Summer Triangle, especially as Cygnus is universally seen as a celestial bird. In other words, the bird shown on the pole at Lascaux is Cygnus marking the celestial pole, with the pole itself representing the vertical axis, or sky pole, which turns the heavens and holds up the sky. As to the birdman, he might well signify a shaman who has attained a trance state and ascended the sky pole in the guise of a bird associated in some manner with astral flight and, of course, the Cygnus asterism, or star group. Moreover, the Shaft Scene is located on a north-facing wall, which corresponds to the direction of the Summer Triangle during this distant epoch. It is almost as if the panel is an imaginary window onto the celestial world it portrays.

This theory suggests that the area of sky in question held a special place in the beliefs and practices of the Ice Age peoples responsible for executing the cave art. Such practices, which perhaps involved a ritual descent into the shaft using the rope provided, very likely acted as a symbolic means of shifting from one level of reality to another. In this way the Paleolithic shamans or initiates could commune with perceived supernatural intelligences in a sky world thought to exist beyond the celestial pole.

On its own, the directing of Lascaux's Shaft Scene toward the stars its panel represents might seem like a happy coincidence. However, elsewhere in the Lascaux Caves other murals have been identified as abstract representations of known asterisms. For instance, Rappenglück and others see the head, horns, and upper torso of a bull in the Salle des Taureaux, or Hall of the Bulls, as a representation of the constellation of Taurus, the bull, with a grouping of six to seven dots next to it being seen as the nearby star cluster known as the Pleiades.[3] As with the Shaft Scene, the animals on the wall of the Salle des Taureaux face toward where the stars in question would have been visible during the epoch in question.

THE VENUS AND THE SORCERER

A third example of the relationship between Ice Age cave art and celestial themes can be found in the Chauvet Cave of southern France, which overlooks an ancient gorge through which the Ardèche River once flowed. Discovered as recently as 1994, its painted galleries, full of breathtaking friezes showing a variety of Ice Age animals, are among the oldest so far discovered, having been executed by Paleolithic cave artists around thirty-two thousand years ago. Of special interest here is the fact that in the Salle du Fond, or End Chamber, located in the deepest part of the complex, a remarkable piece of wall decoration can be found. Called the Venus and the Sorcerer, it appears on a vertically hanging cone of limestone (a form of stalactite) that comes to within 3 feet 6 inches (1 meter) of the cave floor.

The Venus in question is an abstract torso, hips, vulva, and legs of a full-bodied woman, arguably one of the oldest known two-dimensional representations of the female form in existence; it is also the only human figure to be seen anywhere in the caves. The Sorcerer is a young bison, its head overlying the woman's belly or womb, its left front leg doubling as her left leg, indicating a special relationship between the two figures. Completing the scene is the head and upper body of a large feline, perhaps a panther or lion, which extends above and to the left of the woman's body as if the former is emerging from the latter (see figure 6.2).

The strange image is unique, without anything else quite like it in the entire cave complex, and would seem to have been a central focus of the cave artists' ritual activity. Thus any suggestion that the panel might depict abstract representations of celestial objects should be taken seriously, especially when we find that it could well reflect the same region of sky as Lascaux's Shaft Scene.

THE GREAT RIFT

Swiss researcher Franz Gnaedinger has proposed that the woman's torso and genitalia represent the Summer Triangle, within which the young bison's head and shoulders are perfectly framed.* This is an inspiring theory, although a more positive identification would be to suggest that the woman's vulva and scissorlike legs represent the area of the Milky Way known as the Great Rift (also known as the Dark Rift, Cygnus Rift, and Great Cleft), which is framed

*To read more about Franz Gnaedinger's identification of Chauvet's Venus and the Sorcerer panel as the Summer Triangle go to www.seshat.ch/home/homepage.htm, and follow the links for Chauvet.

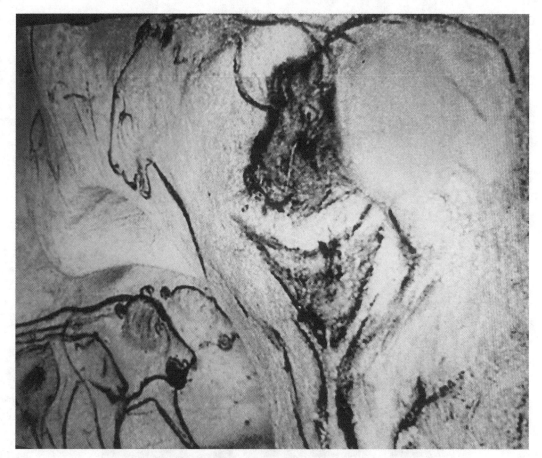

Figure 6.2. The Venus and the Sorcerer panel inside the Chauvet Cave.
Note how the woman and bull share the same leg,
while the large feline seems to emerge from the scene.

within the Summer Triangle (see figure 6.3 on p. 74). This is a dark band of stellar dust and debris in line with the galactic plane that causes the Milky Way to appear to split into two separate streams in the region of the Cygnus constellation. As a dark band it continues to where the ecliptic, the path of the sun, crosses the Milky Way in the region of the stars of Sagittarius and Scorpius, or Scorpio, the celestial scorpion. Here one "leg" of the Milky Way peters out as the other expands in width and continues into the southern sky.

If Chauvet's Venus figure really is an expression of the Milky Way, then the head of the young bison might be viewed as emerging from the Great Rift like a newborn child. As alien as such a concept might seem, there are 3-D representations and murals showing women, goddesses perhaps, giving birth to

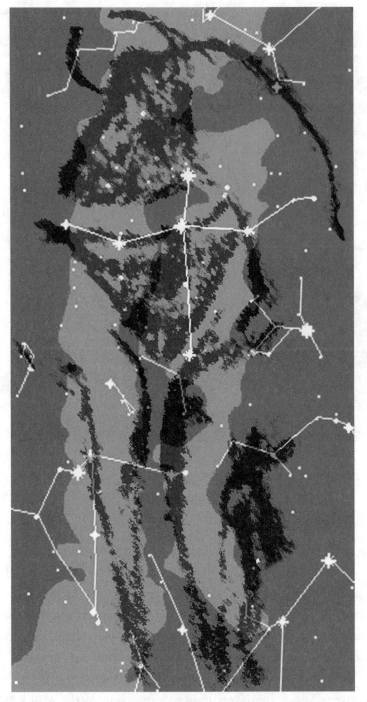

Figure 6.3. The Venus and the Sorcerer from the Chauvet Cave overlaid on the Milky Way, showing that the woman's legs form the twin streams of the Great Rift, while the head of the bull calf in her womb area corresponds to the position of the stars of Cygnus and Cepheus.

Figure 6.4. Three-dimensional panel showing a leopard-headed woman giving birth to a bull calf, from the Neolithic city of Çatal Höyük, ca. 7500–5700 BC.

bull calves at Çatal Höyük, the Neolithic city on the Konya Plain in southern central Turkey, which dates to ca. 7500–5700 BC (see figure 6.4).

In addition to forming the outline of a bird in flight, the arrangement of the Cygnus stars resemble the frontal view of a bovine head, complete with extended horns. It is a realization that probably inspired both the Chauvet Cave's Venus and Sorcerer panel and the ancient Egyptian belief that the sun is reborn each morning in the form of a bull calf, which emerges from between the twin streams of the Milky Way's Great Rift.[4]

Yet if Chauvet's Venus is an abstract representation of the Milky Way in the region of the Great Rift, and the bull calf signifies the Cygnus stars, what does the large feline represent? Its position immediately above the other figures gives the impression that it is either responsible for or connected with what is displayed, suggesting that it too is a representation of something to be seen in the heavens. Universally, large felines, such as panthers, jaguars, pumas, and lions, have been seen as personifications, and even controlling intelligences, of the night sky. Is it possible that the example at Chauvet plays a similar role? Could it be seen as the "father," or progenitor, of the bull calf, with the Venus as its mother—the feline, bull, and woman having some kind of symbiotic relationship?

As with the proposed astronomical frescoes at Lascaux, the Venus and Sorcerer panel at Chauvet is located at the extreme northern end of the cave complex at a position suggesting that it too acted as a symbolic window onto the section of sky represented by the images in question. If this surmise is correct, it could suggest that the Ice Age artists that executed this extraordinary cave art some thirty-two thousand years ago possessed, like those at Lascaux, a highly complex understanding of the night sky that we are only now beginning to comprehend.

CAVE SCENES TO CULT SHRINES

All this is very interesting and might well be correct. Yet linking Ice Age cave art with the design of sacred enclosures created at Göbekli Tepe in southeast Anatolia thousands of years later might seem presumptuous. It is a fact, however, that in the early Neolithic, stalagmites and stalactites were removed from cave interiors and carried back to Çatal Höyük, where they were placed in cult shrines alongside statuettes, bucrania, vulture beaks, and painted frescoes of extraordinary beauty and sophistication. So many fragments from caves were found there that British archaeologist James Mellaart, who excavated the site in the 1960s, proposed that the shrines at Çatal Höyük might have been the realm of chthonic deities; that is, gods of the underworld.[5]

B. C. Dietrich, Ph.D., author of *The Origins of Greek Religion,* went further by suggesting that the ritual activities practiced in Çatal Höyük's cult shrines had formerly been celebrated in primordial cave settings, adding that: "Though the locality of the cult may have changed, its form did not relax its curious hold on the mind of the worshipper who, over many generations, retained the aniconic stalagmite as an image of his goddess."[6] This, of course, resonates with the manner in which the limestone cone in the Chauvet Cave was utilized in the creation of the Venus and Sorcerer panel.

If the sacred enclosures at Göbekli Tepe *do* reflect an interest in the celestial heavens, was it just a symbolic gesture, without any kind of real accuracy, or was there true precision involved in their construction? We examine now the evidence presented by the T-shaped pillars, which reveal a recurring pattern that will leave the reader in little doubt that they were once turned toward something very specific in the night sky.

7

TURNED TOWARD
THE STARS

I n the knowledge that megalithic monuments worldwide have been found to possess alignments toward celestial bodies, such as the sun, moon, and stars, it seems reasonable to look for something similar at Göbekli Tepe, with the most obvious candidates for orientation being the various sets of twin pillars at the center of the different enclosures. These could have acted as astronomical markers, especially as at the time of their construction a clear view of the local horizon would have been visible in all directions from their elevated positions.

Even a cursory glance at the positioning of the different sets of twin pillars in the main enclosures shows them to be aligned roughly north-south. This suggests they are unlikely to have targeted the sun, moon, or planets, which all rise in the east and set in the west. Clearly, if their orientations mean anything, then the enclosures must have been built to target a star or stellar object that either rose or set close to the imaginary north-south meridian line that divides the sky in two and crosses directly overhead.

ANGLES OF ORIENTATION

Establishing the precise orientations of the enclosures' central pillars was put to chartered engineer Rodney Hale, who for the past fifteen years has made a detailed study of stellar alignments at prehistoric and sacred sites around the world. He examined Göbekli Tepe's detailed survey plan and determined that the central pillars in Enclosures B, C, D, and E (the Felsentempel, or rock temple, located to the west of the main group) all seemed to be aligned just west of north, and, equally, just east of south, in the following manner:

Enclosure B   337°/157°
Enclosure C   345°/165°
Enclosure D   353°/173°
Enclosure E   350°/170°

The twin pillars marking the entrance to an apse-like feature at the northern end of Enclosure A were turned much farther west. Indeed, they are oriented 312 degrees/132 degrees, just 3 degrees off northwest-southeast, suggesting that whatever it was they were oriented toward had little to do with the primary alignments of the larger enclosures.

The slight differences in the mean azimuths of the central pillars in Enclosures B, C, D, and E is telling, as it suggests that each set targeted a star or stellar object that was very gradually shifting its position against the local horizon as a result of precession (see figure 7.1). Thus the enclosures were aligned to a celestial object that either set each night on the north-northwestern horizon or, equally, rose each night on the south-southeast horizon.

AN ORION CORRELATION?

Among the southern star groups and constellations looked at by Hale were the Hyades, Taurus, the Pleiades, and Orion (more specifically its three "belt" stars), all of which have been claimed to match the orientations of the twin pillars in the various enclosures at Göbekli Tepe during the epoch of their construction.[1] Out of these, just one candidate emerged as perhaps playing some role at Göbekli Tepe, and this was Orion, the celestial hunter.

Rodney Hale charted the risings of Orion's principal stars between 9500

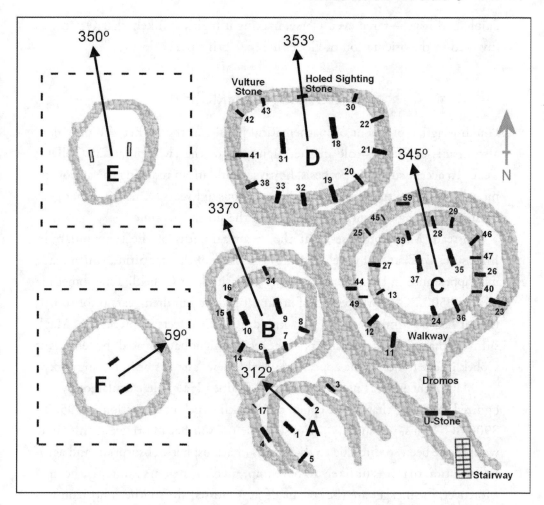

Figure 7.1. The main enclosures at Göbekli Tepe showing the mean
alignments of their central pillars.

BC and 8000 BC, then matched this information against the window of opportunity created by the orientations of the central pillars in the various enclosures
at Göbekli Tepe.* However, the results were disappointing. Although potential alignments existed between Enclosure B and the Orion belt stars between
9000 BC and 8600 BC, the mean azimuths of the central pillars in Enclosures
C, D, and E did not target the rising of *any* of Orion's belt stars between 9500
BC and 8000 BC. The constellation's other key stars—Betelgeuse, Bellatrix,

---

*Dates based on an altitude of 2 degrees including refraction and calculated using Stellarium
planetarium software.

Saiph, and Rigel—fared even worse, making it highly unlikely that Orion was involved in the orientation of Göbekli Tepe's principal enclosures.

ALIGNED TO SIRIUS?

Giulio Magli, a professor of mathematical physics at the Politecnico of Milan, also dismisses Orion's role in the alignment of the twin pillars at Göbekli Tepe. To accept such a hypothesis, he says, would mean reducing the age of the mountaintop sanctuaries by as much as a thousand years, something that goes against all dating evidence emerging from the site at this time.[2]

Instead, Magli proposes that the mean azimuths of the twin pillars in Enclosures B, C, and D were aligned to the rising of the star Sirius, which made its reappearance in the night skies from the latitude of Göbekli Tepe sometime around 9500 BC.[3] For a period of around fifty-five hundred years prior to this time it had been missing from the skies due to the effects of precession. Magli surmises that the hunter-gatherers of the region might have created the temples at Göbekli Tepe to honor the appearance of this new "guest" star in the night sky.

Magli's theory was put to the test by Rodney Hale. He calculated, by recognized methods, that in the epoch of Göbekli Tepe's construction, ca. 9500–8900 BC, Sirius, which only just rose above the southern horizon at this time, would have been so dim due to the effects of atmospheric absorption and aerosol pollution that it is unlikely to have impressed the region's hunter-gatherers.[4] Moreover, the meager arc the star made as it crossed the southern horizon was so brief that in just twenty minutes it would have shifted its horizontal position a full 3 degrees, making it a difficult and highly unrealistic stellar target to use for such a purpose.[5]

In conclusion, it seems totally improbable that the Paleolithic peoples of southeast Anatolia gave up their free lives as hunters to worship such an insignificant star. Clearly, if astronomical phenomena really did inspire these people's building motivations, then it did not involve either the stars of Orion or the lone star Sirius.

NORTH OR SOUTH?

In fact, there is a fundamental problem in even assuming that the main enclosures at Göbekli Tepe are oriented south, for although the humanlike features

of the central monoliths are all turned this direction, there is no reason to conclude that their gaze is fixed toward the southern skyline. More likely, they
greet the entrant approaching from the south in the same manner that statues
in churches face the worshipper approaching the high altar. Church altars are
located in the east, as this is the direction of heaven in Christian tradition,
and also because churches were often aligned toward the position where the
sun rises on the feast day of its patron saint. Just because Jesus, Saint Michael,
or the Virgin Mary faces *away* from the high altar does not mean their gaze is
fixed toward the western skyline.

In Göbekli Tepe's case, if its enclosures did have a high altar or holy of
holies, then it would have been in the north, the direction of darkness, where
the sun never rises. It is also the direction of the celestial pole, the turning point
of the heavens. In southeast and eastern Anatolia, northerly orientations of early
Neolithic cult buildings have been noted at Çayönü, Nevalı Çori, and Hallan
Çemi in the eastern Taurus Mountains (see chapter 23). It thus seems likely that
Göbekli Tepe's enclosures are oriented toward the north, and not the south.

Concluding that Göbekli Tepe's central pillars face south without taking into
account the significance that the north plays in Anatolia's early Neolithic tradition would be very foolish indeed. What is more, the Sabaeans, the pagan star
worshippers of the ancient city of Harran—the ruins of which are overlooked
by Göbekli Tepe—each year celebrated the Mystery of the North, since this was
deemed the direction of the primal cause and the source of life itself.[6] As we saw
in the prologue, the earliest inhabitants of the city, who thrived a full ten thousand years ago, were very likely the direct descendants of the Göbekli builders.

Similar beliefs of the north being the original *qibla,* or direction of prayer,
were held by other ethno-religious groups of the region, including the angel-
worshipping Yezidi, the Mandaeans of Iraq and Iran, and an Ismaili sect known
as the Brethren of Purity.[7] All of them most likely inherited aspects of their
beliefs and practices from much earlier cultures with roots in the Neolithic age.
With these thoughts in mind, Hale now turned his attention to the northern
sky to identify any possible stellar targets there.

TARGET REVEALED

Just one star emerged as a potential candidate, and this was Deneb, the brightest star in the constellation of Cygnus, the celestial bird. Before 9500 BC

Deneb was circumpolar, in that it never set, although after this time, through the effects of precession, it started to set each night on the north-northwestern horizon. As the centuries rolled by, the star's point of extinction moved ever westward in a manner that, as we see below, not only makes sense of the mean azimuths of the various sets of twin pillars at Göbekli Tepe but also offers realistic construction dates for the enclosures in question.

Enclosure D @ 353° = 9400 BC*

Enclosure E @ 350° = 9290 BC

Enclosure C @ 345° = 8980 BC

Enclosure B @ 337° = 8235 BC

These dates should not be seen as absolute, as we have no idea as to what level of accuracy the Göbekli builders employed in their building construction. Even a small error in the positioning of the central pillars could alter the proposed alignment toward a stellar object by as much as a hundred years. Having said this, the construction dates of the various pairs of central pillars—suggested by their alignment to Deneb—correlate pretty well with available radiocarbon dates obtained from key enclosures.

ENCLOSURE DATES

For instance, loam taken from wall plaster found in Göbekli Tepe's Enclosure D has provided a radiocarbon age of 9745–9314 BC,[8] which corresponds perfectly with a date of ca. 9400 BC defined by the alignment of its twin pillars toward Deneb at this time. Interestingly, bone samples taken from Enclosure B have provided a radiocarbon age of 8306–8236 BC,[9] which coincides with a suggested construction date of ca. 8235 BC implied by its twin pillars' alignment toward Deneb. Having said this, radiocarbon specialist Oliver Dietrich of the German Archaeological Institute believes these burials could have been made long after the construction of the enclosure, so no more can be said on the matter until better dating evidence becomes available.[10] Other radiocarbon dates have been obtained from organic

---

*Dates based on an extinction altitude of Deneb at 2 degrees including refraction using Stellarium planetarium software.

materials found within the fill used to cover the major enclosures, and these range from the late tenth to the late ninth millennium BC, the time of the site's final abandonment.[11]

Clearly, the possibility that the central pillars in Göbekli Tepe's main enclosures were aligned to reflect the precessional shift of a single astronomical target across an extended period of time is borne out by the astronomical data presented by Rodney Hale. What is more, there is evidence that cult buildings at other Pre-Pottery Neolithic sites in southeast Anatolia might also have reflected an interest in the star Deneb. For instance, the Flagstone Building, Skull Building, and Terrazzo Building at Çayönü are also aligned north-northwest with entrances in their southern walls (see figure 7.2 on p. 84). Hale checked their orientations, based on available plans, and established that they reflect alignments toward the setting of Deneb between ca. 8825 BC and 7950 BC—shown in the following table[12]—dates that accord well with recent revisions of Çayönü's age based on radiocarbon evidence obtained during the 1960s.[13]

Structure	Azimuth	Deneb Setting Date
Flagstone Building	345.35°	8810 BC
Skull Building	345.86°	8825 BC
Terrazzo Building	336.20°	7950 BC

CELESTIAL MARKERS

Coming to Göbekli Tepe's Enclosure E, the Felsentempel, where all the pillars have been removed and only the slots within the stone pedestals remain, we find that the orientation of its twin pillars targeted the setting of Deneb at a date of ca. 9290 BC, some 110 years later than those of Enclosure D (see figure 7.3 on p. 84). This said, the fact that Enclosure E's standing pillars have been removed makes it impossible to verify whether it really was aligned north toward Deneb. We are, however, on much firmer ground with Enclosure C.

According to Hale's calculations, Enclosure C's central pillars targeted the setting of Deneb around 8980 BC, suggesting that this was the time frame of their construction (no radiocarbon dates are available at present for this

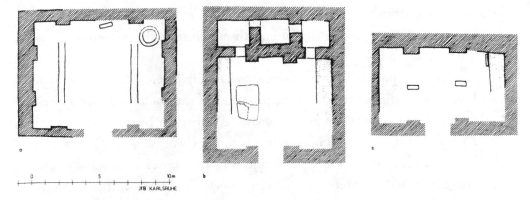

Figure 7.2. The three cult buildings at Çayönü—the Terrazzo Building, Skull Building, and Flagstone Building. All are oriented north-northwest with entrances in the south.

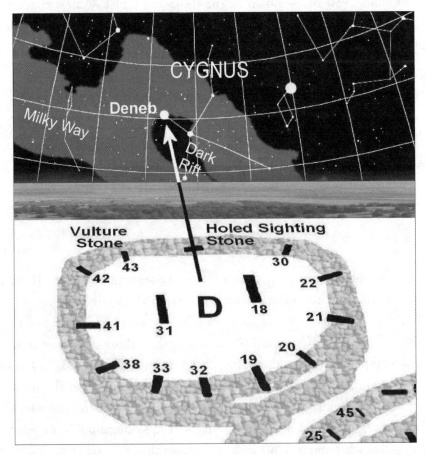

Figure 7.3. The alignment of Enclosure D's central pillars toward the star Deneb in Cygnus and the opening of the Milky Way's Great Rift, ca. 9400 BC.

structure).* Yet the rectangular slots cut out of the bedrock pedestals to support Enclosure C's twin monoliths are aligned slightly more toward north than the pillars themselves. They are askew only by about a degree, although the difference between the stones and their slots is noticeable. This might indicate that the pillars target Deneb at a date slightly later than the construction of the slots, which could reflect the position of the star at an earlier date. If so, then quite possibly the enclosure is older than the 8980 BC date suggested by the proposed astronomical alignment of its twin pillars, perhaps by as much as a century or so. It is even possible that the monoliths were repositioned when it was realized they no longer synched with the setting of Deneb. So around 8980 BC they were turned very slightly to reflect the star's new setting position. If this theory is correct, then it is possible that the Göbekli builders were familiar with the effects of precession, which shifts a star against the local horizon at a rate of around one degree every seventy-two years.

SIGHTING STONE DISCOVERY

Further evidence of Göbekli Tepe's proposed astronomical alignments comes from Enclosure D. A stone pillar standing around 5 feet (1.5 meters) in height has recently been found in its north-northwestern perimeter wall, exactly behind and in line with its central pillars (see figure 10.3 on p. 109). The stone is rectangular, and unlike the rings of radially oriented pillars found in the main enclosures, it has one of its wider faces turned toward the center of the structure. The significance of this stone is that it has a hole some 9 to 10 inches (23–25 centimeters) in diameter bored through it horizontally at a height of around 3 feet (1 meter) off the ground. Covering the stone is a series of curved lines, which flow in pairs and converge just beneath the hole before trailing off toward the stone's right-hand corner. Very likely they are a naïve representation of the human torso complete with legs bent at the knees (see chapter 10).

If the enclosure's twin pillars were indeed oriented toward Deneb, then a person, a shaman perhaps, would have been able to look through the stone's

---

*On the subject of which enclosure uncovered at Göbekli Tepe is the oldest, lead archaeologist Professor Klaus Schmidt is in no doubt—it is Enclosure C (personal conversation September 16, 2012). His reasoning is that Enclosure D's outer perimeter wall abuts that of Enclosure C. Yet a counterargument against Enclosure C being older is easily made. If C was constructed after the latter, then it is possible that D's preexisting boundary wall was reconstructed in order to allow the completion of C's own perimeter wall.

sighting hole to see Deneb setting on the north-northwestern horizon, a quite magnificent sight that cannot have happened by chance alone. Clearly, this is powerful evidence that the enclosure really was directed toward this star during the epoch of its construction.

A similar holed stone exists in Enclosure C, which is also located within the north-northwest section of the temenos wall (see figure 10.1 on p. 106). Designated Pillar 59, it has been turned over onto its eastern side and is fractured across its hole, with the top section now missing. The diameter of the hole is very slightly larger than the one in the corresponding stone in Enclosure D, measuring 11 to 12 inches (28–30.5 centimeters). This is also the approximate width of the stone through which the hole has been bored.

The holed stone in Enclosure C remains only partly exposed. It leans forward so that no indication of whether it bears any carved relief, like its partner in Enclosure D, can yet be determined. What does seem clear is that when in its original position, Pillar 59 would have stood exactly behind and in line with Enclosure C's twin central pillars. This means that it too could have been used to observe the setting of Deneb when standing between the twin pillars during the epoch of its construction (bearing in mind that a second, inner ring of stones was added *after* the original construction of the outer circle, according to Klaus Schmidt.[14] Its construction would quite possibly have obscured the line of vision from the twin central pillars to the holed stone).

SOUL HOLES

So what exactly are these holed stones that once stood in the same positions in Enclosures C and D? The answer almost certainly is that they are *seelen-loch*, a German word meaning "soul hole" (*seelenlocher,* "soul holes," in plural). Across Europe* and also in southwest Asia† megalithic structures, such

---

*Circular porthole stones associated with megalithic monuments exist at the following locations in Western Europe: England (the Tolven Stone in Cornwall and Devils Ring and Finger in Shropshire); Ireland (Cloch-a-Phoill in Ardristan, Co. Carlow); Germany (Züschen in Hesse and Altendorf, Degernau and Schwörstadt in Baden-Württemberg); France (Guiry-en-Vexin in Île-de-France and Trie-Chateau in Picardie/Oise); Spain (Antequera in Andalusia); Belgium (Lüttich and Weris); Switzerland (Courgenay in Jura), and in South Tyrol (Bozen and Riffian in Austria, and Gratsch in Italy).
†Examples of dolmens or chambered tombs in southwest Asia can be found in Syria (Ala Safat, Amman, and Tsil) and Jordan ('Ain Dakkar). Here in the Near East they are ascribed dates ranging from the Chalcolithic age, ca. 5000 BC, down to the Early Bronze Age, ca. 3200 BC.

as dolmens, passage graves, and chambered tombs, often incorporate upright entrance stones into which circular holes have been bored. These holes are usually between 10 and 16 inches (25–41 centimeters) in diameter, which makes them too small for an adult to pass through. This has led to speculation that they must have served some kind of symbolic function.

Prehistorians have suggested that the holes in dolmens might have allowed offerings of food to be made to the dead following their initial interment. This is at least possible. Yet more often than not, holed entrances to megalithic structures are interpreted as seelenloch, holes that are believed to allow the spirit or soul of the deceased to exit the tomb. (Even Klaus Schmidt has suggested that fragmented stone rings found at Göbekli Tepe during the earliest surveys of the site might have functioned as seelenloch.[15] This, however, was long before the discovery of the aforementioned holed stones in Enclosures C and D.)

Holes were also bored into the shoulders or sides of cremation urns in Roman Europe,[16] and also in the Ararat Valley of eastern Anatolia during the Bronze Age,[17] apparently with similar purposes in mind. In places such as the Austrian Tyrol the concept of the seelenloch persisted until the twentieth century. Here, circular "doors" were built into the walls of houses, which were opened only when a person died in the house, the purpose being to allow the soul of the deceased to leave its earthly surroundings and depart for the afterlife.[18]

CAUCASIAN DOLMENS

By far the greatest concentration of dolmens with façades or entrance stones, into which holes have been bored, are to be found in the Caucasus region of Abkhazia and southern Russia, on the northeast coast of the Black Sea. Here as many as three thousand structures of this kind have been noted, many of which have never been properly recorded. Those that have been investigated produce radiocarbon dates and artifacts suggesting a construction date during the Bronze Age, ca. 3000–2000 BC.[19]

Many of the dolmens have paved-stone enclosures with tememos walls that incorporate the porthole stone. The similarity in design between these megalithic enclosures in the Caucasus and Göbekli Tepe's Enclosures C and D, with their own holed stones forming part of the temenos wall, is uncanny and must surely form part of a similar tradition.

Many of the Caucasian dolmens have carved reliefs around their portholes. Often this shows twin pillars or supports capped with a trilithon (like those at Stonehenge), creating the image of a gateway or doorway, similar to the torii entrance gates to Japanese Shinto shrines. These carved gateways are curiously reminiscent of the twin pillars standing at the center of the enclosures at Göbekli Tepe.

It thus seems likely that the holed stones in Göbekli Tepe's Enclosures C and D functioned as seelenloch. If correct, then whether this rite of passage through the stone's bored hole related to souls of the deceased leaving the enclosure or unborn souls entering this world is a matter of debate discussed in chapter 10. More obviously, the seelenloch enabled the soul or spirit of the shaman to exit the structure.

PASSAGE OF THE SOUL

While in an ecstatic or altered state of consciousness a shaman imagines him- or herself entering a hole or tunnel that allows access to otherworldly environments, either in the lower world (underworld) or upper world (sky world). Often these holes, particularly those leading to the lower world, are reached through the visualization of physical holes such as water holes, holes in tree trunks, circular depressions in rocks, entrances to caves, or holes carved in polished circular stones, similar to the jade *bi* or *pi* disks of Chinese folk tradition.[20] These are thought to symbolize the starry vault, with the hole in the center representing the access point to heaven.[21] Siberian shamans often wear on their coats disks with holes, which are usually made of iron. They bear names such as *künjeta* ("sun") and *oibon künga* ("hole-in-the-ice sun") and correspond with invisible holes (*oibone*) in the shaman's body used in spirit communication.[22]

This then is what the porthole stones in Göbekli Tepe's Enclosures C and D most likely signified—points of exit for the shaman's soul on journeys to the sky world, accessed via the star Deneb in Cygnus. Yet why was this particular area of the sky of such interest to the shamans of the early Neolithic? The answer seems to lie in the fact that Deneb cannot take *all* the credit for causing the Göbekli builders to align the various sets of twin pillars toward the north-northwest. For Deneb's role as a stellar marker is in fact secondary to the Milky Way's Great Rift, which, as we find out next, was once seen as an entrance to the sky world.

8

THE PATH OF SOULS

The orientation of the central pillars in Göbekli Tepe's main enclosures toward both Deneb and the Milky Way's Great Rift is by no means unique. All around the globe ancient cultures and societies saw this area of the heavens as an entrance to the sky world. It was considered a place of the gods, a land of the ancestors, and the source of creation in the universe.

For instance, the ancient Maya of Central America pictured Xibalba, their underworld, as accessible from a sky road known as *ri b'e xib'alb'a,* the Black Road, identified as the Milky Way's Great Rift.[1] Its actual entrance or location was represented by cave and mouth imagery, often accompanied by a symbol known as the Cross Bands glyph. This has the appearance of a letter X inside a square frame and has been identified with the Cygnus stars in their guise as a celestial cross, made up of five specific stars.[2] The actual road to Xibalba (a word meaning "place of fear") is shown as a caiman crocodile, its long jaws the twin streams created by the Great Rift, with its head, eyes, and gullet located in the vicinity of the Cygnus region (see figure 8.1 on p. 90).

In Mayan mythology the solar god One Hunahpu was reborn from the mouth of the caiman. The sun god was perhaps imagined as being carried along the length of the creature's open jaws to the place where the ecliptic, the sun's path, crosses the Milky Way in the vicinity of the stars of Sagittarius and Scorpius.[3] This is a point corresponding, visually at least, with the nuclear

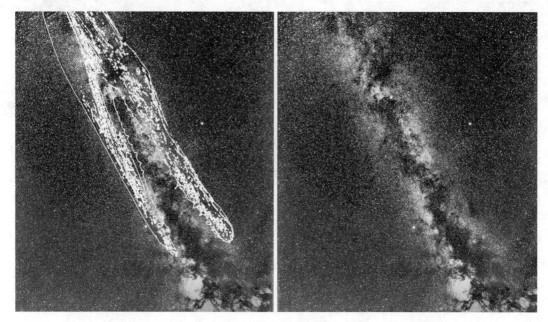

Figure 8.1. Left, caiman crocodile overlaid on the Milky Way's Great Rift, as conceived by the Maya of Central America. Right, the Milky Way's Great Rift on its own for comparison.

bulge in the galactic plane that marks the center of the Milky Way galaxy. The sun god reached this point of rebirth at the moment of sunrise on the winter solstice.

The Olmec of Mexico, whom the Maya might well have seen as spiritual forebears, created grotesque stone offering tables with the likeness of the head and jaws of a monstrous jaguar. From the creature's open mouth (some see it as a cave entrance) a deity identified as a were-jaguar—half human, half jaguar— is seen emerging. Although next to nothing is known about Olmec cosmology, it probably involved mythological ideas similar to those of the Maya.

As the Cross Bands glyph appears on these offering tables, usually either between the teeth of the monster or on the headdress worn by the were-jaguar, it is likely the Olmec also had some concept of the sun god being reborn from the Milky Way's Great Rift, seen as the cavelike mouth of a hideous sky monster.

CLEAVING OPEN THE PORTALS

The Maya manufactured enormous ceremonial ax heads in jade that take the form of abstract were-jaguars, the lips on their human faces downturned in a peculiar and highly exaggerated manner (see figure 8.2). Across the top of the head, going from front to back, is a furrow or cleft, which has a deeply significant meaning, for on the were-jaguar's breech cloth the Cross Bands glyph appears, like the Union Jack emblazoned on a belt buckle. According to the label accompanying the British Museum's own were-jaguar hand ax:

> The crossed bands glyph incised on the breech cloth signifies an entrance or opening. . . . These symbols (i.e., the glyph and the cleft on the top of the head) proclaim the axe's magical power to cleave open the portals into the spirit world.

As that "spirit world" was almost certainly Xibalba, it confirms that the Cross Bands glyph symbolizes its "entrance or opening," which, as we have seen, was marked by the constellation of Cygnus, the Northern Cross. Even the cleft is evidence of this connection, for the Great Rift is known also as the Great Cleft, as it appears to cleave the Milky Way in two, a symbolic act carried out in Mayan tradition by the jade ax in its celestial guise.

Figure 8.2. Left, Olmec altar at La Venta, in Mexico's Tabasco state, showing a figure emerging from the cave-like mouth of the were-jaguar. Note the Cross Bands glyph between the creature's fangs.
Right, Mayan ax in jade fashioned into the likeness of the were-jaguar. Note the cross bands glyph on the belt buckle area of the breeches and the cleft on the top of the head.

THE DENEB PORTAL

Similar ideas regarding a spirit world existing beyond the opening to the Great Rift are held even today by a number of Native American tribes, whose star myths are thought to have a common origin among the Mississippi mound-building cultures, forming what is known as the Southeastern Ceremonial Complex, which thrived ca. AD 1200–1650.[4] The most consistent story that emerges from their beliefs and practices tells of how in death the soul departs to the west, a journey that takes three to four days to complete. When finally it reaches the edge of the Earth's disk, the soul waits for the right moment to make a leap of faith to enter the Milky Way, the so-called Path of Souls, via a star portal, knowing that the consequences of failing this difficult jump will mean being lost forever in the lower world.

The portal is marked by a celestial hand, its fingers pointing downward and made up of stars belonging to the Orion constellation, the three belt stars marking the severed wrist. It is a symbol found again and again in the iconography of the Southeastern Ceremonial Complex and dates back to the Hopewell mound builders of Ohio, who thrived some two thousand years ago.

The actual portal is the stellar object Messier 42, a small, fuzzy nebula located in Orion's "sword." Here the soul joins the Milky Way and travels south and then north until it reaches a fork on the path identified with the twin arms of the Great Rift. Its longer arm, the one bridging the two halves of the Milky Way, is envisioned as a log spanning a celestial river that the soul must cross to reach the sky world.

Yet before the soul can cross the log bridge it has to encounter its guardian, most usually a "forked-eye raptor," a supernatural eagle known as the "Brain Smasher," identified with the star Deneb. Only by receiving the right judgment can the soul avoid Brain Smasher and pass over the log and enter the afterlife. If the judgment is not favorable, the soul is forced to take the Great Rift's shorter, severed arm, which leads only to oblivion. Clearly, the raptor is Cygnus in its role as the celestial bird, its forked eye the Milky Way's Great Rift (see figure 8.3).

STORM DEMON WITH OPEN MOUTH

How exactly the Göbekli builders might have viewed the starry existence beyond the Great Rift is now lost. Yet some idea of their understanding of cos-

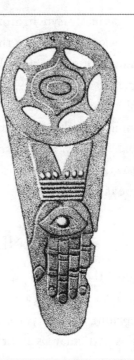

Top: Skull and Bone represent the life soul and free soul. The Raptor is the guardian of the place where the Milky Way splits into two tracks. It is a bird based on the Cygnus constellation. The "forked eye" of the raptor represents the split at the Milky Way. Right: Copper object from Moundville—the hole in the "eye in the hand" is the portal M42. The soul then moves up to the Milky Way and encounters the split creating the Dark Rift. The top circle, often represented as a "Cross," is the star Deneb, the final destination of the soul.

Figure 8.3. Native American symbols from artifacts found at mound sites. Note the raptor, which represents Cygnus, and the eye in the hand, representing Orion, above which is a circle that represents the bright star Deneb in Cygnus (after Greg Little).

mic geography can be gleaned from the star lore recorded in cuneiform script by the astronomer-priests of the civilizations that thrived on the Mesopotamia Plain in what is today Iraq.

Babylonian texts, which contain source material that goes back to the third millennium BC, catalogue dozens of stellar objects, either stars or asterisms, a few of which, such as the Scorpion (Scorpius), the Goat-headed Fish (Capricorn), and the Lion (Leo), are recognizable from their equivalents in the Greek zodiac. The stars of Cygnus would seem to have been combined with others from the neighboring constellation of Cepheus (located immediately above Deneb in astronomical terms) to create a huge griffinlike creature with the head and body of a panther (*nimru* in Akkadian) and the wings, back feet, and tail of an eagle. Its name was [MUL]UD.KA.DUH.A, which means "constellation (MUL) of the storm-demon with an open mouth," and it was seen as the place of reception of dead souls.[5]

With the head of the panther in Cygnus[6] and its tail in Cepheus (making it perfectly synchronized with the Milky Way), it becomes clear that in Babylonian star lore the entrance to the realm of the dead was through the mouth or gullet of ^{MUL}UD.KA.DUH.A, which corresponds to the opening of the Great Rift. This, of course, is similar to the Olmec and Mayan conception of the entrance to the underworld being through the mouth of a gruesome monster, either a jaguar or caiman. For this reason, it seems certain that the Babylonians, and presumably their forebears the Sumerians and Akkadians, saw the entrance to the netherworld, or realm of the dead, as synonymous with the Great Rift.

VENERATION OF THE POLE STAR

From the evidence presented here, it seems likely that the Pre-Pottery Neolithic peoples of southeast Anatolia considered Deneb the visible marker for the opening into a sky world accessed via the Milky Way's Great Rift. Why exactly this particular area of the sky became so important to the mind-set of the Pre-Pottery Neolithic world of southeast Anatolia lies in the fact that there was no Pole Star when Göbekli Tepe was constructed, ca. 9500–8000 BC. In other words, the celestial pole was not marked by any bright stellar object in the night sky. Thus it seems reasonable to suggest that the Göbekli builders adhered to much earlier Paleolithic traditions regarding the location of the sky world that reached back to a time when Deneb was Pole Star, ca. 16,500–14,500 BC. It was, of course, during this epoch that the Lascaux Shaft Scene was created by Paleolithic cave artists. This shows the bird on the pole, perhaps signifying the ascent of the bird-headed shaman (depicted next to it) into a sky world accessed through the celestial pole, marked at that time by Cygnus in the form of a bird.

SHIFTING POLE STARS

Is it really possible that the people of Göbekli Tepe followed a tradition that was more than five thousand years old? As already mentioned, the effects of precession caused the celestial pole to shift away from Cygnus around 13,000 BC. Thereafter it entered the constellation of Lyra, causing its bright star Vega to become Pole Star, ca. 13,000–11,000 BC. So why had the sky watchers of this age not switched their allegiance from Cygnus to Vega? The answer is that some Paleolithic cultures probably did start seeing Vega as the point of entry to the sky world. However, others almost certainly remained loyal to Cygnus, and Deneb in particular, simply because it synchronized with the start of the Milky Way's Great Rift, which was already considered the rightful entrance to the sky world. Visually, the star Vega lies well away from both the Great Rift *and* the Milky Way, explaining why the star might not have attained the same significance as Deneb.

So not only did Vega lose its importance around 11,000 BC, but veneration of Deneb and the Great Rift as the true entrance to the sky world was almost certainly on the increase again, a situation that probably existed when the main enclosures at Göbekli Tepe were under construction in the tenth millennium BC. It thus makes sense that the builders of these monuments, the oldest known star temples anywhere in the world, chose to align them to the opening of the Great Rift, the most obvious point of entry into the sky world at that time.

Yet as we shall see next, the method by which the soul made its journey to and from the sky world was by using Cygnus's most primordial totem, the celestial bird, which we find represented quite spectacularly in the carved art at Göbekli Tepe.

9

CULT OF
THE VULTURE

At Çatal Höyük, the 9,500-year-old Neolithic city in southern central Anatolia, the dead were portrayed in art as headless matchstick men, often seen in the company of vultures. These are carrion or scavenger birds associated with the process of excarnation, the deliberate defleshing of human carcasses, which often took place on wooden mortuary towers, the remaining bones being afterward collected for what is known as a secondary, or disarticulated, burial.

Excarnation is certainly considered to have taken place during the Neolithic age and might even have occurred at Göbekli Tepe, according to Klaus Schmidt. He compares its large enclosures to the Towers of Silence that feature in the funerary practices of the religion known as Zoroastrianism,[1] which thrived in Iran, Armenia, and later India (under the name Parsism) until comparatively recent times. Here the dead were placed at the top of round stone towers, the Towers of Silence, away from a community. The vultures would swoop down and pick the carcasses clean, after which the remaining bones were allowed to calcine in the hot sun before being collected for final burial.

Although such practices are rare today, they do continue under the name sky burials among some remote Tibetan Buddhist communities in the Himalayas.

Eyewitness reports show that first the vultures swoop down to devour the carcasses, then the ravens, hawks, and crows arrive to finish the job, almost as if this honor among birds might be the true origin of the term *pecking order*.

Excarnation almost certainly occurred at Çatal Höyük, where it is depicted on at least one painted fresco (see figure 9.1). This shows two wooden towers, accessed by a staircase, at the base of which are two figures, guardians perhaps of the charnel area. On top of the right-hand tower vultures attack a headless matchstick man, which is very likely an abstract symbol used to represent a dead body. The head was considered the seat of the soul, and because the soul has departed the body, it is portrayed as headless; that is, soulless. The missing head is seen in outline on top of the left-hand tower, where two vultures appear to be taking the head, or soul, under their wings.

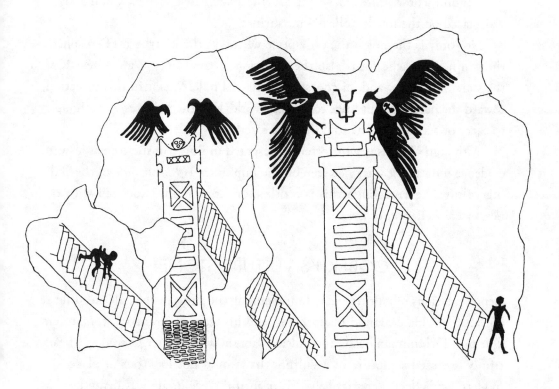

Figure 9.1. Excarnation towers from a reconstructed panel found at the Neolithic city of Çatal Höyük, dating to 7500–5700 BC (after James Mellaart). Note the soul of the deceased depicted as a head, with its denuded body shown as a headless matchstick man.

PSYCHOPOMP

The painting is meant to convey the idea that, even though the human car-
cass might suffer the unsightly (although very efficient) act of excarnation, the
spirits of the vultures accompany the soul into the afterlife. Each bird is thus
acting as a *psychopomp,* an ancient Greek word meaning "soul carrier," used
to describe a supernatural being or creature whose role was to assist a newly
deceased soul reach the next world.

British archaeologist James Mellaart recorded that all panels connected
with death and rebirth at Çatal Höyük were located on either the north or
east walls of cult shrines.[2] East is clearly the direction of rebirth, symbolized
by the appearance of the sun each morning, leaving the north as the direction
of the netherworld, the realm of darkness and the dead. Indeed, some of the
most prominent vulture imagery featuring matchstick men at Çatal Höyük
was placed on the north walls of cult shrines.

Not only is the north the only place where, in the Northern Hemisphere,
the sun never reaches, it is also the direction of the Milky Way's Great Rift,
the stars of Cygnus, and, of course, the celestial pole. Was it in this direction,
toward the perceived entrance to the sky world, that the vultures were thought
to carry or accompany the soul into the afterlife?

Although Cygnus is most often represented in Eurasian star lore as a swan,
evidence indicates it was once seen on the Euphrates as *Vultur cadens,* the "falling vulture,"[3] even though this is a title more commonly associated with the
nearby constellation of Lyra.

GÖBEKLI'S VULTURE STONE

Representations of vultures were found among the ruins of the cult building at
Nevalı Çori. Here Harald Hauptmann and his team uncovered a stone totem
pole on which human heads and vultures are shown together, as well as a beautifully executed sculpture of a vulture that would not look out of place in a
modern art gallery. Yet strangely this beautiful piece of art was being used as
fill within the wall of the cult building, indicating that it belonged to an earlier
phase of building activity, probably ca. 8500–8400 BC.

Vultures are also to be seen among the carved art at Göbekli Tepe, most
obviously on Pillar 43. Located in the north-northwestern section of Enclosure

D, it stands immediately west of the holed stone that would have allowed a person crouching between the twin pillars to observe the setting of Deneb during the epoch in question.

On Pillar 43's western face are three vultures, one of which is a juvenile. Also visible is a scorpion and two long-necked wader birds—flamingos perhaps—and between them and the head of the adult vulture in the upper register is a line of small squares, abutted on each side by a series of V-shapes, possibly signifying the flow of water.

Other strange features are depicted at the top of the stone. Three rectangular forms appear in a line with linked loops that make them resemble handbags. Next to each is a small creature, which in order, from left to right, can be identified as a long-legged bird (a wader perhaps), a quadruped (seemingly a feline), and an amphibian (possibly a frog or toad). An interpretation of this scene is problematic, although the handbags, or "man bags," as some people are calling them, are most likely animal pens or houses, situated on what could be the edge of a river, upon which is a trackway (the lines of squares) underneath which flows water (the accompanying V-shapes).

This, however, is not why Pillar 43 has been singled out as important. It is the vulture positioned at the end of the line of small squares that draws the eye (see figure 9.2 on p. 100). It stands up, with its wings articulated in a manner resembling human arms. It also has bent knees and bizarre flat feet, in the shape of oversized clowns' shoes, indicating that this is very likely a shaman in the guise of a vulture or a bird spirit with anthropomorphic features. Similar vultures with articulated legs are depicted on the walls of shrines at Çatal Höyük, and these too are interpreted either as anthropomorphs or as shamans adorned in the manner of vultures.[4]

HEAD LIKE A BALL

Just above the vulture's right wing is a carved circle, like a ball or sun disk. Klaus Schmidt interprets this "ball" as a human head, and this is almost certainly what it is, for on the back of another vulture lower down the register is a headless, or soulless, figure, just like the examples found in association with the vultures and excarnation towers at Çatal Höyük. And we can be sure that this "ball" *does* represent a human head as similar balls are seen in the prehistoric rock art of the region, where their context makes it clear they

Figure 9.2. Göbekli Tepe's Vulture Stone (Pillar 43). Note the scorpion on the shaft, the headless human figure with erect penis on the neck of the vulture-like bird at the base of the shaft, and the ball above the right wing of the vulture in the upper register.

represent human souls.[5] As Anatolian prehistoric rock art expert Muvaffak Uyanik explains:

> In the Mesolithic age [i.e., in the epoch of the Göbekli builders], it was realized that man had a soul, apart from his body and, as it was accepted that the soul inhabited the head, only the skull of the human body was buried. We also know that the human soul was symbolized as a circle and that this symbol was later used, in a traditional manner, on tomb-stones without inscriptions.[6]

So the headless figure represents not only the human skeleton but also a dead man whose soul has departed in the form of a ball-like head that is now under the charge of the vulture, which is itself arguably a bird spirit with human attributes, a were-vulture, if you like. Clearly, Göbekli Tepe's Pillar 43—the Vulture Stone, as we shall call it—conveys in symbolic form the release of the soul into the care of the vulture in its role as psychopomp, or soul carrier, on its journey into the afterlife (Schmidt's suggestion[7] that the vulture is playing with a human head as part of some macabre game is simply inadequate to explain what is going on here).

VULTURE WINGS

Evidence of vulture-related shamanism has been found also at other sites across the region. For instance, during the 1950s at an open-air settlement called Zawi Chemi Shanidar, which overlooks the Greater Zab River in the Zagros Mountains of northern Iraq, American archaeologists Ralph and Rose Solecki discovered the wings of seventeen large predatory birds, along with the skulls of at least fifteen goats and wild sheep.

Among the species of bird represented by the bones, many of them still articulated, were the bearded vulture (*Gypaetus barbatus*) and griffon vulture (*Gyps fulvus*), as well as various species of eagle. They were found positioned by the wall of a stone structure, which probably served a cultic function.[8] The excavators were in no doubt that the wings had been severed from the birds at the point of death and worn as part of a ritualistic costume.[9] In other words, shamans utilized these wings as "ritual paraphernalia"[10] in order to adopt the guise of the vulture in its role as a primary symbol of the cult of the dead.

The wings were radiocarbon dated to 8870 BC (+/− 300 years),[11] although modern forms of recalibration (due to recent reassessments of the amount of carbon-14 present in organic matter during former ages) means they probably date to the end of the Younger Dryas period, ca. 9600 BC[12]; that is, shortly before the construction of the large enclosures at Göbekli Tepe, which as the crow flies is about 280 miles (450 kilometers) west of Zawi Chemi Shanidar.

STAR MAP IN STONE

If Göbekli Tepe's Vulture Stone *does* show a human soul being accompanied into the afterlife by a psychopomp in the likeness of a vulture, then there has to be a chance that its rich imagery contains themes of a celestial nature. Scholars working in the field of archaeoastronomy have been quick to point out that the scorpion shown at the base of the shaft could signify the constellation Scorpius.[13] Certainly, in Babylonian astronomical texts such as those found on the Mul-Apin tablets, the stars of Scorpius are identified with a constellation named Scorpion (^{MUL}GIR.TAB).[14]

In the cosmological art of the Maya in Central America, a scorpion is often shown at the base of the world tree (see figure 9.3), a symbol interpreted by some scholars as the Milky Way standing erect on the horizon. This has led to the scorpion being identified with the constellation Scorpius, which lies immediately beneath the Milky Way's Great Rift.[15] Thus it is conceivable that there existed a universal identification of the stars of Scorpius with the symbol of a scorpion that originated in the Paleolithic age, the reason it appears on Göbekli Tepe's Vulture Stone, carved ca. 9500–9000 BC.

CYGNUS AS A VULTURE

If Pillar 43's scorpion *does* represent the Scorpius constellation and is thus symbolizing the point of crossing between the ecliptic and the Milky Way's Great Rift, then the vulture with articulated wings and clownlike feet at the top of the stone completes the cosmic picture. Its wings, head, neck, and body have a familiar ring to them, for they form a near perfect outline of the Cygnus constellation, with the vulture's head in the position of Deneb and its outstretched wings matching those of its celestial counterpart as it appeared 11,500 years ago (see figure 9.4). This identification with Cygnus, first noted by Professor Vachagan Vahradyan of the Russian-Armenian (Slavonic) University,[16] is remarkable and unlikely to be coincidence.

Thus the abstract imagery on Pillar 43, with its headless matchstick man next to the scorpion, and the ball-like head above the left wing of the vulture, probably shows the transmigration of the soul from its terrestrial environment, signified by the stars of Scorpius at the base of the Milky Way's Great Rift, to its final destination in the region of the Cygnus constellation at the top of the Great Rift.

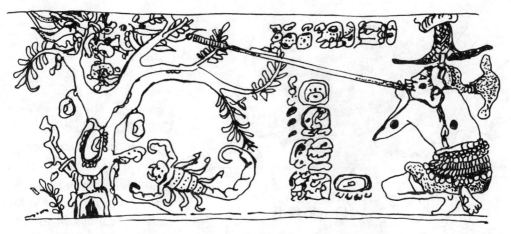

Figure 9.3. Mayan cosmic tree, symbol of the Milky Way, with a scorpion by its base perhaps signifying the constellation Scorpius.

CYGNUS

Figure 9.4. Göbekli Tepe's Vulture Stone (Pillar 43) with the Cygnus constellation overlaid.

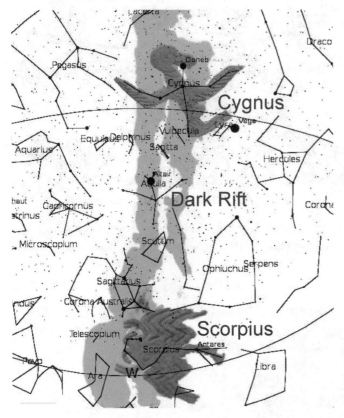

Figure 9.5. The Milky Way's Great Rift overlaid with the scorpion and vulture from Göbekli Tepe's Vulture Stone (Pillar 43), showing their match with, respectively, the stars of Scorpius when just above the western horizon and, at the same time, Cygnus (the vulture) as it crosses the meridian high in the sky.

Absolute confirmation of this pictorial journey into the afterlife comes from the fact that in 9500 BC, when Scorpius came into view on the western horizon shortly after sunset, the Milky Way's Great Rift would have stretched upward into the night sky to highlight Cygnus as it crossed the meridian on its upper transit at an elevation of approximately 70 degrees. It is almost certainly this relationship between the two constellations that is depicted on Göbekli Tepe's Vulture Stone, especially as the pillar's clown-footed vulture and scorpion are in similar positions to their celestial counterparts (see figure 9.5).

The fact that Enclosure D's Vulture Stone is also in the north-northwest, next to the holed stone and on the same basic alignment as its twin pillars, is another potential clue as to its astronomical function, in particular its connection with Cygnus and the Milky Way's Great Rift. Yet how exactly did the Göbekli builders envision the sky world, which seems to have been intrinsically linked to the symbol of the vulture? The greatest clue comes from the holed stone, which, as we have seen, probably acted as a seelenloch, or soul hole, through which the soul had to pass in order to reach its otherworldly destination.

10

COSMIC
BIRTH STONE

If the twin monoliths at the center of Göbekli Tepe's Enclosure D *were* once oriented toward the setting of Deneb in the epoch of their construction, then, as we have seen, a person standing or crouching between them would have been able to view this astronomical spectacle through a holed stone located immediately east of the Vulture Stone. It would have been a similar case in Enclosure C, where the entrant would also have been able to witness the setting of Deneb through the aperture of a holed stone (Pillar 59) when positioned between the twin central pillars.

It is time now to better understand the purpose of these holed stones, focusing our attentions on the example in Enclosure D, which remains in situ. It has carved parallel lines that curve around the hole to form what appear to be naïve renderings of human legs bent at the knee. After coming together beneath the hole the "legs" trail off toward the bottom right-hand corner of the stone, leaving a parallel opening between the knee and the presumed ankles. That the twin sets of parallel lines represent legs, and not something else, is confirmed by the fact that the lower left-hand edge noticeably bulges as if to signify the person's right-hand buttock (see figure 10.1 on page 106).

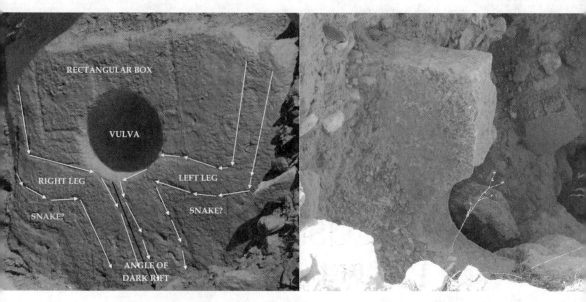

Figure 10.1. Left, decorated holed stone in the north wall of Göbekli Tepe's Enclosure D. Note the lines flowing around the hole, suggestive of an abstract female form. Right, the broken holed stone in a similar position in Enclosure C.

THE KILISIK STATUE

If the incised lines on the sighting stone do show a pair of legs bent at the knees, then the large hole directly above them can only signify one thing—the person's, or should I say the woman's, vulva. A similar hole is seen on the mini T-shaped statue found in 1965 at Kilisik, a village in Adıyaman province, some 46.5 miles (75 kilometers) north-northwest of Göbekli Tepe.[1] In addition to having arms and hands, like the T-shaped pillars at Göbekli Tepe and Nevalı Çori, the statue has an additional line that rises at an angle on both its wide faces to meet the hands on the front narrow face. It seems clear that the figure is lifting up its garment to expose its belly and genitalia (see figure 10.2).

Strangely, the belly or womb area of the statue is sculpted into a much smaller human form represented by a crude head, body, and arms, executed in a style reminiscent of a macabre stone totem pole unearthed at Göbekli Tepe and now in Şanlıurfa's archaeological museum. This too shows smaller human forms in the position of the womb or stomach of a much larger standing figure (see plate 24).

The small figure on the Kilisik statue very likely represents a fetus inside

Figure 10.2. Stone statue of a T-shaped figure found in 1965 at
Kilisik in Adıyaman province, some 46.5 miles (75 kilometers)
from Göbekli Tepe. Note the hole forming the figure's vulva
and the small human figure carved into the stomach area.

a woman's womb, the large incised hole immediately beneath the belly emphasizing not just the position of the vulva but also the birth canal. That a very
similar, although much larger hole, has been bored through Enclosure D's
potential sighting stone, which is itself surrounded by incised lines arguably
signifying the legs of a woman, suggests this hole is also an exaggerated vulva
(presumably the holed stone at the same position in Enclosure C played a
similar role).

This means that when in 9400 BC the setting of Deneb aligned with the
hole in the sighting stone in Enclosure D, the star's presence would have been
framed within the abstract woman's vulva. Clearly, this carefully executed
synchronization between star and stone was created to mark the moment of

alignment with the opening of the Milky Way's Great Rift in its role as the suspected entrance to the sky world, where souls departed to in death and, presumably, emerged from at birth. We can go further, for the angle made by the woman's lower legs, as they trail off toward the right-hand corner of the stone, is similar to the angle of the Milky Way and Great Rift when the star Deneb is at approximately 45 degrees in elevation. In other words, the manner of placement of the woman's legs seems to emphasize that her vulva marks the entrance to the Great Rift (see figure 10.3).

So if the abstract female form seen on the holed stone in Enclosure D symbolizes the Cosmic Mother, is the purpose of the synchronization between star and stone to indicate that she is about to give birth? Should this surmise prove correct, there can be little doubt that this was a highly symbolic act seen to take place both in a material sense within the womblike enclosure, *and* in a celestial form, with the cosmic child imagined as emerging into life from the opening of the Great Rift (exactly like the rebirth of the solar god One Hunahpu in Mayan myth and legend). In this manner, the cosmic child would have been seen to come forth from Cygnus, then descend the Great Rift to the "ground"; that is, the horizon, where the ecliptic, the sun's path, crossed the Milky Way in the vicinity of the stars of Sagittarius and Scorpius.

COSMIC BIRTH

Almost exactly what we see represented in abstract form on the sighting stone in Göbekli Tepe's Enclosure D is found also on the Venus and Sorcerer panel inside France's Chauvet Cave, which, as we have seen, was created by Upper Paleolithic cave artists some thirty-two thousand years ago. Here too the abstract legs of the "Venus" seem to signify the twin streams of the Milky Way on either side of the Great Rift, with the head of a young bovine overlaid upon the position of the womb (see figure 6.3 on page 74). In this context, the bucranium likely represents the Cygnus constellation in its role as the head of a bull calf, which in prehistoric times was seen as an abstract symbol of the female womb or uterus, complete with its hornlike fallopian tubes (see figure 10.4 on p. 110). The uncanny resemblance between the two is something our ancestors would appear to have realized at a very early stage in human development,[2] making the bucranium, and the bull calf in general, primary symbols of birth and death in the Neolithic age.

Figure 10.3. Göbekli Tepe's Enclosure D, showing the location of the holed sighting stone in its perimeter wall. Note the Milky Way's Great Rift on the horizon.

We are reminded also of the 3-D frescoes from Çatal Höyük showing bulls being born from between the legs of divine females (who have the heads of leopards), and the ancient Egyptian belief that the goddess Hathor, in her role as the Milky Way, gave birth each morning to the sun god in the form of a bull calf. The cult of Hathor was virtually synonymous with that of Nut, the sky goddess, who was herself a personification of the Milky Way, her womb and vulva occupied by the stars of Cygnus (see figure 10.5 on p. 110).[3]

Nut was the mother of Osiris, the god of death and resurrection, and also of Re, the sun-god, who was reborn each morning from between her loins. In death, the pharaoh would assume the identity of Osiris and reenter the womb of his mother, Nut, in order to reach an afterlife among the stars. In other words, as the resurrected god Osiris the deceased would return from whence he or she had come originally, which was the Milky Way's Great Rift in the vicinity of the Cygnus constellation.

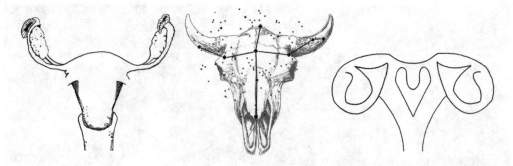

Figure 10.4. Left, womb or uterus, complete with fallopian tubes. Center, the stars of Cygnus overlaid on a bovine head. Right, an abstract uterus design from the Pazyryk culture of Siberia, from approximately the sixth to third century BC.

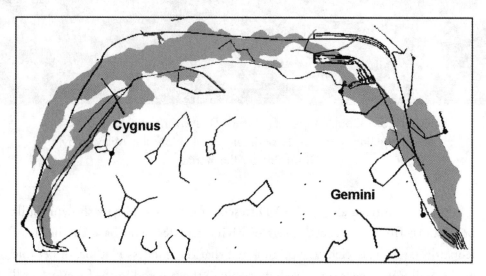

Figure 10.5. Ancient Egyptian sky goddess Nut in her role as a personification of the Milky Way, with the stars of Cygnus marking her womb and vulva, and the Great Rift signifying the gap between her legs (after R. A. Wells).

BIRTH CHAMBER

How exactly the entrants to Göbekli Tepe's Enclosure D, or indeed its neighbor, Enclosure C, might have celebrated the act of cosmic birth is open to speculation. Perhaps the new soul was believed to emerge from the opening of the Great Rift and then in some unimaginable manner enter a pregnant woman waiting between the enclosure's twin pillars. A ritual act like this might have taken place either at the point of conception, sometime during pregnancy, or, perhaps, shortly before birth. It might even be that some births actually took place between the enclosure's central pillars, mimicking exactly what the incised lines on the holed stone were attempting to convey.

So not only were the enclosures at Göbekli Tepe built to honor the departure of the soul in the company of the vulture in its role as psychopomp (remember, the Vulture Stone is next to Enclosure D's holed stone or Cosmic Birth Stone, as we shall call it), but they were also designed to bring forth new life. Presumably souls entering the world would be accompanied by a psychopomp in the guise of a bird, most probably the vulture, which in some painted panels uncovered at Çatal Höyük is shown with an oval inside its back containing a human baby. Today, in many parts of Europe and Asia newborn babies are accompanied into the world by the stork. Yet in the Baltic (and seemingly in Siberia[4]) a white swan replaces the stork.[5] Clearly, in these areas of the globe, the swan or stork plays the same role as the vulture once did in the Near East.

In Egyptian and Hindu myth, a primordial goose or swan brought forth the universe with its call, although in many countries the swan was said to have laid the egg that either formed the universe or became the sun (such as Tündér Ilona, the Hungarian fairy goddess, who "when she was changed into the shape of a swan" laid an egg in the sky that became the sun[6]). This once again ties in with the belief that cosmic creation takes place in the vicinity of the Cygnus constellation and Great Rift, resulting in the rebirth of the sun each day.

COSMOLOGICAL BELIEFS

Everything points toward Enclosure C and Enclosure D's holed stones being not just confirmation of Deneb's place in the mind-set of the Göbekli builders but also of the site's role as a place where the rites of birth, death, and rebirth were celebrated both in its carved art and within the architectural design of its larger enclosures, which formed symbolic wombs complete with twin souls and axes mundi.

The Göbekli builders would appear to have used the holed stones as seelenloch to enter an otherworldly environment associated with both the act of cosmic birth and the creation of human souls, which came forth from there prior to childbirth and returned there in death. During their ecstatic and altered states of consciousness, shamans at Göbekli Tepe perhaps believed they were to become as fetuses in order to reenter the cosmic womb, the source of primordial creation, an act integrally associated with the star Deneb and the Milky Way's Great Rift.

Further confirmation of the holed stones' function as symbolic vulva is found in the work of scholars attempting to understand the cosmic design of megalithic dolmens, which, as we know, often have circular holes in their entrance façades. The burials found inside them are often placed in fetal positions ready for new life, leading to theories that the stone structures are symbolic wombs or uteri, their portholes representing the vulva, prompting one expert on the origins of Judaism and Islam to observe that whosoever "enters or leaves a dolmen [through the hole "drilled with enormous effort"] does this in the posture of a child at delivery through the vagina. The burial-dolmen itself is therefore symbolically a uterus."[7]

These are incredible revelations that entirely alter our current perceptions of the mind-set of those behind the creation of the Pre-Pottery Neolithic world in southeast Anatolia. Yet as we see in part three, such cosmological thinking pales into insignificance when compared with other major factors that might well have been behind the creation of Göbekli Tepe's main enclosures. For it seems likely that monumental architecture on this scale was built in response to something terrible that had happened in the world.

PART THREE

Catastrophobia

11

THE HOODED ONES

Up to twelve T-shaped pillars stood in rings within Göbekli Tepe's large enclosures, all with their faceless gaze focused toward the central monoliths, as if they formed part of some kind of otherworldly gathering of a secret society. For when we come to ask why the human form is being portrayed with T-shaped terminations both here and at other Pre-Pottery Neolithic sites across the region, with the best answer being that they represent individuals with heads that are long and narrow (hyper-dolichocephalic) who also wear cowls, or hoods, that extend to the rear, as if they might cradle a full head of hair.

It is a conclusion strengthened in the knowledge that the life-size statue of a male uncovered during urban development on Yeni Yol Street in Şanlıurfa's Balıklıgöl district in 1993, has a regular face and head, as do the various portable statues found at Göbekli Tepe and Nevalı Çori. So the sculptors of the Pre-Pottery Neolithic world knew very well how to create perfect representations of the human form with all its intricacies. Clearly then, the T-shaped pillars are abstract representations of those remembered as having once *looked* this way, their blank expressions confirming their otherworldliness, or transcendental nature.

Figure 11.1. An example of hooded figures in a circle, like the T-shaped pillars at Göbekli Tepe. Here three men perform a type of dance around a piper. Cyprian limestone carving. Phoenician in origin, date unknown.

THE MINI T-SHAPED STATUE

That the T-shaped pillars show long-headed individuals wearing cowls seems confirmed by the mini T-shaped statue found in 1965 close to the village of Kilisik, some 46.5 miles (75 kilometers) north-northwest of Göbekli Tepe. It appears to be wearing a large hood extended at the rear by the peculiar shape of the skull; indeed, even the start of the hood can be seen as a straight line that divides the rear half of the head from the projecting face (see figure 10.2 on page 107).

Why exactly these figures are depicted with elongated heads is a matter we return to later in this book. Yet why wear hoods or cowls in the first place? Perhaps it was the prevailing climatic conditions, or the fact that these individuals needed to protect their skin from the sun's rays. More likely is that the cowls convey some idea of status among the communities in which they moved, a fact suggesting the presence of elitism; in other words, a clear division between the Göbekli builders, made up of quarry men, stone masons, flint knappers, hunters, and butchers and those who controlled and managed the construction work going on at the site.

Having said this, it seems unlikely that the T-shapes reflect the presence of individuals living when the main enclosures at Göbekli Tepe were constructed around 9500–8900 BC. Like saints and divinities represented as carved art in churches, or the statues of gods and heroes in classical temples, the T-shapes at Göbekli Tepe are perhaps reflections of something that has been. Something that had to be remembered, celebrated, and not forgotten.

We cannot know what might have been going at Göbekli Tepe when the large enclosures were under construction, nor whether the genesis of the T-shaped pillars happened here or elsewhere. It *is* possible, as Schmidt believes, that complex structures like Enclosures C and D were the pinnacle of a long period of development at the site going back many thousands of years. On the other hand, the construction of the monumental enclosures might just as easily have been inspired by a significant event. Perhaps the arrival in southeast Anatolia of representatives from another culture—individuals who helped galvanize the local hunter-gathering population into embarking on this mammoth building project.

A SUDDEN CHANGE IN LIFESTYLE

Is this what really happened in southeast Anatolia sometime either during or directly after the Younger Dryas mini ice age, ca. 10,900–9600 BC? Did some great change occur in the world of the local hunter-gatherers that culminated in the construction of the large enclosures at Göbekli Tepe under the guidance of some kind of "power elite,"[1] as Schmidt refers to them?

Hunter-gatherers would work together in small bands to fulfill their primary functions in life, with these being hunting wild game, foraging for various types of food, and ensuring the well-being and safety of their extended family group. They created temporary settlements that they occupied only at certain times of the year; for the rest of the time the hunters followed the migrational routes of herd animals. They relied on these animals for food; clothes; fat for balms, fires, and lamps; bone, horn, and antler for weapons, tools, and items of personal adornment; and sinew (thin shredded fibers of muscle tendons) for use as cordage, binding points on arrow shafts, and as a backing material on bows.

Epipaleolithic (that is, transitional Paleolithic) hunters used established campsites and work stations, kitted out with basic facilities, before moving on to the next site, and the next site, and so forth, until eventually they returned to their original place of departure. This was their cycle of life, and it would have remained so had neolithization not gotten in the way.

There can have been no obvious advantage in hundreds, if not thousands, of people (Klaus Schmidt believes that between five hundred and a thousand individuals were employed in building construction at Göbekli Tepe at any one time[2]) putting aside their free existence as hunters and foragers and coming together to create monumental architecture on such a grand scale. Something must have spurred the regional population into abandoning their old lives and adopting a completely different way of living, and from the presence in the enclosures of the massive T-shaped pillars, that "something" would appear to have been whoever, or whatever, they represented.

Did the T-shapes represent the memory of powerful individuals, great ancestors perhaps, of those who built Göbekli Tepe?

MESSIANIC MESSAGE

If so, then who exactly were these influential figures—the Hooded Ones, as we shall call them until their likely identity is revealed? Did they come as messianic figures, bringing some sort of message—one that was so clear it could not be ignored? Was it believed that something bad would happen to the local hunter-gatherers, their families, and the world around them if this message were to be ignored?

As much as these ideas might seem at odds with our understanding of the Paleolithic mindset, they will begin to make sense of the evidence being uncovered right now at Göbekli Tepe. This can be seen in the fact that the continuous building of sacred enclosures in the same basic style, albeit in a gradually *declining* fashion, across a period of nearly fifteen hundred years, ca. 9500–8000 BC, argues for the presence at the site of a very rigid belief system attached to the erection of the T-shaped pillars. It implies also a strength of conviction that might be compared to the manner in which Christians, adhering to ancient traditions, have steadfastly built churches in the same basic style across a very similar period of time.

The same can be said for the religious houses of other major religions, with the motivation behind these strictly-adhered-to dogmas always being the words, deeds, and legacy of prophets, saints, and messianic figures. Had something similar been going on at Göbekli Tepe or more particularly in the world that existed immediately prior to the construction of its large enclosures?

If the Hooded Ones did exist, then what might have been their powerful message, and where did they come from? To even start to answer these questions we need to return to the strange symbolism of the T-shaped pillars, in particular those that stand proud in the center of Enclosure D, arguably the most accomplished structure uncovered so far.

12

FEAR OF
THE FOX'S TAIL

The imposing central pillars in Göbekli Tepe's Enclosure D both sport wide belts, at the front of which, beneath a centrally placed belt buckle, fox-pelt loincloths have been carved, the animal's hind legs and long, bushy tail extending down to knee level (see plate 13). Further emphasizing the eastern monolith's vulpine character is the presence on its inner face of a leaping fox, something present also on the central pillars of Enclosures B, the eastern central pillar in Enclosure A, and the western central pillar in Enclosure C.

These images of the fox, along with the high level of faunal remains belonging to the red fox (*Vulpes vulpes*) found at Göbekli Tepe, led archaeozoologist Joris Peters, writing with Klaus Schmidt, to conclude that the interest in this canine creature went beyond any domestic usage and was connected in some way with the "exploitation of its pelt and/or the utilization of fox teeth for ornamental purposes."[1] That this statement was made even *before* the discovery of the fox-pelt loincloths carved on the front narrow faces of Enclosure D's central pillars means that what Peters and Schmidt go on to say in the same paper should not be ignored, for in their opinion "a specific worship of foxes may be reflected here."[2]

That leaping foxes appear also on the central pillars in the large enclosures at Göbekli Tepe suggests that the entrant passing between them would have encountered this vulpine creature upon accessing the otherworldly environment reached through the enclosures' inner recesses. So why foxes, especially as they are usually seen in indigenous mythologies as cosmic tricksters, evil twins of the true creator god, responsible only for chaos and disarray in the universe?

BELT BUCKLE CLUE

Was the fox the chosen animal totem of the Hooded Ones, the faceless individuals portrayed by the T-shaped pillars? If the answer is yes, then what does it mean? The key is the strange belt buckle immediately above the fox-pelt loincloth on the enclosure's eastern pillar (Pillar 18). A similar belt buckle is seen on the western pillar (Pillar 31), although here it is left unadorned, in the same way that the figure's belt, in complete contrast to the one worn by its eastern counterpart, is completely devoid of any glyphs or ideograms.

Only on the eastern pillar does the belt buckle reveal something very significant indeed. It shows a glyph composed of a thick letter U that cups within its concave form a large circle from which emerge three prongs that stand upward (see figure 12.1 and plate 13). That this emblem is worn centrally, on a belt festooned with strange ideograms, suggests that it has a very specific function. If so, then what might this have been?

THREE-TAILED COMET

Having examined the belt buckle glyph at some length, it is the author's opinion that it represents the principal components of a comet. The circle is its head, or nucleus, and the U-shape is the bow shock that bends around the leading edge of the nucleus and trails away as the halo. The upright prongs denote three separate tails, with multiple tails being a common feature of comets (see figure 12.2).

That the comet's "tails" on the belt buckle stand upward also makes sense, for these are often seen to trail into the night sky as the comet reaches perihelion. This is its final approach and slingshot orbit around the sun. As this takes place the solar magnetic fields cause the gaseous particles of the comet to point away from the sun, so when the comet is seen in the sky, either in the predawn

Figure 12.1. The belt on Enclosure D's eastern central pillar (Pillar 18) showing its belt buckle device and fox-pelt loincloth.

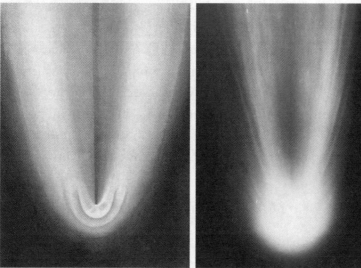

Figure 12.2. Left, comet showing the bow shock around its leading edge and, right, Halley's Comet in 1910. Both resemble elements of Pillar 18's belt buckle.

Figure 12.3. The Great Comet of 1861 showing its triple tail.

light (before perihelion) or, alternatively, just after sunset (following perihelion), its tail or tails point upward from the horizon, creating an unforgettable sight (see figure 12.3).

The idea that the belt buckle glyph shows a comet is strengthened by its similarity to three-tailed comets seen in an ancient Chinese silk text. The Mawangdui cometary atlas (also known as the *Book of Silk*), created ca. 300–200 BC and named after the Han Dynasty mound tomb in which it was discovered in the 1970s, lists, in all, twenty-nine different cometary forms and the disasters associated with them. In figure 12.4, we see that in more than one example there is a striking resemblance to the Göbekli Tepe belt buckle design, especially as the comets are drawn with their tails pointing upward.[3]

MARK OF THE COMET

Yet even assuming that the belt buckle glyph *does* show a comet, could this not simply be a personal device without any connection to the function of Göbekli Tepe? This appears unlikely, as the pillar is festooned with ideograms of a probable celestial nature. The belt's C and H glyphs would appear to have

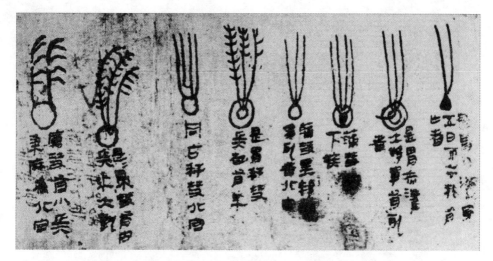

Figure 12.4. The Chinese Mawangdui atlas (or *Book of Silk*) from ca. 300–200 BC, showing the entry for the various different types of comet, some resembling the belt buckle on Göbekli Tepe's pillar.

cosmological values, as does the carved eye held within a slim crescent worn around the "neck" of the T-shaped monolith. In addition to this, it does seem as if Enclosure D's eastern central pillar has a greater function than its western neighbor, almost as if one twin is alive, while the other functions as a ghost or echo of the other.

Regardless of these facts Pillar 18's belt buckle is simply not enough to demonstrate that comets held some special importance at Göbekli Tepe. There is, however, another tantalizing link between the symbol of the comet and Enclosure D—this being the fox-pelt loincloths seen beneath the belt buckle on both monoliths. Universally the fox, *and the fox tail in particular,* has been seen as a metaphor for comets, due to the hairlike appearance of their long tails. Even in British heraldry the device known as the comet or blazing star is drawn to resemble the fox's tail (see figure 12.5 on p. 124). It is for this reason that comets have occasionally been personified as having clear vulpine and—as we shall see—canine (doglike) and lupine (wolflike) qualities of a dark, foreboding nature.

COMETARY CANINES

Chinese myths and legends, for instance, speak of mountain demons called *t'ien-kou* (*tengu* in Japanese), "heavenly dogs." Folk tradition asserts that these

Figure 12.5. Medieval heraldic device known as the comet or blazing star with its distinctive "fox tail."

supernatural creatures derive their name from comets or meteors falling to earth, for it is said they resemble the tails of dogs or foxes. One account speaks of t'ien-kou as:

> a huge dog with a tail of fire like a comet. Its home was in the heavens, but it sustained itself by descending to earth every night and seeking out human children to eat. If it could not catch any children it would attack a human adult and consume his liver.[4]

It is this dreaded fear of comets, seen in terms of malevolent supernatural creatures in canine form, that brings us to a fascinating account recorded by a Spanish Jesuit priest who journeyed through northern Mexico in 1607–1608. While staying in the town of Parras in the state of Coahuila, Andrés Pérez de Ribas (1576–1655) witnessed the priests of the local tribe, perhaps the Tlaxcalan Indians, conduct a powerful and somewhat macabre ceremony to ward off the baleful influence of a comet (almost certainly it was Halley's Comet, which made an appearance in 1607). According to him:

> The end of the comet (some of them said) was in the form of plumage: others said it had the form of an animal's tail. For this reason some came with feathers on their heads, and others with a lion's or fox's tail, each of them mimicking the animal he represented. In the middle of the plaza there was a great bonfire into which they threw their baskets [containing dead animals] along with everything in them. They did this in order to burn up and sac-

rifice these things, so they would rise up as smoke to the comet. As a result, the comet would have some food during those days and would therefore do them no harm.[5]

Although this strange ceremony to negate the influence of a comet took place on another continent nearly ten thousand years after the abandonment of Göbekli Tepe, the very specific use of fox (and lion) tails not just to represent the comet but also to connect with its supernatural nature, cannot be ignored. This form of sympathetic magic was the domain of the priest or shaman, and there can be little question that very similar ceremonies took place on other continents in past ages.

That the twin central pillars of Göbekli Tepe's Enclosure D both display fox tails, while the eastern example additionally possesses a belt buckle that might well show the symbol of a comet, begs the question of whether the Göbekli builders might in some way have been concerned by the influence and presence of comets in our skies. Moreover, because the comet symbolism only appears in full on one of the central pillars, was this particular figure seen to have a special dominion over comets, an ability connected with the proposed message or doctrine introduced to the hunter-gatherers of southeast Anatolia in the epoch immediately prior to the construction of the first stone enclosures at Göbekli Tepe?

I PREDICT A COMET

Is it possible that this imposing stone figure at the center of Enclosure D, whoever or whatever it represents, was seen to have delivered the means by which the Epipaleolithic peoples of southeast Anatolia, with the help of his shamanic-based elite, could combat the baleful influence of comets? That the hunter-gatherers of southeast Anatolia so readily gave up their nomadic lifestyles to build monumental architecture in an unprecedented manner argues persuasively that this incoming elite must have had some kind of hold or influence over the people. Perhaps they claimed they had direct contact with the supernatural creature behind the manifestation of comets. If so, then such claims would have needed to be backed up with some convincing displays of proof for the hunter-gatherers to have so readily abandoned their old ways. So what might this have been?

One realistic answer is that, like the ancient Chinese astrologers behind the creation of the Mawangdui atlas ca. 300–200 BC, the incoming elite had a very real knowledge of comets, which might have included information on periodic comets, those that make their return within one to two human generations. A perfect example is Halley's Comet, which makes its return every seventy-five to seventy-six years (its last appearances were in 1910 and 1986). Indeed, even though the gravitational influence of the solar system's larger planets, such as Saturn and Jupiter, means that the orbit of a short-period comet can fluctuate somewhat, it *is* possible that its reappearance might have been calculated to some degree of accuracy in just a few centuries of observation.

It is not known whether Halley's Comet graced our skies in the tenth or eleventh millennium BC, although some sources do suggest that it has been in its current orbit for between sixteen thousand and two hundred thousand years.[6] So the likelihood of Göbekli Tepe's founding elite being able to calculate the return of a short-period comet was therefore pretty high. If they *were* able to do this, then using this valuable information to their advantage might have been enough to convince the hunter-gathering communities that they had real influence over these fearful celestial objects.

Such ideas might help explain why Enclosure D's twin central monoliths wear fox-pelt loincloths, why leaping foxes are present on the inner faces of key central pillars at Göbekli Tepe, and why Joris Peters and Klaus Schmidt considered that "a specific worship of foxes may be reflected here." These thoughts also perhaps have some bearing on why the large enclosures seem to incorporate symbolism of a clearly celestial and cyclic nature.

Is it possible that the enclosures embody a belief, offered by the Hooded Ones and, through them, their lineal descendants (responsible perhaps for the continued construction and management of Göbekli Tepe), that by synchronizing the enclosures with cosmic time cycles it would help provide the builders with enough information to control the influence of comets on a supernatural level? Was it these communities' absolute fear and loathing of comets that motivated them to abandon their old lifestyles to build monumental architecture on such a dramatic scale? More pertinently, how did any of this relate to the apparent alignment of the main enclosures at Göbekli Tepe toward the Milky Way's Great Rift, marked out in the heavens by the star Deneb? These are matters that must be addressed next.

13

COSMIC TRICKSTER

I t was the Greek Neoplatonist and celebrated philosopher Proclus of Athens (412–485 AD) who warned that "the fox star nibbles continuously at the thong of the yoke which holds together heaven and Earth,"[1] with German folklore adding that when the fox succeeds, the world will come to an end.[2] Proclus was referring here to the faint binary star Alcor, which in Babylonian star lore was known as [MUL]KA.A, the Fox Star.[3] In astronomical terms Alcor is located next to a much brighter quadruple system of binary stars, collectively known under the name Mizar. Together Alcor and Mizar make up the kink in the "handle" of the Plough, or Big Dipper, which forms part of the constellation of Ursa Major, the Great Bear (see figure 13.1 on p. 128).

Some semblance of Alcor's mythical origin is revealed in Greek star lore, which tells how the star was once part of the Pleiades, or Seven Sisters, the cluster of seven stars located in the proximity of Taurus, the Bull. According to the Greek writer Hyginus (or one of his pupils writing under his name), a Pleiade named Elektra was so distraught at seeing the death of her descendant, King Dardanus, during the fall of Troy, that she withdrew her light and took flight as a "hair star," a comet, and became Alopex, the Fox, called by the Arabs Al Suha (the "forgotten" or "neglected one"), all names for Alcor.[4]

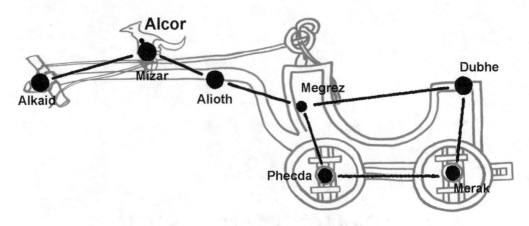

Figure 13.1. The stars of Ursa Major, or the Big Dipper, as the ancient asterism known as the Wain, with Alcor in its role as the Fox Star (after Gavin White).

TURNING THE HEAVENS

Even though there are no astronomical explanations behind these puzzling myths featuring the star Alcor, they do reinforce the connection between the fox, as a symbol of the cosmic trickster, and the destruction of the world caused by the intrusion of a comet, or comets in plural. Why should this have been so? The answer seems to lie in the fact that the seven main stars of Ursa Major, which includes the Alcor/Mizar combination, were once universally seen as the plow, yoke, mill, handle, wain, or mechanism that quite literally turned the sky pole or world pillar holding up the heavens. This belief came about because the stars of Ursa Major are seen to revolve around the celestial pole in an unerring fashion, a role played by the constellation in every human age, despite the fact that none of its stars ever occupy the position of Pole Star.

Proclus's warning about the Fox Star nibbling "continuously at the thong of the yoke which holds together heaven and Earth" is an allusion to the fox attempting to sabotage the universe's turning mechanism, which, of course, was seen to have its terrestrial point of origin wherever an axis mundi was established on the ground. The fox, if allowed to carry out its mischievous deeds, would eventually bring about the collapse of the imagined sky pole, and with it would follow the end, not just of the world but also of time itself. The fact that Alcor, or Alopex, the Fox Star, was additionally seen as a comet inbound from the Pleiades is revealing indeed and conjures the idea that as a "hair star" it might have been seen as responsible for this perceived cosmic catastrophe.

Fox, star, comet, pole, destruction. These are the key elements in this puzzling enigma of ancient Greek star lore, which might easily have had its origins in ancient Mesopotamia, among one of the great civilizations that rose up on the banks of the Tigris and Euphrates rivers around 3000 BC. Indeed, it is just possible that certain aspects of this seemingly naïve vision of the cosmos might reflect something of the proposed strategy adopted by the Epipaleolithic hunter-gatherers of southeast Anatolia prior to the construction of Göbekli Tepe. Interestingly, Professor Klaus Schmidt compares the leaping foxes carved on the twin central pillars in the various enclosures at Göbekli Tepe with Reynard the Fox, a trickster of French folklore,[5] as well as with the Mesopotamian Fox Star Alcor, which he says belonged to Enlil, the highest god of the Sumerian pantheon, who was patron also of the ancient city of Nipper in Lower Iraq.[6]

MAN VERSUS DEVIL

So if the Fox Star Alcor appears on the inner faces of key central pillars Göbekli Tepe, why are they aligned toward Cygnus, and not Ursa Major? The answer seems to lie in the fact that there was once a close interrelationship between the Fox Star and the power and influence of Cygnus in its role as guardian of the celestial pole.

It is a relationship brought out in a complex Romanian sky myth that begins with the formation of the earth and heavens and leads into a search by humankind to find the creator. For the journey "the Man" gathers together various tools, objects, and creatures, which are identified with different constellations of the night sky. Among the items taken on the journey are "the Great Cross of the church" and "the Fountain of the Crossroads," identified, respectively, as Cygnus and the constellation's bright star Deneb,[7] the crossroads being a metaphor for both the axis mundi and the corresponding cosmic axis in the sky.

Thereafter, the Man sets off on his voyage and eventually reaches "the middle of the Sky's road," with the "Sky's road" being the Milky Way.[8] Here the Man encounters "He Who Will Be Killed By The Cross." This is the Devil, identified as the Fox Star, Alcor, whom the Man fights and eventually defeats.[9] The story implies that in Christian times the mischievous sky fox was transformed into the Devil himself.

RESTORING COSMIC ORDER

What takes place during the cosmic battle between the Man, as the bearer of the Cross, and the Devil, as the Fox Star, seems to relate to the former regaining control of "the cosmic world axis or world tree of other myths,"[10] after the Devil sends the heavens spinning out of control. Thus the story implies that the Devil, that is, Alcor, is "killed" or stopped by the Man wielding the Cross, which is Cygnus in its role as guardian of the "cosmic world axis."

This restoration of cosmic order is achieved, however, only after chaos and mayhem have taken place, for we are told that once the "brave Man" began fighting with the Devil, their battle "created a great storm beneath the Sky, called by us on Earth 'the rabid wind.'"[11] There are no indications of what this "great storm" or "rabid wind" might have been, although it clearly implies some sort of mass upheaval in the heavens, which either affected the earth or was witnessed from the ground.

It seems feasible that this Romanian sky myth reflects the role played at Göbekli Tepe by Cygnus, and Deneb in particular. The leaping foxes on the pillars, along with the fox-pelt loincloths on the central monoliths of Enclosure D, certainly suggest there was some connection between the Fox Star Alcor as the cosmic trickster and the area of sky toward which the pillars were directed, in other words the Cygnus star Deneb. These precision alignments toward the perceived opening to the upper world enabled the shaman or astral traveler immediate access to the sky realms. Beyond here, in otherworldly terms, would have been a world inhabited by a whole host of strange creatures. They would have been seen to roam freely within this sky world and could thus be encountered during vision quests or shamanic journeys made during altered states of consciousness. Many of these sky creatures, denoted by stars and star groups spread out along the Milky Way, are almost certainly represented in carved relief on the T-shaped pillars at Göbekli Tepe.

Yet for these people living in southeast Anatolia during the tenth millennium BC one of the greatest considered threats to the stability of the sky pole or cosmic axis was, it seems, the fox, who as the cosmic trickster had the ability to create chaos and mayhem—activities that could lead to the collapse of the sky pole and the destruction of the world. It is almost certainly for this reason that the fox appears on the inner faces of the pillars at Göbekli Tepe, which Schmidt was probably correct to identify with the Fox Star Alcor. Very likely the foxes shown within the bent arms of the anthropomorphic figures represented by the twin pillars—particularly those in Enclosure D, who wear the fox felt loincloths—are displaying absolute control over the trickster influence of the sky fox, whose astronomical form is the Fox Star, Alcor.

In the Romanian sky myth quoted above, the shaking of the heavens is all that results from the Man battling against the Fox Star Alcor in its form as the Christian Devil. However, this perceived threat from the heavens multiplies exponentially when we realize that it is not just the fox that can cause comets to bring about world destruction but also the wolf, a much more dangerous creature by far.

14

FROM A FOX
TO A WOLF

In the star lore of Estonia, on the Baltic coast of Northern Europe, we again encounter Alcor, the Fox Star, although now its zoomorphic form has changed to that of the wolf (*bar* in Estonian). As the Wolf Star it stands alongside the Ox, or Bull, identified with the nearby star Mizar.[1] Once again they constitute the kink of the "handle" of the Big Dipper, or Plough, which in Estonia is known as the Great Wain (that is, a cart or wagon).

Slovenian star lore tells the story of Saint Martin, who uses the Great Wain (Ursa Major) to carry a great pile of logs.[2] Along comes the mischievous Wolf (Alcor), who proceeds to kill the Ox (Mizar) and break the vehicle's shaft. The saint repairs the Wain and, as punishment, harnesses the Wolf to the Ox in order to make the animal take the load. Yet the Wolf does nothing more than pull the cart backward.

THE CESSATION OF COSMIC TIME

Once more the star Alcor, here in the guise of the Wolf, is seen to interfere with the turning mechanism of the heavens, symbolized in this instance by the shaft of the Wain. Not only this, but he also disrupts the natural order of the heavens by dragging the wagon backward, an allusion to the collapse or reversal of time. Clearly, in European star lore the figure of the sky wolf was interchangeable with that of the sky fox.

The harnessing of the Wolf (Alcor) by Saint Martin is simply a variation of the Romanian sky myth in which the Man defeats the Devil to restore cosmic order. Clearly, the wolf, the fox, and the Devil play nearly identical roles in this myth cycle, with the human intercession being necessary to prevent any kind of catastrophe taking place (the role played by the shaman at Göbekli Tepe).

Saint Martin's feast day is November 11, when swans and geese are roasted and eaten across Europe. The date corresponds also to the return of migrating swans and geese from their breeding grounds in the north. Indeed, the idea of swans and geese carrying souls to and from a northerly placed "heaven" played a major role in European folklore until fairly recent times, the connection with Cygnus in its capacity as the entrance to the sky world being the obvious next step.[3] Thus if Saint Martin might be seen as a Christian patron of the Cygnus constellation, then his role in the Slovenian sky myth makes complete sense. Like the Man in the Romanian story, he is the guiding intelligence of the Cygnus constellation in its struggle against the cosmic trickster symbolized by the star Alcor in Ursa Major. More incredibly, these beliefs almost certainly go back to a time when the constellation of Ursa Major revolved around either Deneb or Delta Cygni in their role as pole stars, ca. 16,500–13,000 BC.

Yet even if this unprecedented vision of the beliefs and practices of those who inspired the construction of Göbekli Tepe in the tenth millennium BC is correct, why go to all this trouble in order to avert the baleful influence of comets? What was the real motivation behind all this work and effort, which must have completely changed the lifestyles of the hunter-gatherers of the region? Why did anyone at the end of the Upper Paleolithic age live in fear that a sky fox, or indeed a sky wolf, might disrupt the turning mechanism of the heavens and in so doing bring about the destruction of the world?

The answer would seem to be that in the minds of the Göbekli builders, there was a genuine fear that if they did *not* do everything in their power to curtail this perceived threat from the sky, then something bad would happen. Whatever that "something" was, it was so deeply entrenched in the collective psyche of the peoples of southeast Anatolia that they were willing to abandon their old lifestyles and adopt new ones in order to deal with the problem.

Accepting such a scenario only makes sense if there had already been a terrifying incident involving the sky fox or sky wolf—one that had brought chaos to the world during some former age of humankind. As we see next, a search through the folklore, myths, and legends of the ancient world tells us that just such a catastrophe might well have taken place in fairly recent geological history.

15

TWILIGHT
OF THE GODS

I
t was the American congressman, popular writer, and amateur scientist Ignatius Donnelly (1831–1901), most remembered for his best-selling work *Atlantis: The Antediluvian World* (1882), who first publicly explored the possibility that a comet impact caused untold devastation on earth during some former geological age. More significantly, he thought that humans living at this time might well have preserved a memory of this catastrophic event that was passed down through countless generations in the form of myths and legends.

Donnelly's theories on a comet impact in recent geological history became the subject of a book entitled *Ragnarök: The Age of Fire and Gravel,* published in 1883, just one year after *Atlantis: The Antediluvian World*. It contains myths, legends, stories, and traditions from around the world that preserve chilling accounts of something immensely bad that happened in our skies, involving the sun, moon, and intruding celestial phenomena. As a result the earth is decimated by an all-encompassing conflagration, accompanied by noxious clouds, an extended period of darkness, and a subsequent deluge, responsible for putting out the fires *and* drowning humankind. Invariably, just a few righteous people survive, either by boarding a vessel or by hiding in a cave. Very often the world is repopulated either by a single family or a couple, usually a brother and sister, who become the progenitors of a new group of humans. Some accounts even speak of the survivors erecting great temples as a direct response to what has happened.

THE EDDAS

One source of material utilized by Donnelly to outline the actions of what he saw as a rogue comet, or cluster of comets, that brought destruction to the world, was that preserved by the peoples of Scandinavia and Iceland. Two primary sources are cited—the *Prose Edda* and *Poetic Edda* (known also as the *Younger Edda* and *Elder Edda*)—both recorded in their present form by Christian scholars during the medieval period. The *Prose Edda,* attributed to Snorri Sturluson, who lived ca. 1178–1241, derives from an Icelandic text known as the *Codex Upsaliensis,* which dates to the early 1300s, while the *Poetic Edda* is found in a thirteenth-century manuscript, written in Icelandic and known as the *Codex Regius.*

Both Eddas feature a much prophesized event that acted as the climax to the age of the gods, who are known as the Æsir, or Asa. This catastrophic event is referred to as Ragnarök, an Old Icelandic word meaning "doom or destruction of the gods; the last day, the end of the gods."[1] Another variation of the name, Ragnarøkkr, means "twilight of the gods" or "world's end."[2] Put simply, it is the Norse version of Armageddon, a fatalistic judgment, where key gods actually die fighting hellish monsters that rise up intent on bringing about the end of the world.

So important was the account of Ragnarök to Donnelly's mounting evidence for a comet impact in some former age of humankind that it provided him with the title for his book. As there is today overwhelming scientific evidence to confirm his forward-thinking conclusions (see chapter 17), it seems appropriate to allow the U.S. congressman's often poignant comments to set the scene as we review the account of Ragnarök as given in the *Prose Edda,* Donnelly's own source for the events described in his book, cited here using the English translation by American author, professor, and diplomat Rasmus Björn Anderson (1846–1936).[3]

THE DEVOURING OF THE SUN AND MOON

The twilight of the gods began, according to the Scandinavian account, after the human race had become foul murderers, perjurers, and sinners, shedding each other's blood. Humanity's descent into depravity is a common theme in catastrophe myths that generally stress that divine intervention was necessary to purge the world of a wicked or evil strain of humanity.

Thus the scene is set for the coming destruction, and shortly afterward a terrible sight is seen in the skies—the wolf named Sköll opens its jaws and eats the sun. "That is, the Comet strikes the sun, or approaches so close to it that it seems to do so,"[4] was how Donnelly put it.

The Edda tells us next how another wolf named Hati Hróðvitnisson (his first name means "he who hates, enemy"[5]) devours the moon: "and this, too, will cause great mischief. Then the stars shall be hurled from the heavens, and the earth shall be shaken so violently that trees will be torn up by the roots, the tottering mountains will tumble headlong from their foundations, and all bonds and fetters will be shivered to pieces."[6]

These words Donnelly saw as describing the appearance of a second comet, its blazing debris now falling to earth, causing absolute devastation.[7] There is a hint here also of the loosening of the bonds that hold up the sky pole, or world pillar, preventing the world from falling apart.

After this the monster known as the Fenris Wolf, the offspring of the trickster god Loki, breaks free of his shackles, which had held him firm up to this time (see figure 15.1 on page 138), prompting Donnelly to comment: "This, we shall see, is the name of one of the comets."[8] Fenris himself is the father of Sköll and Hati, wolves that pursue and devour the sun and moon.

THE MIDGARD SERPENT

The account of Ragnarök continues: "The sea rushes over the earth, for the Midgard-serpent writhes in giant rage, and seeks to gain the land."[9] This is a mythical snake that curls around the base of the world tree, known as Yggdrasil, which unites heaven, earth (Midgard), and underworld. The Midgard Serpent is for Donnelly "the name of another comet; it strives to reach the earth; its proximity disturbs the oceans."[10] However, once again we can see here the actions of a terrible monster intent on destroying the physical world by bringing about the downfall of Yggdrasil, the Norse form of the world pillar.

We are told next that the "Fenris-wolf advances and opens his enormous mouth; the lower jaw reaches to the earth and the upper one to heaven, and he would open it still wider had he room to do so. Fire flashes from his eyes and

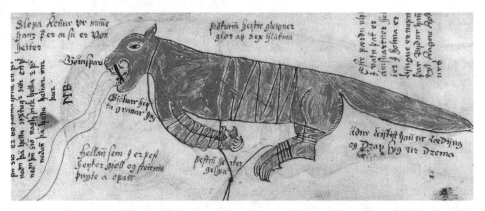

Figure 15.1. The Fenris Wolf bound with magical cord, from a seventeenth-century Icelandic manuscript in the possession of the Árni Magnússon Institute in Iceland. Note the Van River emerging from the creature's mouth.

nostrils. The Midgard-serpent, placing himself by the side of the Fenris-wolf, vomits forth floods of poison, which fill the air and the waters."[11]

These then, the Fenris Wolf and the Midgard Serpent, are to be seen as the two principal comets of destruction, side by side, Donnelly suggested, "like Biela's two fragments, and they give out poison—the carbureted-hydrogen gas revealed by the spectroscope."[12]

Biela was the name given to a short-period comet first recorded in 1772 and observed again in 1805. It was not, however, recognized as being the same object until 1822, when Wilhelm von Biela, an army officer from Vienna, finally identified it as a periodic comet with an orbit of just 6.6 years. During its appearance in 1852 the comet split in two, prompting Donnelly's comment about the two comet fragments moving together.

Biela's comet was never seen again, and presumably it has now broken up into undetectable pieces that periodically fall to earth as harmless meteors whenever the earth passes through the orbit of its remaining fragments. Illustrations of the comet after its breakup into two separate fragments make for a very ominous picture indeed (see figure 15.2), helping us to understand the dread that the appearance of such celestial bodies might have instilled in the peoples of former ages.

After this time the *Prose Edda* states that "Surt rides first, and before and behind him flames burning fire. His sword outshines the sun itself. Bifrost (the rainbow), as they ride over it, breaks to pieces."[13] Surt is said to have been a fire giant, although for Donnelly it is the "blazing nucleus of the comet,"[14] with

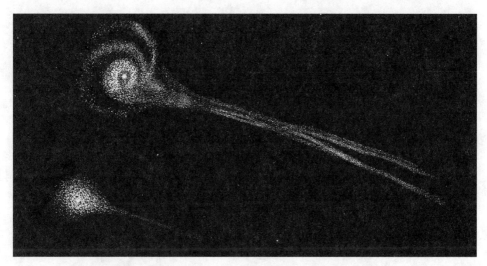

Figure 15.2. Biela's comet in 1846, soon after it split in two.

swords being common metaphors for comets. For example, an illustration of comet types in Johannes Hevelius's *Cometographia,* published in 1668, shows them as swords and daggers of various shapes and sizes (see figure 15.3 on p. 140).

THE MONSTROUS REGIMENT

The *Prose Edda* account reveals next how the monstrous regiment "direct their course to the battle-field called Vigrid. Thither repair also the Fenris-wolf and the Midgard-serpent, and Loki with all the followers of Hel, and Hrym with all the frost-giants."[15]

For Donnelly this implied that "all these evil forces, the comets, the fire, the devil, and death, have taken possession of the great plain, the heart of the civilized land. The scene is located in this spot, because probably it was from this spot the legends were afterward dispersed to all the world."[16]

This is an interesting statement since it supposes that somewhere in the ancient world there existed a heartland, a place where all these great tragedies were played out and witnessed by those who survived this tumultuous ordeal.

BATTLE OF LIGHT AND DARKNESS

It is after this time that the gods, as the defenders of the world, begin to fight back and start to win the day against the hellish terrors, although not without casualties

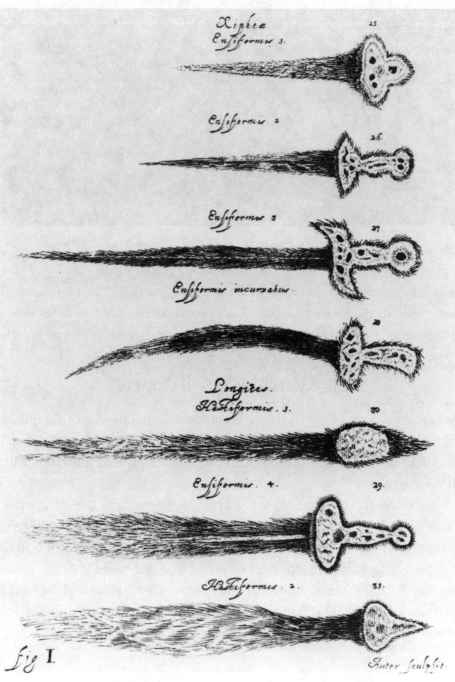

Figure 15.3. A page from Johannes Hevelius's *Cometographia* of 1668 showing comets as daggers and swords.

on their own side. Heimdal, the guardian of Bifrost Bridge, blows the Gjallarhorn, which had been hidden beneath Yggdrasil. It awakens the gods, allowing the battle of Ragnarök to commence. The sky god Odin takes flight to Mimir's Well, a sacred pool at the foot of Yggdrasil. Here lurks the head of his friend Mimir, which he asks to grant him advice. After that we are told the "ash Yggdrasil begins to quiver, nor is there anything in heaven or on earth that does not fear and tremble in that terrible hour."[17] It is a hint once more that the world pillar is being shaken, tilted even, by the events transpiring both on the ground and in the air.

Thereafter, the gods enter Vigrid and engage in battle: "That day the dog Garm, that had been chained in the Gnipa-cave, breaks loose. He is the most fearful monster of all, and attacks Tyr, and they kill each other."[18] At the same time, the god Thor is able to slay the Midgard Serpent but dies as a consequence of the poisonous venom the monster breathes on him. Inevitably, Donnelly saw Garm, described as a bloodstained hound that guards "Hel's gate," as alluding to yet another comet fragment.[19] Its appearance marks the entry of a fourth canid into the Ragnarök story.

THE EARTH SINKS

At this point in the battle Odin takes on the Fenris Wolf but is swallowed by the monster, which he himself had helped to rear (is this "because Odin had a connection with wolves?" asks one commentator[20]). On seeing the death of his father, Odin's son Víðarr rushes at the beast and, wearing a magic boot prepared specially for the confrontation, stamps his foot into the Fenris Wolf's mouth and holds open its lower jaw. He then uses brute force to pull up on the beast's jaw, an action that brings about its instant demise (see figure 15.4).

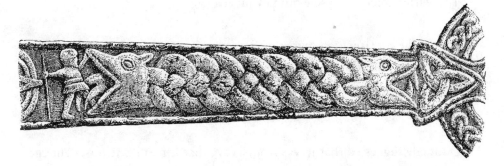

Figure 15.4. Shaft of the Gosforth Cross in Cumbria, England, showing Odin's son Víðarr killing the Fenris Wolf. Note its knotted serpentine tail.

The Fenris Wolf's father, Loki, comes up against the god Heimdal, and they kill each other, at which: "Surt flings fire and flame over the world. Smoke wreathes up around the all-nourishing tree (Yggdrasil), the high names play against the heavens, and earth consumed sinks down beneath the sea."[21] Once more, this is a clear sign of some kind of global conflagration, as well as an all-encompassing deluge that begins to engulf the earth, making it appear as if it is sinking beneath the waves.

THE FIMBUL-WINTER

Just in these few lines we see telltale signs of the aftermath of a major cataclysm that is set to decimate the earth and everything upon it, a surmise affirmed by the fact that the *Prose Edda* speaks also of the world being plunged into an age of ice:

> The growing depravity and strife in the world proclaim the approach of this great event. First there is a winter called Fimbul-winter, during which snow will fall from the four corners of the world; the frosts will be very severe, the winds piercing, the weather tempestuous, and the sun will impart no gladness. Three such winters shall pass away without being tempered.[22]

Donnelly easily recognized these words as describing the onset of a glacial age, following the impact of the comets. This great freeze, which seems to come on quickly, does eventually begin to thaw, as the clouds of darkness disappear and a new sun and moon are born. The floods recede also, leading to a complete renewal of nature.

Thereafter emerge the sole human survivors:

> During the conflagration caused by Surt's fire, a woman by name Lif (life) and a man named Lifthraser lie concealed in Hodmimer's forest. The dew of the dawn serves them for food, and so great a race shall spring from them that their descendants shall soon spread over the whole earth."[23]

Donnelly suggested that it was from a cave that Lif and Lifthraser emerged because caves feature worldwide in the regeneration of humankind in the wake of catastrophes, while the reference to them giving birth to a great "race" implies that, in Scandinavian tradition at least, the current human population derives from these two individuals. Others survive the cataclysm as well, including Víðarr and Vale, the sons of Odin, and Mode and Magne, the sons of Thor. Yet these are not mortal beings like Lif and Lifthraser. They are offspring of the Æsir, who are destined to dwell on the plains of Ida, where stands the world tree, Yggdrasil, alongside Mimir's Well and Asgard, the home of the gods.

DONNELLY'S DATES

From what we read here, it does seem possible that the Eddas, like very similar myths and legends from around the world, contain echoes of a devastating catastrophe that engulfed the world during some distant epoch. Donnelly envisaged this sequence of events beginning around thirty thousand years ago, at the height of the last ice age, and culminating around eleven thousand to eight thousand years ago.[24] As we shall see, his later dates correspond pretty well with the proposed timescale of cosmic catastrophes now believed to have taken place globally toward the end of the last ice age, triggered by a major impact event around 10,900 BC (see chapter 17).

Donnelly was convinced that a comet, or indeed a series of comets, was responsible for these cataclysms, and once again he was bang on the money, as we shall see soon enough. His proposal that these global killers were portrayed in ancient myths and legends as supernatural creatures of the earth and sky also seems to be right, a theory advanced since that time by a number of different catastrophists, who have each put a unique spin on the subject.

NUCLEAR WINTER

In the Ragnarök account, various monsters are cited as being responsible for destruction in this world, including the Midgard Serpent, the fire giant Surt, and at least four canids, three of them wolves. Two of the wolves are accused of having swallowed the sun and moon, and this quite possibly describes the temporary disappearance of the heavenly bodies that would inevitably follow a catastrophe of this scale. A comet or asteroid impacting the earth would create unimaginable clouds of smoke, dust, and microparticles of various kinds that would be thrust into the upper atmosphere, creating what is known as a nuclear winter, a total blackout of available light. This debris, which would probably remain airborne for some considerable length of time, would be joined by a thick layer of toxic ash produced by the intense firestorms that would engulf entire regions of the planet in the days, weeks, and months after the initial event.

To our ancestors this period of absolute darkness might have led them to assume that the sky wolves, in other words, the comet fragments, had quite literally devoured the sun and moon. Clearly, the lack of any sunlight heating up the planet would have resulted in an immediate drop in temperature, helping to trigger the onset of an ice age in a matter of days. Indeed, it would have happened in a manner quite similar to that portrayed in Roland Emmerich's disaster movie *The Day After Tomorrow* (2004). Although fiction, this film adequately shows what would happen under such severe weather conditions and how quickly our world would be turned on its head by an initial catastrophe of global consequences.

The effect of all this would have been to bring humankind to its knees as it strived to survive from day to day, all this being "caused" by the intrusion into their midst of perceived supernatural creatures, including deathly serpents and terrifying sky wolves that could quite literally swallow the sun and moon whole.

It must have been an unimaginably frightening time to live in. Never would this dreadful age be forgotten; nor should it be forgotten. As Donnelly so aptly put it:

> What else can mankind think of, or dream of, or talk of for the next thousand years but this awful, this unparalleled calamity through which the race has passed?
>
> A long-subsequent but most ancient and cultivated people, whose memory has, for us, almost faded from the earth, will thereafter embalm the great drama in legends, myths, prayers, poems, and sagas; fragments of which are found to-day dispersed through all literatures in all lands.[25]

The peoples of Northern Europe almost certainly preserved their memory of this "unparalleled calamity" in their accounts of Ragnarök. Its existence helps strengthen the case for canids—wolves, hounds, and foxes—being seen by our ancestors not just as dangerous cosmic tricksters with the power to bring about death and destruction but also as outright enemies of the world pillar, or sky pole, that connects this world with both the underworld and sky world. Yet as we see next, these myths existed not only in "legends, myths, prayers, poems, and sagas"[26] handed down from some forgotten age. They lingered on in fragmentary sky lore that once again reveals the great threat that the sky wolves were seen to pose in destabilizing everything that we have ever held dear in this world.

16

THE WOLF PROGENY

The dual relationship between order and chaos in the heavens is high-lighted in the "magnificent song of Eirek," ca. 950 AD, which has the Norse god Odin say: "Evermore the wolf, the grey one, gazes on the throne of the gods," an allusion to the Pole Star, which in Anglo-Saxon tradition was the "divine seat where the north star Tir (or Tyr) . . . 'never flinches.'"[1]

There is a strange echo of this scenario in the Scandinavian story of Ragnarök. The main battle is most often described with Odin coming up against Loki's son, the Fenris Wolf, and losing his life, and then how Odin's son Víðarr is finally able to kill the demonic creature. However, less attention is paid to the story of the Germanic, Old English, and Norse war god named Tíw, Týr, or Tir. He is willing to sacrifice his life to ensure the safety of humankind by placing his arm in the Fenris Wolf's jaws after the gods had asked the beast to try on various fetters, or shackles, to test his strength against them, the real purpose being to trick Fenris into bondage so that he could never wreak havoc in the world (see figure 16.1).

Fenris was easily able to break free of two sets of fetter, the second one twice as strong as the first. Yet he becomes suspicious when he sees the next fetter, which seems to be little more than a silk ribbon. So to make sure this is not a ruse, Fenris asks one of the gods to step forward and put his arm in his mouth. Tíw agrees to do so, after which the wolf is bound.

Figure 16.1. Helmet plate die from Torslunda on Oland in Sweden showing the Norse god Tíw binding the Fenris Wolf, seventh century AD.

Of course, it *is* a trick, as the silk ribbon has been forged by dark elves from six different magical substances, which when combined make an utterly unbreakable fetter. Once the Fenris Wolf realizes he has been tricked, he bites off Tíw's right arm.

Although simply a tale, it is a story containing much deeper symbolism relating to the stability of the world, and in particular the world pillar. In the Norse magical alphabet known as the runes, Tíw is represented by the T-rune named Tiwaz. It is composed of an upright pole at the top of which are two downward turned lines that show the rune to be an arrow. The Tiwaz rune

Figure 16.2. Left, the German world pillar known as the Irminsul and,
right, the Tiwaz rune, showing its likeness to the world pillar.

is popularly considered to be a representation of the "vault of heaven held up
by the universal column,"[2] as well as the Irminsul, the "world column" of the
Saxons, that "has its heavenly termination in the pole star."[3] (See figure 16.2.)

This identification fits well with Tíw's role as personification of the North
Star, suggesting that originally he was the genius loci, or guardian spirit, of
the axis mundi, protecting it against attacks by adversaries such as the Fenris
Wolf. Even though Tíw is killed by the helldog Garm in the *Prose Edda* rendi-
tion of Ragnarök, in the *Poetic Edda* this act is never fulfilled—Tíw's earlier
sacrifice for his warriors and humanity permitting him the title "Leavings of
the Wolf"[4]; in other words, the one that the wolf left alone, that is, didn't kill.

SAVIOR OF THE WORLD

Tíw was a very early sky god. His name is thought to derive from the same
route as *deus,* or *dei,* meaning "god,"[5] although he is also the "hanged" god.
This suggests he is to be seen as some kind of savior who fought and won the
battle against the cosmic trickster in the guise of a supernatural wolf, when it
attacked the world pillar and almost brought about the destruction of not only
the Æsir gods, but also humankind, an abstract memory, seemingly, of a very
real comet impact event in some former age.

In Nordic folklore the twin streams formed by the Milky Way's Great Rift, in the vicinity of Cygnus, have been identified as the "two streams of saliva" that fall from the Fenris Wolf's jaws, one named Wil, the other called Wan, or Van, known also as "Hell's stream" or the "road of the dead"[6] (see figure 15.1 on p. 138). Fenris's alternative name, Vanargandr, actually means monster guardian of the River Van,[7] so there is tantalizing evidence that the wolf was linked in some manner with the Milky Way's Great Rift, and through this to the celestial pole and axis mundi, from which the monster was finally able to break free of his bonds to wreak havoc in the world.

BLACK DOG

And the Fenris Wolf was not the only supernatural canid of European folklore to have been perceived as a threat to the stability of the world pillar. Ukrainian sky lore relates how the constellation of Ursa Major, which includes the seven stars making up the Plough or Big Dipper, is a team of horses tethered to a harness and that "every night a black dog tries to bite through the harness, in order to destroy the world, but he does not achieve his disastrous aim: at dawn, when he runs to drink from a spring, the harness renews itself."[8] Since the Big Dipper circles around the celestial pole, the horses tethered to the sky pole are the method by which the heavens turn. The "black dog" is, of course, the cosmic trickster attempting to break the horses free in order to collapse the sky pole and bring about the destruction of the world.

Variations of the Ukrainian sky myth say that the black dog was bound in chains beside the constellation of Ursa Minor, the Little Bear, which is the location of the current Pole Star, Polaris. Here the animal attempts to gnaw through its shackles, and when this occurs the world will end,[9] a clear comparison with the actions of the Fenris Wolf in Norse sky lore.

THE ETERNAL STRUGGLE

In a similar vein, Russian philologist Dr. Vyacheslav Ivanov wrote that the eternal struggle against the dragon in Slavonic folklore derives from a much older tradition in which heroic blacksmiths were able to bind and chain "a terrible dog." Ivanov goes on to say that "over the whole territory of Eurasia, this mythological complex is associated . . . with the Great Bear . . . (and) with a star near it as a dog which is dangerous for the Universe."[10]

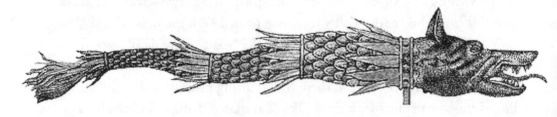

Figure 16.3. Dacian battle standard known as the Draco, or Drago.
Note its cometlike tail.

Although it's not stated which star "near" Ursa Major the infernal dog is to be identified with, almost certainly it is Alcor, the Fox Star, or Wolf Star. It is a conclusion confirmed by the fact that this canine "is dangerous for the Universe" and has the ability to bring about the destruction of everything. As sky monsters, the wolf and dragon are essentially one and the same, as is shown by the battle standard of the Dacians, the pre-Roman peoples of Romania. With a wolf's head and serpent-like tail, it is called the Draco, or Drago, the dragon, and has been identified as a possible representation of a comet (see figure 16.3).[11]

TEUTONIC MYTHOLOGY

The great philologist and mythologist Jacob Grimm (1785–1863) in his multi-volume work *Teutonic Mythology* discusses the role of the supernatural canid in catastrophe folklore. He saw the Fenris Wolf as quite simply the trickster god Loki "in a second birth . . . (although now) in the shape of a wolf."[12]

Grimm cites also an old Scottish story about "the tayl of the wolfe and the warldis end,"[13] a reference to the world falling apart following the appearance of a wolf's tail, which we can be pretty sure is a metaphor for a comet. Grimm wrote that much fuller stories of how a great wolf or dog had brought destruction to the world must once have existed "all over Germany, and beyond it," adding that, "we still say, when baneful and perilous disturbances arise, 'the devil is broke loose,' while in the North they would say '*Loki* er or böndum (Loki is out of control).'"[14]

Grimm quotes other examples of catastrophe-based folklore and folk beliefs among the peoples of medieval Europe. They include a popular French song about King Henry IV that "expresses the far end of the future as the time when the wolf's teeth shall get at the moon"[15]; in other words, the wolf will cause it to be extinguished, bringing about the world's end. All these stories seem to be fragmented memories of a terrible cataclysm, coupled with an unerring fear that one day it could all happen again.

THE BUNDAHISHN

That these examples of canine cosmic tricksters, manifesting in the skies as planet killers such as comets and asteroids, come from Europe and not Anatolia need not concern us, for similar cosmological themes exist in sky lore much closer to Göbekli Tepe. The Bundahishn, a sacred text of Zoroastrianism, a religious doctrine that once thrived in Iran, India, and Armenia, contains its own graphic account of a Ragnarök-style scenario, which includes the following somewhat enigmatic lines: "As Gokihar falls in the celestial sphere from a moon-beam on to earth, the distress of the earth becomes such-like as that of a sheep when a wolf falls upon it."[16]

Gokihar is generally translated as "meteor,"[17] that is, an incoming comet fragment, asteroid, or bolide of some sort, while the name itself has been interpreted as meaning "wolf progeny."[18] The double allusion in this statement to the wolf is significant, and one can envisage, and even feel, the force of the assumed impact, here likened to the manner that a sheep's legs bend and collapse when pounced on by a wolf.

That Gokihar's appearance heralds some kind of apocalyptic event seems confirmed in the verse that follows: "Afterward, the fire and halo melt the metal of [the archangel] Shatvairo, in the hills and mountains, and it [the molten metal] remains on this earth like a river."[19] If the impact of a comet fragment or asteroid *is* implied, then the presence afterward of firestorms and rivers of molten "metal" caused by the eruption of volcanoes would be inevitable.

After the destruction of the seven evil spirits under the rule of the evil principle, named Ahriman, Gokihar "burns the serpent in the melted metal, and the stench and pollution which were in hell are burned in that metal, and it (hell) becomes quite pure."[20]

Once again these are indications that Gokihar, the "wolf progeny," is involved directly with apocalyptic events described in the Bundahishn, and although they focus on a day of reckoning for both the gods and humanity, there is a sense of them forming part of a repeating cycle. In other words, the Bundahishn describes a replay of events that have already taken place. Christians in countries where the Norse myths remained strong associated the events of Ragnarök with the coming Day of Judgment, described in the book of Revelation; in other words, they saw them as events to come, not events that had occurred during some previous age.

Gokihar ably takes the place of the Fenris Wolf in the Norse myths, although in the Bundahishn there is a strange twist—the comet, or bolide, personified as a supernatural wolf, actually becomes a cleansing agent, clearing away the wicked in order to make the world "immortal forever and everlasting."[21]

It is a disturbing account of a past that is to be repeated in the future, and if all this is true, then the cataclysm that Donnelly envisaged as having taken place in some former epoch of humankind must have been so powerful, so all encompassing, that it affected not just a few isolated communities here and there, but human populations all over the world. What then was this event, and how did it come to affect the mind-set of the Epipaleolithic peoples that occupied southeast Anatolia in the age immediately prior to the construction of Göbekli Tepe?

As we see next, those who lived in the Near East at this time might have had every reason to be suffering from catastrophobia (as publisher, visionary, and mysteries writer Barbara Hand Clow so aptly put it in her book of the same name[22]), for the great cataclysm did not pass them by. Instead, it engulfed them in a quite terrifying manner that the scientific world is only now piecing together for the first time.

17

A DARK DAY IN SYRIA

Tell Abu Hureyra is an archaeological site of great importance on the Middle Euphrates of northern Syria. It was occupied from the late Epipaleolithic age, ca. 11,340 BC, to the Neolithic age, ca. 5500 BC, although today it lies beneath the waters of Lake Assad, created in 1973 following the completion of the Tabqa Dam.

Investigation of Abu Hureyra began in 1972 under the leadership of Andrew Moore from the University of Oxford. Yet as the rising waters began to lap around the base of the tell during the second digging season, the excavation changed into a frantic salvage operation as the British archaeologist's team desperately attempted to understand the significance of the occupational mound before its final submergence.

THE BIG CHILL

Even after the first season's expedition it was clear that Abu Hureyra was a quite extraordinary site that would reveal much about the transition from the age of the hunter-gatherer to the establishment of settled farming communities across the Near East. The second year of excavation, along with the subsequent work continued both in Syria and at various foreign universities, enabled Moore to get a pretty good picture of what had been going on at the site at the end of the Paleolithic age. He concluded that the first people to occupy the region arrived as the climate warmed during the Allerød interstadial, which heralded the end of the last ice age, around 13,000 BC.

In the two thousand years that followed there was a population boom throughout the Fertile Crescent, and it was during this new golden age that Abu Hureyra was established. Its inhabitants—who belonged to the Natufian culture, which inhabited the Levant region, ca. 12,900–9500 BC—lived mainly by hunting, fishing, and cultivating lentils and wild cereals, such as einkorn, emmer, and rye.

With the onset of the big chill, known as the Younger Dryas, around 10,900 BC, there was a sudden and unexpected disruption to migratory animals across the region. One animal that all but disappeared from the Fertile Crescent was the Persian gazelle, which until that time had formed a major part of the diet of the hunter-gatherers at Abu Hureyra.

Adding to the problems of the Epipaleolithic hunter-gatherers was the disappearance of forageable foods, such as wild grain and pistachio nuts, almost certainly caused by the rapid climate change, which had brought with it a severe drought, revealed by an analysis of plant remains recovered from Abu Hureyra. In the end, its inhabitants were left with no alternative but to seek warmer climes. It was the same throughout the Fertile Crescent, Natufian settlements being abandoned to the elements, their distinctive style of living vanishing completely.

The mini ice age lasted for approximately 1,300 years. After its cessation around 9600 BC, just before the creation of the first large enclosures at Göbekli Tepe, the temperatures began to rise again. A new community was established at Abu Hureyra, which built mud brick houses on the site of earlier dwellings. The inhabitants, now classed as members of the Pre-Pottery Neolithic A culture, used much fatter grain seeds for cultivation, making this perhaps one of the oldest sites where the domestication of cereal crops is thought to have occurred.[1]

MICROSPHERULES AND SLOS

Theories about Tell Abu Hureyra and its role in the birth of agriculture at the point of transition from the Epipaleolithic age to the earliest Neolithic farming communities remain controversial. Yet none of the scholars attempting to understand the evolution of the site, and its place in the emergence of the Pre-

Pottery Neolithic world, can have been prepared for what an eighteen-member international team of researchers, including James Kennett, professor of earth science at the University of California, found after examining sediment materials removed from the site during Moore's excavations in 1972 and 1973.

Soil taken from a depth of 11.8 feet (3.6 meters) below the surface revealed, quite astonishingly, that it contained large quantities of almost nano-sized magnetic and glass balls known as *microspherules,* along with something called *SLOs,* short for "siliceous scoria-like objects." These are microscopic glassy particles up to a quarter of an inch (roughly 6.5 millimeters) in size that are highly porous and *vesiculated,* which means they are full of small sacs created by gas bubbles. In appearance the SLOs resemble *scoria,* the name given to jagged rock fragments ejected from volcanoes.

What is so remarkable about SLOs is that they form only under incredibly high temperatures, in the range of 3,100 to 3,600 degrees Fahrenheit (1,700 to 1,980 degrees Celsius),[2] which, believe it or not, is the boiling point of quartz, a form of silica. This, in its molten form, is one of the main constituents of SLOs, which can appear dark brown, green, white, or black. The extraordinary heat needed to create these glassy objects rules out their manufacture by either human activity or volcanic action—or by any other natural process connected with the earth itself.

Also discounted was the possibility that the tiny glass objects were produced in space, then fell to earth as micrometeors. Results show that 90 percent of the microspherules and SLOs are composed of elements not only distinct from cosmic material, but also closely match the geochemistry of the rocks and sediment in the area of their recovery, clearly indicating their *terrestrial* origin.

MELT PRODUCTS

The microspherules and SLOs are also geochemically and morphologically comparable with each other; in other words, they derive from the same or very similar source materials. More significantly, they both show evidence of "high-energy interparticle collisions" of the sort that occur inside impact plumes.[3] Both are also comparable with *melt products,* tiny objects of molten glass, found at Meteor Crater, Arizona, the site of an impact event around fifty thousand years ago, and also at tektite-strewn fields in Australasia (*tektites* are glassy objects created from a mixture of terrestrial and extraterrestrial matter ejected during impacts).

More disturbingly, the SLOs found at Abu Hureyra and two other sites in the United States (Blackville, South Carolina, and Melrose, Pennsylvania) resemble "high-temperature materials"[4] found at the Trinity site, which forms part of the Alamogordo Bombing Range, New Mexico, following the detonation there of the first atomic bomb in 1945. Apparently, the thermal blast melted 0.5–1 inch (1–2.5 centimeters) of the desert floor for a radius of approximately 500 feet (150 meters) and left puddles of melted silica glass objects across a wide area.

MULTIPLE IMPACTORS

Nature herself creates such unbelievably high temperatures only during lightning strikes. Under such conditions microspherules and SLOs can result, although when this occurs, the lateral spread of glassy objects is only around 60 inches (1.5 meters); none generally reach beyond this point. However, the SLOs discovered at Abu Hureyra indicate a minimum spread of 14.5 feet (4.5 meters), ruling out lightning as their cause.

All this supports the slightly disturbing conclusion that the microspherules and SLOs found at Abu Hureyra were the product of an unimaginable impact plume or fireball cloud. Moreover, the fact that similar microparticles were discovered at three of the eighteen sites where evidence of an impact event was found by the team tells us there must have been "multiple impactors," air blasts caused by a fragmenting comet or asteroid, most likely the former.[5] Most significant to this debate are the final words in the published paper containing the findings of the international team:

> Because these three sites in North America and the Middle East [i.e., Syria, where SLOs were found] are separated by 1,000–10,000 km, we propose that there were three or more major impact/airburst epicenters for the YDB [Younger Dryas Boundary] impact event. If so, the much higher concentration of SLOs at Abu Hureyra suggests that the effects on that settlement and its inhabitants would have been severe.[6]

The Younger Dryas Boundary (or YDB) impact event is the name given to this proposed comet collision with Earth, which is believed to have occurred around 10,900 BC. This date marks the "boundary" or "horizon" between the Allerød interstadial and the Younger Dryas mini ice age. The glass microspherules and SLOs found at Abu Hureyra were located at this Younger Dryas Boundary, immediately beneath an organic-rich layer referred to as the "black mat," which, the report claims, has been found at a number of sites in North and South America, Europe, and now Syria.

TOO CLOSE FOR COMFORT

We can only imagine how the Epipaleolithic hunter-gatherers of Abu Hureyra felt around 12,900 years ago, gazing out of their subsurface round houses and seeing one or more blinding balls of fire crossing the open sky (like the meteor caught so spectacularly on film as it passed over Russia's Chelyabinsk region in February 2013) before exploding shortly before impact with the ground and as a result causing thunderous explosions, unlike anything ever imagined before in the lives of these people. Moments later, everything—livestock, buildings, and people—are hit by a shock wave of soaring heat and wind that peppers everything in its path with microscopic glassy objects, like the discharge of a hundred thousand shotguns all fired at once.

This is just a glimpse of what might have happened at one location on the Euphrates River, but other Natufian settlements in the Levant and elsewhere could also have been affected by the Younger Dryas impact event. Indeed, we have no real idea just how widespread the proposed devastation might have been, with the only clue being the Usselo horizon. This is a "charcoal-rich layer" measuring 8 inches (20 centimeters) in thickness that has been detected at the Allerød–Younger Dryas Boundary at sites in the Netherlands, France, Germany, Belgium, Belarus, Poland, India, South Africa, Egypt, and Australia.[7]

This strange black layer has been found to contain magnetic grains, microspherules, iridium (an element commonly found in cosmic impactors), and nanodiamonds,[8] that is, pure carbon, all of which supports the conclusion that the Usselo horizon is the result of multiple impact events that sent ash, soot, and other debris high into the atmosphere. This mixture would eventually have fallen back to earth to create the Usselo horizon, which now becomes a telltale marker for the effects of the impact event around 12,900 years ago.

In addition to the evidence presented here, other scientific teams have uncovered similar evidence of microspherules at the Younger Dryas Boundary in Venezuela, South America, and various other parts of the world.[9] It is thus clear that something very major did go down at this time and that it involved a series of bolides, most likely fragments of a comet that perhaps broke up during its slingshot orbit of the sun. The inhabitants on Earth would have seen all this—the arrival of the comet, or comets, in the sky, its reappearance and fragmentation, along with the incoming waves of fireballs and the terrifying air blasts as the fragments reached the lower atmosphere, causing maximum devastation on the earth itself.

KILL, CHILL, ILL, AND NOW GRILL!

The effects of the Younger Dryas Boundary impact event would have been felt on every continent, although the true extent of the damage can only be guessed at today. What we do know is that it coincided with the disappearance of the Ice Age megafauna, such as mammoths, mastodons, giant ground sloths, dire wolves, and saber-toothed tigers. All of these animals existed in abundance until the end of the Allerød interglacial, then vanished with the onset of the Younger Dryas mini ice age. How exactly they disappeared remains a complete mystery, with three main theories being proposed: they died through overhunting (the overkill theory); they died because of the sudden change in temperature at the beginning of the mini ice age (the overchill theory); or they suffered some kind of mass epidemic, which wiped out whole species (the overill theory). Recently, a fourth contender has entered the debate, this being the overgrill theory, which proposes that they were decimated in the wildfires caused by the comet impact.

None of these theories—kill, chill, ill, or grill—is ever going to account for the extinction of so many different Ice Age animals, and indeed there is a good chance that all four scenarios played some role in their demise.

Also around the same time North America's Paleo-Indians, represented by the Clovis culture, abruptly disappear from the archaeological record. With the knowledge that some of the larger fragments of the disintegrating comet are thought to have impacted with the Laurentide Ice Sheet—which had covered hundreds of thousands of square miles of North America for much of the last glacial age—causing the ice to vaporize and fall back to earth as acid rain, it becomes increasingly likely that the Clovis population might have been greatly reduced by the events of the Younger Dryas Boundary impact event.[10]

That some kind of cataclysm really did occur at the Allerød–Younger Dryas Boundary seems inescapable, both from the evidence presented by science today,[11] and from the wealth of catastrophe myths preserved in ancient texts and by indigenous societies worldwide. All of this tells us very clearly that something terrible happened in the world around this time, and very likely these legends refer, at least in part, to the same catastrophic event. Most likely a disintegrating comet was the culprit, although we cannot discount other possibilities, such as an asteroid or meteor impact, or a close supernova event. What *is* important, however, is its impact on the mind-set of the peoples existing in the Euphrates Basin at the termination of the Paleolithic age, for there is compelling evidence that a memory of this devastating cataclysm lingered on in the minds of the Göbekli builders themselves.

18

AFTERMATH

One of the major problems for farmers in southeast Turkey is that the landscape is littered with basalt boulders of all shapes and sizes, making it difficult to plow or sow a piece of land unless the rocks are first moved to the edge of the field. Since many of these boulders can be anything between several hundred pounds and a couple of tons apiece, this can often be a near impossible task.

The sources of these boulders are local volcanoes, which are known to have erupted in fairly recent geological history. Exactly when this might have been differs from volcano to volcano, although some kind of pattern might eventually emerge. One such volcano is Karajeddah Dağ, part of the Karaca Dağ massif, which lies between the cities of Diyarbakır in the east and Şanlıurfa to the west. It is Karaca Dağ, we should recall, that geneticists have identified as the point of origin of sixty-eight modern strains of wheat, suggesting that it was here, in the heart of the *triangle d'or,* that the Neolithic revolution had its inception.

A BEDOUIN CATASTROPHE MYTH

With this information in mind, it is interesting to find that Karajeddah Dağ is the setting for a highly significant folktale preserved by Bedouin tribespeople,

160

who inhabit the area even to this day. The tale, told to the author in 2004 by a Bedouin driver as they came within sight of the mountain,[1] speaks of how once, long ago, when humankind first began to till the land, a dragon with seven heads lived in a hole.

One day, the tillers' plows revealed the monster's lair, making the creature extremely angry. It emerged into the light and began torching the forests with its fiery breath until all the trees had been razed to the ground. Fearing for their lives, the people called upon Allah to stop this misery. This he did by carrying the monster up through the seven heavens until it reached the highest one, and here the dragon exploded with a great burst of fire, scattering rocks across the entire region.

SEVEN-TAILED COMET

Even though this story exists to help explain the countless boulders ejected by the now-extinct volcano, elements within it hint at a meaning on a much deeper level. The aerial detonation of the great dragon in the seventh heaven smacks of the sudden entry into the atmosphere of a fiery bolide, a comet perhaps. The seven heads of the dragon suggest that the comet might have fragmented into seven pieces or that it had multiple tails. In 1907 Comet Daniel appeared in our skies with seven tails, leading one astronomer to refer to it as "this awesome, seven-tailed monster."[2] That the seven-headed dragon of the story torched the forests with its fiery breath until all the trees had been razed to the ground is another clear sign that this was more than simply the action of a volcano.

If this Bedouin folktale does recall some memory of the Younger Dryas Boundary impact event, as well as an eruption of Karajeddah triggered at the same time, then this is very important indeed, especially as the mountain, although a full 50 miles (80 kilometers) away from Göbekli Tepe, is just about visible on the northeast horizon. Even more significant, however, is the reference in the story to the first tillers of the land disturbing the lair of the fiery dragon, resulting in it wreaking havoc on the world. Does this allude to the first people to begin cereal cultivation in the *triangle d'or* at the beginning of the Neolithic age? The fact that this tilling of the land was said to have *triggered* these catastrophic events need not worry us, as after thirteen thousand years confusion as to what happened in which order is understandable.

Behind this archaic story is one final piece of useful information. The folktale tells us that it was the tillers' actions that caused the release of the dragon. In other words, the inhabitants of the region, whose descendants we know became the first farmers, blamed themselves for the destruction it caused. If correct, then we can better understand why the Epipaleolithic hunter-gatherers of southeast Anatolia so feared a repeat of these events, for in their minds it was their actions that had caused the original catastrophe, in which case it could all happen again if they were not careful, the definition perhaps of Barbara Hand Clow's catastrophobia. No wonder these people might have accepted the offer of an incoming elite to rid them of this constant fear, a decision that led, eventually, to the construction of Göbekli Tepe.

PROFESSOR SCHMIDT'S OPINIONS

Whether there is a connection between Göbekli Tepe and the Younger Dryas Boundary impact event is something the author put to Professor Klaus Schmidt during an impromptu interview in September 2012. His immediate response was an emphatic "no, no connection." It was, however, pointed out to him that there was now firm evidence that the Natufian settlement at Tell Abu Hureyra on the Middle Euphrates, just 100 miles (160 kilometers) away, might have been an impact zone, and that in the opinion of the scientists who made this discovery, "the effects on that settlement and its inhabitants would have been severe."[3]

Schmidt's dismissal of the subject is, however, understandable. Even if the proposed impact event of 10,900 BC really did occur in the manner described, then this was a full 1,400 years before the construction of the oldest known enclosures at Göbekli Tepe, ca. 9500 BC. Surely, the hunter-gatherers of the region would have forgotten what had happened so many centuries after this supposed catastrophe took place.

This is a valid point, although scientific evidence indicates that something catastrophic continued to happen in the world for many hundreds of years after the commencement of the Younger Dryas cold spell. Drilled cores taken from the Greenland ice sheet reveal that ammonium levels in the atmosphere, arguably caused by the spread of wildfires, rose suddenly around 12,900 years ago, coincident to the proposed impact event, and then remained high for hundreds of years afterward.[4] They then spiked again around 12,340 years ago, that is

10,340 BC, suggesting that something else occurred at this time, prompting Dr. Richard Firestone of Lawrence Berkeley National Laboratory of Nuclear Science and his coauthors in their book *The Cycle of Cosmic Catastrophes* to comment, "We think that [10,340 BC] may be the date of one of the impacts."[5]

In other words, we could be looking at another major impact on or around 10,340 BC, which brought to a climax a sequence of events that had been happening on and off since the initial impact some five centuries earlier. Firestone and his team propose that at least part of the ammonium content in the Greenland ice cores came from a disintegrating comet, the rest from the wildfires it caused.

In addition to the massive spike in ammonium corresponding to a date of 12,340 years ago detected in the Greenland ice cores, the levels of nitrate they contain also peaked at exactly the same date—12,340 BP. Nitrate is another chemical produced by wildfires, although when the levels shoot up for both ammonium and nitrate together, it could mean that the fires in question were burning fiercely, as opposed to smoldering after the event.[6]

Compounding the mystery still further is the fact that another chemical, oxalate, also spikes in the Greenland ice core samples for the date 12,340 BP, and this too is associated with wildfires. Apparently this peak is the highest on record for the entire four hundred thousand years covered by the ice cores.[7] The importance of these findings is made clear by Firestone and his coauthors when they write, "The researchers tested a lot of ice, and they did not find any event as severe as that one, which spanned about four ice-age cycles. We think that it was no ordinary fire; it was a cosmic one."[8]

Whether a comet *was* responsible for the wildfires raging some 12,340 years ago remains a matter of speculation, although the ice core samples make it clear that the world was not at all stable at that time. Remember too that this is a full 560 years after the proposed Younger Dryas impact event of 12,900 years ago, and just 850 years, arguably less, before the construction of the first large enclosures at Göbekli Tepe.

A REMEDY FOR CATASTROPHOBIA

Mammoth building projects like Göbekli Tepe were initiated, most probably, after the inhabitants of southeast Anatolia came into contact with other parties, most likely displaced peoples from some other part of the ancient world.

They perhaps brought with them a virtual messianic message explaining how they had the power to put an end to the prevailing state of fear. We have called them the Hooded Ones and suspect that it is their memory, and the memory of their own great ancestors, embodied in the T-shaped pillars erected at Göbekli Tepe. Most likely, this power elite was shamanic in nature and believed it had some special relationship with either the fox or the wolf, a connection that gave them control over the sky fox or sky wolf responsible for bringing destruction to the world.

It is time now to examine the archaeological record in the hope of identifying this incoming group who would appear to have had such a big impact on the Epipaleolithic peoples of southeast Anatolia. Where did they come from, and how were they so easily able to convince communities of hunters to give up their free lives to build huge stone monuments, the oldest known astronomically aligned temples anywhere in the world? The answers, as we shall see in part four, might well lie on a different continent together, with that continent being Europe.

PART FOUR

Contact

19

THE REINDEER
HUNTERS

D r. Alice Roberts is a British anatomist, anthropologist, and osteo-archaeologist (bone specialist), as well as an author and TV presenter. In her book *The Incredible Human Journey* (2009), written to accompany a BBC documentary series of the same name, she visited Göbekli Tepe and chatted at some length with lead archaeologist Professor Klaus Schmidt. During the interview Roberts made a poignant observation, based on a sound knowledge of ancient stone tool technologies. She noted that the toolkit in use at Göbekli Tepe "was similar to some of the tanged point cultures of Central Europe, in the late Paleolithic and Mesolithic."[1]

In response, Schmidt suggested that "perhaps there was some kind of connection or communication between the societies of Turkey and those around the Black Sea and the Crimea,"[2] noting also a similarity between the style of game hunting in southeast Anatolia in the epoch of Göbekli Tepe's construction and the "reindeer hunters of the North."[3] Yet as if, immediately, to distance himself from any proposed connection between Europe and Göbekli Tepe, Schmidt pointed out that there is nothing "even vaguely like it in Europe . . . until well into the Neolithic."[4]

TANGED POINT CULTURES

This is true; there is absolutely nothing to compare with Göbekli Tepe any-where in Europe or, indeed, anywhere else in the ancient world until much later, when megalithic architecture begins in earnest at places such as Malta, Sardinia, Brittany, Ireland, and, of course, Britain. Yet that doesn't rule out the tantalizing possibility that the Göbekli builders came in contact with peo-ples from Europe, and from what Dr. Roberts and Klaus Schmidt were both implying, perhaps we should be looking toward the "tanged point cultures" and "reindeer hunters of the North" for some answers.

In the late Upper Paleolithic age reindeer hunters who occupied the forests and plains of Northern Europe, often operating on the sandy terrains of loess left behind by the melting glaciers, started different hunting strategies because their perennial prize, the reindeer herds, were abandoning their old territories and moving ever northward and northeastward. The animals undertook these continual migrations so that they could remain within the forests and tundra (land with small trees and plants) essential for their continued survival. Even with the onset of the Younger Dryas mini ice age, ca. 10,900 BC, the rein-deer kept moving, even though the worsening weather conditions were forcing human populations to migrate ever southward.

As part of their change in strategy, the reindeer hunters at the termina-tion of the Upper Paleolithic age, which in Europe quickly transformed into the Mesolithic age, adopted the use of a very specific type of weapon, usually made of flint and known as the tanged point. This is a type of arrowhead, either shaped like a willow leaf or geometric (that is, triangular) in form. These points have distinctive "shoulders," or "tangs," delicately chipped away from the base so that they could more easily be hafted onto an arrow shaft. Sometimes the points have only one tang, or shoulder, while at other times they have two. Clearly, the use of the bow and arrow gave Paleolithic hunters the advantage not only during the chase but also over human enemies.

THE CASE OF MARY SETTEGAST

So could there have been some kind of contact between these reindeer hunt-ers of the North European Plain and the Epipaleolithic peoples of southeast Anatolia in the lead up to the construction of the first large enclosures at

Göbekli Tepe? The answer is almost certainly yes. In 1987 a fascinating book entitled *Plato Prehistorian,* by archaeological writer Mary Settegast, attempted to paint a picture of the turmoil that might have existed in Europe in the aftermath of a global catastrophe at the end of the last ice age. Settegast linked this event with the account given by the Greek philosopher Plato in his works *Timaeus* and *Critias,* written around 350 BC. He, of course, describes the destruction of a mythical island empire called Atlantis that was said to have existed beyond the Pillars of Hercules, out in the Atlantic Ocean.

According to Plato the main island of Atlantis sank beneath the waves around 9500 BC following a day and night of earthquakes and floods, sent by the sky god Zeus to punish the Atlanteans for having become too haughty and arrogant. Prior to this time they had made incursions into the Mediterranean and attacked major city-ports as far east as Italy's Tyrrhenian Sea, then under the control of the Athenians.

Plato's account of Atlantis might well be based on some kind of historical reality, although the wars between the Atlanteans and the Athenians are much more difficult to prove, especially given that Athens and its inhabitants, the Athenians, did not exist in 9500 BC. For this reason, some of Settegast's proposals are quite obviously biased toward accepting the validity of Plato's account. That said, the evidence she presents for bloodshed and turmoil in Europe at the end of the Ice Age is stunning.[5]

THE SWIDERIAN CULTURE

Crucially, Settegast recognized that during the Younger Dryas period, ca. 10,900–9600 BC, major migrations were taking place all over Europe, seemingly in the aftermath of the proposed cataclysm. Among those on the move was a specific group of reindeer hunters known as the Swiderians. They began pushing farther and farther eastward and southward until they were quite literally knocking on Anatolia's door.

Mary Settegast realized that as they moved across Europe at the onset of the Younger Dryas cold spell, the Swiderians left behind a noticeable trail of finely carved tanged points. It stretched all the way from the Carpathian Mountains of Central Europe right across to the Crimean Mountains, located on a peninsula immediately west of the Sea of Azov, a northerly extension of

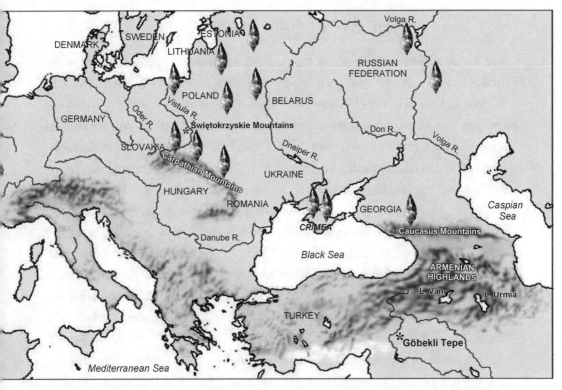

Figure 19.1. Map showing the eastern migration of tanged, or shouldered, points, most likely arrowheads, belonging to the Swiderian culture, which emerged ca. 11,000 BC.

the Black Sea, in what is today Ukraine. She noted also that around this same time strikingly similar tanged points started to appear at Epipaleolithic and proto-Neolithic sites in the Near East, something that is unlikely to be a simple coincidence.[6]

To better argue her case, Settegast included in her book a map that shows the trail of Swiderian points across Europe,[7] a version of which is included here (see figure 19.1). Her compelling evidence prompted the question of what exactly these Paleolithic hunters were doing crossing Eastern Europe so boldly, with the standard explanation being that they were following the flight of the reindeer herds, but as Settegast herself noted, many of their campsites show very little evidence of the spoils of the chase,[8] so clearly something else was going on in their lives. So who exactly were the Swiderians, and how do they fit into the gradually emerging picture painted so far in this book?

THE SWIDERIAN LANDSCAPE

The Swiderians take their name from an occupational "type" site where their unique style of stone tool technology was first recognized. This is Świdry Wielkie in Otwock, near Warsaw in Poland, which now forms one of the thousands of campsites, work stations, and settlement sites that the culture created across a vast territory, stretching from Poland in the west across to Belarus, Lithuania, Latvia, Estonia, Moldova, and Ukraine. They make their presence known for the first time at the beginning of the Younger Dryas period, occupying the forests, steppes, and glacial loess of the East European Plain, and settling on major rivers including the Vistula, Oder, and Warta in the west, and the Dnieper, Volga, Oka, and Don in the east.[9] In addition to this, they are known to have occupied the northern and eastern foothills of the Carpathian Mountains,[10] which embrace Slovakia, Poland, Hungary, Ukraine, and Romania (which is made up of the former kingdoms of Transylvania, Wallachia, and western Moldavia).

The culture's principal calling cards, so to speak, were their distinctive tanged points, along with their exquisitely finished leaf-shaped points. Prehistorians propose that the Swiderians were an offshoot of one of the preexisting reindeer-hunting traditions of Northern Europe, either the Hamburgian-Ahrenburgian cultures of North Germany or, more likely, the Brommian-Lyngby cultures of Denmark and the Scandinavia Peninsula (together they form what is known as the Tanged Point Technocomplex). Yet as we see next, the Swiderians had ancient roots that mark them out as more successful than their contemporaries. They would seem also to have had a great motivation and drive that has allowed them to be credited with the foundation of various subgroups that were instrumental in the establishment of European culture and language on a number of different levels. It is a long road from Central Europe to Anatolia, but it is one we must now take to create a better picture of why exactly the Swiderians are so crucial to the story of Göbekli Tepe and the rise of civilization in the ancient world.

20

SWIDERIAN DAWN

The effect the Younger Dryas Boundary impact event of 10,900 BC might have had on Europe remains unclear. Yet evidence of its aftermath can be found at sites across the continent as the Usselo horizon, the 8-inch (20-centimeter) charcoal-rich layer lying between soils signifying the termination of the Allerød interstadial and the commencement of the Younger Dryas mini ice age, ca. 10,900 BC.[1] Listed among the countries in Europe where this black layer has been found are the Netherlands, France, Germany, and Belgium, as well as known Swiderian territories such as Belarus and, as we shall see now, Poland.

THE WITÓW PEOPLE

At the beginning of the 1960s, archaeologists working on a site at Witów, near Łęczyca, in the Polish province of Łódź, were puzzled to find "a charcoal layer in late-glacial dune, comparable to [the] Usselo-layer."[2] This layer was found to contain flint artifacts "forming a hitherto unknown assemblage,"[3] while in the sand immediately above this black mat, archaeologists came across stone implements belonging to the "middle Swiderian industry,"[4] showing that the Swiderian reindeer hunters were here at this time.

In addition to the flint implements, archaeologists found at Witów four large ovoid "huts," all aligned east-west. Each one contained various finds, including a noticeable amount of hematite, which is a highly magnetic, iron-based mineral, usually rust red in color. It is crushed to make a pigment called ochre, used in rock art and human decoration, such as tattoos and body paint.

Radiocarbon analyses for the charcoal layer provided dates in the region of 10,820±160 BP, or 8820 BC. However, when these tests took place it was not realized that recalibration is necessary to bring raw radiocarbon dates in line with the true trend of carbon-14 release from organic materials, so when this is applied the charcoal layer offers dates in the range of 11,000–10,500 BC, well within the proposed time frame of the Younger Dryas Boundary impact event of ca. 10,900 BC.

SWIDERIANS IN CRIMEA

The stone tools found inside the huts at Witów in Poland were initially quite a mystery to archaeologists, leading them to announce the discovery of a previously unknown culture.[5] What they did notice, however, were similarities between the assemblage's curved-back knives and blade segments with examples found over 850 miles (1,400 kilometers) away in the Shan Koba cave in Crimea.[6] These are now recognized as belonging to a Crimean Swiderian culture, responsible also for the manufacture of Swiderian points found at other sites in the Crimean Highlands, immediately north of the Black Sea.[7]

Here in a rock shelter known as Syuren 2, tanged blades have been unearthed "with direct analogies to the Polish Swiderian."[8] In other words, they are more or less identical to those found at the culture's mostly open air sites in their original heartland of Poland and the Carpathian Mountains. More crucially, the examples found in the Syuren 2 rock shelter are so similar to the real thing that two Russian prehistorians were led to conclude that a "direct migration of a group of Swiderian population in the Crimea is not excluded."[9] In other words, the Swiderian peoples who inhabited these caves might well have been the immediate descendants of reindeer hunters who had arrived in this region from Poland.

If these migrations really did take place, then it is unbelievable evidence of the sheer endurance and willpower of these people, who crossed the entire length of Eastern Europe to end up on the Black Sea. What is more, there is tentative evidence that they did not stop their journey there. In 1959 Russian prehistorian Aleksandr Formozov saw evidence of stone tools of the Swiderian-European style as far east as the Caucasus Mountains of Georgia,[10] which stretch between the Black Sea in the west and the Caspian Sea in the east. If correct, then this brings the reindeer hunters within striking distance of the Armenian Highlands, just a couple of hundred miles away from Göbekli Tepe.

TANGED POINTS IN THE NEAR EAST

Supporting the idea that the Swiderians reached even beyond the Caucasus Mountains is, as Mary Settegast realized, the fact that a great many tanged points strikingly similar to those manufactured in Europe have been found at Epipaleolithic and early Neolithic sites across the Near East. Indeed, if they had been found on European soil, archaeologists would have had no qualms in identifying them as belonging to one or another of the North European reindeer-hunting traditions.

Clearly, there are certain differences in style. Sometimes the tang is trapezoid in shape, or with a slight barb. Alternatively, notches are made on either side of the blade, making it easier to haft onto an arrow shaft. Despite these variations, there are enough similarities to suggest that the Swiderian reindeer hunters were somewhere in the background. Indeed, leaf-shaped tanged points that easily compare with those created as part of the Swiderian tradition have been found at Göbekli Tepe (see figure 20.1 on p. 174).[11] This opens up the possibility that the European reindeer hunters, or at least their direct descendants, really were present in southeast Anatolia and might well have influenced the development of its earliest Neolithic cultures, something they certainly did in other parts of the ancient world.

POST-SWIDERIAN CULTURES

Having established many hundreds of settlement sites as far east as the Don and Upper Volga rivers of Central Russia, Swiderian groups spread into new territories, where they created post-Swiderian cultures, such as the Kunda and Butovo, which thrived between the middle of the tenth millennium and the end of the seventh millennium BC in Estonia, Belarus, Latvia, and northwest Russia.[12] Here they adopted an advanced toolmaking technique known as surface pressure flaking, a process so unique that when discovered at a Mesolithic site in north or northeast Europe it is seen as clear evidence of a Swiderian presence there.

Pressure flaking is a process whereby a bone tool or antler is used to trim a biface (an implement shaped on both faces) by very carefully applying pressure to

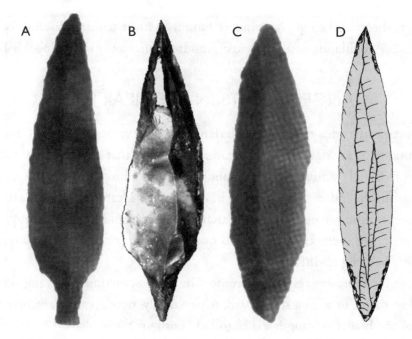

Figure 20.1. Comparison of tanged points found in the fill at Göbekli Tepe (A and C) against two examples (B and D) from the Swiderian culture.

its edges in order to prize off rows of tiny flakes. This produces equally spaced, concave troughs, each one generally overlapping the next in line, which can reach as far as the center of the implement, giving it a perfect geometric finish.

Although stone tools dating back seventy-five thousand years found at the Blombos Cave in South Africa show evidence of having been finished using pressure flaking, it is a technique not usually associated with European cultures at the end of the Paleolithic age. This said, pressure flaking was being used in eastern Anatolia to process obsidian (see chapter 22) during the Pre-Pottery Neolithic B period, ca. 8700 BC and 6000 BC, and was present at the Neolithic city of Çatal Höyük by 7000 BC.[13]

FINNO-UGRIC PEOPLES

There is firm evidence also that post-Swiderian groups entered Finland and established key settlements during the ninth millennium BC. Here their traditions are associated with the country's Finno-Ugric speaking peoples, including the Sámi, a shamanic-based, reindeer-herding culture that exists to this day.[14] Additionally, newly discovered settlement sites in Norway, dating to roughly the same age as those in neighboring Finland, have revealed evidence of a blade technology identified as post-Swiderian in nature.[15] Similar tools have been found at a Mesolithic site in Lapland, northern Sweden, dated to ca. 6600 BC.[16] What is more, extraordinarily accomplished stone tools finished using pressure flaking techniques were manufactured during the late Neolithic/early Bronze Age, ca. 3000–2500 BC, in parts of Scandinavia (Denmark in particular), and this can be put down to the presence of technologically advanced cultures deriving from the post-Swiderian tradition.

All this implies that some of the earliest influences on Finnish, Scandinavian, and Baltic ethnicity, culture, stone technology, and, very likely, mythology might well have originated with the Swiderian reindeer hunters, whose original homeland was the forests, steppes, and river valleys of Central and Eastern Europe. Yet who exactly were the Swiderians? Where did they come from, and what did they look like?

HUMAN HYBRIDS

Anatomically speaking, the Swiderians have been described as "tall . . . long-headed, [and] thin faced."[17] It is something confirmed by noted Lithuanian anthropologist Marija Gimbutas (1921–1994), who in 1956 detailed the discovery eight years earlier, in 1948, of a partial cranium, minus its lower jaw, at Kebeliai, near Priekulė in Lithuania. Dating to the end of the Paleolithic age, when Swiderian settlements occupied the area, it is said to have been "massive, dolichocephalic [that is, long headed], with strong proclivity [inclination] of the forehead, prominent and massive brow ridges and a narrow forehead." In her opinion the strange skull "was *sapiens,* but had Neanderthaloid elements, in other words, [it] was a Neanderthal-*sapiens* hybrid."[18] Gimbutas spoke also of a "closely related" cranium dating again to the end of the last glacial age, this one discovered on the Skhodnia River, northwest of Moscow,[19] where Swiderian groups are known to have existed at this time.

A third skull of interest, attributed to the post-Swiderian Kunda culture and found in a pit paved with stones at Kirsna in the district of Marijampolė in southern Lithuania, Gimbutas describes as "hyperdolichocephic [that is, extremely long headed] . . . narrow faced, high-orbited," and resembling the "Brünn skull of central Europe."[20]

The "Brünn skull" mentioned refers to one of a number of examples, all very similar, unearthed in 1891 at Brünn (modern Brno), the capital of Moravia in what is today the Czech Republic. Here human remains dating back as much as twenty-five thousand years were found that had a slightly different physiognomy to the pre-existing Cro-Magnon population that had entered Europe from Africa around forty-three thousand years ago.[21] Whereas the Cro-Magnon were broad-faced, large-headed individuals, the Brünn skulls displayed "extreme elongation and dolichocephaly,"[22] that is, their craniums were long and narrow. They also had strong chins, high cheekbones, low, wide-set eye orbits, and, like the Kebeliai example, prominent brow ridges.[23]

Similar skulls from the same human population were unearthed three years later in 1894 at Předmost (modernly spelt Predmostí), also in the Czech Republic. Fourteen complete skeletons and the remains of six others had been placed in a tight circle within a pit, their bodies contracted into a squatting position and surrounded by a bank of stones. The size of the limbs of these individuals indicated that they were of "large stature."[24] The finds at Předmost led anthropologists of the period to start referring to this unknown human type as "Brünn-Předmost man" and even *Homo předmostensis*.[25]

Speculation mounted in the early twentieth century that the Brünn population of the Upper Paleolithic age were in fact "Neanderthaloids," either Neanderthal-human hybrids and/or the remnants of an intermediary stage between the two species,[26] ideas that almost certainly influenced the observations made by Marija Gimbutas in 1956 regarding the strange physiognomy of the Kebeliai skull.

It is thus possible that the Swiderians of Central and Eastern Europe were directly related to the Brünn population and that both either evolved from or contained within their communities Neanderthal-human hybrids of quite striking appearance, having elongated heads, long faces, high foreheads, prominent brow ridges (a specific Neanderthal trait), high cheekbones, large jaws (a Cro-Magnon trait), and an increased height. It was a physiognomy inherited by post-Swiderian cultures, such as the Kunda, who are elsewhere described as tall with elongated skulls and narrow faces.[27]

That the Swiderians might have been related to the Brünn population that appeared in Central Europe sometime around twenty-five thousand years ago is an extraordinary realization. Yet it is a conclusion strengthened in the knowledge that the Swiderians might well have inherited one of the most accomplished and mysterious traditions of the Upper Paleolithic age—that of the Solutrean, a matter we explore next.

Plate 1. The fig-mulberry tree that stands on the summit of Göbekli Tepe in southeast Turkey. This place has long been sacred to the native Kurds of the region, as seen from the presence here of a small cemetery.

Plate 2. View of Göbekli Tepe from the northwest, showing the main group of sanctuaries built more than eleven thousand years ago. The two giant monoliths in the foreground belong to Enclosure D, the most sophisticated structure uncovered to date.

Plate 3. Archaeologists survey the bedrock impression left by the former presence there of the Felsentempel (German for "rock temple"), otherwise known as Enclosure E.

Plate 4. Pillars belonging to Göbekli Tepe's Enclosure A, the first structure to be uncovered, during the 1995–96 digging seasons. Visible in the center is Pillar 2, showing an auroch, a leaping fox, and a wading bird, most likely a crane.

Plate 5. Göbekli Tepe's Enclosure B, which lies immediately to the north of Enclosure A. The two T-shaped pillars to the right stand at its center, each one with a leaping fox on its inner face. Do they represent the cosmic trickster?

Plate 6. The leaping fox on the inner face of Enclosure B's Pillar 10. Note the graffito boar carved immediately beneath it.

Plate 7. Göbekli Tepe's Enclosure C from the north. Note the remains of its twin central pillars (the eastern one encased in wood), as well as the twin standing stones acting as its southern entranceway.

Plate 8. One arm of the U-shaped portal, dubbed the "Lion's Gate," that marked the entrance into the long corridor, or dromos, that enabled access to Enclosure C. The strange quadruped that caps its termination is thought to be a feline of some sort.

Plate 9. Pillar 37, the western of the two great monoliths that stand at the center of Enclosure C. Like the twin pillars in Enclosure B, it has a leaping fox carved on its inner face. This animal faces south, toward the entrant who walks between the twin monoliths in order to access the sky world.

Plate 10. The author surveys Göbekli Tepe's unfinished monolith, partly hewn out of the bedrock around a quarter of a mile (400 meters) from the main enclosures. It is as much as 22 feet (6.9 meters) in length and 6.5 feet (2 meters) broad, with an estimated weight of 50 metric tonnes (approximately 55 U.S. tons).

Plate 11. Decoration on the right-hand side of the waist belt on Pillar 18, the eastern central monolith in Enclosure D. It shows a combination of C and H glyphs.

Plate 12. Pillars 31 and 18, the central monoliths of Enclosure D. Note the long arm of the eastern pillar, which seems to be almost holding the fox. See also the way that the T-shaped head is tilted toward those who approach from the south.

Plate 13. Pillar 18's belt buckle, with its three-tailed comet design, surrounded by a group of H-shaped ideograms. Note also the fox-pelt loincloth hanging directly beneath the belt buckle.

Plate 14. The twin pillars at the center of Enclosure D. Note the holed stone centrally positioned behind the monoliths, which might well have targeted the bright star Deneb in Cygnus as it set on the horizon around 9400 BC.

Plate 15. The holed sighting stone at the rear of Enclosure D. Note the lines suggestive of the legs and buttocks of the female form, which if correct makes the hole a representation of the vulva.

Plate 16. The seven flightless birds, identified as dodos, carved into the southern face of the bedrock pedestal holding up Enclosure D's Pillar 18.

Plate 17. One of the roaring lions carved on the inner faces of the twin pillars marking the eastern end of Göbekli Tepe's Lion Pillar Building. Built ca. 8500–8000 BC and aligned east-west, its advancing felines could well represent both the might of the sun and the constellation of Leo, the celestial lion.

Plate 18. Göbekli Tepe's Lion Pillar Building, located at the summit of the occupational mound some 50 feet (15 meters) higher than the site's main enclosures, suggesting that it was constructed as much as 1,000 to 1,500 years after these earlier structures.

Plate 19. The author, left, with Professor Klaus Schmidt, who has been excavating Göbekli Tepe on behalf of the Museum of Şanlıurfa and the German Archaeological Institute since 1995.

Plate 20. One of the most recent pillars to be uncovered at Göbekli Tepe. It was discovered during excavations in the northwest section of the occupational mound and could well be eleven thousand years old. It shows a south-facing lion on what is presumably the inner face of a central pillar in a previously unexplored enclosure.

Plate 21. Göbekli Tepe's Enclosure F, built probably ca. 8500–8000 BC. Notice how reduced in size the sanctuaries have become by this time. Some of them are no bigger than a bathroom, with stones no more than 5 feet (1.5 meters) in height.

Plate 22. Strange carved head found among the fill that covered the enclosures at Göbekli Tepe, now in the Museum of Şanlıurfa. Its teeth show it to be a predator, most likely a wolf.

Plate 23. Life-size human statue dating to around 9000 BC. It was discovered in 1993 within the Balıklıgöl district of Şanlıurfa, the oldest part of the city, and is now in the archaeological museum. Tradition asserts that Şanlıurfa, ancient Edessa or Orhay, was founded either by the prophet Enoch or by "Orhay son of Hewya"; that is, the "Serpent," a clear allusion to the Watchers of the book of Enoch.

Plate 24. Carved stone totem pole discovered in one of the minor structures at Göbekli Tepe, and now in the Museum of Şanlıurfa. Its damaged head is that of an animal, while its body is of a human. A smaller human figure emerges from its stomach, and from the womb area of the second figure comes a child that holds in its hands a vessel of some sort. Twin snakes rise up on either side, possibly as guardians of the child. This is one of the strangest pieces found so far and shows the virtually alien mindset of the Göbekli builders.

Plate 25. Left, a Solutrean laurel-leaf spearhead, 13 inches (33 centimeters) long and around twenty thousand years old, on display at the British Museum. Right, Swiderian tanged point made of chocolate flint, eleven thousand to twelve thousand years old. Not to scale. Were the Swiderian hunters of Central and Eastern Europe, as successors of the Solutrean tradition, instrumental in the rise of Göbekli Tepe around the end of the Younger Dryas period, ca. 9600 BC?

Plate 26. Medieval painted wooden panel in All Saints Church, Kempston, Bedfordshire, UK. It shows the removal of Adam and Eve from the Garden of Eden and the angel who wields the flaming sword. Note the serpent crawling on the ground and the Mountain of God behind Adam, both in the left-hand scene.

Plate 27. Tenth-century encaustic painting from Saint Catherine's Monastery in Egypt's Sinai Peninsula, showing, left, the disciple Thaddeus, and, right, the disciple curing Abgar, king of Edessa, using a handkerchief that Jesus wiped across his face. Thaddeus continued his journey, reaching Armenia in AD 43/45. At Yeghrdut, near Mush in historical Armenia (eastern Turkey), he is said to have deposited a piece of the Tree of Life, as well as other important holy relics.

Plate 28. The remains of the Yeghrdut monastery, now known as Dera Sor (the Red Church), on the northern slopes of the Eastern Taurus Mountains of eastern Turkey. It was here that Thaddeus apparently deposited his precious cache of holy relics.

Plate 29. The west wall of Dera Sor, the ruins of the Yeghrdut monastery, said to have been located in the Garden of Eden itself. Muslims and Christians alike came here to sit beneath its holy tree and partake of its sacred waters to rejuvenate their bodies by as much as twenty years.

Plate 30. The view from Dera Sor, the ruins of the Yeghrdut monastery in eastern Turkey, looking out over the plain of Mush, through which flows the Euphrates River. Is this the true site of the Garden of Eden as described in the book of Genesis?

Plate 31. Bingöl Mountain in the Armenian Highlands of eastern Turkey, the source of the Araxes and Euphrates rivers. Evidence suggests it is the true site of the Mountain of Assembly of the Watchers, as well as Kharsag, the home of the Anunnaki in Sumerian tradition. It can be identified also with Charaxio, the mountain in which Seth concealed the secrets of Adam, according to Sethian Gnostic tradition.

Plate 32. Two examples of snake-headed statues, found in graves belonging to the Ubaid culture, which thrived in Mesopotamia ca. 5000–4100 BC. They are now thought to be representations of a long-headed elite group that controlled the Bingöl/Lake Van obsidian trade during the earlier Halaf period, ca. 6000–5000 BC. Did this elite group model itself on a memory of those responsible for the construction of Göbekli Tepe?

Plate 33. The Alevi holy site of Hızır Çeşmesi (the Fountain of Hızır), at Muska (modern Beşikkaya Köyü) in the northern foothills of the Bingöl massif in eastern Turkey. Is this the original Ab'i Hayat, the Waters of Life, where Alexander the Great is said to have gained immortality upon reaching Bingöl? The building on the right is a dream incubation house, where people come to spend the night and dream of Hızır, the Turkish form of al-Khidr, the Green One.

Plate 34. View from Muska looking south toward the western foothills of the Bingöl massif. Is this the original location of Dilmun, the paradisiacal realm of the Anunnaki gods of ancient Sumer, as well as the site of the terrestrial Paradise in Judeo-Christian tradition?

21

THE SOLUTREAN CONNECTION

The Solutreans are the key to the emergence of high culture across Central and Western Europe during the Upper Paleolithic age. Their campsites, work stations, and cave sites date to between 25,000 and 16,500 years ago and span from England (especially East Anglia) in the north, to northern Spain, Portugal, and France in the south. Like the Swiderians much later, the Solutreans mastered the use of surface pressure flaking to create highly unique willow-leaf-shaped projectile points and much larger, laurel-leaf-shaped lance heads, which share similarities to the Swiderians' own leaflike points. Moreover, like the Swiderians, the Solutreans—who were themselves reindeer hunters—fashioned shouldered (i.e., tanged) points, with either one or two shoulders (see figure 21.1 on p. 178) and thus almost certainly used bows and arrows.

So thin and so finely worked are the Solutreans' laurel-leaf lance heads, which can be up to 14 inches (36 centimeters) in length, translucent, and just a quarter of an inch (0.6 centimeter) thick (see plate 25), that Sharon McKern, an anthropological consultant, writing with her husband, Dr. Thomas McKern, professor of anthropology at the University of Kansas, was moved to observe: "This delicately flaked tool technique is the most aesthetic—and the most mysterious—known from prehistoric times."[1] The fact that a number of these

177

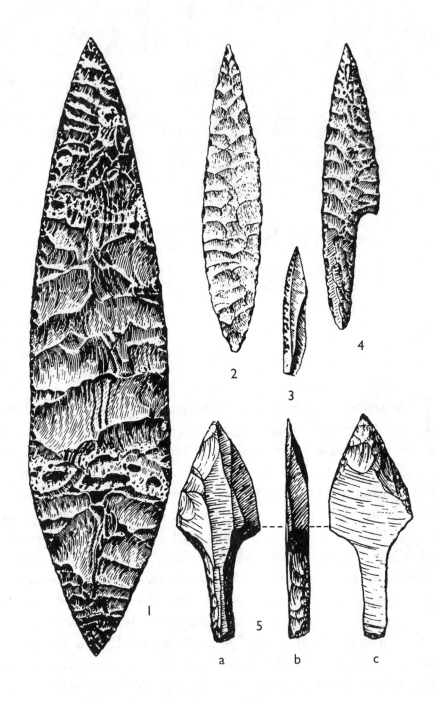

Figure 21.1. A selection of finely worked Solutrean points, ca. 20,000–14,500 BC, many finished using the pressure flaking technique.

unique blades have been found in groups within caches and are regularly made of nonlocal, exotic materials (including chalcedony, jasper, and quartz crystal) has led to speculation that they were not used for any practical purpose but instead served some ritual or symbolic function.

RIMUTÈ RIMANTIENÈ'S COMMENTS

So what exactly is the connection between the Solutreans and the later Swiderians? In 1996 Lithuanian archaeologist Rimutè Rimantienè proposed grouping together the various North European cultures that thrived in the Upper Paleolithic under a single umbrella term—the Baltic Magdalenian, or the "Group of Baltic Magdalenian cultures," because they all display signs of having a common origin.[2] Just one culture was to be excluded from the list, and this was the Swiderian, "where the relations with the Solutrean are outstanding, though also indirect."[3]

Rimantienè recognized the remarkable similarities between the stone tool technologies of the two cultures and felt the need to put this in writing, even though making such a connection was clearly anathema in the scholarly community in which she moved.* The problem is simple—the Swiderian culture does not enter the scene until the beginning of the Younger Dryas period, ca. 10,900 BC. This is thirty-five hundred years *after* the Solutreans disappear from the pages of European history to make way for the Magdalenians, an altogether different culture whose principal legacy is the beautiful Ice Age cave art of southwest Europe.

As to the fate of the Solutreans, no one really knows, although some prehistorians propose that they departed for the North European Plain when the reindeer herds migrated northward at the end of the last ice age. If so, then they might easily have formed the core of much later reindeer-hunting traditions, in particular the Brommian-Lyngby cultures of Denmark and the Scandinavian Peninsula. Certainly, laurel-leaf points and shouldered points, identical to those of the Solutreans, have been found in the south and west of Sweden and Norway,[4] suggesting strongly that this is where the Solutreans came looking for the reindeer herds. Here their descendants would have remained until the onset of the Younger Dryas mini ice age, when with the worsening climate they were forced southward into Central Europe, paving the way for the emergence of the

*Rimutè Rimantienè (b. 1920) was a friend and colleague of Lithuanian-born anthropologist Marija Gimbutas (see chapter 20).

Swiderian tradition in places such as Poland, Slovakia, and the foothills of the Carpathian Mountains.

ANCIENT MARINERS

All this is quite plausible, although there is now mounting evidence to suggest that the Solutreans also took to the high seas and ended up in North America, having navigated the southern limits of the sea ice that clogged large areas of the North Atlantic Ocean some twenty thousand years ago.[5]

In North America, beyond the Laurentide Ice Sheet, which reached as far south as Missouri and the Ohio River Basin, the Solutrean hunters became the forerunners of the Clovis culture, producing laurel-leaf-shaped blades very similar to those manufactured in Western Europe. It was a tradition continued in the production of the exquisite Clovis points, manufactured using the pressure flaking technique by the Clovis people, who thrived in many parts of North America around the same time as the emergence of the Swiderian culture some thirteen thousand years ago. Yet unlike the Clovis culture that flourished for just five hundred to seven hundred years before disappearing during the Younger Dryas period, the Swiderians continued to thrive, creating all manner of post-Swiderian cultures, which, as we have seen, went on to occupy large areas of north and northeast Europe during Mesolithic times.

THE BRÜNN CONTROVERSY

Strengthening the connection between the Solutrean and Swiderian traditions still further is the fact that the two cultures might once have shared the same territories and the same physiognomy. It has long been known that a stone tool industry identical to that of the early Solutrean existed in Germany and the modern Czech Republic, and even further east in Hungary and Poland.[6]

Anthropologists of the early twentieth century became convinced that the Solutreans derived not from Cro-Magnons but from the Brünn peoples, who emerged onto the scene in places such as Hungary and the Czech Republic around twenty-five thousand years ago, where they formed part of the much larger, and far older, Eastern Gravettian culture. This connection was no idle speculation either, for quite distinctive Solutrean tools and laurel-leaf blades were found in association with human remains of the Brünn type at two separate sites, one of them being Předmost in the Czech Republic, leading Princeton paleon-tologist and geologist Henry Fairfield Osborn (1857–1935) to observe: "There is no question that the human remains [found at Předmost] belong to the middle Solutrean stage."[7] It was a link that seemed confirmed with the discovery in the late nineteenth century of skulls similar to those of the Brünn type at Solutré, west of Mâcon in France's Saône-et-Loire region,[8] which, as the name suggests, was the original "type-site" of the Solutrean tradition.

Yet when, in the second half of the twentieth century, typological thinking regarding the racial origins of humankind became unfashionable, if not down-right distasteful, any proposed connections between the Brünn type and the Solutrean tradition were dropped. Not only did this leave the Solutreans with-out any definitive physical characteristics, but any notion that the Solutreans of Western Europe were related to the Solutreans of Central Europe was aban-doned. Indeed, those of Central Europe were stripped completely of their Solutrean status and reclassified as a separate culture that evolved quite inde-pendently of the Solutreans of Western Europe.

Despite this awkward and somewhat strange reclassification process, it remains possible that the Solutrean tradition really is tied in with the sudden appearance in Central Europe of the Brünn population around twenty-five thousand years ago. Having said this, modern anthropological thinking has the Solutreans enter southwest Europe from Africa where, it has been suggested, they formed part of a Saharan culture known as the Aterian, which employed the use of strikingly similar toolmaking techniques. Yet equally likely is that the Solutreans and the human population of Central Europe categorized as the Brünn type came from the east, not the south.

Paleolithic stone tool expert Bruce Bradley, Ph.D., of the University of Exeter, and his colleagues have proposed that the Solutreans' highly sophisti-cated stone technology originated among the peoples who occupied a region stretching from the cold forest steppes north and northeast of the Black Sea as far north as the central Russian Plain. Here between ca. 30,000 BC and 19,000 BC thrived an advanced culture known as the Kostenki-Streletskaya, which formed part of the much larger Eastern Gravettian tradition and produced stone tools and projectile points with close parallels to those manufactured by the Solutreans in both central and southwest Europe.[9]

These Ice Age peoples of the Russian steppes and plain inhabited a series of settlement sites, including Kostenki, the culture's principal type-site, on the west bank of the Don River, and Sungir on the Klyazma River. At this last site, located on the outskirts of the city of Vladimir, some 110 miles (177 kilometers) east-northeast of Moscow, three extraordinary human burials were uncovered in 1956. Each was adorned with thousands of ivory beads, which had been attached to tailored garments of immense sophistication. Radiocarbon evidence shows that the burials took place as early as 30,000 BC.[10] One of the skulls, Sungir 1,[11] bears similarities to some of the skulls found at the Předmost site in the Czech Republic, in particular an example known as Předmost 3. With its prominent brow ridge and pronounced jaw, it bears distinct characteristics of not only the Brünn population that entered Central Europe around twenty-five thousand years ago and perhaps kickstarted the Solutrean culture, but also the Neanderthal-human hybrid skulls found in Russia and Lithuania (see chapter 20), which might well have belonged to individuals stemming from the Swiderian culture. It is a supposition supported by the observations of one of the twentieth century's greatest prehistorians, V. Gordon Childe. In his book *The Prehistory of European Society,* published in 1958, he writes:

> In Western and Central Europe the "Solutrean" seems a brief episode that exercised no recognizable influence on subsequent developments. In Eastern Europe on the contrary Solutrean techniques were applied at times to the later East Gravettian (Kostienki) flint-work and survived locally even in the Mesolithic Swiderian industry."[12]

Childe recognized the close similarity between the "flint-work" of all three traditions and believed that the Swiderians and Solutreans derived their characteristic toolmaking capabilities from the Kostenki-Streletskaya culture of Central Russia. In other words, their true point of origin was not to be looked for in Central Europe, but much further east, on the Russian Plain, where highly advanced peoples, almost certainly related to the Brünn population, existed at places like Kostenki and Sungir as much as thirty-two thousand years ago.

Thus it is exciting to think that the legacy of these technologically advanced societies of the Upper Paleolithic might have had some influence on the events that led eventually to the construction of Göbekli Tepe during the tenth millennium BC. It is a surmise strengthened in the knowledge that one of the *only* known uses of carved stone blocks prior to the Neolithic age was among the Solutrean cave artists of southwest Europe.

SOLUTREAN STONE FRIEZES

In the collapsed rock shelter of Roc-de-Sers, located in France's Poitou-Charente region, in the southwest of the country, archaeologists in the 1920s uncovered a series of huge limestone blocks, their front faces covered with deeply carved bas-reliefs of Ice Age animals and human forms. Ibexes, deer, bison, and boars are represented, as are reindeer and horses. All come together to form part of a multipiece rock frieze originally positioned in a semicircle on a natural ledge located at the rear of the shelter. In addition to this, lumps of manganese used to create a black pigment for painting were also found at Roc-de-Sers, suggesting that its elaborate rock frieze was originally painted in some manner. This incredible stone art, thought to be around nineteen thousand years old, has been firmly identified as belonging to the Solutrean occupation of the shelter, even though it would not look out of place among the gothic architecture of Chartres Cathedral or Notre Dame de Paris (see figure 21.2).

Two more carved stone blocks were found at the Fourneau du Diable rock shelter in France's Dordogne region, and these have also been identified as belonging to the Solutrean tradition. In addition to this, archaeologists found

Figure 21.2. Carved stone block from the Roc-de-Sers shelter in France's Poitou-Charente region, showing a horse (on the left), and bull, its head recarved as a boar. Solutrean period, ca. 17,000 BC.

within the Solutrean layers in the Cueva del Parpalló rock shelter, situated on the slopes of Montdúber Mountain in Valencia, Spain, literally thousands of painted stone slabs.

Although direct evidence of ritual activity, and even burials, is sadly lacking when it comes to the Solutreans, it is proposed that the "placement of engraved blocks at some sites, the accumulation of painted slabs at Parpalló, and even the abundance of elaborate worked stone points at a number of sites all reflect some type of ceremonial or ritual activities."[13] In other words, the unique rock friezes found at Solutrean sites might well have had a magico-religious function similar to that of the decorated T-shaped pillars at Göbekli Tepe.

PURSUED BY A BULL

One block is of particular significance at Roc-de-Sers. It shows a human figure, a male it seems, with a pudding-basin haircut and slightly bent legs (see figure 21.3). He appears to be either baiting or escaping from a pursuer in the form of a huge musk ox, its three-dimensional head lowered in readiness to charge. The clear relationship between this human form and an aggressive bovine has

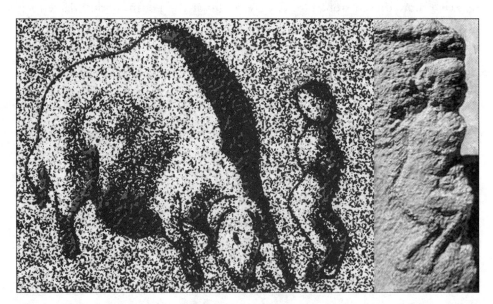

Figure 21.3. Left, drawing showing a musk ox pursuing a human figure from the rock frieze found at Roc-de-Sers. Right, the aforementioned human figure as seen on the rock frieze. Solutrean period, ca. 17,000 BC.

led to comparisons with the Shaft Scene in the Lascaux Caves. This, as we shall recall, shows a reclining birdman being confronted by a wounded bison.

Yet the connection with Lascaux goes deeper, for stylistic and dating evidence indicates that its famous Shaft Scene was executed not by Magdalenian cave artists, as most prehistorians assume, but by Solutreans who entered the well shaft as early as 16,500 BC.[14]

SOLUTREAN BIRD CULT?

More incredibly, the only other human figure depicted among the stone blocks forming the frieze at Roc-de-Sers appears to be wearing a bird mask. It is carved on the very same block as the aforementioned musk ox and figure with pudding-basin haircut. This mask-wearing figure, which also has slightly bent legs, might well have an erect phallus, like the birdman in Lascaux's Shaft Scene (see figure 21.4 on p. 186 to judge for yourself). Clearly, bird totemism, perhaps involving ecstatic states and mask-wearing rituals, could have been important to the Solutrean peoples of southwest Europe.

This conclusion is strengthened by the presence in various caves decorated during the Solutrean period of a strange abstract symbol known as the aviform. This is a long, thick, horizontal line, with downward-turned lines at each end and a vertical extension, either up or down, at its center.

Aviform means "birdlike," and there is no denying the birdlike appearance of these devices, which are found so often that they might well be a sign of recognition among a particular Solutrean grouping or subculture. Yet if these *are* birds, then their downturned outer wings suggest they have adopted a gliding position, usually seen when birds are kept aloft by thermals generated by columns of warm air (see figure 21.5 on p. 186). It is a method of flight used particularly by raptors, vultures, seagulls, and storks, as well as by smaller birds such as swallows and swifts. Thus the aviform could represent either astral flight or the soul of the shaman in the form of a bird.

THE SKY PEOPLE

Maybe it was believed that a mask-wearing shaman could project his or her soul into a soaring bird to observe the herd animals below, providing vital information in advance of the chase. In this manner, high-flying birds taking advan-

Figure 21.4. Comparison of different bird-headed figures: left, the birdman from the Lascaux Shaft Scene, Solutrean period, ca. 16,500–15,000 BC; center, birdman from the rock frieze at Roc-de-Sers, Solutrean period, ca. 17,000 BC; and, right, ceramic bird goddess from the Vinča culture of southeast Europe, ca. 5500–4500 BC.

Figure 21.5. Left, two examples of Solutrean aviform signs from the Grotte du Placard rock shelter in France's Poitou-Charente region, ca. 18,000 BC, and, right, a silhouetted kite gliding in flight for comparison.

tage of warm air thermals might themselves have been identified as shamans that had adopted an avian form. If correct, then with the existence of the bird-men at Lascaux and Roc-de-Sers, we could be looking at evidence among the Solutreans of a semiorganized cult of the bird, which might easily have become associated not just with the sky but also with an imagined sky pole linked to the cosmic axis, something that seems depicted in the Lascaux Shaft Scene.

Perhaps the Solutreans were the original sky people, with the aviform a visible sign of their sky-based religion.

That the Lascaux Shaft Scene might be the handiwork of Solutrean artists is incredibly important, for it could suggest they were carriers of the tradition that identified Cygnus as a celestial bird, with its bright star Deneb marking the entrance to a sky world reached through the Milky Way's Great Rift. Remember, Deneb occupied the position of Pole Star from ca. 16,500 BC to 14,500 BC, precisely when Solutrean cave artists created the Lascaux Shaft Scene.

Thus it becomes possible that Solutrean knowledge regarding the execution of stone friezes in cave sanctuaries, along with their profound understanding of cosmic geography, bird totemism, and avian shamanism, might well have found its way to southeast Anatolia via the Swiderians. This enabled much earlier traditions, which all had their roots in the Kostenki-Streletskaya culture of the Russian Plain, to flower once more with the construction of the large sanctuaries at Göbekli Tepe, an event that undoubtedly helped catalyze not just the Neolithic revolution but also the rise of civilization.

SWANS AND WOLVES

Despite their compelling links to the Solutreans, the religious ideologies of the Swiderians have been more difficult to ascertain. The ancient rock art of the Russian Republic of Karelia, which borders Finland to the west, does, however, throw some light on the matter. Close to the shores of Lake Onega—where in 1936 a nine thousand-year-old cemetery was found and identified as belonging to the post-Swiderian Kunda culture—exposed rock surfaces are covered in carved petroglyphs, many of which belong to the Mesolithic age. Some show swans with exaggerated necks, like long poles. Others show swans sitting on top of poles that are being climbed by a small human figure. As at Lascaux, the poles almost certainly symbolize axes mundi, while the human figures are perhaps the souls of shaman travelling between the physical world and sky world. This suggests that the Swiderians, like the Solutreans before them, saw birds, and swans in particular, as symbols of a sky world reached via the Cygnus constellation (a belief probably going back to a time when Cygnus marked the celestial pole, ca. 16,500–13,000 BC).

Interestingly, a large number of bird bones, including those of the swan, have been recovered from the Mesolithic cemetery of Oleni Ostrov (Reindeer

Island) on Lake Onega. Their deliberate placement alongside human burials has been compared with the shamanic practices of the indigenous Sámi population, who utilize bird and animal bones in rituals and see the spirit of the bird as associated with otherworldly journeys.[15] Also, as we saw in chapter 10, the swan replaces the stork in the Baltic countries as the bringer of newborn babies into the world, another intimation that the swan was associated with the soul's passage to and from the sky world.

Also of value is an examination of the beliefs and practices of those who much later occupied Swiderian territories in Central Europe. For instance, in the first millennium BC a collective of fierce tribal nations known as the Dacians, or Getae, inhabited the region between the Carpathian Mountains and the Black Sea, which was known as Dacia. They honored the "spirit wolf" and saw themselves as "wolf people."[16]

The Dacians venerated the wolf as "lord of the animals" and utilized its supernatural power against all they saw as evil, in which role it became their "guardian warrior."[17] In fact, the Dacians' bond with the lupine influence was so strong that they were apparently able to transform themselves into wolves to become werewolves, a connection with Romania and more specifically Transylvania and the Carpathian Mountains, all too familiar to Western popular culture. According to the Romanian historian Mircea Eliade (1907–1986), the Dacians conducted carefully orchestrated rituals featuring wolf pelts and psychoactive mushrooms in order to undergo "a total psychological transformation into wolves," the origin most likely of lycanthropy, the belief that certain people can, quite literally, become wolves.[18]

Although the Dacians thrived a full nine thousand years *after* the Swiderians hunted the same territories, there is a distant echo of what could be a memory of a distant cataclysm in the Dacians' use of the Draco, or Drago, battle standard. Its description as a wolf's head with the tail of a serpent and its proposed identification as a comet[19] are too close to the Fenris Wolf's role in Ragnarök for this to be a simple coincidence. Were the Geto-Dacians unconsciously recalling the manner in which the world was brought to its knees by a comet likened to a heavenly wolf with a serpent's tail? If so, did they inherit these ideas from indigenous peoples whose own ancestors inhabited the Carpathian Mountains as far back as Paleolithic times?

HUNTING WITH WOLVES

What we do know is that the Paleolithic hunters of Central and Eastern Europe actually began to work alongside wolves, training the animals to accompany them on hunting expeditions. Modern scholarship says that this act of cooperation between human and beast cannot be seen as simply a matter of taming friendly wolves to turn them into man's best friend. Instead, it should be viewed as the adoption of "a new technology," a new "weapon,"[20] which, like the bow and arrow, would have increased the efficiency of the hunter during the chase. Yet from this taming of the wolf the relationship between human and beast emerged, and there is evidence for this even among campsites belonging to the Swiderian hunters.*[21]

Perhaps the Swiderians thus felt it necessary to quite literally take on the mantle of the wolf to ensure both the success of the chase and the safety of the herd against predators. Then, when the comet terrorized the planet in the guise of a sky wolf or sky fox, they played an active part in attempting to counter the supernatural creature's baleful influence to prevent the sky pole from toppling and the world from coming to an end.

Might some memory of this supernatural sky creature have passed from the post-Swiderian cultures of northeast Europe into the myths and legends of their descendants in Scandinavia? Was a representation of this cosmic trickster, identified in Norse myth as the Fenris Wolf, carried aloft by the Geto-Dacians in the form of the Draco battle standard, and was it this knowledge that the Swiderians took with them all the way to Göbekli Tepe? If so, what motivated members of this Post-Solutrean culture to journey to such distant lands, and how exactly did they come to so strongly influence the peoples of southeast Anatolia? The answer, as we see next, seems to be the exploitation of minerals, in particular obsidian.

---

*In the suspected Swiderian level at the Epipaleolithic site of Erbiceni, near the city of Iasi in Romania, evidence of canine domestication has been found.

22

OBSIDIAN OBSESSION

Not only were the Swiderians an advanced hunting society with a unique stone-tool technology, but they also established sophisticated mining operations, some of the only accepted examples anywhere in the world during the Paleolithic age. At various locations within the Świętokrzyskie (Holy Cross) Mountains of central Poland they extracted "exotic" forms of flint, as well as hematite, used as ochre. In addition to becoming efficient miners, the Swiderians established long-distance trading networks to export high-quality stone tools as well as the "pre-form" cores to make new ones. Yet in addition to flint and ochre, one other mineral coveted by the Swiderians was the black volcanic glass known as obsidian.

Obsidian is a natural glass, usually black or gray, created when volcanic lava solidifies very quickly, without allowing any time for a crystalline matrix to form. Throughout the Middle and Upper Paleolithic ages, obsidian was a highly prized commodity all around the world. It was used by prehistoric cultures in Africa, Asia, the Americas, Australia, and Europe. The Solutreans also used obsidian to create their unique projectile points.[*1]

In Europe, there are only a handful of obsidian sources. Two can be found on small volcanic islands forming part of the Sicilian archipelago off the south coast

---

*Obsidian bifaces were found at Laugerie-Haute in France's Vézère Valley in the Dordogne.

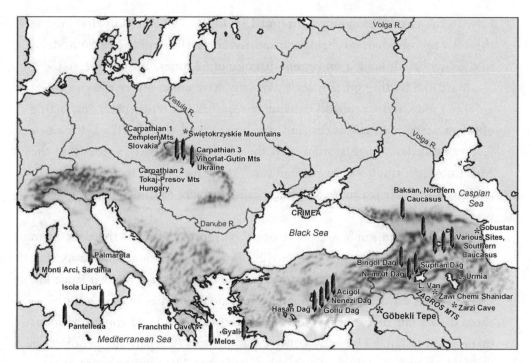

Figure 22.1. Map of obsidian sources in Europe and southwest Asia, along with sites mentioned in connection with the distribution of obsidian in the same regions.

of Italy. Another is located on a tiny island off the west coast of Italy, with a further source on the island of Sardinia. There is also an important ancient source on the Greek Cycladic island of Melos (or Milos), with another on the volcanic Greek island of Gyali, close to the southwest coast of Turkey.* The only other sources in mainland Europe are located in the Carpathian Mountains, the "land of obsidian,"[2] within the Tokaj and Zemplén Mountains, which straddle the border between, respectively, northeast Hungary and southeast Slovakia (see figure 22.1).[3]†

THE FRANCHTHI CAVE

The obsidian trade was big business in the Upper Paleolithic, with examples from the island of Melos reaching an occupational site known as the Franchthi

---

*Obsidian sources also exist in Iceland and, possibly, in the Balkans.

†A further source of Carpathian obsidian exists in Ukraine, within the Vihorlat-Gutin Mountains, much farther to the east.

Cave in the Greek Peloponnese around 13,000 BC.[4] This tells us that even at this early age, obsidian was being transported across the Aegean Sea from Melos to the Greek mainland, a minimum distance of 62 miles (100 kilometers).

Maritime trading on this scale can only have come under the control of an elite group, most probably a band of complex hunter-gatherers exporting obsidian across vast distances, initially by sea, and then by land. Professor Catherine Perlès, a prehistorian with the University of Paris, argues that the Melos obsidian trade was in the hands of "specialists," who had the ability to navigate a familiar sea route and knew exactly where to find the raw material on the island.[5]

Melos obsidian might well have been transported as far as the Balkans in Neolithic times,[6] confirming its incredible importance throughout Europe. For the Swiderians too it would seem to have held a special place in their stone kit. One survey of exotic materials found at late Paleolithic sites in the Carpathians showed that out of twenty Swiderian centers examined, *all* contained items made of obsidian.[7] The only other contemporary Carpathian people that would seem to have taken a noticeable fancy to obsidian were the Swiderians' neighbors in Hungary, the Epigravettians (i.e., late Gravettians), with a large number of items made from the volcanic glass being found in their settlement sites as well.[8]

LETHAL WEAPON

The Swiderians used obsidian to create super-sharp tanged points, such as the one found at a site in Wolodz, Subcarpathia, Poland.[9] Being fashioned out of obsidian would have made these arrowheads among the most lethal weapons in the world. So sharp is obsidian that surgeons today use scalpel blades tipped with the black volcanic glass to make near-perfect incisions during operations.

Experts in Stone Age tool production often cite the story of Don Crabtree, one of the people responsible for the rebirth of stone knapping in the 1960s and 1970s.[10] He apparently insisted that during an operation surgeons use obsidian blades that he himself had made. Incredibly, obsidian slices through tissue with such efficiency that it enables healing to take place easily. Metal blades, in contrast, make micro-rips in body tissue that can take much longer to heal.

CROW-FLINT FIRE

It might not have been just the sharpness of obsidian that appealed to the Swiderians, or indeed their neighbors, the Epigravettians. We cannot say exactly how the peoples of the Upper Paleolithic viewed obsidian on a subtle level, but the fact that it was found on the slopes of volcanoes, some of which might still have been active, tells us that it could have been associated with the element of fire.

Indeed, Hungarians living in the Carpathian Basin would use obsidian—picked up at prehistoric settlement sites—to kindle fire. They referred to it as *varjúkova,* "crow-flint,"[11] as well as *isten nyila,* "thunder bolts" (or "godly arrowheads"),[12] associating it with the god of thunder and lightning. They even described obsidian as *lebkövek,* "meteorite-like stones," in the belief that these shiny gray or black pieces of rock came from the sky.[13]

OBSIDIAN RELIGION

In Mesoamerican tradition obsidian was said to be blood that had congealed and gone black. Both the Aztecs and Maya used obsidian to create sacrificial knives, as well as blades and implements for autosacrifice; that is, bloodletting through self-inflicted incisions.

Scottish folklorist Lewis Spence (1874–1955) wrote in *The Magic and Mysteries of Mexico* (1922) that the Mesoamerican fixation with obsidian—what he called the "obsidian religion"—emerged from an epoch of human history when prehistoric hunters used obsidian weapons to hunt deer:

> The deer was slain by the obsidian weapon, which, therefore, came to be regarded as the magical weapon, that by which food was procured [by the prehistoric hunters of Mexico]. In the course of time it assumed a sacred significance, the hunting-gods themselves came to wield it, and it [obsidian] was thought of as coming from the stars or the heavens where the gods dwelt.[14]

Even though Mexico lies thousands of miles away from the Carpathian Mountains, can we envisage the existence of similar beliefs in the magical potency of obsidian among the Upper Paleolithic peoples of Central and

Eastern Europe? Did the Swiderians see obsidian as a magical weapon, linked integrally with their role as reindeer hunters?

THE SEARCH FOR NEW SOURCES

In all likelihood, the Swiderians' fascination with obsidian could suggest they had some kind of control over its collection and distribution in the Carpathian Mountains, the "land of obsidian," prior to any kind of forced migration to north and northeast Europe caused either by the Younger Dryas Boundary impact event, ca. 10,900 BC, or the thirteen-hundred-year mini ice age that followed it. Not only was obsidian to be found in the Caucasus Mountains, which the Swiderians reached as early as the eleventh millennium BC, but as we see next, it was the sources in and around the Armenian Highlands that become crucial to making the connection between the Swiderians and the power elite thought to be behind the construction of Göbekli Tepe.

23

THE BINGÖL MASTERS

In 2008 it was determined that obsidian tools found at Göbekli Tepe derive from three primary sources—one of them being Göllü Dağ in central Anatolia, where there are several major sources of obsidian, with the other two coming from locations near Bingöl Mountain.[1] This is a north-south aligned massif with twin peaks located some 30 miles (50 kilometers) south of the city of Erzurum in the Armenian Highlands of eastern Anatolia.

A separate survey completed in 2012 determined that another source of the raw material used to fashion many of the obsidian tools and blades found at Göbekli Tepe was Nemrut Dağ, an extinct volcano close to Lake Van, Turkey's largest inland sea, which lies to the southeast of the Armenian Highlands.[2] This latest discovery has led to speculation that Göbekli Tepe might have been a cosmopolitan center, a kind of Neolithic Mecca or Jerusalem for people coming from central Anatolia, some 280 miles (450 kilometers) away, and from the Bingöl/Lake Van area, which lies around 200 miles (320 kilometers) to the northeast.[3]

Supporting evidence for the cosmopolitan center theory includes the countless flint tools found scattered about Göbekli Tepe's artificial mound, which are hardly likely to have been dropped by the builders. They are everywhere; you cannot help but tread on them. The sheer quantity suggests they are offerings left by visitors across an extended period of time.

Clearly, Göbekli Tepe *was* a center of pilgrimage. However, the presence here of obsidian tools from central Anatolia and the Bingöl/Lake Van area might well have other implications. As we have seen in Mexico, Central Europe, and Greece, obsidian was a prestige item, one endowed with great magical properties, including the ability to produce fire. Its presence at Göbekli Tepe tells us two things: first, that it might have been employed in rituals due to its special qualities, and, second, there must have been lines of communication between Göbekli Tepe and the obsidian sources in the Bingöl/Lake Van area. This connection with Bingöl Mountain in particular was most obviously through proto-Neolithic centers such as Hallan Çemi in the foothills of the eastern Taurus Mountains, which dates to ca. 10,250–9600 BC, and Çayönü, ca. 8650–7350 BC, both of which acted as clearinghouses for obsidian reaching southeast Anatolia from the Armenian Highlands.

THE EMERGENCE OF HALLAN ÇEMI

Hallan Çemi exhibited a level of cultural sophistication that easily matched anything going on in the Levant at this time. Although the people here were hunters and foragers, eating wild game (mostly sheep, goats, red deer, foxes, and turtles), they would appear to have domesticated the pig, the earliest evidence of this form of animal husbandry anywhere in the world.

The discovery of a substantial number of stone querns, used to grind seeds, has led some prehistorians to suggest that the inhabitants of Hallan Çemi were engaged in protoagriculture, or certainly the exploitation of wild cereals. However, very few cereal seeds have been found at the site, casting doubts on this theory. In fact, all the indications are that the main food here, in addition to game meat, consisted of wild lentils, bitter vetch (a type of pea), and nuts. These included pistachios and wild almonds, which had first to be roasted before consumption to remove their toxicity. Evidence of pistachio and almond consumption has also been found at Göbekli Tepe.

Excavators at Hallan Çemi worked frantically to explore the site from 1991 to 1994 in advance of its disappearance beneath the rising waters of the nearby Batman River, following the construction of a nearby dam. Before its final submergence they were able to uncover two semisubterranean, circular structures of great significance. Each one was around 20 feet (6 meters) in diameter, with walls faced with sandstone ashlars, as well as stone benches, plastered floors, and central hearths. Archaeologists found inside them a large number of prestige items, including pieces of copper ore and obsidian tools, along with evidence of food preparation, most likely for ceremonial feasts cooked on the hearths.

One of the structures contained a massive auroch's skull, which had hung at its northern end, indicating that the building was almost certainly used for cultic purposes. The discovery of this bucranium supports the theory that the north was the preferred direction of orientation of proto-Neolithic cult buildings even before the construction of much more complex structures at both Göbekli Tepe and Çayönü.

Indeed, there is a good case for Hallan Çemi having some direct bearing on what came later at Göbekli Tepe, as does the basic design and carved art of other cult centers in the region, such as Jerf el-Ahmar in North Syria and Qermez Dere in the Jezirah Desert of northern Iraq (see chapter 1).

Hallan Çemi, where almost half the stone tools found were made of obsidian, is 75 miles (120 kilometers) south-southwest of Bingöl Mountain and just under 140 miles (225 kilometers) away from Göbekli Tepe. To date, Hallan Çemi is the closest known proto-Neolithic site to Bingöl, and the sheer amount of obsidian found here has prompted prehistorians to suggest that trade networks must have existed across the region. If so, then Hallan Çemi was very likely a main distribution center, the raw obsidian arriving here from workshops much closer to the mountain.

EUROPEAN TAKEOVER

These realizations take us into interesting territories, for if the trade in obsidian was indeed regulated by some kind of elite group, is it possible that Swiderian peoples entered eastern Anatolia from the north during the Younger Dryas period and assumed control of the regional obsidian trade, introducing new forms of tool manufacture, such as the pressure flaking technique? Curiously, this is the exact same time that the local culture, the Zarzian, vanish from the scene, having thrived in the region for as much as nine thousand years.

The Zarzians are a very compelling group. Not only were they the founders of Hallan Çemi, but evidence suggests they also domesticated dogs.[4] In addition to this, they were one of the first cultures in the Middle East to employ the use of bows and arrows, which they utilized to hunt red deer, onager (or wild ass), cattle, sheep, and wild goats. They kept on the move, living mainly in temporary campsites, and most important of all, they had access to major obsidian sources in the Armenian Highlands.

Obsidian from the Bingöl sources has been found at various Zarzian camps as far south as the Zagros Mountains, including the cave of Zarzi (the culture's type site), near Sulaymaniah in Iraqi Kurdistan, and the Zawi Chemi Shanidar settlement site, which overlooks the Greater Zab River in northern Iraq. It was here during the 1950s that American archaeologists Ralph and Rose Solecki discovered the wings of seventeen large predatory birds, mostly vultures, along with the skulls of at least fifteen goats and wild sheep (see chapter 9). Although this ritual deposit is assigned to the proto-Neolithic community that occupied the site, chances are it represents a continuation of beliefs and practices that had been prevalent among the Zarzian peoples, whose legacy lived on among the proto-Neolithic populations of southeast Anatolia and northern Iraq. In other words, the Zarzians were most likely carriers of the tradition that included the utilization of the vulture in shamanic practices, something that later appears at cult centers such as Göbekli Tepe and Nevalı Çori. This is despite the fact that the Swiderians held specific knowledge regarding bird- and canine-related shamanism derived, at least in part, from both their suspected Solutrean background *and* their likely contact with the descendants of the Kostenki-Streletskaya culture of the Russian steppes and plain, whom they would have encountered on their journey to eastern Anatolia. Yet their beliefs and practices do not appear to have included the use of the vulture as a primary symbol of birth, death, and rebirth. That seems to have come from the Zarzian peoples, who occupied the region before their arrival.

As to their origin, British archaeologist James Mellaart felt that the Zarzians had started their journey on the Russian steppes, then moved gradually southward into the Caucasian Mountains and Armenian Highlands, before eventually reaching the Zagros Mountains of northern Iraq and northwest Iran.[5] Yet this was a migration that had started as early as 19,000 BC, as much as nine thousand years before the Swiderians would appear to have traveled exactly the same route to reach eastern Anatolia during the Younger Dryas period.

So did the Swiderian hunters overrun Zarzian camps, decimating the inhabitants? Certainly, there is compelling evidence that some kind of power struggle occurred around this time in the Zarzian territories of Gobustan in

Azerbaijan, right where the eastern termination of the Caucasus Mountains meets the Caspian Sea.

THE GOBUSTAN WARRIORS

Rock art in the Gobustan (or Kobystan) National Park, located 40 miles (64 kilometers) southwest of the Azerbaijani capital of Baku, shows warriors with bows and arrows slung across their backs (see figure 23.1). Some figures appear to be wearing fringed waistbands and even animal loincloths with the tails

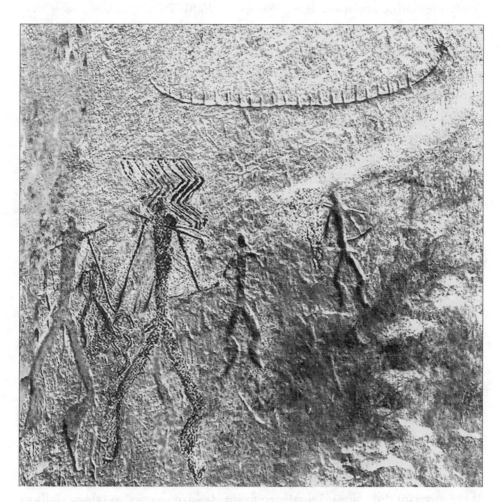

Figure 23.1. Rock art from Gobustan, Azerbaijan, close to the west coast of the Caspian Sea, showing warriors wielding bows and arrows. Mesolithic period, ca. eleventh to tenth millennium BC. The boat in the upper register is thought to have been added at a later date.

hanging between their legs, similar to those seen on the anthropomorphic twin pillars in Göbekli Tepe's Enclosure D.

The lifelike manner in which the warriors are drawn, with smaller figures behind them, gives the impression of arrival—as if they are arriving from somewhere else in the ancient world. This seems emphasized by the fact that in the background of some of the engraved panels are high-prowed boats of a type common to the Neolithic rock art of Egypt's Eastern Desert and the Bronze Age rock art of Scandinavia. So much do these vessels resemble those of later cultures that prehistorians suggest that, whereas the Gobustan warriors are "early Mesolithic age at the latest,"[6] thus ca. 9600–9000 BC, the vessels were added later, most probably during the Bronze Age.

Mary Settegast, the author of *Plato Prehistorian,* argues that the Gobustan rock art shows the arrival of incoming warriors, most likely bow-and-arrow-wielding reindeer hunters from Europe.[7] So are we looking at Swiderians seizing control of Zarzian territories? Whoever these warriors represent, their presence would not seem to have been greeted cordially, for some of the engraved panels show open conflict between two separate groups of individuals.

Even if the Gobustan rock art does show Swiderian hunters coming up against their Zarzian counterparts, there is no reason to assume that one decimated the other. Perhaps after some initial skirmishes, the two factions came to some kind of understanding regarding the exploitation of the region's rich mineral resources, including the all-important obsidian. In doing so, it is possible that the Zarzians amalgamated with the incoming European hunters to become the driving force behind the emergence of the proto-Neolithic world at key settlements like Hallan Çemi in the Eastern Taurus Mountains. As mentioned earlier, Hallan Çemi acted as a workshop and clearinghouse for obsidian coming from Bingöl Mountain and Lake Van, and so its Zarzian vulture shamans might well have had some hand in the rise of early Neolithic cult centers in the *triangle d'or* such as Göbekli Tepe, Çayönü, and Nevalı Çori.

DISTANT COUSINS

If the Zarzians did come originally from the Russian steppes, as James Mellaart suspected, sometime around ca. 19,000 BC, the chances are they were related to the highly advanced Kostenki-Streletskaya culture, which disappears around exactly the same time. So if the Solutreans and their proposed successors, the

Swiderians, really were related to the Kostenki-Streletskaya culture (as was proposed by V. Gordon Childe, see chapter 21), then it means that the Zarzians were in fact distant cousins of the Swiderians, a factor that might just have allowed them to find some common ground. Both used bows and arrows, and both might well have domesticated dogs and/or wolves, while the Kostenki-Streletskaya culture is thought to have held a special interest in the fox, one of the primary totemic animals seen at Göbekli Tepe.

For example, a male burial uncovered at Sungir in Russia in 1956 (designated Sungir 1) had a number of perforated arctic fox teeth on his cranium when uncovered, suggesting they were sewn into a cap of some sort. Another burial of a boy aged around thirteen (Sungir 2), interred in a shallow grave head-to-head with an adolescent female (Sungir 3), was found to have around 250 drilled arctic fox teeth around his waist. These probably came from a decorated belt, similar to those seen on the central pillars in Göbekli Tepe's Enclosure D.

Burials at Kostenki itself have also been found to contain unusual amounts of teeth and bones of the arctic fox. This includes the 150 fox teeth found wrapped around the head of a child, aged about six to seven years old, uncovered at a site known as Kostenki 15. Covering the burial was a huge mammoth scapula (shoulder blade), a feature common also among the contemporary, and unquestionably related, Pavlovian culture of Moravia. Today Moravia is part of the Czech Republic, which includes the sites of Brünn (modern Brno) and Předmost, where evidence of the Brünn-type human population was reported in the nineteenth century.

Among the Pavlovians—their name deriving from Pavlov, a village situated in the Pavlov Hills, around 22 miles (35 kilometers) from the city of Brno—the arctic fox also features heavily among burials. At a site named Dolní Věstonice one child burial contained twenty-seven arctic fox teeth, while a triple burial made up of two men, with a woman in between them, revealed that both males had been wearing headdresses of arctic fox teeth when interred. Within the mass grave uncovered at Předmost in 1894 (see chapter 20), excavators came across large amounts of wolf and fox remains, which seemed to line the perimeter of the pit. Among the remains were a number of unperforated arctic fox canines as well as various wolf skulls. Most pertinently, a woman, aged around forty, discovered at Dolní Věstonice site 1, and known popularly as "the shamaness," was found to be holding five unperforated fox incisors in her right hand and various fox bones in her left hand.

Although the use of wolf and arctic fox remains as items of personal adornment among the Eastern Gravettians, ca. thirty-two thousand to twenty-one thousand years ago, might easily be attributed to the large-scale capture of these carnivores for their meat and pelts, the presence in the graves of unperforated fox teeth hints at the importance of this animal on a cosmological level. Arguably the arctic fox, and the wolf also, was seen as an otherworldly creature that needed to be appeased by the newly dead on their journey into the afterlife. Such ideas, if realistic, might easily have been inherited by the descendants of the Eastern Gravettians, including the Swiderians, who came to occupy the same territories during the Younger Dryas period.

Should this quite fantastic scenario prove realistic, then it seems likely that incoming Swiderian groups entered eastern Anatolia and assumed control of the obsidian trade, giving them direct access to settlement sites not just in the Eastern Taurus range and Zagros Mountains, but also in southeast Anatolia, much closer to Göbekli Tepe. Now they were in a position to introduce their own religious ideologies to the local inhabitants, which would seem to have included new ways to counter the baleful actions of the cosmic trickster in its guise as the sky wolf or sky fox.

Because the center of the Armenian obsidian trade was Bingöl Mountain, there is every chance that this is one of the locations the Swiderian hunters settled so that they could exploit their newly acquired sources of exotic materials, including the all-important obsidian find sites. If this is correct, then we should find evidence of their presence in this region, and this, as we see next, is exactly what we do find.

24

WOLF STONE MOUNTAIN

I n the religion of Zoroastrianism, a native form of which flourished in historical Armenia before the spread of Christianity in the fourth century, the wolf was an animal of Ahriman, the evil principle, who engages in a constant struggle with Ohrmazd (also known as Ahura Mazda), the creator of the universe. The Bundahishn, one of the holy books of the Zoroastrian faith, speaks of how Ahriman planned to create the wolf species as "disembodied, unseen evil spirits." Yet Ohrmazd got wind of Ahriman's plan and created the wolf himself, along with the elephant and the lion, which were all made creatures of the evil principle.

Ormuzd showed what he had done to Ahriman, who being pleased, "attached the evil spirits to these forms saying, 'Ohrmazd did what I was going to do.'"[1] Elsewhere, Ahriman is cited as the progenitor of the "wolf species," the leader of whom is the lion,[2] a predator interchangeable with the wolf in the Zoroastrian tradition.

There is a reason for citing these facts, for in historical Armenia, the region we know today as eastern Turkey (the modern Republic of Armenia lies immediately north of here), there once existed a mountain called Gaylaxaz-ut, which means "abounding in *gaylaxaz*," or "wolf's stone" (from *gayl*, "wolf").[3] Usually this refers to flint, the principal material used during the Stone Age to make tools and weapons. Yet *gaylaxaz* can also mean obsidian,[4] even though in Armenian tradition this black volcanic glass is known also as *satani elung,* "Satan's nail,"[5] or perhaps "Satan's claw."*

SERVANTS OF SATAN

Previously, Gaylaxaz-ut had been called Paxray,[6] which in the Armenian language means "hind, deer, stag,"[7] with the deer being a creature synonymous in local folk tradition with both Satan and the wolf.[8] Aristakes Lastivertc'i, an eleventh-century Armenian cleric and historian, relates an archaic story that speaks of how on this mountain a "village" was established named Xač (pronounced something like "hack"), which means "holy cross." This was destroyed, he said, by the "servants of the Satan,"[9] who afterward returned "to their snake-dwelling lairs,"[10] located elsewhere on the mountain.

Trying to get to the bottom of this strange story, Armenian linguist Hrach K. Martirosyan wondered whether the mountain Gaylaxaz-ut might be Baghir Dağ,[11] a peak at the end of a mountain chain to the west of Bingöl Mountain. On its eastern side is the ominously named Shaitan Dağ, "Satan's Mountain," leading Martirosyan to ask:

> Bearing in mind that the mountain of Paxray = Gaylaxaz-ut is said to be dwelled by "servants of the Satan" [in "snake-dwelling lairs"], one may assume that the "devilish fame/nature" of the mountain is conditioned by the abundance of *gaylaxaz*-stones as is seen in the name of the mountain and is also reflected in its earlier name Paxray, if this indeed is identic with *paxray* "hind, deer."[12]

In other words, the name Gaylaxaz-ut alludes, most probably, to a mountain where "*gaylaxaz*-stones," that is, flint or obsidian, is found, and that the "servants of the Satan" are in fact reflections of the mountain's inhabitants. Although Martirosyan identifies this location with Baghir Dağ,[13] there are no notable flint or obsidian sources nearby. More likely is that Gaylaxaz-ut, which quite literally means Wolf Stone Mountain, is Bingöl Mountain, around 45 miles (72 kilometers) east of Shaitan Dağ. This, as we saw in

---

*This name for obsidian is cited on various Internet sites with the following words: "Ancient people called Obsidian 'Satan's claws' fragments." This sounds so similar to "Satan's nail" that it has to be the same.

chapter 23, has been the region's primary source of obsidian since Paleolithic times.

Confirmation that Gaylaxaz-ut is Bingöl Mountain comes from its earlier name of Paxray, recorded also as Paxir, Parxar, and Parxaray.[14] According to the Roman naturalist and philosopher Pliny the Elder (AD 23–79), the beginning of the Euphrates on Monte Aba (an ancient name for Bingöl Mountain) was called the Pyxirates,[15] which almost certainly derives from the same root as Paxray, suggesting that Bingöl Mountain really is Gaylaxaz-ut, Wolf Stone Mountain.

That obsidian was known in Armenia as wolf's stone implies, quite clearly, that the creature was associated in some manner with this black volcanic glass. Might the wolves not have been animals originally, but groups or individuals who identified themselves with the wolf and prized this black volcanic glass? Did the memory of these "wolves" degenerate over time until they became nothing more than the "servants of the Satan," minions of the Zoroastrian evil principle Ahriman, who lived in "snake-dwelling lairs" on Wolf Stone Mountain?

LAND OF THE PERI

That mythical beings associated both with obsidian and the wolf might once have inhabited the region is affirmed by the fact that one of the rivers that takes its rise on Bingöl Mountain is the Peri Şu, which means "river of the Peri," with Peri being "one of a large group of beautiful, fairy-like beings of Persian mythology."[16] Peri Şu is the river's name in the local Kurdish language, although to the region's Armenian population it is the Gail, or Kyle, from *gayl,* meaning "wolf."[17] Linking the wolf still further with Bingöl is a narrow gorge through which the fledgling river passes after leaving the mountain, which is called in Turkish Kurt-Duzi, meaning "wolf (*kurt*) plain (*duzi*)."[18]

So how then did a river named Gail, or wolf, come to be called Peri Şu by the region's Kurdish inhabitants, and did this information have any obvious bearing on Bingöl's long association with obsidian?

Kurdish folklore asserts that the mountains and valleys around the Peri Şu were once the haunt of the Peri, the offspring of fallen angels in Persian myth and legend. They are said to have been tall, strong, beautiful, "super human beings that could cohabit with mortal kind."*[19] It was even believed that certain communities of Kurds, particularly those that included pale-looking females, were the descendants of Peri that had mated with mortal kind.[20] According to a Kurd who was born and raised in a rural village close to the obsidian route between Bingöl and Diyarbakır, the Peri were linked to the local obsidian trade in stories once told by the most elderly members of the community.[21] How exactly, unfortunately, has now been lost.

Yet the fact that the Peri Şu, or Gail River, rises on Bingöl Mountain links these various traditions with mythical individuals who might well have been identified not only with the Peri of Kurdish folklore, but also with both the wolf and obsidian. It is even possible that we have here a dim recollection of the arrival in the region of Swiderian peoples from central and eastern Europe.

If all this is correct, then how would these European hunters, whose totem animals included the wolf and reindeer, convince the indigenous peoples of southeast Anatolia to embark on the construction of monumental architecture unlike anything ever seen before in the ancient world? It is time now to examine just how exactly the hunting magic of the Swiderians might have gone on to influence the strange world that emerged at Göbekli Tepe in the aftermath of the Younger Dryas mini ice age ca. 9600–9500 BC.

---

*For instance, my Kurdish contact, Hakan Dalkus, says: "Unlike Genie, the Peri are not our religious beliefs. We, Kurds, believe the Peri were human beings who really lived. I also think they were a beautiful race" (February 10, 2012). He adds: "When I was a kid, my grandmother and some other women from old generation told us many stories of Cin (Genie) and Peri. Those women hardly left the village in all their lives, they could not speak Turkish. They had no influence of the outer world. So their stories wholly reflected old beliefs. I vaguely remember those stories now but I certainly remember that the Peri were human beings. Some kind of super human beings. Human beings could marry the Peri and have kids from them. . . . My knowledge of our old stories is only confined to the region around my village. My village has a proved history of at least 13 thousand years old. On Bingöl road. I read that the region around my village was a center of obsidian trade" (February 28, 2012).

25

SAVIORS OF THE WORLD

Polish anthropologist Maria Czaplicka (1884–1921) made a study of the Koryak reindeer herders of Siberia's Kamchatka Krai, which is in the extreme northeast of Russia (a krai is a federal subject, or political division, of Russia). One ceremony she recorded involved the slaughter of a wolf and then the killing of a reindeer. The latter was decapitated, and its head and body placed alongside that of the slain wolf on a raised platform. The rite was a sacrifice to Gicholan, "The-One-on-High," the Koryak supreme being, upon whom they called to prevent the wolf from attacking the herd. A feast was afterward prepared and eaten, at which "the wolf is fed"; that is, its spirit was appeased. Czaplicka goes on:

> The night is spent without sleep, in beating the drum, and dancing to enter-
> tain the wolf, lest his relatives come and take revenge. Beating the drum
> and addressing themselves to the wolf, the people say, "Be well! (Nimeleu
> jatvanvota!)," and addressing The-One-on-High, they say, "Be good, do not
> make the wolf bad!"[1]

Yet in answer as to whether this ritual was done to ward off wolves, the Koryak insisted that the animal was not dangerous in its visible state, especially as the northern wolf generally avoids human contact. Czaplicka said it was dangerous only in its "invisible, anthropomorphic form"; that is, as a werewolf, a half-human, half-wolf. With this in mind, she noted that in Koryak tradition:

> The wolf is a rich reindeer-owner and the powerful master of the tundra . . . [and] avenges [himself] particularly on those that hunt [wolves]. The Reindeer Koryak, who have special reason to fear the wolf on account of their herds, regard this animal as a powerful shaman and an evil spirit.[2]

Thus for the Koryak the wolf was both a "powerful shaman and an evil spirit," a force to be reckoned with on a supernatural level.

WOLF-STICK FESTIVAL

In another ritual celebration practiced by the Koryak, called the Wolf-stick Festival (Elhogi Çayönüin), a wolf was killed, skinned, and decapitated. Moving across to a hearth the participants would then place a pointed stick in the ground, to which they would tie an arrow. Alternatively, the arrow was driven into the earth, with its point sticking upward. A man would then adorn himself in the wolf's skin and walk in circles around the hearth to the beat of a drum played by someone standing nearby. When questioned as to why they conducted this ritual, the Koryak would simply shrug their shoulders and say: "Our forefathers did [it] this way."[3]

THE SHAMAN'S POLE

Czaplicka was mystified as to why during the Wolf-stick Festival the Koryak stuck a stick in the ground with an arrow tied to it or used an arrow instead. Yet an explanation is actually quite simple, for it cannot be coincidence that shamanistic practices in Siberia, and many other parts of the world, involve the erection of a stick or pole that represents the axis mundi, the axis of the earth.

The shaman's pole, which can even be the central support of a skin-covered tent, then becomes the means by which the shaman gains entry to the sky world, either by ascending it in astral form and/or by actually *climbing* the pole, like some weird circus act in a big top. As Czaplicka herself pointed out in connection with the cosmological views of the Chukchi, a Siberian tribe whose territories border those of the Koryak:

A hole, under the pole-star, forms a passage from one world to the other, and through this hole shamans and spirits pass from one to another of the worlds.[4]

Such beliefs and practices are likely to have existed in Paleolithic times, and if this is correct, then there is no reason they cannot have survived into the modern era in remote parts of Siberia. The existence of rituals such as the Wolf-stick Festival of the Koryak demonstrates the absolute necessity of a tribal group in countering the malefic intentions of their enemies; not here, but in the spirit world, where they can be confronted head-on by the shaman, who might well take on the mantle of the wolf to deal directly with a feared and respected rival or enemy.

OCCULT BATTLE

These are psychological processes most assuredly, but it is as well to recall that during the Second World War British witches and occultists—most famously Dion Fortune (1890–1946), who lived at Glastonbury at the time—became entangled in what they saw as a magical battle of life and death in order to counteract the threat of Nazi Germany to British freedom. Those taking part conducted regular rituals, meditations, and psychic battles to ensure an Allied victory. These individuals believed that what they were doing was very real indeed, and no amount of skepticism would have convinced them otherwise. It is extremely likely that something similar was going on in the aftermath of the Younger Dryas Boundary impact event involving European reindeer hunters and wolf shamans countering the baleful influence of the cosmic trickster in the form of the wolf or fox.

Did the Paleolithic peoples eventually claim victory over the forces of the sky wolf, or sky fox, in a manner echoed in the outcome of the Scandinavian account of Ragnarök, the Twilight of the Gods? Did their claims, handed down from one generation to the next, have any bearing on the story of how the god Tíw, or Tyr, sacrificed his right arm in order that the Fenris Wolf might be bound forever, saving the lives not just of the remaining Æsir, or Asa gods, but also the fledgling strains of humanity? Remember, this was seen as a compassionate act of self-sacrifice that gained Tíw the epithet "leavings of the wolf."

Not only was Tíw considered a divine protector of the North Star or celestial pole, but his symbol, the T-rune Tiwaz, is the outline of an arrow, and, as we saw in chapter 16, a representation of the "vault of heaven held up by the universal column,"[5] as well as the Irminsul, or "world-column of the Saxons that terminates in the pole star."[6] The symbolism is thus the same as the arrow and pole used in the Koryak Wolf-stick Festival, with all of it being done to counter the trickster wolf and ensure the future stability of the world.

STRANGE CUSTOMS OF THE SÁMI

Further evidence of this surmise comes from the Sámi, the shamanic-based tribal culture and, until fairly recently, reindeer herders who have existed in Finland, northern Scandinavia, and the Kola Peninsula of Russia since Mesolithic times (see figure 25.1 on p. 211). According to noted Swedish ethnologist Uno Harva (1882–1949), the Sámi practiced a "strange custom" whereby they made sacrifices to a sky god "so the sky or the world would not fall down."[7] For this they erected a forked tree, or tall pole, on the top of which they placed an iron nail, symbolizing the "world pillar," next to which an altar was created so that the god "could support and keep the world, that it would not grow old and fall from its former position."[8] Harva compared the Sámi's sky pole with the Irminsul of the Saxons, linking it back to the Tiwaz rune, which was known both to the Scandinavians and the Germanic peoples.[9]

According to an eighteenth-century missionary named Jens Kildal (1683–1767), the Norwegian Sámi believed in a high god called Maylmen Radien, in whose honor a world pillar or axis mundi called Maylmen Stytto was erected and "smeared with the blood of a sacrificial reindeer oxen."[10]

Here we have clear evidence of shamanic rituals taking place among the Sámi to preserve the stability of the sky pole, or world pillar (the Maylmen Stytto was thought to connect with the celestial pole). This was done in order that it might "not grow old and fall from its former position" or that "the sky or the world would not fall down"; that is, so that it would not be destroyed, either through neglect or, might we say, through the intrusion of some kind

---

*Intriguingly, the Sámi once played a board game called tablo, whereby one person plays as the wolf or fox and the other as the hunter. Players moved around their pieces, with the hunter attempting "to corner the predator before he or she 'eats' all the hunter's pieces." See "Sami," Countries and Their Cultures, www.everyculture.com/wc/Norway-to-Russia/Sami .html#b#ixzz2J0bfenar.

Figure 25.1. Antique line drawing showing Sámi reindeer herders.

of supernatural agency, such as a sky wolf or sky fox* (the reindeer, wolf, and fox are key animals depicted on Sámi shaman drums, alongside a central cross variously described as the world tree [Saiva Moura], the world pillar [Maylmen Stytto], and even the Cross of Christ).

FINNO-UGRIC ORIGINS

The significant point about the Sámi is that they belong to an ethnic group that forms part of the Finno-Ugric language family. Not only is there a relationship between the Finno-Ugric language and both Armenian and Hungarian, but there is evidence also that the Sámi inherited traditions from a post-Swiderian culture responsible for the spread of the Finno-Ugric group of languages into Scandinavia, Estonia, and Finland.[11]

Thus there exists some small chance that the beliefs and practices of the Sámi owe some debt to those practiced by the Swiderian reindeer hunters, including, we can only assume, shamanic rites to preserve the stability of the sky pole so that the world does not come to an end.

With all this in mind, can we go on to imagine Swiderian groups reaching the Armenian Highlands in the wake of the catastrophic events that would appear to have affected the world in the eleventh millennium BC and claiming that their hunting magic and their understanding of the sky wolf or sky fox, had, quite literally, brought humankind back from the brink of destruction? Did they offer to reveal how the hunter-gatherers of southeast Anatolia could themselves stabilize the world pillar and counter the baleful influence of the cosmic trickster so that "the sky or the world would not fall down"?

Such speculation might seem crazy, but we have to imagine ourselves in the position of the hunter-gatherers of southeast Anatolia at the end of the Paleolithic age and attempt to understand why they might have embarked on mammoth building projects such as Göbekli Tepe. If the large enclosures, built ca. 9500–8900 BC, are not the end product of hundreds, if not thousands, of years of gradual evolution, then it is possible they were inspired not only by the fear of a further cataclysm taking place but also by new ideas carried into the region by outsiders. As we have seen, by far the best candidates for this role are the Swiderians, who would seem to have been carrying traditions inherited from their likely forebears, the Solutreans and Kestenki-Streletskaya culture of the Russian Plain, in particular a knowledge of cosmic geography and shamanistic practices involving the concept of the sky pole used to reach a sky world existing in the area of the Cygnus region.

FOX, NOT WOLF?

One question remains before we can move on: If Fenris is a wolf, and the European reindeer hunters arrived in Anatolia claiming an association with this animal, why don't we see the wolf depicted more at Göbekli Tepe? The answer is that the wolf *is* represented among the carved art at Göbekli Tepe. It is very likely the identity of at least three "predators" or "quadrupeds" represented by 3-D statues found at the site, which are today on display at the Şanlıurfa archaeological museum. That said, it is the fox that predominates among the carved art seen in the enclosures, especially on the inner faces of the central pillars. It was this realization, along with the large number of faunal remains belonging to the red fox found at the site, that prompted archaeozo-ologist Joris Peters and Klaus Schmidt to conclude that "a specific worship of foxes may be reflected here."[12]

The reason behind this noticeable switch from wolf to fox, both of which were forms of the cosmic trickster and the star Alcor in Ursa Major, is easily explained. Whereas the wolf was important to the reindeer hunters of the East European Plain, the fox appears to have played a cosmological role among the Eastern Gravettian peoples of both Central Europe and the Russian Plain. The fox was also important among the Natufian communities of the Levant. Here the bones and teeth of the red fox have often been identified among the faunal remains found at occupation sites.[13]

It was arguably for similar reasons that the fox and wolf were interchange-able in their role as cosmic trickster, since the animals meant different things to different cultures in different localities. In ancient Egyptian tradition, for example, the trickster god is Seth, whose animistic form is the *fenekh,* or desert fox, while for the Dogon of Mali in West Africa the trickster is Ogo, the pale fox.

The cosmic trickster, in all its forms, whether as the wolf or fox (or, indeed, the dog, dragon, lion, or any other type of animal) has the potential to quite literally bring about the death of the world through the collapse of the sky pole that holds up the heavens. The crucial knowledge of how to prevent this from happening was, quite possibly, the all-important remedy for the catastropho-bia rife among the hunter-gatherers of southeast Anatolia in the wake of the Younger Dryas Boundary impact event.

This then was the knowledge very likely made available to the Epipaleolithic peoples of southeast Anatolia some twelve to thirteen thousand years ago. Those who offered this solution were, most probably, members of a Swiderian ruling elite—hunters, warriors, tool specialists, and shamans—whose journey probably begins as far west as Poland's Vistula River and the obsidian sources of the Carpathian Mountains and ends with their entry into eastern Anatolia sometime during the Younger Dryas mini ice age, perhaps around 10,500 BC or slightly later. They are the face of the Hooded Ones, whose own great ancestors are most likely immortalized in the twelvefold rings of T-shaped pillars, not just within the large enclosures at Göbekli Tepe but also at the various other Pre-Pottery Neolithic sites throughout the *triangle d'or.*

Yet we still need to better understand how exactly the incoming groups of Swiderians were able to convince the Epipaleolithic hunter-gatherers of southeast Anatolia to come together to create the first truly megalithic architecture in human history. How did this happen? It is a matter we address next.

26

STRANGE-LOOKING PEOPLE

Can we imagine the sense of fear and uncertainty that must have existed in the minds of the Epipaleolithic peoples who lived in the vicinity of Göbekli Tepe during the Younger Dryas mini ice age, ca. 10,900–9600 BC? The golden age once spoken about by the elders was now little more than a utopic dream. Since the great fire from the sky and the time of perpetual darkness and constant rain, when the land had sunk beneath the waters, the world had been an entirely different place—cold, bleak, dry, and almost devoid of the herd animals that had provided life and sustenance to so many.

It almost seemed as if the animal spirits that had addressed their every need had now deserted them, perhaps through their misdeeds in the years leading up to this terrible change in the world. What is more, there was no assurance that these great catastrophes would not happen again and again, until finally nothing more was left, only the darkness that prevailed before time began.

Then one day a group of tall, strange-looking people of striking appearance, with elongated heads, long faces, high cheekbones, strong jaws, and prominent brow bridges due to their ancestry as Neanderthal-human hybrids, enter the settlement. Perhaps they wear long, hooded garments made of linen, flax, or hide, as well as belts decorated with strange symbols, leather

215

Figure 26.1. 3-D digital sculpts by artist Russell M. Hossain depicting the Hooded Ones—the Swiderian power elite behind the creation of Göbekli Tepe. Their physical traits are derived from anatomical evidence of the Brünn population and the Sungir burials of Russia, coupled with a knowledge of Swiderian physiognomy, which suggests Neanderthal-human hybridization.

leggings, and boots made out of animal skin (a reconstruction by graphic artist Russell M. Hossain is offered in figure 26.1). They are clearly hunters, with bows and arrows slung over their backs and items of personal adornment gained from the chase. They have necklaces of wolf or fox teeth; strings of beads made from ivory, bone, shell, antler, and stone; as well as insignia of office that hang like medallions around their necks. Alongside them are others, peoples of the region, identified as post-Zarzian shamans, warriors, and tradesmen.

Leaders of the group will have addressed representatives of the community, showing them examples of exotic materials such as obsidian from Bingöl and Lake Van and flint from farther afield. They might have offered to supply these and other valuable commodities, and then, after gaining the community's trust, the hooded strangers will have revealed the true purpose of their mission. Their sky magic had successfully combated the baleful influences of the canine trickster, who had attempted to destroy the world at the time of the great fire from the sky. This knowledge they would now pass on at a price. However, to successfully bind the cosmic trickster and ensure the future stability of the sky pole that supported the heavens, the community would have to give up their hunting lifestyles and learn to work together to put into practice this powerful magic.

COMMUNITY NETWORKING

The chances are that this incoming group, of Swiderian descent, visited other Epipaleolithic communities as well, offering exotic materials to their inhabitants while at the same time spreading their potent message and showing their control and influence over the cosmic trickster, perhaps by predicting the appearance of short-period comets. Eventually the Hooded Ones gained control of each and every one of the settlements they entered. When simple exchanges did not work, open conflict might have ensued, although very likely the strangers set existing allies against confrontational groups or tribes to quell any unrest.

This then was very likely the beginning of a type of regional supremacy instigated by the incoming power elite to bring about the building projects that would eventually lead to the creation of major cult centers such as Göbekli Tepe. These stone sanctuaries would function as axes mundi, terrestrial turning points of the heavens, their central pillars acting as gateways or portals to a perceived sky world existing in the direction of the constellation of Cygnus. From these enclosures rites of birth, death, and rebirth would be enacted and the baleful influence of comets countered by shamans.

THE WALLS OF JERICHO

How exactly the ruling elite might have convinced the indigenous peoples to create monumental architecture on such a grand scale remains a mystery. Fear is the most obvious answer—fear that it would all happen again if they did *not* create these monuments in exactly the fashion prescribed. Yet as Klaus Schmidt is at pains to point out, nothing like Göbekli Tepe existed anywhere else in the world at this time. That said, monumental architecture *was* being built contemporary to the construction of Göbekli Tepe 420 miles (675 kilometers) away at Jericho, in what is today the Palestinian territories.

A Natufian site existed at Jericho during the Younger Dryas period, but it was not until the arrival of a Pre-Pottery Neolithic A culture that the place was transformed into a major town complex. Very quickly the inhabitants felt the need to surround the 10-acre (4 hectare) settlement with a stone wall 10 feet (3 meters) thick and 13 feet (4 meters) high, which extended around the entire occupational mound for a distance of nearly half a mile (800 meters).

In addition to the great wall, the Jericho inhabitants constructed an enormous stone tower 33 feet (10 meters) in diameter and 28 feet (8.5 meters) high, accessed through a west-facing doorway that connected with a stone staircase of twenty-two steps.

As well as the almighty stone tower and perimeter wall, a gigantic ditch was cut out of the limestone bedrock around the outside of the settlement. This was 9 feet deep (2.75 meters), 27 feet wide (8 meters), and more than half a mile (over 800 meters) long, with one prehistorian describing it, aptly, as "a considerable feat in the absence of metal tools."[1]

Clearly, something major was occurring at Jericho. The inhabitants seemed eager to keep something out, and it was not simply wild animals or the elements. An aggressor lurked out there somewhere, who was perceived as a potential threat to the well-being and lifestyle of the Jericho population, which numbered in the hundreds.

The existence of sites such as Jericho tells us that the capability to super-size monuments and structures *was* present among the Pre-Pottery Neolithic peoples of the Fertile Crescent at this time. Yet clearly, before the construction of Göbekli Tepe and Jericho, the motivation to create large-scale stone buildings for specific magico-religious purposes was simply not present. Something then changed, and all the indications are that the hunter-gatherers of southeast Anatolia and the Levantine corridor were responding to events happening in their world, and in the opinion of the author that was the Younger Dryas Boundary impact event and the incredible state of fear it left in the world's human population in its aftermath. However, even then it had taken the intrusion of a powerful elite of European descent to inspire the creation of monumental architecture with the intent of curbing wide-scale catastrophobia once and for all.

SCHMIDT AND THE SWIDERIANS

As controversial as these theories might seem, even Klaus Schmidt has had his eye on the Swiderians as being in some way instrumental in what was going on in southeast Anatolia at the commencement of the Pre-Pottery Neolithic age. Not only does he acknowledge the similarity between the Natufian gazelle hunters and the "reindeer hunters of the North,"[2] that is, those in Europe, and admit that "perhaps there was some kind of connection or communication between the societies of Turkey and those around the Black Sea and the Crimea,"[3] but in a paper written for the journal *Neo-lithics* in 2002, he even names the Swiderians[4] when he writes:

> The late Paleolithic Swiderian reindeer hunters of eastern Europe had a similar hunting strategy [to the Pre-Pottery Neolithic peoples of the Upper Euphrates] using the seasonal wandering of reindeer and their crossing of big rivers such as the Vistula (Weichsel).[5]

Schmidt obviously recognizes something of the European hunting tradition in the Pre-Pottery Neolithic world that existed in the lead-up to the construction of Göbekli Tepe and other religious centers in southeast Anatolia during the tenth millennium BC. He singles out the Swiderians as an example of these hunting strategies, when he could have mentioned the Hamburgian-Ahrenburgian cultures of North Germany, the Brommian-Lyngby cultures of Denmark and Scandinavia, or indeed any one of a number of other Paleolithic hunting traditions that thrived in Europe toward the end of the Upper Paleolithic age. Why? Was it that he had just read an article on the Swiderian culture and wanted simply to use them as an example of this hunting strategy, or does he too have a sense of their presence at Göbekli Tepe?

The greatest clue is in the German archaeologist's suggestion that "perhaps there was some kind of connection or communication between the societies of Turkey and those around the Black Sea and the Crimea."[6] When he said these words to osteoarchaeologist and TV presenter Dr. Alice Roberts, he almost certainly had in mind the incursions of the Polish Swiderian tradition into the Crimean Highlands, immediately above the Black Sea. A simple boat journey along its eastern coast, or a gradual migration overland through the Caucasus Mountains and the Armenian Highlands, would have brought these European hunters directly into contact with the Epipaleolithic peoples of southeast Anatolia, and Schmidt knows this very well. However, I suspect that until now he has found nothing concrete at Göbekli Tepe that might help confirm these surmises, despite the fact that worked flints have been found that are more-or-less *identical* to Swiderian tanged points.

THE END OF GÖBEKLI TEPE

The world of Göbekli Tepe remains truly bizarre, and so far we have only been able to scratch the surface of what was really going on here nearly twelve thousand years ago. Having started with grand structures featuring monoliths 18 feet (5.5 meters) high, the Göbekli builders ended up settling for bathroom-size rooms, with standing stones no more than a few feet in height and communal benches like something you might find in a family-size Jacuzzi.

It seems clear that whatever incentive there had been to remain loyal to a particular style and design gradually diminished as the centuries rolled by. It is almost as if the Göbekli builders, although still committed to following an established tradition, which included the erection of anthropomorphic T-shaped pillars, were now downsizing in their choice of architectural styles. By the end they were simply going through the motions, without the original motivation being there any more.

It has been suggested that the entire complex at Göbekli Tepe was buried hurriedly around 8000 BC, as if there was some urgency involved. It has even been speculated that the large enclosures were covered over to protect them from another cataclysm, either a comet strike or some kind of plasma-induced event, brought about by a coronal mass ejection from the sun.[7]

As attractive as such disaster scenarios might seem, there is at present nothing that has been discovered at Göbekli Tepe that might support such claims. The site's final decommissioning involved the remaining sanctuaries, cult buildings, shrines, and other structures being buried beneath thousands of tons of imported earth, quarry chippings, and refuse matter. Yet even then, very occasionally, the heads of stones would be exposed by soil erosion and tilling of the land. The rest, however, remained encased within the tell's swollen belly for a full ten thousand years until Klaus Schmidt realized the site's incredible importance in 1994. We owe him a great debt for bringing back to life this unimaginable stone complex that reveals to us the mind-set of our ancestors during an age of uncertainty and change.

Yet we cannot end the story here, for even after the final abandonment of Göbekli Tepe its legacy lived on, and there is every reason to believe that the role its founders, *and maintainers,* played in the instigation of the Neolithic revolution was preserved in the myths and legends of the cultures that thrived in these same regions during much later times.

Some of these ancient accounts are still with us today, and it is time now to see how exactly they address the strange world that existed in southeast Anatolia and the Armenian Highlands during the formative years of the Neolithic era. As we shall see, they seem to preserve dim echoes of the Younger Dryas Boundary impact event and the existence of the Hooded Ones—the Swiderian elite whose memory is encapsulated in the rings of T-shaped pillars and twin central monoliths at Göbekli Tepe.

For the next part of our journey the author would like to ask the reader to excuse him as he now switches from a third-person narrative to, where necessary, a first-person delivery that much better fits the quest of discovery that befell him in the wake of an extraordinary sequence of events that will culminate with the finding of Eden itself.

PART FIVE

Convergence

27

IN THE GARDEN OF EDEN

The overwhelming aroma of incense hung heavy in the air of the church's darkened interior. Low chanting, almost like a murmuring, filled the open space, where lamps burned, a few candles flickered, and the soft light pouring in through the high windows revealed a strange but compelling sight.

Illuminated on the cold stone floor, close to the center of this archaic house of God, was a group of Armenian monks, dressed from head to foot in thick, dark garments. They were the source of the melancholic chanting that continued unabated, like some primal tone, essential to the success of their ritual actions. It was unlike any singing ever heard before, even in the strange, secluded monasteries of Mount Athos in Greece. Their combined voices made the whole place seem like a slowly building powerhouse of divine energy.

The monks were engaged in a religious ceremony, yet one without any congregation. It seemed to involve the elevation of an object high above their heads, as if offering it up for God to acknowledge its presence here in this monastery. It was an act that had been performed for countless generations to celebrate the gift of eternal life, given to our First Parents in the Garden of Eden, but taken away from them at the time of the Fall.

*For these monks believed that their monastery was located on the very
spot where the terrestrial Paradise could once be found. It was an unerring conviction that, although they could never have realized it themselves,
was linked integrally with the location, just a couple of hundred miles
away, of the hidden world that would one day be uncovered at Göbekli
Tepe, the site of the oldest temple in the world.*

I t was an unprompted dream I awoke from on Wednesday, April 20,
2011, triggered no doubt by the fact that I had just agreed with the publisher to write a book on the story of Göbekli Tepe and its impact on myth,
religion, and the origins of civilization. I had already submitted a detailed
synopsis and chapter breakdown and knew pretty well what I was going to
write.

Yet now I sensed that something was missing, a major piece of the jigsaw
that my vivid dream suggested I would find if I looked in the right places.
Somewhere in eastern Turkey, not far from the huge inland sea named Lake
Van, a couple of hundred miles east of Göbekli Tepe, was, I felt, a church and
monastery where the monks believed that the landscape thereabouts was the
actual Garden of Eden. These were thoughts now going through my mind,
even though twenty years of research into the origins of the Genesis account of
the Fall and its geographical relationship to eastern Turkey, for books such as
From the Ashes of Angels (1996) and *Gods of Eden* (1998), had failed to uncover
anything even remotely like this tradition.

TEMPLE IN EDEN

There seemed only one thing to do, and this was for me to reexamine the evidence that had led me to conclude that eastern Turkey, the former Greater
Armenia, or Armenia Major, was the true site of the Garden of Eden, and to
see if I could turn up any new leads that might throw further light on this
puzzling mystery. This seemed especially important to do, as in 2009 there
had been reports that Professor Klaus Schmidt had told British journalist Sean
Thomas (writing under the pseudonym Tom Knox) that "Göbekli Tepe was
not the Garden of Eden: it is a temple in Eden."[1]

Although Klaus Schmidt told me in September 2012 that Sean Thomas
had misquoted him (the German archaeologist had actually said that Göbekli

Tepe was an Eden-*like* place, not "a temple in Eden"), the story became a news sensation, with headlines such as "Do These Mysterious Stones Mark the Site of the Garden of Eden?"[2] appearing worldwide. The German archaeologist obviously played down the matter, and eventually it did all die down. (I actually apologized to Schmidt as it was me who'd given Sean Thomas instructions on how to get out there, after he became interested in Göbekli Tepe through reading material I'd written on the subject.)

So if Göbekli Tepe was not the Garden of Eden, where was it really located, and how did the Genesis story of Adam and Eve and the Fall fit into the emergence of the Pre-Pottery Neolithic world of southeast Anatolia?

THE EXISTENCE OF PARADISE

It was really not until medieval times that people started looking for the Garden of Eden. Prior to this time it was considered a paradisiacal realm created by God for the benefit of our First Parents, Adam and Eve, who had lived in a state of perpetual bliss and happiness, not knowing death, pain, or hunger. Yet when they committed the original sin by eating of the Tree of Knowledge of Good and Evil, and knew immediately that they were naked, God removed Paradise from the reach not only of our First Parents, but also of humanity as a whole. Never again would humans gaze upon the garden until the Final Judgment, when all righteous souls would be reunited with God in the heavenly Paradise. In other words, there was no point looking for Eden as it had no material presence in the mundane world. In fact, so detached from the physical world was it considered to be that some medieval theologians and church leaders thought that God had removed it to the vicinity of the Moon.[3]

Even if Paradise *had* existed in a material sense, there was no way it was accessible to humankind. It existed as a place beyond physical existence, almost like a parallel world, guarded by angels called cherubim, whose flaming swords protected its entrances with an impenetrable wall of fire. This was the manner in which Paradise was portrayed on medieval maps of the world—as a walled garden surrounded by fire, existing just beyond the eastern limits of the Eurasian landmass. Adam and Eve, the Serpent of Temptation, the Tree of Good and Evil, and the cherubim with flaming swords would all be present, as if to remind the onlooker where humanity might now be if the original sin had not been committed.

Those church leaders or theologians who *did* propose that the Garden of Eden might once have had a physical existence would be informed that if this were the case, then it would have been destroyed in the Great Flood. According to the Genesis account, this all-encompassing deluge engulfed the entire earth, right to the highest mountaintops. Only Noah and his family survived by taking to the ark and eventually finding the sole piece of land that God had set aside to remain above water, and it was from here that the world began anew.

THE GREAT REFORM

These were the generally accepted views that the Church of Rome held regarding the existence of Paradise, and very few scholars or church leaders dared challenge these opinions for fear of being branded as heretics. It was not until the religious reforms of the sixteenth century and the birth of Lutheranism and Protestantism that attitudes began to change regarding the concept of Paradise. This was helped by the discovery of the American continent, which confirmed that the known world was not surrounded by an expanse of water, beyond which there was nothing, a realization that led eventually to the abandonment of the long-held belief that the world was flat. The earth was a globe, and every part of it could be mapped and explored without fear of falling off into an abyss that existed beyond God's creation. So everything in the world became more tangible and fixed, and even the inspired word of God transmitted through the prophet Moses to create the Pentateuch, the first five books of the Old Testament, became subject to question for the first time.

Church leaders, travelers, and cartographers began now to find firm geographical clues in the Bible that revealed the true location of the Garden of Eden, which many now concluded had existed in the Bible lands themselves. According to the book of Genesis, as well as various apocryphal and pseudepigraphical works of Jewish, Christian, and Muslim origin, the Garden of Eden was watered by a single stream that took its rise from a spring or fountain that emerged from the base of the Tree of Life. After exiting the garden, the stream then split into four heads that became the sources of four great rivers (see figure 27.1), each of which are named and described in chapter two of the book of Genesis (I shall quote from *Young's Literal Translation of the Bible,* which exactly reproduces the original Jewish and Greek text, so that nothing is lost in translation):

And a river is going out from Eden to water the garden, and from thence it is parted, and hath become four chief [rivers]; the name of the one [is] Pison, it [is] that which is surrounding the whole land of the Havilah where the gold [is], and the gold of that land [is] good, there [in Havilah, is] the bdolach and the shoham stone; and the name of the second river [is] Gibon [or Gihon], it [is] that which is surrounding the whole land of Cush; and the name of the third river [is] Hiddekel, it [is] that which is going east of Asshur; and the fourth river is Phrat. (Gen. 2:10–14)[4]

Figure 27.1. Adam and Eve in the terrestrial Paradise, from the Hereford Mappa mundi (Map of the World), ca. 1300 AD. Note the four rivers of Paradise, each one named, which emerge from a fountain of four heads positioned in front of the Tree of Knowledge of Good and Evil, complete with the Serpent of Temptation.

Identifying these four rivers has always been key to locating the terrestrial Paradise, and two of them are easily found. The last one mentioned, the Phrat (Kurdish Firat, Armenian Aratsani, Greek and Roman Arsanias), is the Euphrates, the longest river in Western Asia. It has two main branches, the Kara Şu, or Western Euphrates, and the Murad Şu, or Eastern Euphrates, which rise, respectively, to the north and northwest of Lake Van in the Armenian Highlands. They then snake their way through southeast Turkey and merge together before passing into northern Syria and entering the Mesopotamia Plain in what is today Iraq. Just before emptying into the Persian Gulf, the Euphrates joins the Tigris River.

There can be little question that the Euphrates was one of the four rivers of Paradise, and this information alone should always have been enough to establish the geographical position of Eden as being somewhere along its course. Yet we find again and again that this was often not the case, with the Garden of Eden being placed not just in the Bible lands but also in every other part of the ancient and new world. Ceylon, the Americas, equatorial Africa, Australia, and even the North Pole have all been proposed as the setting for the terrestrial Paradise, based on arguments that seem more related to personal theories and the beauty of the place than to the facts presented in the Genesis account.

THE HIDDEKEL

Another river of Paradise easy to identify is the Hiddekel, which flows to the "east of Asshur"; that is, Assyria, in what is today northern Iraq. This is unquestionably the River Tigris (from the Persian *tigra,* meaning "arrow"), originally called the Hiddekel (from the Akkadian *id Idikla,* "the river of Idikla"), which does indeed flow through the eastern parts of the ancient kingdom of Assyria. The river, which takes its rise northeast of the city of Diyarbakır, immediately south of the main sources of the Euphrates, is fed by a series of tributaries that rise in the Eastern Taurus Mountains of eastern Turkey.

The Tigris then leaves Turkey and flows southeastward through Iraq, parallel with the Euphrates on its western side. The two rivers bend toward each other in the vicinity of Baghdad, close to the site of the ancient city of Babylon. Yet instead of coming together they run parallel for a few miles before parting again, only to merge finally into one giant estuary that empties into the Persian Gulf.

So if both the Euphrates and the Tigris form two of the four rivers of Paradise, this should confirm that the Garden of Eden was either where they take their rise in the Eastern Taurus Mountains and Armenian Highlands or where they come together in southern Iraq; no other possible location should even be considered based on the evidence provided by the book of Genesis. Indeed, the matter can be pinned down still further by pointing out that the Garden of Eden was situated at the *source* of the four rivers, meaning that the terrestrial Paradise can only have been located in historical Armenia, modern eastern Turkey. Where exactly is provided by the identities of the remaining two rivers.

GIHON AND THE LAND OF CUSH

Identifying the Gibon or, more commonly, the Gihon, another of the rivers of Paradise, is slightly more of a challenge, although the fact that it is said to flow "around the whole land of Cush" is a major clue. Usually, the land of Cush is identified with an ancient kingdom of this name in Ethiopia, the reason the word *Ethiopia* appears instead of *Cush* in the King James Bible. It is also why the Gihon is identified with the River Nile, which rises in Ethiopia and was called the Geion by the Coptic Christians of Egypt.[5]

Yet these identifications are fundamentally wrong, and very misleading too. Cush, or Kush, is more likely to be a kingdom named in Assyrian inscriptions as Kusu. It was the land of a people called the Kusai, who lived "in the celebrated hill country to the north of Syria, whence came the Kusai breed of horses."[6] Indeed, it was apparently from Kusu that the Assyrians obtained their horses.[7]

English Assyriologist George Smith (1840–1876), in *The Chaldean Account of Genesis* (1876), notes that in the book of Genesis the father of Nimrod, the builder of the Tower of Babel, is given as Cush, and that this too might be an allusion to the land of Kusu.[8] Nimrod is a legendary figure of Armenian folk history said to have cast the patriarch Abraham into a fiery furnace because he would not bow down to pagan idols. This is supposed to have taken place in the ancient city of Edessa, modern Şanlıurfa, celebrated as the birthplace of Abraham. It is also, as we have seen, just 8 miles (13 kilometers) away from Göbekli Tepe, a connection that should not be forgotten. If Kusu was north of Assyria, then it must have been located somewhere in the vicinity of Lake Van and the Armenian Highlands.

Historical Armenia was overrun by the Turkish Ottoman Empire in the mid-fifteenth century, and although it kept its cultural, religious, and geographical identity until the twentieth century, the entire country was wiped off the face of the map following the Armenian Genocide of 1915. In antiquity, however, it was a kingdom in its own right, with the separate kingdom of Armenia Minor to its west. Today the modern Republic of Armenia, the former Soviet Armenia, is the only remaining part of Greater Armenia (or Armenia Major), with the rest of "historical Armenia" now being simply the eastern provinces of Turkey.

Back in the first millennium BC, at the height of the Assyrian Empire, the kingdom of Armenia was famous for its horses. The Greek geographer Strabo reported that it was very good for "horse pasturing" and that "Nesaean horses," favored by the Persian kings, were bred there.[9] Moreover, Strabo recorded that every year the Persian king was sent by way of a tribute from Armenia twenty thousand foals.[10] He noted also that: "The passion for riding and the care of horses characterize the Thessalians, and are common to Armenians and Medes."[11] The Medes were the inhabitants of Media, a kingdom located on the southern shores of the Caspian Sea, northeast of Armenia, in what is today Azerbaijan and northwest Iran.

So the land of Kusu, where Kusai horses came from, was almost certainly a reference to the Armenian Highlands, which makes sense, for the Gihon River has long been identified with the Araxes (the modern Aras) River. Along with a major branch of the Western Euphrates, the Araxes takes its rise on Bingöl Mountain, the center of the obsidian trade, located some 30 miles (48 kilometers) south of the city of Erzurum. It then flows eastward, past the base of Mount Ararat, joining eventually another great river called the Kur before emptying finally into the Caspian Sea. Its mouth is near Baku, the capital and largest city of Azerbaijan, ancient Media, close to Gobustan, the site of the incredible rock art described in chapter 23.

Where exactly the name Gihon came from is unclear, although during the Arab invasion of the Caucasus in the eighth century the river was known as the Gaihun,[12] with nineteenth-century Persian dictionaries referring to the Araxes as the Jichon-Aras.[13] Moreover, American theologian and educationist John McClintock (1814–1870) recorded in his multivolume biblical encyclopedia that the Gihon "to this day bears the same name among the Arabs. This [i.e., the Araxes] is a large river in Armenia Major, which takes its rise from a number of sources in Mount Abus (the present Bin-Gol), nearly in the centre of the space between the east and west branches of the Euphrates."[14]

Strangely, not only was the Araxes identified with the Gihon by Dutch philologist and scholar Hadrian Reland (1676–1718) more than three hundred years ago, but he also proposed that the land of Cush, through which it passed, was "the country of the Cussaei of the ancients,"[15] a perceptive observation that is almost certainly correct.

So from the evidence provided so far we can be pretty certain that if one specific location *is* being identified as the site of the terrestrial Paradise then it is the Armenian Highlands, where the Euphrates and Araxes take their rise, with the source of the Tigris just a short distance to the south.

IN SEARCH OF THE PISON

The final river of Paradise, called the Pison, or Pishon, is a little more tricky to identify, so the clues offered by the book of Genesis are worth examining a second time: "the name of the one [is] Pison, it [is] that which is surrounding the whole land of the Havilah where the gold [is], and the gold of that land [is] good, there [is] the bdolach and the shoham stone."

To begin with, the land of Havilah is completely unknown, although Havilah as a personal name also appears in the book of Genesis, where it is cited, like Nimrod, as being a son of Cush (Gen. 10:9). If these names are, as seems possible, references both to kingdoms and their founders, then the fact that Cush is synonymous with the land of Kusu, an ancient name for Armenia, suggests that this is where we should look for the Pison River.

THE LAND OF GOLD

Adding weight to this conclusion is the fact that Armenia was well known for its gold, as is recorded by Strabo, who in the section of his *Geography* on Armenia speaks of the gold mines of "Syspiritis and Caballa, to where Menon was sent by Alexander with soldiers, and he was led up to them by the natives."[16] Dutch chemist and science historian Robert James Forbes proposed that the mines of "Syspiritis and Caballa" were on the Black Sea near Batumi in southwest Georgia, the site of Colchis, legendary land of the Golden Fleece.[17]

It is an interesting theory. However, the site of Caballa is completely lost to us. Syspiritis, on the other hand, is a little more easy to track down, for although some classical scholars like to see its gold mines as existing somewhere in the vicinity of the ancient city of Erzurum, north of Bingöl Mountain, Syspiritis was most likely close to Adiabenê.[18] This is a former kingdom and Assyrian city (the modern Arbil, or Erbil) located between the Upper Zab and Lower Zab rivers of northern Iraq, which flow down from the direction of the Thospites, or Arsene Lake,[19] ancient names for Lake Van, and merge eventually with the Tigris River. Interesting in this respect is the fact that Robert Forbes mentions that "other deposits [of gold] known are south of Lake Van,"[20] doubly confirming that Syspiritis is to be looked for here, and not farther north.[21]

SEAT ON THE RIVER OF EDEN

This information becomes a major clue to the identity of the last river of Paradise, for the ancient Assyrian Church, also known as the Nestorian Church, recognized the Greater Zab as the River Pison. This information comes from the seat of their patriarch and head bishop, or Catholicos, located from the seventeenth century until the Assyrian Genocide of 1915 at Kotchanes (modern Konak) in the Hakkari. This is a remote region in the foothills of the Zagros Mountains in the southeast corner of Turkey, close to the borders with Iraq and Iran. Here the patriarch would sign off his letters "from my cell on the River of the Garden of Eden."[22]

Valuable clues like this should not be taken lightly, as the Assyrian Church was one of the oldest forms of Christianity existing in the region, being founded as early as the first century.[23] This seems to affirm that the land of Havilah, through which the Pison flowed, was an area defined by the course of the Greater Zab, which embraces the Turkish provinces of Van and Hakkari, as well as the Iraqi governorate of Arbil.

The "bdolach" that we are told was found in the land of Havilah can easily be identified as a resinous exudation produced by shrubs of the *Astragalus* genus, called gum tragacanth or astragalus manna.[24] This was collected in the Mush, Erzurum, and Lake Van districts of Greater Armenia[25] and then transported to the city of Mosul, close to where the Greater Zab joins the Tigris.[26] However, the province most commonly associated with the *Astragalus* shrub is the Hakkari,[27] the suspected heartland of the land of Havilah.

As for the shoham stone mentioned in the Genesis account, this is probably a reference either to onyx (its usual identity), which is found in the Ararat district of Armenia, or to obsidian, which was very often confused with onyx in ancient times. Having made all these statements, there is one further tradition regarding the identity of the Pison that, due to its compelling yet conflicting implications, is best left until chapter 29.

RELAND'S CHOICE

The Genesis account of the Garden of Eden indicates, very clearly, that if it *did* exist as a physical location, then it was to be found somewhere in the vicinity of Lake Van and the Armenian Highlands, where the sources of the four rivers of Paradise take their course (see figure 27.2). It is a conclusion that anyone can achieve, simply by following the clues on offer, and it was something that Dutch

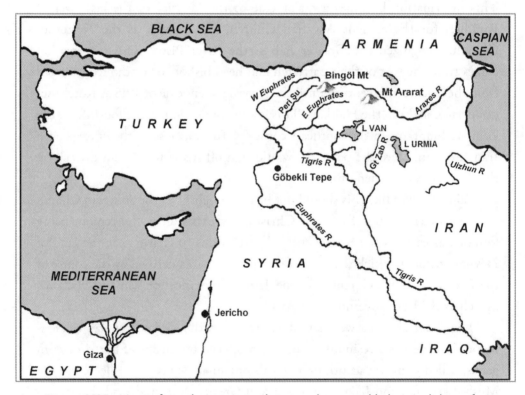

Figure 27.2. Map of southwest Asia showing the most likely candidates for the four rivers of Paradise: the Euphrates (Phrat), Tigris (Hiddekel), Araxes (Gihon), and Greater Zab (Pison). The modern trend in identifying the Pison with the Uizhun River of Iran is rife with problems due to its great distance from the sources of the other three rivers.

scholar Hadrian Reland worked out at the beginning of the eighteenth century.[28] However, having identified the Euphrates, Tigris, and Araxes as three of the rivers of Paradise, he chose to correlate the final one, the Pison, with the Phasis, a river mentioned in ancient Greek sources, which is usually associated with the Rion, or Rioni, which rises in Georgia and empties into the Black Sea.

Choosing the Phasis as the Pison pulls the imaginary epicenter for the terrestrial Paradise much farther north, toward the northern extremes of the Armenian Highlands, whereas identifying the Pison with the Greater Zab places the epicenter much farther south, close to the northern edge of the plain of Mush, which separates the Armenian Highlands from the Eastern Taurus Mountains to the south (see figure 27.3).

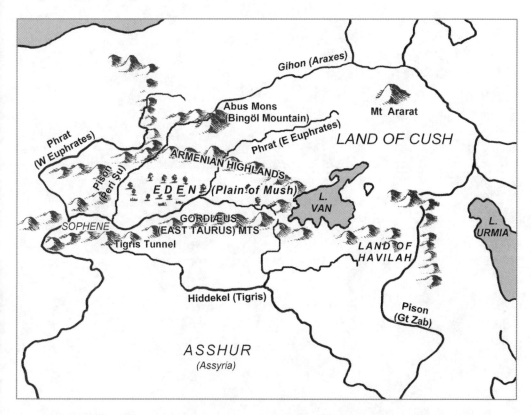

Figure 27.3. Map showing sources of the four rivers of Paradise with their epicenter in the vicinity of the Mush Plain in eastern Turkey. Note the locations of the land of Cush, through which the Gihon flowed, and the land of Havilah, associated with the Pison River. Note also the Peri Şu, or Gail ("Wolf") River, which in Armenian tradition is identified with the Pison (see chapter 29).

Was this where I would find the Armenian monastery where, according to my dream, the monks believed they served God in the Garden of Eden itself? As we shall see next, the Mush Plain becomes one of the most likely candidates for the site of the terrestrial Paradise, information that, although available long ago, has not stopped theologians and scholars from locating Eden everywhere but where the four rivers of Paradise take their rise.

28

THE FOUNTAIN
OF PARADISE

The book of Genesis's description of the four rivers of Paradise indicates very strongly that the Garden of Eden was located in historical Armenia, modern-day eastern Turkey, with the epicenter being somewhere in the vicinity of the enigmatic plain of Mush, a vast expanse of congealed lava, created across tens of thousands of years by the outpouring of the various volcanoes that surround it. After crumbling to dust, the lava was transformed into a rich soil that has made Mush one of the most fertile regions in eastern Turkey, noted in the past for its wheat and tobacco. Vineyards were also once numerous, with a fair wine apparently being produced.[1]

THE PLAIN OF MUSH

The plain itself lies at a height of just over 4,100 feet (1,250 meters) above sea level and is approximately 40 miles (64 kilometers) in length from east to west and 10 miles (16 kilometers) broad. Visible at its eastern end is the extinct volcano Nemrut Dağ (Mount Nimrod), which takes the form of a gigantic caldera half a mile (800 meters) in diameter, within which is an enormous crescent-shaped lake. Obsidian from Nemrut Dağ has been found at Göbekli Tepe.

The Murad Şu, or Eastern Euphrates, cuts right across the plain, dividing it in two, before vanishing into a narrow gorge at its western end. This creates a pass through the Eastern Taurus Mountains, along which the somewhat hazardous road to Diyarbakır winds its way. This was the old obsidian route from Bingöl and Lake Van to the various proto-Neolithic and Pre-Pottery Neolithic centers, such as Hallan Çemi, Çayönü, Nevalı Çori, and, of course, Göbekli Tepe.

Another gorge at the plain's southeast corner forms a pass through the Eastern Taurus range, providing access to the university city of Bitlis (ancient Baghesh) and Lake Van while another pass, carved out by the Murad Şu, opens the way north toward Bingöl, both the town and the mountain, beyond which is the old Armenian city of Karin, modern-day Erzurum.

MONASTIC FOUNDATIONS

Some miles to the northwest of the town of Mush, the capital of the province of the same name, are the remains of Surb Karapet, or more correctly Surb Hovhannes Karapet Vank, the Monastery of Saint John the Baptist. Before its destruction at the time of the Armenian Genocide in 1915, it was a major place of pilgrimage, with Christians coming here from all over Armenia to venerate holy relics belonging to John the Baptist. According to tradition, Armenia's great crusading churchman Gregory the Illuminator built the monastery on the site of important pagan temples destroyed by him and his army at the beginning of the fourth century. Today, Surb Karapet, which from old pictures looks more like a fairy-tale castle than a monastery, is little more than a few pathetic walls in the middle of a bustling Kurdish village, which has long since lost interest in its rich Armenian heritage.

Apparently, several monasteries were once to be found on the plain of Mush, which formed part of a royal kingdom called Taron, or Turuberan, where Armenian Christianity had its beginnings even before the arrival of Gregory the Illuminator in the fourth century.[2] I could find information about just one other notable monastic ruin in the area, and this was Surb Arakelots (Holy Apostles), located in a mountain valley southeast of the town of Mush. However, an examination of what was known about Surb Karapet and Surb Arakelots, or, indeed, any of the other monasteries that once existed in the region, did not in any way feel similar to what I had seen and experienced in my dream.

THE TREE OF LIFE

Yet the more I recalled the strange ceremony taking place inside the gloomy church interior, the more I became convinced not only that the Eden monastery existed, but that the monks there had been elevating an object of great spiritual value. It had been removed from a plain, wooden box that acted as a reliquary (a relic holder). As to the nature of the relic, this seemed to be a blackened piece of wood, like a short, round section of a tree branch, some 2.5 inches (6 centimeters) in diameter and 7 to 8 inches (18 to 20 centimeters) in length.

Initially, I thought the monks might have identified this relic as a piece of the Tree of Knowledge of Good and Evil, which the Genesis account tells us was to be found in the Garden of Eden. However, this did not sit right with me, and very quickly I realized that I had this wrong. The relic was in fact thought to be a fragment of the Tree of Life, the *other* tree in the Garden of Eden. That felt absolutely right, especially as I had seen it being elevated during a ritual that seemed to celebrate life itself.

The monks, I suspected, believed that simply possessing this holy relic invoked a sense of the eternal life that Adam and Eve experienced before their expulsion from the Garden of Eden. The couple's existence was sustained through their proximity to the Tree of Life, which, situated within the garden, was seen as a powerhouse of divine energy that transcended the normal laws of nature. Yet without the benefits of the Tree of Life, Adam and Eve, along with all their descendants, were doomed to suffer mortality in all its ugly ways, a just punishment for committing the original sin, or so the book of Genesis tells us.

That the monks of the monastery drew some kind of spiritual power from what they saw as a fragment of the Tree of Life made absolute sense. Combining the religious potency of this relic with the fact that the monastery was thought to have existed in the Garden of Eden would only have increased their faith in what they believed they were achieving here in this spiritual powerhouse. No wonder I could so vividly recall this archaic ritual that must have taken place before the assumed destruction of the monastery at the time of the Armenian Genocide.

I sensed strongly that the monastery in question existed somewhere in the vicinity of the plain of Mush. It was a perfect setting for the Garden of Eden, especially as high mountains surround it on all sides and from these come streams that feed all four rivers of Paradise.

FINDING OTHER EDENS

Despite this information, the most often quoted solution regarding the where-abouts of the Garden of Eden stems from the somewhat puzzling conclusion, first proposed by influential French theologian and pastor John Calvin (1509–1564), that the terrestrial Paradise was located in the vicinity of Basrah, in southern Iraq. Here the Euphrates and Tigris rivers were once thought to have come together and then parted again to form all four rivers of Paradise. The fact of the matter is that although these two great rivers do indeed converge here to form the Shatt al-Arab waterway, into which flows Iran's Karun River (which some take to be the Gihon[3]), this hardly fits the evidence offered for the location of the Garden of Eden in the book of Genesis.

Others have suggested that the four "heads" of the rivers of Paradise refer to their mouths, meaning that we should be looking for the Garden of Eden where the Euphrates and Tigris empty into the Persian Gulf. This has prompted all sorts of complicated theories involving now-vanished rivers, with the most persuasive being that the Pison once ran through Arabia's Wadi al-Rummah, emptying into the Persian Gulf close to the Shatt al-Arab waterway.[4] As far-fetched as these claims might seem, they remain the most popular theo-ries regarding the true site of the Garden of Eden.[5]

More incredible still is the view that the holy city of Jerusalem is the terrestrial Paradise, based on a few brief references in the Old Testament comparing the city to the Garden of Eden, along with a Jewish legend that speaks of Jerusalem as the center of the world.[6] Once again, this is not simply the belief of lay people, but the opinion of theologians and historians, even though Jerusalem is located nowhere near *any* of the easily identifiable rivers of Paradise.

These theories have been put forth despite the fact that Armenian schol-ars have for many years attempted to convince the outside world that the ter-restrial Paradise was located in their historical homeland. Their arguments go unnoticed because they are usually written in Russian Armenian, which very few non-Armenians can read. Even when their work *is* published in English, something is lost in translation, resulting in very few people taking it seriously.[7]

THE REVEREND MARMADUKE CARVER

Yet, as we have seen, Westerners do occasionally conclude that the area around the *sources* of the four rivers of Paradise constitutes the most likely site of the Garden of Eden. Dutch scholar Hadrian Reland worked this out at the beginning of the eighteenth century, although he was certainly not the first to do so. One of the earliest individuals to come to the same conclusion was the rather grandly named Marmaduke Carver (d. 1665), a former rector of Harthill in South Yorkshire. His fascinating work on the subject, entitled *A Discourse of the Terrestrial Paradise, Aiming at a More Probable Discovery of the True Situation of That Happy Place of Our First Parents Habitation,* was published posthumously in 1666, one year after his death.

Having learned that the Reverend Marmaduke Carver had identified the site of the Garden of Eden as Armenia Major, I decided to find out more about the churchman's life and theories, so went in search of him and his book, beginning with his former parish of Harthill, near Sheffield. Yet here, in the local parish church, I found no mention of him, other than his name entered in a long list of rectors from medieval times to the present day.

One thing I did manage to establish was that toward the end of his life Carver had spent much of his time in the city of York, just 60 miles (97 kilometers) from Harthill. Here he had become chaplain to Sir Thomas Osborne (afterward Duke of Leeds), high sheriff of the county, delivering sermons in York Minster, the city's famous cathedral. More significantly, I found that on his death in August 1665 Carver's body had been laid to rest in the south aisle of the cathedral choir.

So after leaving Harthill, I traveled to York Minster, hoping to find some evidence of Carver's gravesite. Yet no evidence of his interment remains today, not even the wall plaque that marked the spot. This was obviously a great disappointment, so after sitting down briefly in the choir area to meditate on what I should do next, I made the decision to visit the York Minster Library, located within the cathedral grounds. Here I was finally able to find out a little more about the fate of Marmaduke Carver's memorial plaque. Originally it had borne an inscription in Latin, written by James Torre, an early historian of the minster, but this had been destroyed during restoration work in 1736. It was subsequently replaced with a new plaque, its inscription now in English. This, however, along with the site of Carver's grave, has since been lost due to subsequent restoration work in the south aisle. Mercifully, both versions of the inscription have been preserved.*[8] As you can see, it is a fitting epitaph to the churchman's life and work, in particular his search for the terrestrial Paradise:

> Reader, if you love piety, if you know how to value learning, you should know what a treasure lies under this stone, Marmaduke Carver, formerly rector of the Church of Harthill, but very well versed in . . . chronology and geography, an accomplished linguist, a fine speaker—the man, to wit, who . . . pointed out to the world the true place of the terrestrial paradise, (yet in death) made of the object of his admonitions, the celestial (paradise) which he recommended to the praise of his hearers to attain which we are filled with great longing. He was translated on this day of August 1665.[9]

During his stay in York, Carver had apparently spent much of his time conducting research for his book in the cathedral library, which is the largest of its kind in the country. It has a collection of around 120,000 volumes, 25,000 of which were printed before 1801, including 115 incunabula (tracts printed before 1501).

So it seemed only fitting that I should find that York Minster Library has two of the only remaining copies of Carver's book in the country. Some cunning persuasion helped overturn the librarian's decision not to allow me to view the title at such short notice, so I sat down ready to read what I hoped would provide me with some valuable insights regarding the true whereabouts of the Garden of Eden. I was not to be disappointed.

THE GREAT FIRE OF LONDON

The small, leather-bound book placed before me on the reading desk felt very special indeed. It was printed in April 1666 by James Flesher of London and sold by one Samuel Thomson "at the Bishop's head in St. Paul's Church-yard" (see figure 28.1). Now, it is important to conjure a vision of the time, for 1666 was the

---

*James Torre's original Latin inscription is as follows: "*Lector si Pietatis amator, si Doctrinae estimator, scias quantus sub hoc lapide thesaurus situs est, Marmaducus Carver, Ecclesiae Hartilluncis Rector, C(h)ronologiae et Geographiae scientissimus, Linguarum peritus, concionando prepotens; hic scilicet, qui cum scriptis ad invidiam usque, verum terrestris paradisi locum orbi monstrasset, ad coelestem quem predicando Auditoribus commendaverat, cujus adeunti ingenti desiderio tenebatur moriendo translatus est, die Aug. 1665.*"

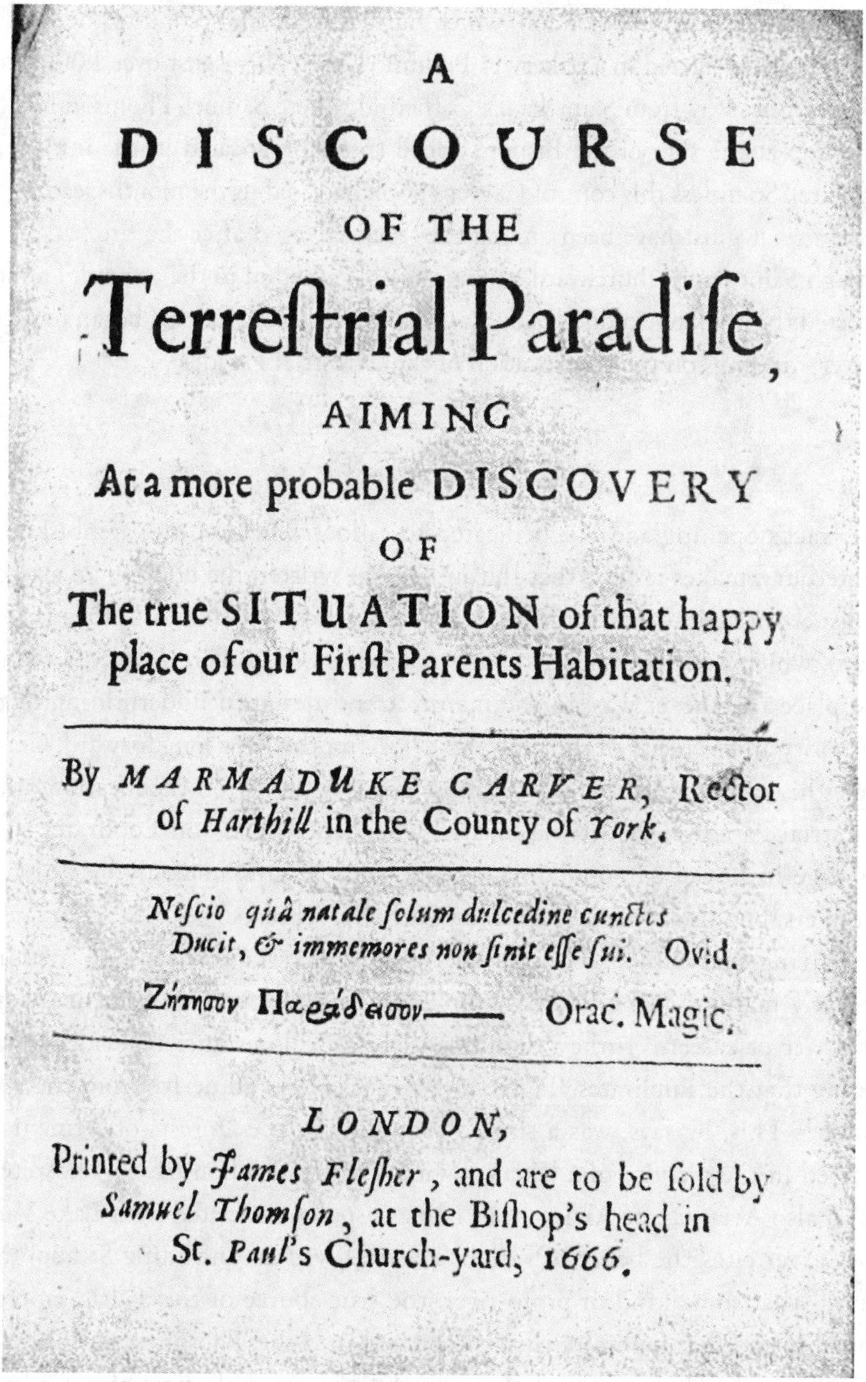

A

DISCOURSE

OF THE

Terreſtrial Paradiſe,

AIMING

At a more probable DISCOVERY

OF

The true SITUATION of that happy
place of our Firſt Parents Habitation.

By *MARMADUKE CARVER*, Rector
of *Harthill* in the County of *York*.

*Neſcio quâ natale ſolum dulcedine cunctis
Ducit, & immemores non ſinit eſſe ſui.* Ovid.

Ζήτησον Παράδεισον —— Orac. Magic.

LONDON,
Printed by *James Fleſher*, and are to be ſold by
Samuel Thomſon, at the Biſhop's head in
St. *Paul*'s Church-yard, *1666*.

Figure 28.1. The cover of *A Discourse of the Terrestrial Paradise*, by the
Reverend Marmaduke Carver, published in London, England, in 1666. It was
arguably the first book to build a solid case for the terrestrial Paradise being
located in historical Armenia.

year of the Great Fire of London, which burned from the second to the fifth of September and started in a bakery in Pudding Lane. This is just over 1,000 yards (1 kilometer) away from Saint Paul's Cathedral, where Samuel Thomson had his bookshop at the sign of the Bishop's Head (probably located in the inn's thoroughfare). So unless this copy of Carver's book had sold in the months leading up to the fire, it must have been among the stock salvaged after the fire had swept through Saint Paul's churchyard, razing the old cathedral to the ground. I almost expected the book to exude a residual aroma of smoke and fire as I began to digest Carver's findings on the true location of the terrestrial Paradise.

A MERE UTOPIA

The tract's opening address, dedicated to Gilbert Sheldon, the archbishop of Canterbury, makes it clear that the author has written the book in an attempt to dispel antiscriptorial thinking, begun in earnest by Martin Luther (1483–1546), which asserted that the Garden of Eden was "a mere *Utopia,* a Fiction of a place that never was, to the manifest and designed undermining of the Authority and Veracity of the Holy Text."[10] After this, in a long forward, Carver makes his case against the current most popular theory on the location of the terrestrial Paradise, that it was located where the Tigris and Euphrates rivers converge in Lower Mesopotamia, a view held, he says, not only by Calvinist reformers, but also by some Papist, or Catholic, scholars.[11]

Having successfully rebutted this theory, Carver proceeds, in a sound, scholarly manner, to build a case for Eden being located in Armenia Major, now part of eastern Turkey. Significantly, he explores ancient evidence suggesting that the Euphrates, Tigris, and Araxes rivers all derive from the same source.[12] This, he says, was a single "fountain" in the "forests of Armenia,"[13] situated in the vicinity of a lake known anciently as Thonitis, or Thospites,[14] called also Arianias, or Arsissa,[15] all names usually associated with Lake Van.

Carver cites the belief of various classical writers, including Strabo[16] and Pliny,[17] that some kind of proto-river, the true source of the Tigris, emerged from a primordial fountain, then discharged into the Thospites, or Lake Van, its waters so rapid, so powerful, that they did not mix with those of the "nitrous lake." The proto-Tigris then reemerged beyond the lake's southwest corner and sank down into a subterranean cave, only to reappear on the south side of the Eastern Taurus Mountains in the former Armenian province of Sophene, north of Diyarbakır. This then becomes the open source of the Tigris, which is known today as the Tigris Tunnel, or Birkleyn, from the Arabic *birqat al-'ayn*, "source of the river."

Carver believed it was this primordial fountain, the true source of the Tigris, that brought forth the four rivers of Paradise.[18] With this in mind, he concludes his scholarly discourse by proposing that the site of Eden, or "Heden" as he marks it on the accompanying map (see figure 28.2), was to be found between Sophene "and the fountains of Tigris, in the midst whereof, and upon the bank of the river, stood the *Tree of Life*. . . . Just about which place . . . we see . . . the nitrous Lake Thospites."[19]

CHERUBIM WITH THE FLAMING SWORDS

Carver points out that after the proto-Tigris passes through the Thospites, it was said by the classical writers to reemerge in the region of Mount Niphates.[20] This is the ancient name for Nemrut Dağ, the volcanic caldera situated just beyond Van's western shoreline. Having concluded that the Fountain of Paradise lay between here and Sophene, or immediately south of the plain of Mush, he proposes that the cherubim, which God set up to guard the Tree of Life with flaming swords turning every way, were in fact the "flashings issuing out of some Lakes."[21]

This is a very clever solution. Such "flashings" might easily describe the volcanic activity attached to Nemrut Dağ, which has erupted periodically since ancient times, the last time being in 1891, when the summit started "vomiting forth flames and lava," destroying the villages at the base of the mountain.[22]

On this same matter, the Reverend W. A. Wigram and Sir Edgar T. A. Wigram in their book *The Cradle of Mankind,* published in 1914 following their celebrated travels in Kurdistan (eastern Turkey, northern Syria, northeast Iraq, and western Iran), observed:

> It is held by many commentators that the site of the Garden of Eden was near modern Van and Bitlis, round about the headwaters of the Euphrates, the Tigris, the Araxes, and the Zab. If so, then the Garden of Eden now lies buried beneath the lava of these volcanoes; and where could we find fitter antitypes of the Cherubim with the flaming swords?[23]

It is unlikely that the Wigrams were aware of Carver's work when they wrote their book. However, their statements suggesting that the volcanoes, as natural boundaries to the Garden of Eden, were themselves the cherubim wielding the flaming swords echo Carver's thoughts completely.

And if the Garden of Eden is not encased in volcanic lava, then it could equally have been drowned, for one old Armenian legend asserts that it lies "at the bottom of Lake Van," where it has been since the time of the Great Flood.[24] This conclusion reflects the medieval belief that even if a terrestrial Paradise *had* once existed, then it would surely have been destroyed at the time of the Flood, which covered everything to the height of the highest mountains.

CARVER'S MAP OF PARADISE

Turning next to Marmaduke Carver's detailed, though rather fantastic, map of Greater Armenia (see figure 28.2), we see the terrestrial Paradise marked under the Latin legend *Heden regio quae et anthe* (Eden region and caves). These words are sandwiched between the Thospites, or Lake Van, in the east, and Sophene in the west. Indeed, the inscription appears in the vicinity of the Eastern Taurus Mountains, which lie immediately beneath the plain of Mush, with *eden* deriving most probably from the Akkadian word *edinu* (Sumerian *eden*), meaning "plain" or "steppe."[25] Having said this, a recent academic trend sees *eden* as stemming from the West Semitic root *'dn,* meaning "to enrich, make abundant,"[26] which remains possible, although less likely.

MOUNT ABUS

Passing across Thospites Lake on Carver's map are two parallel lines that run north-south, representing the proto-Tigris flowing unaffected through its waters. They continue as dotted lines beyond the lake's northern shores, indicating that this is the incoming subterranean river alluded to in the writings of classical writers, such as Strabo and Pliny, and that at its source was the primordial foundation from which all four rivers of Paradise took their course. Geographically, the lines originate from between a line of mountains, one of which is marked with the legend "Abus Mons."

Abus Mons, or Mount Abus, also spelled Monte Abas,[27] or Aba,[28] is mentioned in the works of both Pliny[29] and Strabo, the latter of whom writes that

Figure 28.2. Section from Marmaduke Carver's *A Discourse of the Terrestrial Paradise* showing "Heden," or Eden, between Lake Van (the Thospites, in the center) and the ancient kingdom of Sophene. Note the proto-Tigris coming down from the north, close to Abus Mons (Bingöl Mountain), and flowing uninterrupted through the lake.

from its summit "flow both the Euphrates and the Araxes, the former towards the west and the latter towards the east."[30] This can only be a reference to Bingöl Mountain, of which it is said: "The Araxes rises near Erzurum (Turkey) in the Bingöl Dağ region: there is only a low divide separating it from the head-waters of the Euphrates river."[31] We should recall that Bingöl was the center of the obsidian trade in the Armenian Highlands in the proto-Neolithic age and can also be identified with Gaylaxaz-ut, or Paxray, the Wolf Stone Mountain of Armenian folklore (see chapter 24).

THE SOURCE OF MANY RIVERS

Dutch scholar of Semitic studies Martijn Theodoor Houtsma (1851–1943), in the *Encyclopaedia of Islam,* made it even clearer in 1927, when he wrote:

"No fewer than six important water-courses rise in this erosion [i.e., Bingöl Mountain's innumerable glacial pools], in which Armenian tradition for this reason places the site of the biblical Paradise."[32] These "water-courses" are broken down in the following manner: in the northwest is the source of the Araxes, in the west is the Tuzla Şu, which becomes a major branch of the Western, or Northern, Euphrates, and the Bingöl (or Peri) Şu, which, as we saw in chapter 24, was known to the native Armenian population as the Gail, or "Wolf," River. It too rises on the west side of Bingöl Mountain, then heads off in the direction of Baghir and Shaitan Dağ. In the southwest part of the massif rises the Gönük Şu; in the south, the Çabughar Şu; and in the east and northeast, the Khınis Şu. The last four mentioned rivers, including the Peri Şu, all join the Eastern, or Southern, Euphrates.

What was it that led the Reverend Marmaduke Carver to conclude that the primordial fountain that gave rise to the four rivers of Paradise existed in the same mountain range as Abus Mons, in other words Bingöl Mountain? Was he aware of Strabo's reference to Abus Mons as the source of both the Euphrates and Araxes?[33] It is possible, although if this were the case then surely he would have mentioned it. More likely is that it was quite simply an intuitive decision based on whatever evidence he had in hand when he came to write his fascinating book.

Strangely, Carver does not identify the Gihon with the Araxes, nor does he associate the Greater Zab with the Pison. Instead, he sees major waterways that split away from the Tigris and Euphrates as evidence for the existence of these other two rivers. The Pison, for instance, he has entering neighboring Persia and linking, eventually, to the Indus, one of the longest rivers in Asia. Yet this vagueness should not detract from Carver's remarkable insights into the geographical location of the Garden of Eden, and we are by no means finished with his findings quite yet.

I felt the need now to focus my efforts more toward Bingöl Mountain, the Abus Mons of antiquity, in an attempt to better understand why Carver believed that here somewhere was the primordial fountain of life, and why the Dutch scholar Martijn Houtsma concluded that this was "the site of the biblical Paradise."

29

THE WORLD'S SUMMIT

Bingöl is a Turkish place-name that means "a thousand (*bin*) lakes or springs (*göl*)," an allusion to the many mountain streams that take their rise from the glacial lakes that grace its summit. In the Armenian language, Bingöl Mountain is known as Biurakn, which means "a million (*bir, byur*) eyes (*akn*)," a reference, once again, to the countless springs, or "eyes," that take their rise on its summit (although see chapter 33 for a clearer interpretation of this Armenian name).

Bingöl is mentioned also in Armenian texts under the more enigmatic name of Mount Srmantz, or Srmanç[1] (again, see chapter 33 for a discussion of the meaning of this name), described as Katar Erkri, the Summit of the Earth,[2] or the World's Summit,[3] or, indeed, the Top of the World, from which flowed the "four rivers to the four corners of the world."[4] Bingöl was also a "place of the gods,"[5] the habitation of mythical beings identified, almost certainly, with the Peri of Kurdish and Persian folklore (the region's population until the early twentieth century were mainly Armenians, Kurds, Turks, Yezidi, and Kızılbaş [Alevi], the last two being ethno-religious groups quite separate from the others mentioned here).

Very probably, the Judeo-Christian belief in the four rivers of Paradise flowing out of the Garden of Eden (see figure 29.1, for instance) is simply a variation

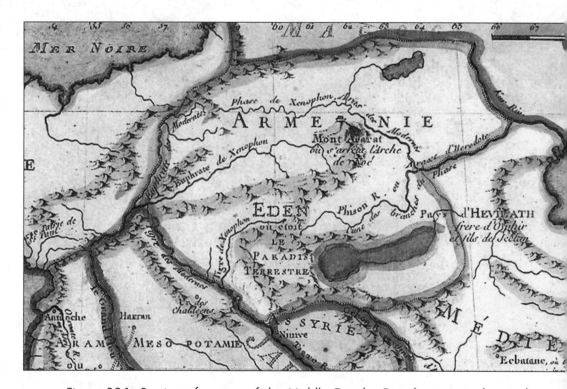

Figure 29.1. Section of a map of the Middle East by French cartographer and geographer Philippe Buache (1700–1773), published in 1783. Eden is shown to the west of Lake Van, placing it in the vicinity of the Mush Plain and Armenian Highlands. Confusingly, the identities of the Pison and Gihon rivers are transposed: the Araxes is shown as the Pison (written "Phison"), while the Greater Zab becomes the Gihon (written "Gehon").

of the cosmic mountain theme preserved in connection with Bingöl Mountain by the Armenian inhabitants of the region. It was probably for this reason that Martijn Houtsma, in 1927, noted that Armenians considered it "the site of the biblical Paradise,"[6] which, if correct, should be extended southward to include the plain of Mush, the proposed site of the Garden of Eden itself.

Having said this, we know that the Genesis account of the earthly Paradise describes real rivers, three of which—the Tigris, Euphrates, and Araxes—were considered to take their rise from the same primordial fountain that existed somewhere in the vicinity of the Bingöl massif. Only one of the rivers, the Pison, remains somewhat of an enigma, even though the Assyrian Church, as we saw in chapter 27, identifies it with the Greater Zab, which rises in the mountains southeast of Lake Van.

THE PISON RIVER—NEW EVIDENCE

Having said this, compelling evidence suggests that the Pison was also once seen to take its rise on Bingöl Mountain and is to be identified with the Peri Şu, or Gail River. This flows initially westward before turning south to merge, eventually, with the Eastern Euphrates just north of the ancient fortress town of Kharput, thought to be Carcathiocerta, the lost capital of Sophene.

This connection between the Pison River and the Peri Şu is recorded in a book written in 1870 by German cartographers Wilhelm Strecker and Heinrich Kiepert.[7] It examines the geography of the *Anabasis,* a seven-volume work penned by Greek professional soldier and writer Xenophon (ca. 430–354 BC). He marched with the ten thousand Greek mercenaries hired by Cyrus the Younger, who sought to wrest the throne of Persia from his brother, the king, Artaxerxes II.[8] The route of the Ten Thousand, as they are known, to and from the Battle of Cunaxa on the banks of the Euphrates, some 45 miles (72 kilometers) north of Babylon, took them through Colchis (modern Georgia), Armenia, and Mesopotamia. The identity of the rivers, towns, and cities Xenophon describes encountering on this two-way journey has been the subject of debate among scholars for hundreds of years.

The Ten Thousand are known to have marched through the foothills of the Bingöl massif, and discussing the sights they might have encountered Streker and Kiepert make the following observation:

> The native people spoken to on my trips to Armenia Major, call this river [i.e., the Peri Şu] Phison, and see it as a river of Paradise, [which they say] lies on Bingöl Mountain.[1] That this is not an arbitrary adoption of modern times is proved by the ancient Armenian writer who indicates the existence of a Castell Phison in Sophene, probably identical with the area between the two Euphrates.[9]

The superscript number 1 after the word "Mountain" in the original text refers the reader to the base of the page. Here we read that although the inhabitants of the region assert the Peri Şu to be the "Phison," the authors have been unable to verify this claim among the works of the Armenian writers.[10]

This is a shame. Yet we are still left with the tantalizing possibility that the

Peri Şu *is* the Pison, even though this new information is unlikely to constitute a major challenge to the Greater Zab's claim to being the self-same river. As stated in chapter 27, the word of the ancient Assyrian Church should not be taken lightly, especially as the Armenian Church seems to have a tendency to move around holy places (the case of the ark's Place of Descent being a prime example—see chapter 30).

Having said this, the fact that the Armenian population of Armenia Major *believed* that the Peri Şu was the Pison now links the sources of *all four* rivers of Paradise with the area around Bingöl Mountain, which, we should not forget, was known in Armenian tradition as Katar Erkri, the Summit of the Earth, its waters carrying the "four rivers to the four corners of the world."*[11]

FOUNTAIN OF LIFE

Quite independent of Judeo-Christian tradition, Muslim Kurds revere Bingöl Mountain as the site of another heavenly, paradisiacal fountain of great renown. Here is to be found Ma'ul Hayat, the Fountain of Life, the waters of which can rejuvenate youth and provide everlasting life.[12]

According to popular legend, Alexander the Great (called in Persian Iskender and in Turkish Zülkarneyn, meaning "the Horned One" or "the Two-horned," a reference to the ram horns on his helmet) traveled to "the land of darkness," beyond the setting sun, in search of the Fountain of Life, which was said to exist "in the north, beneath the Pole Star."[13] His guide and vizier on the journey was the mysterious al-Khidr, a wise man; however, when they came to a fork in the road, both men went in different directions. Only al-Khidr ended up finding the Fountain of Life and drinking from its waters (or eating a fish that swims in the fountain in another version; see figure 29.2). Even though al-Khidr waited for Alexander to catch up, the fountain disappeared as he approached. Al-Khidr also then vanished, having been granted immortality by Allah.

Although the Persian and Turkish accounts of Alexander's journey do not

---

*In 1989 Egyptologist David Rohl, in his book *Legend*, identified the Pison with the Uizhun River in Iran (the modern Qezel Uzun). Yet realistically this is untenable, as the Uizhun takes its course a full 250 miles (400 kilometers) southeast of Lake Van. Why have the sources of three of the rivers close together, only for the fourth one to be so far away? It just doesn't make sense, especially given that the heads of the four rivers are said to emerge from a single stream that waters the Garden of Eden.

Figure 29.2. Al-Khidr (Turkish Hızır), the Green One, who gains immortality at the Ma'ul Hayat, *the Fountain of Life,* thought to be located in the vicinity of Bingöl Mountain.

mention Bingöl by name, local Kurdish folklore does. Its version of the story tells how Alexander, with deep wounds and pains in his body, went in search of the Ab'i Hayat, the Waters of Life, which he found in the vicinity of Bingöl Mountain (named Jabal-i-çur). Here he either drinks or bathes in its waters, an act that cures his ailments. In honor of this miracle Alexander chooses a spot on a nearby river and builds a castle called Çapakçur,[14] this being the old name for the town of Bingöl, which lies a short distance from the mountain.

AL-KHIDR, THE GREEN ONE

Al-Khidr, called in Turkish Hızır, means the "Green One." He features in the Holy Qur'an,[15] as well as in Persian literature and various non-Islamic sources, as a mysterious figure, an ever-youthful "servant of Allah" who appears at the right moment to avert a disaster or rectify a fatalistic situation. There are many accounts of people who encounter a bearded holy figure only to find afterward that it was al-Khidr. He is a saint and a holy man, as well as the spiritual head of the Sufi movement, the so-called *qutb,* the intermediary between Allah and humankind. He is also identified with Saint George and shares the same feast date as him, which is April 23. Some even see the presence of al-Khidr in the proliferation of carved foliate heads, or Green Men, in Norman churches and cathedrals.[16]

THE CULT OF ENKI

Al-Khidr himself was originally, most probably, a deity belonging to Mesopotamian myth and legend. Very likely he is linked with Enki, the Sumerian god of creation, water, and intelligence, known in the Akkadian and Babylonian language as Ea. In art Enki is generally shown as a human figure wearing a horned helmet with streams of water emerging from his shoulders, like twin fountains (see figure 29.3). Within the flow fish swim upstream, like salmon trying to reach the source of a river. These twin streams represent the Tigris and Euphrates,[17] over which Enki presided as god of Eridu, an ancient Mesopotamian city located on the shores of the Shatt al-Arab waterway, where the two rivers come together before emptying into the Persian Gulf. However, there is no reason why Enki should not also have been connected with the *sources* of these mighty rivers.

Figure 29.3. The Sumerian Anunnaki god Enki (Akkadian Ea, Armenian Haya), with the twin streams of the Euphrates and Tigris emerging from his shoulders.

In Sumero-Akkadian mythology the Tigris and Euphrates were said to take their rise from a primordial water source, a subterranean lake that was the source of all "sweet water" called the Abzu (also written Apsu), which came under the patronage of Enki.

In his Semitic form as Ea, Enki was venerated in Urartu, the ancient kingdom that thrived between the Eastern Taurus Mountains and the Armenian Highlands during the last quarter of the second millennium BC and the first half of the first millennium BC, under the name Haya or Hayya.[18] His importance at that time is preserved in Armenia's Persian name, which is Hayastan, and also in its original Urartian name, which is Hayasa.[19] Even today the Armenian term for "Republic of Armenia" is Hayastani Hanrapetutiun. This indicates very strongly that this region, which includes Bingöl Mountain, was formerly associated with the cult of Haya, or Ea, the patron of the Tigris and Euphrates rivers, which, as we have seen, emerge as twin streams from his shoulders.

In Armenian folklore Haya was transformed into the culture hero Hayk,[20] who was said to have slain Bel, a Titan and king of Babylon synonymous with the biblical character Nimrod. Tradition asserts that before the battle Hayk visited Bingöl Mountain and here immersed his sword in the icy waters of one of its glacial lakes in order to sharpen it.[21] After Hayk had killed Bel on the shores of Lake Van, the Titan's body was apparently buried on the summit of nearby Nemrut Dağ, which is named in honor of Nimrod.

DILMUN— GARDEN OF THE GODS

Enki, Ea, or Haya, was associated with a mythical location called Dilmun, a kind of garden of creation, inhabited by him and his wife in an act that initiated "a sinless age of complete happiness," where animals lived in peace and harmony, humans had no rivals, and the god Enlil "in one tongue gave praise."[22] It was also a pure, clean, bright "abode of the immortals," where death, disease, and sorrow were unknown,[23] and some mortals were given "life like a god."[24] One text describes Dilmun as a place "where the raven did not croak and wolves and lion did not devour their prey."[25]

Even though Dilmun was a name given by the Sumerians to the island of Bahrain in the Persian Gulf, originally it was a mountainous region that overlooked the Mesopotamia Basin. One text speaks of "the mountain of Dilmun. The place where the sun rises."[26]

Some texts refer to Dilmun as the "land of Cedars," and Mehrdad Izady, professor of Near East studies at New York University, has successfully shown that this is a reference not to distant Lebanon, the country normally celebrated for its cedar forests, but to the Upper Zagros Mountains as far north as Lake Van.[27] Cedar forests grew here in abundance until the end of the Neolithic era, when they were cut down and used by the Sumerians and Akkadians to build their towns and cities, which thrived down on the Iraqi plain.

THE DIMLI KURDS

The Bundahishn, the holy book of the Zoroastrians, actually locates a place called Dilamân "at the headwaters of the Tigris,"[28] while the archives of the Assyrian Church, located in the ancient city of Arbil in northern Iraq, refer to Beth Dailômâye, the "land of the Daylamites" as existing in the same region.[29] The Daylamites were a Kurdish tribal dynasty whose original homeland was Daylamân, or Dilamân, a region of the Armenian Highlands,[30] where their modern descendants, the Dimila, or Dimli, Kurds live today. Their actual territory extends from the city of Erzincan and the province of Tunceli in the west, across to the Murad Şu, or Eastern Euphrates, in the east.

It is an area that includes Bingöl and the northern parts of the plain of Mush, making it clear that the geographical location of the terrestrial Paradise appears to be synonymous with the Mesopotamian concept of Dilmun; the two most likely deriving from the same culture that once saw the region as the location of the Abzu, the primordial water source that fed every river, lake, and sea in the ancient world.

The Dimli Kurds are a distinct ethnic community with very few connections to the Muslim Kurds of the region. They have their own language, called Zâzâ or Gurani, and belong to a very ancient religion called Alevi (also known as Kızılbaş, meaning "red heads," a reference to their distinctive red headgear). Although considered to have been introduced to eastern Turkey from southwest Iran, Alevism probably contains religious elements deriving from the beliefs and practices of the Arevordi, or Arewordik, the "children of the sun,"[31] who are classed as a type of Armenian Zoroastrian.[32] They practiced exposure of the dead on rooftops (i.e., excarnation) and entered subterranean "pits" for their rites—practices reminiscent of the early Neolithic peoples who lived in this same region thousands of years earlier.[33]

THE FOUNTAIN OF HIZIR

More significantly, the Alevi revere Hızır (pronounced *his-sheer*), the Turkish form of al-Khidr, whose most sacred shrine is Hızır Çeşmesi, the Fountain of Hızır, a mountain spring with accompanying fountain that emerges from the base of a tree in the foothills northwest of Bingöl Mountain, close to the town of Varto (ancient Gimgim). Alevi come from all over Turkey to venerate

Hızır at this shrine. They take water from the fountain, which is believed to have rejuvenating properties, and spend the night in a small, unassuming building next door in order to experience dreams of the saint. This practice, known as dream incubation, is an extremely ancient means of communication with supernatural forces, and to find that it still occurs at the base of Bingöl Mountain is quite extraordinary.

Whether the Fountain of Hızır is considered to be the original Ma'ul Hayat, Fountain of Life, or the Ab'i Hayat, Waters of Life, is unclear, although the connection is indisputable. Clearly, this holy spring cannot have been the actual source of the rivers of Paradise, because each river rises from a different location on the mountain's summit. Perhaps some kind of primordial fountain, as imagined by the Reverend Marmaduke Carver, was thought to exist within the mountain itself. Perhaps this was seen to feed the glacial lakes that are the true source of the many rivers and streams that take their rise on the mountain, accounting for the name Bingöl, which, as we have seen, means "a Thousand Lakes"; that is, boundless sources of water.

Was this also the origin of the concept of the Abzu, the primordial water source of Mesopotamian mythology presided over by Enki, who lived with his wife in the paradisiacal realm of Dilmun? Was the Alevi shrine of Hızır Çeşmesi, the Fountain of Hızır, some distant echo of these beliefs, which we can only assume sprang from this very region many thousands of years ago?

The fountain's current genius loci, certainly among the Alevi, is Hızır, a figure that can almost certainly be identified with Haya, the Armenian form of Enki or Ea, guardian of the Abzu. Might the Alevi, as the descendants of the Daylamân, or Dilamân, hold some special knowledge regarding the former existence in their midst of Dilmun? As we see next, this paradisiacal realm was synonymous with another location in Mesopotamian myth and legend, this being the Duku mound, birthplace of the Anunnaki gods.

30

RISE OF THE ANUNNAKI

Klaus Schmidt may have regretted talking to British journalist Sean Thomas, who would later write that the German archaeologist claimed that Göbekli Tepe was a "temple in Eden." It has not, however, stopped Schmidt from speculating about the effect the site might have had on the civilizations that flourished on the Mesopotamia Plain from around 3000 BC onward.

In his book *Göbekli Tepe: A Stone Age Sanctuary in South-eastern Anatolia,* published in its English language version for the first time in 2012, Schmidt speculates that the Göbekli builders may have derived from a shamanic society and that the T-shaped pillars perhaps represent their great ancestors. Much later, the memories of these powerful individuals were transformed into stories relating to deities called the Anunna gods of heaven (an) and earth (ki), known also as the Anunnaki.

According to the myths and legends of the Sumerians and Akkadians— the peoples that thrived down on the Mesopotamian Plain during the third millennium BC—the birthplace and abode of the Anunnaki was the Duku, a Sumerian word meaning "holy mound." Here was created the first sheep and grain, which were then given by the gods Enki and Enlil to humankind, who lived down below. This is very clearly an allusion to the origins of animal husbandry and agriculture, which, as we have seen, took place in the *triangle d'or* at the time of the Neolithic evolution. As Klaus Schmidt puts it himself:

Can these arguments be connected, is it possible that behind Göbekli Tepe there hides Mount Du-ku, and are the anthropomorphous pillars of Göbekli Tepe—suddenly surprisingly real—the ancient Anuna Gods?[1]

Incredibly, these same ideas regarding the origins of the Anunnaki being a memory of the prime movers behind the Neolithic revolution in southeast Anatolia were put forward by the current author in his book *From the Ashes of Angels,* published in 1996, and written as Schmidt was surveying the mountaintop sanctuary of Göbekli Tepe for the first time. That the German archaeologist now also believes the catalyzing events of the Neolithic revolution might well be preserved in the accounts of the Duku mound and the Anunnaki giving humankind the rudiments of civilization is highly significant. Consequently, it is essential to ascertain the foundation point of these mythological traditions, and to find out whether they really do relate to Göbekli Tepe and its enigmatic T-shaped pillars.

Although in the Sumerian language Duku means "holy (*ku*) mound (*dul*)," the equivalent of *dul* in Akkadian is *tillu,* cognate with the Arab *tell,* that is, an occupational mound, very like Göbekli Tepe itself.[2] In fact, Mesopotamian scholar Jeremy Black thinks it likely that as a mythological concept the Duku was seen as a prototype of the many tells found scattered across the Mesopotamian Plain, many of which would already have been abandoned, even by the commencement of the Sumerian and Akkadian civilizations in the third millennium BC.[3]

Just a riffle through the dirt and soil of any occupational mound very quickly produces potsherds, worked flints, and even human remains, which might easily have been seen as material evidence of the former presence on earth of the gods. The existence of these tells is most likely the root behind not only the Duku mound of Sumerian mythology but also the primeval mounds featured in the myths and legends of other ancient civilizations, where they are seen as the first built structures to occupy the earth (those that feature in ancient Egyptian texts as the foundation points of pharaonic civilization being prime examples). The Duku was therefore a primeval mound, the place of origin of the earliest ancestor gods, built where earth and heaven come together. These ancestor gods were so old that when eventually superceded by later deities, they were seen to have withdrawn into a nebulous world existing within the mound itself, which thereafter acted as a conduit into this netherworld, known as the *Kur.*[4]

The holy mound thus became an entrance to the Kur, a word meaning also "foreign land" and "mountain." Indeed, some scholars see the word *kur* as the origin of "kurd," the name given to the foreign inhabitants of the north, from which we derive the term Kurds and Kurdistan.[5] Yet having said this the Duku also came to be identified, like Dilmun, with the "Mountain of the Spring," from which the sun emerged each morning.[6] This association comes from the fact that, like the sun-god in ancient Egyptian tradition who was thought to pass through the *Duat,* or underworld, from sunset to sunrise, the sun-god in Mesopotamian tradition similarly passed through the Kur, or netherworld, to emerge from a cavelike opening in the Duku mound. Thus the Kur, as both the mountainous land of foreigners and the realm of the dead, came to be associated with the land of darkness, in other words the north, the only direction that the sun does not reach in the Northern Hemisphere.

Although ancient Mesopotamian cities often possessed their own representations of the Duku mound, somewhere out in the mythological world was the original one, where the genesis of the Anunnaki gods took place. So was Schmidt correct to identify the Duku with Göbekli Tepe?

MOUNTAIN OF THE GODS

Ancient texts tell us the Duku mound existed as part of a much larger hill or mountain called Kharsag (or *hursaĝ*), known as Kharsag-gal-kurkura, "great mountain of all lands."[7] It acted as a support on which the heavens rested and around which the stars revolved in an unerring fashion, showing it to be a cosmic mountain or world mountain.

Although Kharsag, like the Duku mound, is sometimes described as the Mountain of the East,[8] an allusion to the direction of the rising sun, it is also occasionally situated in the north,[9] the direction of the Eastern Taurus Mountains and the Armenian Highlands. So where exactly was Kharsag, if indeed it was a physical location?

THE NIPPUR FOUNDATION CYLINDER

One Sumero-Akkadian inscription, dating to around 2600 BC and found on a terra-cotta cylinder deposited in the foundations of the "Mountain House"

(E-kur) of the god Enlil in the city of Nippur in southern Iraq, speaks of Kharsag in direct association with the Tigris and Euphrates rivers:

> *The holy Tigris, the holy Euphrates,*
> *The holy scepter of Enlil*
> *Establish Kharsag;*
> *They give abundance.*
> *His scepter protects (?);*
> *[to] its lord, a prayer . . .*
> *the sprouts of the land.*[10]

Unless this is a reference to the *mouths* of the Tigris and Euphrates, it implies that the two great rivers were seen to sprout forth from Kharsag, the Mountain of the World. That Kharsag might be an actual mountain to the north or northeast of Mesopotamia has long been realized, although most usually it is identified with Mount Ararat,[11] a sacred mountain in eastern Turkey of paramount importance to Christian tradition.

It was here, we are told, that Noah's ark came to rest after the Great Flood, although this, as we shall see, is a complete misnomer. The original Genesis account says only that the ark came to rest "on [the] mountains of Ararat (Gen. 8:4)," a reference to the kingdom of Ararat. This is the Hebrew name for Urartu, which appears in Assyrian and Babylonian literature for the first time around the thirteenth century BC. At its height Urartu stretched from the Eastern Taurus Mountains in the south all the way to the Caucasus Mountains in the north, with its main heartland being in the region of the Armenian Highlands and Lake Van. Never does the Bible allude directly to Mount Ararat. Yet this has not stopped overzealous clergy members, theologians, and scholars identifying the so-called Place of Descent, where Noah's ark made landfall, with the tallest mountain in Armenia, which is Mount Massis, popularly known today as Mount Ararat.

MOUNT AL-JUDI

Mount Massis is unquestionably a mountain very sacred in Armenian tradition, and evidence of human activity here goes back to prehistoric times. Yet nothing before the fifth century AD associates it with the story of Noah's ark.

Indeed, the inhabitants of the region point out another mountain as the true Place of Descent. This is Mount al-Judi, the modern Cudi Dağ, close to the Turkish-Syrian border. At the foot of the mountain is the town of Cizre, which tradition asserts is the site of Thamanin, the settlement established by Noah and his family after leaving the ark.

Mount al-Judi is the Place of Descent recognized by Babylonian Jews, Christians of the Assyrian Church, Muslims (as stated in the Holy Qur'an's Sura 11:44), Yezidis (a Kurdish angel-worshipping religion), and "Chaldeans,"[12] a reference to the peoples of Northern Mesopotamia. This same mountain is asserted to be the landing place of Noah's ark by Berossus (a Babylonian historian, ca. 250 BC) and Abydenus (a Greek historian, ca. 200 BC), who stated that inhabitants thereabouts "scraped the pitch off the planks as a rarity, and carried it about them for an amulet," while "the wood of the vessel (was used) against many diseases with wonderful success."[13]

According to English Orientalist George Sale (1697–1736), who made an English translation of the Holy Qur'an published in 1734, relics of the ark were "seen here in the time of Epiphanius [a famous church leader who lived at the end of fourth century AD], if we may believe him; and we are told the [Byzantine] emperor Heraclius [who ruled AD 610–641] went from the town of Thamanin up to the mountain al Jûdi, and saw the place of the ark."[14]

Sale mentions also that there was once an ancient monastery on the summit of Mount al-Judi, which was destroyed by lightning in AD 776. After this time, belief that the mountain was the Place of Descent declined, its place taken by Mount Massis, called by the Turks Agri Dağ and by the Christians Mount Ararat.[15]

THE SWITCH TO MOUNT MASSIS

The Armenian Church was directly responsible for transferring the Place of Descent from Mount al-Judi to the more northerly Mount Massis,[16] a holy mountain under the jurisdiction of the Mother See of Holy Echmiadzin, a church and monastery located in Vagharshapat, near the city of Erivan, or Yerevan, the capital of the Republic of Armenia (see figure 30.1). As the seat of the Catholicos, or head of the Armenian Church, Holy Echmiadzin is to the Armenians what the Vatican is to the Catholic Church. When viewed from Echmiadzin, Mount Massis seems to rise up from the surrounding plain to dominate the southern skyline.

The change in location of the Place of Descent from Mount al-Judi to Mount Massis was almost certainly political and occurred following the ruling of the Council of Ephesus in 431, which banned the ancient Assyrian Church from the Orthodox Catholic Church because of its unorthodox views on Christ's dualist nature. At the time Mount al-Judi was under the jurisdiction of the Assyrian Church, the Armenian Church's southern rival, so a switch of interest away from Mount al-Judi to Mount Massis was deemed appropriate, as the Armenians did not want the Assyrians to have control of this important place of pilgrimage.

Yet before this time the Armenian Church was, seemingly, happy to accept Mount al-Judi as the site of the Place of Descent. This is brought out in an Armenian chronicle known as the *Epic Histories,* attributed to an Armenian historian named Faustus of Byzantium, who lived in the fifth century. The book chronicles the visit of Jacob (or James), the second bishop of Nisibis in Northern Mesopotamia, to Mount al-Judi. Here the "Armenian saint," who was born at the end of the third century, is said to have found the "wood of Noah's Ark."[17]

Today, only Christians believe that Mount Ararat is the site where Noah's ark came to rest. Yet the sheer potency of this belief remains so strong that it has inspired a number of high-profile attempts to locate the remains of the ark on the slopes of Mount Ararat. All of these expeditions have either come to nothing or resulted in clandestine video footage of the alleged remains of a petrified boat, which becomes impossible to verify.

The reason for diverting from the main theme of the chapter to cite these facts is that the Christian belief in the power of Mount Ararat has over the past three hundred years seriously clouded scholarly judgment regarding the geographical placement of legendary locations connected with either Northern Mesopotamia or the Armenian Highlands. For instance, it was almost certainly the Christian obsession with Mount Ararat that led to its being identified with Kharsag.[18] Yet no major rivers take their rise there, especially not the Tigris and Euphrates mentioned in the inscription recorded on the Nippur foundation cylinder.

Since it was anciently believed that the Tigris and Euphrates stemmed from the same source, it is more likely that Kharsag should be identified with

Figure 30.1. Old print of Mount Ararat as seen from Erivan, modern Yerevan, the Republic of Armenia's capital and largest city.

the Bingöl massif, which is located around 150 miles (240 kilometers) west-southwest of Mount Ararat. Just as the Armenians saw Bingöl Mountain as the Place of the Gods, the Sumero-Akkadians saw Kharsag as "where the gods were born"[19] or "where the gods had their seat,"[20] an allusion to the presence thereabouts of the Duku mound, which, as we have seen, was very likely envisaged as a tell, an abandoned occupational mound, dating back to the age of the gods.

Interestingly, some accounts of the Duku mound speak of something called the Ancient City,[21] which was believed to have been built right on top of it, underneath which was the Abzu.[22] Although scholars consider that this account relates to the ancient city of Eridu, which was under the patronage of Enki and had its own representation of both the Duku mound and Abzu, chances are that the concept of the Ancient City relates to a built structure existing on the original Duku—one that was seen to sink down into the hill when its ancestor gods withdrew into the mound.

THE NIPPUR FOUNDATION CYLINDER

In the 1980s British historical writer and geologist Christian O'Brien (1914–2001) made a careful study of the Nippur foundation cylinder (correctly entitled the Barton Cylinder, after George A. Barton [1859–1942], the Canadian clergyman and professor of Semitic languages who first translated its text). He concluded that its inscription alluded to some kind of settlement of the Anunnaki existing in Kharsag, which he interpreted as meaning "principal fenced enclosure" or "lofty fenced enclosure."[23] It was a conviction reinforced by the fact that the Akkadian word *edin,* meaning "plain," "plateau," or "steppe," is twice used in connection with this highland "settlement."[24] Was this the "Ancient City" existing on top of the Duku mound?

Among the Anunnaki named in the Nippur foundation cylinder is the great lord Enlil, along with Enki, whom we have already met; Utu, or Ugmash, the sun god; Anu, whose name means "heaven"; and Enlil's (usually Enki's) consort, Ninkharsag, a name that translates as "Lady of the Sacred Mountain." Significantly, she appears also under the Akkadian name Šir (the equivalent of the Sumerian Muš, pronounced *mush*),[25] meaning "Serpent," and is given the epithet Bê-lit, meaning "Divine Lady."[26] Even though Mesopotamian scholar George A. Barton assumed that Šir was a "serpent goddess" venerated in the city of Nippur,[27] O'Brien interpreted her name as meaning "Serpent Lady"[28] and identified her as one of the Anunnaki living in Kharsag.

CULT OF THE SNAKE

It is curious that Ninkharsag, also called Šir (or Muš), the wife of Enlil or Enki, is seen as one of the Anunnaki living at Kharsag, for a cult of the snake is known to have thrived on the plain of Mush (which in Turkish is written Muş). A medieval translation of a work by the fourth-century Armenian abbot Zenob Glak says that snake worship was introduced to the kingdom of Taron, the ancient name of Mush, by "Hindoos," who arrived from the east in 149 BC.[29] They built cities and temples here that were destroyed by Gregory the Illuminator during his crusade against the pagans at the beginning of the fourth century AD. Apparently, the temples were located at Ashtishat, close to the road between Mush and Bingöl Mountain, where afterward Surb Karapet, the Monastery of Saint John the Baptist, was built.

This story suggests that Mush derives its name from the Sumerian Muš, the Akkadian Šir (pronounced *shir*), both meaning "snake" (even though in Armenian popular tradition Mush, as the word *mshush,* means "fog," a name deriving from a story in which the Armenian goddess Anahita raised a mist so that her daughter Astghik, goddess of love and beauty, could bathe without any mortal setting eyes on her nakedness). If so, then the ancient snake cult known to have existed at Ashtishat (the principal seat of the goddess Astghik, whose symbol was the *vishap,* a word meaning "snake" or "dragon") probably predates the arrival of the "Hindoos" and most likely relates to a time when the region was under the control of one of the Mesopotamian civilizations. If so, then this has profound implications for the identification of Kharsag with Bingöl Mountain, and the Garden of Eden with the Mush Plain, for in his book *The Genius of the Few,* Christian O'Brien argues that the account of Kharsag preserved in the Nippur foundation cylinder was perhaps the origin of the Genesis account of the terrestrial Paradise:

> The parallels between this epic account and the Hebraic record at the Garden of Eden are highly convincing. Not only is "Eden" twice mentioned, but the reference to the "Serpent Lady", as an epithet for Ninkharsag . . . [is]

clear confirmation of the scientific nature of the work carried out by the equivalent Serpents in the Hebrew account.[30]

We shall meet with those Serpents of Hebrew tradition shortly, but for the moment it is important to explore O'Brien's conclusions regarding Kharsag's identification as the original Garden of Eden. He located this mountain settlement of the Anunnaki not at Bingöl Mountain in the Armenian Highlands but at Mount Hermon (modern Jabal al-Shaykh, "Mountain of the Chief"), which forms part of the Anti-Lebanon range and straddles the border between Syria and Lebanon, extending as far south as the Israeli-occupied Golan Heights.

NO CEDAR FORESTS

O'Brien identified Mount Hermon with Kharsag primarily because the text associates it with cedar forests. So even though the Sumero-Akkadians located their world mountain in the north, northeast, or even the east of what is today Iraq, O'Brien chose to place it in the extreme west, the direction of Lebanon's celebrated cedar forests, because, in his opinion, there were no cedar forests in the Zagros Mountains. Yet as we have seen, cedar forests existed in abundance throughout the Zagros Mountains at the start of the Sumerian and Akkadian civilizations. So thorough, however, was their extermination that much later scribes interpreted references to cedar forests in ancient texts as alluding to Lebanon in the far west. This was simply because the scribes were not aware that cedar forests had once existed in the mountains to the north and northeast of their kingdoms. As a consequence, some versions of the famous *Epic of Gilgamesh* have its hero embarking on his quest for the plant of immortality and ending up in the vicinity of Lake Van and the Armenian Highlands, while others have Gilgamesh in Lebanon, traveling as far as Mount Hermon.[31]

If Kharsag is to be geographically placed anywhere, then it is going to be in the direction of the Eastern Taurus Mountains and Armenian Highlands, close to Lake Van. What is more, if Kharsag really was established where the Tigris and Euphrates sprouted forth, as the Nippur foundation cylinder suggests, this locates it in the vicinity of the Bingöl massif, making it the true "place of the gods," in both Armenian and Mesopotamian tradition. Here too was the site of the terrestrial Paradise, which O'Brien was almost certainly right to identify with Kharsag, and thus the Duku mound, where the Anunnaki lived and were first created.

Whether or not Göbekli Tepe can claim some credit as the original inspiration behind the Duku mound, as Klaus Schmidt surmises, remains to be seen. Undoubtedly, it would have had some influence on the development of the various myths featuring the Duku mound, just in the same manner that the story of the first sheep and grain created on the Duku mound and given by the Anunnaki to humankind is an abstract memory of the introduction of animal husbandry and sedentary farming in the *triangle d'or*. Having said this, the vision of the Duku as an abandoned tell situated in a hilly or mountainous environment, on which was built the "Ancient City," fits Göbekli Tepe perfectly. So in summary we can say that the concept of the Duku—as handed down across the millennia, until it became a feature in the cosmological world of the Sumerians, Akkadians, and later Babylonians and Assyrians—most likely constituted an amalgam of sites that included Göbekli Tepe in the *triangle d'or,* and another now lost site in the vicinity of Bingöl Mountain in the Armenian Highlands.

So who exactly were the Anunnaki, and what were they doing in the terrestrial Paradise, where in biblical tradition Adam and Eve are placed after being created by God? As we see next, in Mesopotamian tradition it was not God, but the Anunnaki who were responsible for the creation of the first humans.

31

THE MAKING OF
HUMANKIND

As to who the Anunnaki might have been, we shall learn soon enough, and as to what they were doing in the terrestrial Paradise, the answer is clear—Kharsag, Eden, and Dilmun, as geologist and writer Christian O'Brien suspected, are all one and the same, and in Mesopotamian tradition it was here that the Anunnaki are said to have "made" humankind.

One story in particular talks about mythical beings called the Igigi being burdened with labor by their masters, the Anunnaki, and rebelling, only to be replaced by human beings.[1] The account appears in the myth of Atrahasis, the Assyrian flood hero, where we find the Igigi being told to dig a watercourse in a paradise seen in terms of a garden.[2] The environment is actually very similar to the setting imagined by Christian O'Brien in his own translation of the Nippur foundation cylinder.

THE CREATION OF MAN

After "3600 years" of digging out the Tigris and Euphrates river beds to create water channels, seen as "the lifelines of the land,"[3] the Igigi decide they are not going to suffer this toil any longer and so rebel against the Anunnaki,

270

who are under the leadership of Ellil (the Old Babylonian and Assyrian form of Enlil).[4] Apparently, they set fire to their tools and lay siege to Ekur, Ellil's mountain house, where the other Anunnaki are also to be found. On learning why exactly the Igigi are up in arms, the Anunnaki council decides to make the first humans in order to carry out all further manual work on behalf of the gods.

The humans are created by the Anunnaki through the intervention of "far-sighted Enki" and some of the other Anunnaki.[5] To achieve this, the god Illawela "who had intelligence" (the god Kingu in other accounts) is sacrificed, and the Anunnaki immerse themselves in his blood to purify themselves.[6] Enki then provides clay to the womb goddess Nintu, also called Mami, who calls upon more womb goddesses to start molding together the blood of the god to create the first human beings "to bear the yoke . . . to bear the load of the gods." From the god's flesh a ghost comes into existence, so that the slain god might never be forgotten.[7]

In another version of the Mesopotamian creation myth, the first man is said to have been Adapa, a name reminiscent of Adam, the first man of Hebrew myth, who is modeled from clay that is the color of blood.[8] In this instance it is not only Enki who provides clay for the creation of the first humans, but also his wife Ninkharsag, who is synonymous with Nintu and Mami. Together they mold together the blood and clay to create the likeness of the human form.

Ninkharsag, we must remember, is one and the same as the wise snake goddess Šir, or Muš, of the Nippur foundation cylinder, meaning that in Mesopotamian myth a goddess identified as a snake is involved in the creation of the first human beings. George A. Barton, the original translator of the Nippur foundation cylinder, sensed the biblical connection with this story when he wrote: "She [Muš] was very wise. Her counsels strengthen the wise divinity of Anu [the god of heaven], a statement which reveals a point of view similar to that of Genesis 3,"[9] a reference, very clearly, to Eve's role as the progenitor of humankind in the Genesis story.

EVE, THE GIVER OF LIFE

Strangely, in Aramaic, the West Semitic language used in the Bible lands during the first millennium BC, the word for Eve (חַוָּה, *chava* or *hava*) is more or less identical to the word for snake (חוה).[10] In Arabic also the name Eve, *hawwa,* means "snake," although it can also mean "giver of life." Life, Eve, and the Serpent of Temptation are ultimately bound together, reflections of each other, and if this is the case then the fact that Eve bears correspondences with the goddess Ninkharsag, Muš, or Šir, the wife of Enki, is significant. Could Eve simply be a Hebrew form of this snake goddess who was responsible for the creation of humanity, the same way that in biblical tradition Eve is considered to be the First Mother of humankind?

If so, then it strengthens still further the case for the Mush Plain being the Garden of Eden and Bingöl Mountain being not only Kharsag, and the Duku mound, where the Anunnaki lived and were created, but also the true "place of the gods" in Armenian tradition. Perhaps as both Klaus Schmidt and the current author surmise, the Anunnaki are to be seen as the instigators of the Neolithic revolution, whose memory is immortalized in the T-shaped pillars found in the various large enclosures at Göbekli Tepe. As we have seen, there is every chance that these divine ancestors are a memory of Swiderian groups who entered eastern Anatolia sometime during the Younger Dryas mini ice age, ca. 10,900–9600 BC, and went on to catalyze the Neolithic revolution in the *triangle d'or.*

Yet there remains a stratum of activity concerned with this transformation of humanity from simple hunter and forager to animal herder and agricultural laborer that needs addressing, and this is the memory of the founders of civilization contained in the forgotten, fringe, and often heretical literature of the Judaic world. Here the mythical beings that provide humanity with the rudiments of civilization are named as *'îrîn,* "Watchers." As we see next, their story is told in the book of Enoch, one of the strangest yet most compelling holy books ever written.

32

THE COMING OF
THE WATCHERS

While researching the myths and legends of Bingöl Mountain I became intrigued by its ancient name of Srmantz, or Srmanç, which appears occasionally in old Armenian texts without explanation.[1] In Greek, I found it written Σερμάντου (Sermantou),[2] which I asked writer and journalist Jonathan Bright, a colleague from Greece, to investigate on my behalf. He possesses a sound understanding of the origins of the Greek language and stood a good chance of identifying the root components behind this curious place-name. Without knowing anything about my findings concerning Bingöl Mountain, he felt compelled to respond in the following manner:

> I cannot avoid noticing the resemblance of the word [Σερμάντου (Sermantou)] with the Enochian 'Ερμώμ' (Sherman-tu/Shermon-/Hermon-/Hermom-. . .), where the 200 watchers have supposedly descended, so although Mt Hermon is identified as the one standing at the borders between Syria, Lebanon and Israel (Golan Heights), one cannot help but wonder . . .[3]

One cannot help but wonder, indeed. Mount Hermon does indeed feature in "Enochian" texts, such as the enigmatic book of Enoch. This is a pseudepigraphical (falsely attributed) work of immense age, the oldest fragments of which have been identified among the Dead Sea Scrolls, which in their earliest form date to the third century BC.

One of the book of Enoch's internal texts, known to scholars as the book of the Watchers, tells the story of the 'îrîn, a name given to angels in certain Hebrew works of early manufacture and meaning something like "those who are awake" or "those who watch" (in Greek, ἐγρήγοροι [egrêgoroi]; in Latin and Slavic, Grigori; and in English, Watchers).* It is said that two hundred of their number came together in an assembly on top of a mountain and swore an oath of loyalty before descending to the plains below. Here they took mortal wives and revealed to them the secret arts of heaven. For this they became outcasts, rebels, and reprobates—the first fallen angels, a crime for which they were rounded up, incarcerated by the heavenly angels, and forced to watch the slaughter of their giant offspring, the Nephilim, a word that means "those who have fallen" or the "fallen ones."

FIRSTS FOR HUMANITY

The secret arts and sciences of heaven revealed to humanity by the rebel Watchers, as I first noted in *From the Ashes of Angels,* correspond with a number of firsts for humanity in the centuries and millennia after the initial Neolithic revolution. This we can see beginning with the construction of Göbekli Tepe in the mid-tenth millennium BC and continuing in one form or another across the Near East and Middle East for the next four thousand years.

In addition to the earliest expression of animal domestication and agriculture, the earliest use of beaten and smelted metal took place in the Near East, as did the earliest manufacture of linen fabric, the first brewing of beer and fermenting of wine. Some of the earliest creation of figurines using fired pottery occurred in this region, as did the first known construction of stone buildings for both secular and religious purposes.

This very same epoch saw the first use of stone drills, arguably made of flint, to penetrate large, polished beads made from semiprecious stone, such as quartz, agate, and carnelian, to create beautiful necklaces. At the same time, we find the first use of green malachite powder for cosmetic purposes.

---

*Many thanks to Jonathan Bright for clarifying the Greek variations of the name for Watcher.

Interestingly, the Watchers were accused of teaching women how to beautify themselves, just as they are said to have introduced humanity to working with metal,[4] something that took place for the first time at Çayönü in southeast Anatolia.

THE SONS OF GOD

So who were the Watchers, and how do they fit into the bigger picture? Bible scholars are convinced that the book of Enoch and other similar examples of Enochian literature derive from a few brief passages in Genesis 6, which speak of how the *bene ha-Elohim,* the "Sons of God," who are synonymous with the Watchers, came upon the "daughters of men" and, finding them fair, lay with them to produce *gibborim,* "giants," generally interpreted as alluding to the Nephilim. However, this is the original account:

> The fallen ones [Nephilim] were in the earth in those days, and even afterwards when sons of God [bene ha-Elohim] come in unto daughters of men, and they have borne to them—they [are] the heroes, who, from of old, [are] the men of name [gibborim]. (Gen. 6:4).

Clearly, the Nephilim were actually already existent when the Sons of God, that is, the Watchers, took mortal wives, and there is good reason to suggest that the Watchers and Nephilim are simply different names for the same antediluvian population that thrived in the Bible lands prior to the Flood of Noah. Yet to think that these meager lines should have inspired the story of the Watchers in the book of Enoch seems unlikely. More plausible is that it was the other way around: the few lines in the book of Genesis are interpolations, later insertions, based on quite separate source material, most likely some variation of the Watchers story.

After reading the book of Enoch, I became convinced that these Watchers, or "fallen ones," like the Anunnaki of Sumero-Akkadian tradition, were very powerful human individuals who lived during some distant age of humankind. They were advanced enough to give us the rudiments of civilization, recalled in the manner in which the fallen angels revealed to mortal kind the forbidden arts and sciences of heaven. What is more, their sexual liaisons with the "daughters of men" expressed their quite obvious human nature, as well as their ability to cocreate in order to produce flesh and blood offspring that resembled both themselves and their mortal wives.

VISAGE LIKE A VIPER

Yet these rebel Watchers, or fallen angels, bore no recognizable wings. In Enochian literature they are described only as tall in stature, with long, white hair, pale skin, ruddy complexions, and mesmeric eyes that quite literally shine like the sun.[5] One crucial passage in a fragmentary text known as the Testament of Amram likens the visage of one Watcher to that of a "viper," suggesting a long, narrow face of apparent serpentine appearance.[6]

At other times, the Nephilim, as the offspring of the Watchers, are called Awwim, "Serpents,"[7] while in one instance a Nephilim is described as the "son of the serpent named Tabâ'et,"[8] with Tabâ'et being one of the rebel Watchers. A Watcher named Gâdreêl is even cited as the serpent that "led astray Eve,"[9] implying that the serpent of Eden was in fact a Watcher, or fallen angel. More crucially these strange beings are occasionally described as flying like birds,[10] or they are described as wearing iridescent dark cloaks,[11] or garments with "the appearance of feathers"[12] (see figure 32.1). Very clearly it suggests the Watchers are in fact quite human shamans, or some kind of ruling elite, and not simply heavenly beings that have become flesh and blood in order to lie with mortal women.

As we have seen, vultures feature heavily in the early Neolithic art of central and eastern Anatolia, often in humanized form, where they seem to be associated with the passage of the soul into the sky world, a path taken also by the shaman after entering trancelike states. It is likely that to achieve these astral journeys the shaman put on the paraphernalia of the vulture, like the articulated wings found at Zawi Chemi Shanidar in the Zagros Mountains of northern Iraq, a site more or less contemporary with Göbekli Tepe.

HUMAN ANGELS

Is it possible that the memory of how a shamanic or ruling elite seen as responsible for humanity's sudden leap forward at the beginning of the Neolithic age has been preserved in Judaic literature as the story of the Watchers and Nephilim? Were these fallen angels remembered in Mesopotamian myth as the

Figure 32.1. Left, artist Billie Walker John's conception of a Watcher based on descriptions given in Enochian material, and, right, a 3-D sculpt by graphic artist Russell M. Hossain of a Watcher based on Billie Walker John's 1995 illustration.

Anunnaki, the gods of heaven and earth, that "fashioned" the first humans from blood and clay, and later revealed to us the rudiments of civilization?

Once again we find that Klaus Schmidt has had something interesting to say on the subject. Having separately speculated on the myths of the Anunnaki being some distant memory of the divine ancestors portrayed as the T-shaped pillars at Göbekli Tepe, in an interview given to the *Turkish Times* in 2006 he spoke of the stones as representing the "watchman [*sic*] of the period."[13] Watchmen is simply another form of the name Watcher and actually appears in the book of Enoch ("And I related before them all the visions that I had seen in my sleep, and commenced to speak those words of justice and to upbraid the watchmen of heaven"[14]).

Whether Schmidt had in mind the Watchers of the book of Enoch when he said these words is not clear; either way, it is an interesting admission and one that does make complete sense. For instance, Christian O'Brien, in *The Genius of the Few*, not only identifies the Anunnaki with the Watchers but concludes that the Anunnaki's highland settlement of Kharsag was one and the same as the earthly abode of the Watchers described in the book of Enoch.[15] These, it must be said, were incredibly forward-thinking ideas for 1985, when his book was published, particularly as the most popular theory at the time was that the Watchers and Anunnaki were ancient astronauts who came here in rocket ships two hundred thousand years ago and created human beings as slave labor to mine South African gold, which was then taken off planet.

These fanciful notions continue to prosper today. However, at least now we have a realistic alternative that with the discovery of Göbekli Tepe is becoming acceptable even among the academic community, thanks to the very bold stance taken on the subject by scholars such as Professor Klaus Schmidt. He recognizes that stories and legends preserved in ancient texts relating to mythical beings, accredited with being the founders of civilization, could well reflect a memory of the prime movers behind the initiation of the Neolithic revolution.

So if the Watchers were, in fact, not heavenly angels but human beings, then where exactly was their earthly abode? Where was the Mountain of Assembly on which the two hundred rebels swore allegiance before descending on to the plains below and taking mortal wives? As we shall see next, it was certainly not where the book of Enoch tells us, but much farther north in a mythical realm known as the Land of Darkness.

33

MOUNTAIN OF
THE WATCHERS

There is a general belief that the events portrayed in the book of Enoch, if they do have geographical correspondences in the real world, must have occurred in the vicinity of Mount Hermon, where the Watchers are said to have made their pact before descending on to the plains below. Indeed, some of the place-names featured in the text can be found in the foothills around the mountain, which lies on the northern border of Israel in the Anti-Lebanon range. There is no denying that the stories acted out in the book of Enoch are *meant* to be seen as having occurred in the Promised Land of the Israelites, occupied in the wake of Abraham and his family's departure from the city of Harran.

More likely, however, is that the setting for the events featured in the book of Enoch was eastern Anatolia, historical Armenia, where almost all the stories contained in the book of Genesis prior to the age of Abraham are played out. Not only is it the suspected setting for the fall of Adam and Eve in the Garden of Eden, but it is also where Noah's ark came to rest; where Abraham was brought up in Ur of the Chaldees (which was most likely Şanlıurfa, and not a city in southern Iraq, as is generally believed today); where Enoch built the first city (identified with Şanlıurfa—see chapter 34); and where Nimrod, the builder of the Tower of Babel, came up against Abraham and was later defeated by the Armenian cultural hero Hayk.

All of these biblical characters supposedly lived their lives in this region—their shrines and monuments still revered today. So if eastern Turkey *is* the geographical setting for the stories of the book of Genesis, then this is where we should start looking for the home of the Watchers and Nephilim, and not the area around Mount Hermon in the Levant.

ARMON
NOT HERMON?

Although such an assumption might seem ludicrous to some, there is confirmation of this surmise in the book of Enoch itself. Whereas in some extant copies Mount Hermon is cited as the mountain where the rebel Watchers assemble to swear allegiance, in others it is called Armon, which introduces an entirely different ball game. For instance, the translation of the book of Enoch by German scholar Andrew Gottlier Hoffman reads:

> Their [i.e., the rebel Watchers'] whole number was two hundred, who descended in the days of Jared, upon the top of Mount Armon. Therefore they called the mountain Armon, because they had sworn upon it, and bound themselves by mutual execrations.[1]

Now, it could be argued that *Armon* is simply a corruption of *Hermon,* but this was not the conclusion of John Baty, who made an English translation of Hoffman's German language edition of the book of Enoch, published in 1836. He was sure that using the name Mount Armon for the Watchers' Mountain of Assembly revealed its true geographical significance, for Armon, the name "the evil angels called that mount . . . in Hebrew signifies both the top of a mountain, and the residence of a famous chief,"[2] adding that "the land of Armenia received its name from Armen, the third of the leaders of the evil angels, who taught the signs of the earth."[3] This, he felt, confirmed the origin of the name, for "the land of Armenia is in Hebrew the land of Ararat, and mount Ararat of the Armenians has been clearly shewn to be the mount on which the angels swore, the top of which was called Armon."[4]

MOUNT ARARAT AGAIN

So here Baty not only locates Armon in Armenia but identifies it also with Mount Ararat, the tallest mountain of the region, which, as we have seen, is taken by Christians to be the landing place of Noah's ark. Yet as outlined in chapter 30, much older traditions, accepted by Babylonian Jews, Muslims, and Assyrian Christians, as well as indigenous Kurds belonging to various ethnoreligious groups, identify the ark's Place of Descent as Mount al-Judi, the modern Cudi Dağ, near the town of Cizre in southeast Turkey.

This absolute conviction in Mount Ararat's role as the resting place of Noah's ark has allowed it to be identified with all manner of legendary mountains thought to be located in this region. Any story relating to a nonspecific holy mountain in either Northern Mesopotamia or Armenia is automatically assumed to refer to Mount Ararat, simply because it is seen as the sole piece of land that God set aside to become the place of renewal of humanity following the receding of the waters at the time of the Flood. In the eyes of the Christian faith, no other holy mountain even comes close to the religious significance played by Mount Ararat in the emergence of humankind.

So much did Ararat become a sponge for myths and traditions attached to the mountains of Armenia that Abus Mons, or Mount Abus, modern Bingöl Mountain, the acknowledged source of the Euphrates and Araxes rivers, has been assumed to be Mount Ararat. This is despite the rather obvious fact that the sources of the Euphrates and Araxes do not take their rise on this mountain. The closest source of the Euphrates to Mount Ararat is 50 miles (80 kilometers) away, while the Araxes flows only through its foothills, having taken its course some 150 miles (240 kilometers) to the west on Bingöl Mountain, the true site of Abus Mons.

So absurd did this situation become that some maps of Armenia show a mountain in the approximate geographical position of Bingöl, from which emerge the Euphrates and Araxes rivers. However, instead of its being labeled Bingöl, or even Abus Mons, it is named Mount Ararat! (See figure 33.1 on p. 282.) This general confusion even led, as late as 1907, to the Araxes being cited as "rising in Mt. Ararat,"[5] when clearly its source is on Bingöl Mountain.

Figure 33.1. Section of a map of Armenia by French cartographer Alain Manesson Mallet (1630–1706), published in 1683. It misnames Bingöl Mountain, the clear source of the Euphrates and Araxes rivers, as Mount Ararat.

MOUNTAIN-LAND OF THE MINYAS

Bearing all this in mind, Baty's assertion that the book of Enoch's Mount Armon has been ably identified as Mount Ararat is completely groundless. Despite this, he was probably right to link this mythical location, where the Watchers swear their allegiance, with Armenia. In the book of Enoch, Armen, the root of the name Armenia, is the name of one of the rebel Watchers. He is said to have "taught the signs of the earth,"[6] this being a form of divination whereby the perturbations of the heavens are reflected also on earth, and vice versa, the rudiments, of course, of astrology.

The name of this Watcher derives most probably from another mythical figure named Armen, who is considered to be the legendary founder of Armenia. Quite possibly, the inclusion of Armen's name in the book of Enoch relates to an Armenian location mentioned by classical writers under the name Armon,[7] or Armona,[8] a corruption of Har-minni, that is, Mount Minni (with variations such as Minyas and Minyadis).[9] In this form it is found in the Bible's book of Jeremiah, which reads:

> *Lift ye up an ensign in the land,*
> *Blow a trumpet among nations,*

> *Sanctify against it nations,*
> *Summon against it the kingdoms*
> *of Ararat, Minni, and Ashkenaz.*[10]

Here the Armenian kingdoms of Ararat and Ashkenaz are clearly separate to that of Minni, so where exactly was it to be found? English lexicographer William Smith (1813–1893) in his celebrated *Bible Dictionary,* published in 1884, states on the matter: "[In the Bible] MINNI only occurs in Jeremiah (51:27). It is probably identical with the district Minyas, in the upper valley of the Murad-su branch of the Euphrates."[11]

The Murad Şu, or Eastern Euphrates, flows westward through the Armenian Highlands and gradually turns south below the town of Varto before finally entering the plain of Mush. This places Minyas, or Minni, in the vicinity of the town of Varto, immediately south of the Bingöl massif, implying, if correct, that Har-minni, or Mount Minni, was most likely Bingöl Mountain itself.

HEAVENLY MOUNTAIN

German theologian Christian Abraham Wahl (1829–1901), whose biblical lexicons were published in the early nineteenth century, translated the name Har-Minni as meaning:

> "Heavenly Mountain, the mountain whose top reaches to heaven, meaning Ararat; for *mino* in Zend, and *myno, myny* in Parsee, signify heaven, heavenly. And hence the ancients called the whole province of Ararat, Minyas."[12]

Once again a biblical scholar is beguiled by the magnetic draw of Mount Ararat, for as Jeremiah as well as Latin and Greek scholar William Smith make clear, the kingdom of Minni was *not* Ararat. Har-minni was thus another mountain, and although its exact location cannot be verified with absolute certainly, the fact that Ararat's main rival Bingöl was once called Mingöl[13] seems a little beyond coincidence.

Since the Turkish root *bin,* "a thousand," coupled with *göl,* "lake," provides Bingöl's normal translation of "a thousand lakes" or "a thousand springs," it means that the root *min,* as in Mingöl, is either a corruption of *bin* or it relates to something else. Wahl's second option seems more likely, as the name Bingöl Dağ is unattested before the writings of Jean-Baptiste Tavernier (1605–1689), a French diamond merchant and traveler who visited the region in the second half of the seventeenth century.[14]

Perhaps as the German theologian Christian Wahl proposes, the name Har-minni (i.e., Mingöl) derives from a time when Armenia was under the control of the Persian Empire, which was between the sixth century BC and the time of Alexander the Great in the fourth century BC, and again from AD 301 until the sixth century AD. Thus the word root *min* derives most probably from *mino,* which in the language of the Persian Zoroastrian holy books known as the Avesta means "heaven" or "heavenly." It is a conclusion supported by the fact that in Persian *minú* means "azure heaven,"[15] while in Hindustani or Urdú, a language that includes many Persian words, *mína* means "heaven,"[16] while *minú* means "paradise."[17] Thus in Persian, Mingöl probably means something like "lake of heaven" or even "waters of paradise."[18]

All this tells us very firmly that the mountain named Armon, or Har-mini, upon which the rebel Watchers assembled and swore an oath of allegiance before descending on to the plain below, was located in Armenia, and not in the Levant, and is most probably Bingöl Mountain, the center of the Armenian obsidian trade during the age of Göbekli Tepe (see figure 33.2).

THE MOUNTAIN OF GOD

There is yet more evidence that the setting for the book of Enoch was the Armenian Highlands and not Mount Hermon in the Anti-Lebanon range. Polish-born Orientalist and scholar Edward Lipinski (b. 1930), who specializes in biblical and ancient Near Eastern studies, conducted a major investigation into the origins of the Mountain of God, the place where the Canaanite god El was said to dwell. Even in biblical times, this was deemed to be Mount Hermon, although Lipinksi found compelling evidence that it was originally located much farther north, in the kingdom of Armenia.

The first thing that the Belgium-based scholar observed was that the name of El's abode was *gr-ll,* the "mountain of the night."[19] This is derived from the fact that its recesses were "toward the meeting place of the assembly" in the north where the sun never reaches, the Land of Darkness, as viewed from the perspective of the southerly placed Mesopotamian Plain, home of the

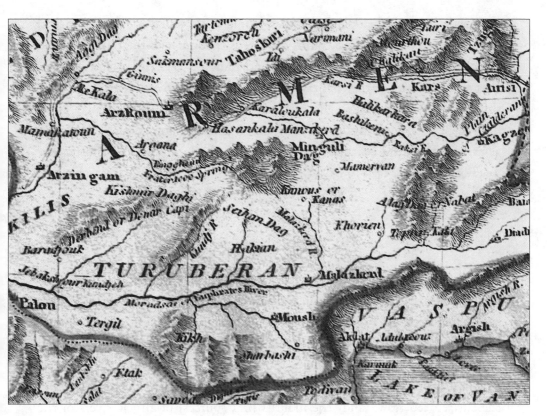

Figure 33.2. Section of a map of Armenia by Scottish cartographer John Tomson (ca. 1777–1840), published in Edinburgh in 1814. Here Bingöl Mountain is called Minguli Dağ, which derives from the Turkish for mountain (*dağ*) and the Persian *minjul*, meaning "lake of heaven" or "waters of paradise."

Sumerians, Akkadians, and later Babylonians and Assyrians.[20] Lipinski was able to draw parallels between the name of El's abode and the Sumerian place of God known as kur-suh-ha, "the dark mountain," as well as "the mountain of darkness" in the Jewish Talmud, which contains teachings and lore relating to the contents of the Torah, the first five books of the Old Testament.[21] The Talmud speaks also about a place called Gehenna, a kind of Jewish underworld, lying "behind the land of darkness," somewhere in the Armenian Highlands.[22]

BENEATH THE POLE STAR

This was also where, Lipinski realized, Alexander the Great must have come seeking immortality in "the land of darkness,"[23] which was said to exist "in the north, beneath the Pole Star."[24] According to the story, Alexander reached "'the way of the Armenians' country, where is the source of the Euphrates and of the Tigris,' [here] he entered the wonderland, traversed the land of darkness, proceeded up to the country of the blessed ones, where 'the sun does not shine,' and, without knowing it, he reached the spring of life,"[25] located, as we have seen, on Bingöl Mountain. This story, Lipinski points out, was known as early as the third century BC, because the Greek philosopher and teacher Teles of Megara in ca. 240 BC says that humans want "as Alexander to become immortal."[26]

ENOCH IN PARADISE

All this was just a prelude for Lipinski's investigation of the locations described in the book of Enoch, for he instantly recognized the same mythical locations cited here. At the beginning of the story, Enoch journeys to Paradise in the company of two angels, or Watchers, and comes "to a dark place and to a mountain, the point of whose summit reached to heaven."[27] Here he saw "the mountains of the darkness of winter and the place whence the waters of the entire deep flow," and "the mouths [i.e., sources] of all the rivers of the earth and the mouth of the deep."[28] Additionally, after having "passed above a land of darkness," Enoch "came next to the Paradise of righteousness,"[29] which Lipinski says, "has to be identified with the high mountain of God"[30]; that is, the aforementioned abode of El, who is a form of the Hebrew god Yahweh. This "Paradise of righteousness" is, of course, the Garden of Eden or terrestrial Paradise of the Genesis account, for here, we are told, "the throne of God was fixed where the Tree of Life was."[31]

TIGRIS TUNNEL

From this Lipsinki concluded that the entrance to the Land of Darkness, beyond which was the Mountain of God, was reached through "a gate of darkness, whose geographical origin is likely to be looked for in the tunnel at the source of the Western Tigris."[32] This, of course, was the Reverend Marmaduke Carver's western corner of his proposed terrestrial Paradise, its eastern corner being Lake Van, with its apex in the mountain range that included Abus Mons; that is, Bingöl Mountain.

The Tigris Tunnel, through which the river passes, was originally about a mile long (1.5 kilometers) and ran all the way through the mountain, although today it has been shortened due to landfalls at its northern end. Yet thousands of years ago this mysterious passage, which is in part a deep gorge, was seen as a symbolic gateway from the world of the living to a realm of myth and legend, a wonderland, beyond which was Paradise itself.

THE MOUNT OF ASSEMBLY

It would be impossible to do full justice to Lipinski's incredible contribution to this subject (for instance, he shows that the Tigris Tunnel features in the *Epic of Gilgamesh* as the long tunnel through which the Mesopotamian hero, on his quest to discover the plant of immortality, passes to reach the Land of the Ever Living, situated in a region of perpetual darkness).[33] However, I'll let him give you his conclusions on the presence in Armenia of the mountain abode of the god El.

Talking about the Old Testament's book of Isaiah, where the king boldly proclaims: "Above the stars of El I will exalt my throne, and I will sit down upon the Mount of Assembly, in the recesses of the north (Is. 14:13)," Lipinski writes:

> The recesses of the north are here the high mountains of Urartu [the Armenian highlands], where the divine assembly, presided by El, was believed to gather. . . . In the light of these mythological allusions to the abode of the gods in the mountains of Armenia, the only explicit mention of El's abode at the sources of the Euphrates acquires new dimensions.[34]

In other words, as he says himself: "El's abode . . . *is not to be looked for near Mount Hermon [in the Levant], but midst the mountains of Armenia* [current author's emphasis],"[35] near the sources of the Euphrates.

BABYLONIAN MAP OF THE WORLD

Strengthening the case still further for the Mountain of Assembly of the rebel Watchers existing somewhere in the vicinity of the Armenian Highlands is the oldest known map of the ancient world. Dating from the sixth century BC, it is contained on a Babylonian clay tablet found during the nineteenth century at the ancient city of Sippur in southern Iraq and is currently on display in the British Museum (BM 92687).[36] (See figure 33.3.)

The map shows a large central disk, representing the known world, beyond which is a circular band labeled *mar-ra-tum,* which means "ocean," this being the primordial waters that were thought to exist beyond the world landmass. Various triangles extend from the "ocean," like the rays of a star, each representing a *nagû,* or "region," either a mythical realm or distant land. Smaller circles positioned just inside the perimeter of the disk indicate real geographical locations as observed from the perspective of Babylon, which is marked as a large rectangle just above the center of the map.

Running through the landmass are parallel lines representing the Euphrates River, which begins at the top of the circular landmass within a semicircle labeled *šá-du-ú,* meaning "mountain," a reference to the northerly placed Eastern Taurus range. This identification is confirmed by the presence just below and to the right of the semicircle labeled *ur,* "city," next to which is the word Urartu, the ancient kingdom that embraced territories from the Eastern Taurus Mountains north to the Armenian Highlands (the land of Ararat of the Bible) and beyond to the Caucasus Mountains. Just below this, to the south, is another small circle labeled [kur]aš+šur[ki], "Assyria," which, like Urartu, is correctly placed.

Yet it is what lies outside of the semicircle marked "Mountain" that is of interest here, for the triangle extending away from the primordial ocean bears the name BÀG.GU.LA, meaning "great wall," accompanying which is the legend "6 leagues in between where the sun is not seen."[37] Its location, in the north, corresponds perfectly to the direction of Lake Van and the plain of Mush, suggesting that the "great wall" is in fact a seemingly impenetrable wall of mountains, either the Armenian Highlands or perhaps even the more northerly Caucasus Mountains, which do indeed form a virtually impenetrable barrier stretching from the Black Sea in the west to the Caspian Sea in the east.

That the sun does not shine here shows it to be, as Mesopotamian scholar Wayne Horowitz surmises, a "region of perpetual darkness" in the extreme north. Like Lipinski, he thinks it likely this is the same wonderland encountered by the hero Gilgamesh on his journeys and mentioned also in literary traditions concerning the travels of the celebrated king of Akkad, Sargon the Great, who ruled ca. 2334–2279 BC.[38] Almost certainly this distant *nagû,* or region, was thought to be accessed, as Lipinski also realized, through the fabled Tigris Tunnel, which acted as a kind of passage or gateway from the material world in the south to the

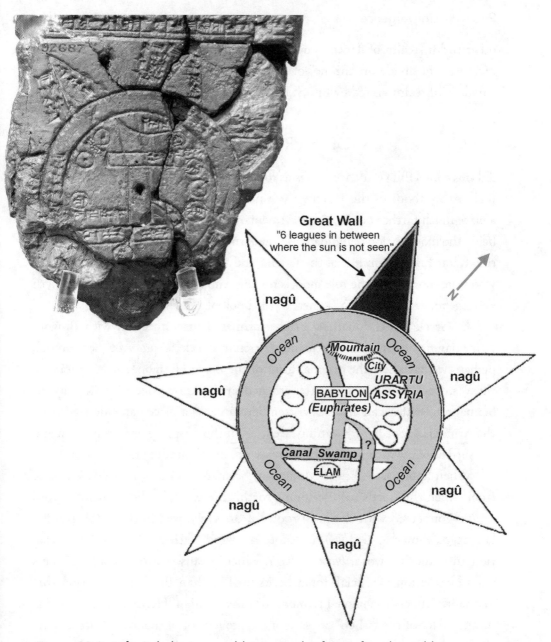

Figure 33.3. Left, Babylonian world map in the form of a clay tablet, now in the possession of the British Museum (BM 92687), and right, the translation of key terms used on this map. Note the northerly placed "Mountain," most likely the Eastern Taurus range, beyond which is the nagû, or "region" (triangle shown in black), labeled "Great Wall," indicating either the Armenian Highlands or the more northerly Caucasus Mountains. As the legend states, this was "where the sun is not seen"; that is, the Land of Darkness, the location of both the Mountain of Assembly of the Watchers and Kharsag, the mountain home of the Anunnaki gods.

otherworldly realm of darkness existing beyond the Eastern Taurus Mountains. Here was the abode or "throne" of God, the Garden of Righteousness, and the paradisiacal realm visited by Enoch in the company of angels.

GOD'S PROMISED LAND

All this compelling evidence brings us to one powerful conclusion—that the original earthly abode of the Watchers was not Mount Hermon in the Levant, but a place much farther north, in the Armenian Highlands, with Bingöl Mountain being the most obvious candidate. As the Armenian world-mountain, it bore the title Katar Erkri, "Summit of the Earth," and was seen as the abode of the gods, who were most likely the role models for the Anunnaki of Mesopotamian myth and legend, as well as the Watchers of the book of Enoch.

As Greek writer Jonathan Bright intimated in connection with Bingöl's Armenian name Srmantz, or Srmanç, written in Greek Σερμάάντου (Sermantou), perhaps we have here the original form of the name Hermon, the Mountain of the Watchers. It is a surmise strengthened in the knowledge that Srmantz, or Sermantou, which can also be written Sermantz, is a place-name derived from the Armenian root *serm,* meaning "seed," as in the offspring of a progenitor, and the suffix *antz,* which means either "place of" or "abounding in."

When applied to Bingöl Mountain, Sermantz reflects its role as a place from which the "seeds" of life sprang forth. Interestingly, the Armenian word *serm* is connected with the word root *her,* or *herm,* used in the old Armenian language (known as *Grabar*) to denote the word "father," through its association with another word, *hayr,* or *hai'r,* which means the root of a hair.* This word association is crucial, for it backs up Jonathan Bright's suggestion that Sermantz reflects the name Hermon, for in Armenian, Hermontz or Hermanz means "place of the father," or place of the progenitor of the seed of life, exactly the same as Sermantz.

So both Sermantz and its variation Hermontz not only help explain Bingöl's classical name of Abus Mons, which means "Mountain (Latin *mons*) of the Father (Aramaic and Greek *abba*)," but they also make better sense of the mountain's most common Armenian name Biurakn. This, as we saw in chapter 29, means "a

---

*Many thanks to Gagik Avagyan for all facts regarding the etymology and meaning of Bingöl's Armenian place-names, which were gleaned from correspondence in May–June 2013.

million (*bir, byur*) eyes (*akn*)," with "eyes" here meaning sources, most obviously the countless springs that take their rise on the mountain's summit. However, Armenian correspondent Gagik Avagyan has informed the author that there is a much deeper meaning behind the name Biurakn that expresses the idea of the mountain being the root, source, or fount of life itself. He says that this same sentiment is conveyed in the mountain's suspected Persian name, Mingöl, which means "heavenly waters" or the "waters of paradise," with Paradise or Heaven being the source of all life on earth.

Apparently, Armenians from all over the country would arrive at Bingöl Mountain every spring to give thanks to Anahita, the Armenian goddess of fertility, for the sprouting forth of new seeds (*serm*) following the harsh winter months. Many of them would remain camped in its foothills until summer.

So in the context of Bingöl's role as the source of the four rivers of Paradise in Judeo-Christian myth and legend, we can now see that in Armenian tradition this concept related to the mountain being the place of beginning, the place of original creation, the garden of God himself. He was the "father" who brought forth the "seed" of all life, which was then, symbolically, carried toward the four directions by the rivers themselves. How exactly Bingöl gained this wondrous association is today lost. Most probably it is connected with the fact that the mountain was the center of the region's obsidian trade during the age of Göbekli Tepe and that it was from here that the forerunners of the Göbekli builders, identified as incoming Swiderian groups, emerged as the ruling elite sometime around 10,500 BC. It was the memory of their deeds that were mythologized into the stories of the Anunnaki—who dwelt in Duku, Kharsag, or Dilmun— and the Watchers, the human angels, who descended from Mount Hermon to take mortal wives and reveal the forbidden arts of heaven. That the Armenian Highlands were also once known as Yerkir Nayiri, "Land of (the) Watchers,"[39] supports this theory.

Curiously, the name Anunnaki itself might also be of Armenian origin, for in the old Grabar language (which bears some comparisons to Akkadian) its root components break down as *anun,* "name"; *ak,* "root, beginning, river root, seed"; and *e,* "the,"[40] which when put together makes "the name is the beginning," *an allusion most assuredly to the genesis of the gods themselves.* Yet just what was the role of the Watchers at Göbekli Tepe? Could it really be said that the Watchers, or, indeed, the Anunnaki, are immortalized in the dozens of anthropomorphic pillars being uncovered there today?

34

WALKING WITH
SERPENTS

So exactly who were the Watchers of the book of Enoch? Their recorded appearance as being extremely tall, like "trees," with long white hair, pale skin, ruddy complexions, eyes that seem to shine like the sun, and visages with the appearance of vipers, conjures a strange creature indeed, and one that has all the hallmarks of an albino. So were the Watchers albinos? It is a compelling theory, although there is a far easier explanation.

Such distinctive traits might simply be exaggerated descriptions of the Swiderian population, whose suspected presence in eastern Anatolia in the aftermath of the Younger Dryas Boundary impact event might well have catalyzed the creation of Göbekli Tepe and the later accounts of mythical beings such as the Watchers and Anunnaki. As we saw in chapter 20, Swiderian communities certainly included "tall . . . long-headed, [and] thin faced" individuals,[1] while among the post-Swiderian groups of Central Russia and the Baltic region were people of increased height with elongated (hyper-dolichocephalic) skulls and narrow faces.[2]

Additionally, Swiderians would also seem to have carried the distinctive physiognomy of the Brünn population. They too possessed heads that were long and narrow, plus they bore traits that marked them as likely Neanderthal-human hybrids, most obviously prominent brow ridges.[3] Similar traits were identified in the Swiderian-linked Kebeliai skull, found in Lithuania in 1948, suggesting that among the Swiderian groups entering eastern Anatolia were strange-looking people indeed.

In fact, the unique physiological features of the Brünn population derived, most probably, from prolonged contact with Neanderthal communities, either in Central Europe or at places like Kostenki and Sungir in Central Russia (the first settlement sites at Kostenki go back at least 40,000 years, arguably even earlier). It is even possible that cross-contact between the different human species began much further away, in the Altai region of Siberia, where anatomically modern humans shared the world with Neanderthals, as well as other types of extinct human types, before their final disappearance sometime around thirty to forty thousand years ago.

All this tells us that when the Swiderians entered eastern Anatolia their striking physical appearance might have contrasted greatly with that of the local Epipaleolithic population. Did this lead, eventually, through consistent storytelling, to gross exaggerations that have made the Watchers into superhuman albinos the size of trees? If so, then we can understand also how the the Swiderians' elongated heads led to their being represented not only as abstract statues with T-shaped heads at Göbekli Tepe but also as human angels with visages like vipers in myths and legends. Was it a memory that across the millennia became so abstract that eventually they became Awwim, quite literally walking "serpents"?[4] It is a staggering possibility. What is more, compelling evidence now suggests that the peoples of the Near East preserved an abstract memory of the existence of a serpent-faced elite for thousands of years after the construction of Göbekli Tepe.

THE MYSTERY OF TELL ARPACHIYAH

Following the Pre-Pottery Neolithic age came the Pottery Neolithic, which in eastern Anatolia and Northern Mesopotamia was represented by the Halaf culture, ca. 6000–5000 BC, and the Ubaid people, ca. 5000–4100 BC, both of whom probably influenced the emergence of the Sumerian and Akkadian civilizations down on the Mesopotamia Plain. At a Halaf and later Ubaid site known as Tell Arpachiyah, situated in the Khabur Valley, just outside the city of Mosul in northern Iraq, Max Mallowan and John Cruikshank Rose of the British School of Archaeology in Iraq, in the company of writer Agatha Christie, made an amazing discovery. They uncovered evidence of an advanced village setting with cobbled streets, rectangular buildings, and round buildings with domed ceilings like the tholoi tombs of Mycenaean Greece.[5]

Mallowan and his team also unearthed a number of burials, many in poor condition. Thirteen skulls, however, were better preserved, and these were examined by anthropologists Theya Molleson and Stuart Campbell.[6] Six were found to be artificially deformed, in that they had been deliberately elongated to create an extended cranium. This must have been done when the individuals were still in their infancy using a combination of boards and linen wrappings. These findings had earlier been predicted by Max Mallowan and fellow archaeologist Hilda Linford, who in 1969 wrote:

> We appear to be confronted with long heads, and there are certain pronounced facial and other characteristics which . . . would have made them exceptionally easy to recognize.[7]

What seemed important about these deformed skulls is that some of their unique features were not artificial but natural. In other words, the deformation had merely accentuated what was already there. It was a realization that led Molleson and Campbell to conclude that "several of the individuals (including some without deformations) were related to each other,"[8] in that they formed part of an extended caste, or family group. Moreover, because the site covered the transition phase from Halaf to Ubaid, ca. 5200–4500 BC, and the characteristics were present in remains belonging to both cultures, there was evidence of a direct genetic descent from one culture to the other across an extended period of time.

SNAKELIKE HEADS

Molleson and Campbell went on to state that this type of deliberate cranial deformation within a specific group of people "has considerable potential for elitism."[9] In conclusion, they wrote that head accentuation among the Halaf and later Ubaid peoples was done to "demarcate a particular elite group, either social or functional," who were of "close genetic relationship" and as such were part of a hereditary group that was "closely inbred."[10]

Furthermore, Molleson and Campbell speculated that the "shapes of the head may have had some meaning,"[11] adding, incredibly, that these individuals were perhaps recalled in the fired clay figurines found in various Ubaid cem-

Figure 34.1. Heads of serpent-like statues from ancient Mesopotamia in the British Museum. Their extended heads and coffee-bean eyes indicate that they are abstract representations of the long-headed elite known to have existed among the Ubaid and Halaf cultures, ca. 6000–4100 BC.

eteries, which have snakelike heads (see plate 32).[12] In addition to this, they wrote that a number of small ceramic heads with elongated cranial features and strange coffee-bean eyes dating from the Halaf period were also most likely representations of this elite group (see figure 34.1).[13]

CULT OF THE SNAKE

So who exactly were these long-headed individuals, who would seem to have been members of a genetically related group seen as snake-headed in appearance? The greatest clue comes not from the ancient world, but from Central America. Among the Maya of Mexico's Yucatan Peninsula, a hereditary line of priests called the *chane,* or "serpents," would deliberately deform the heads of their infants to give them what was known as a *polcan*—an elongated serpent-like head. Doing this made the child eligible for a hereditary priesthood known as the People of the Serpent, who perpetuated the cult of the rattlesnake.[14] They honored Itzamna, or Zamna, a form of Ahau Can, the "Lordly Serpent," a great wisdom bringer and legendary founder of the chane priesthood.

Had something similar been occurring at Tell Arpachiyah in northern Iraq—a hereditary group, arguably an elite caste, that deliberately elongated the heads of their children so that when they came of age they were demarked as special among the communities in which they moved? Was this done to honor or celebrate a divine ancestor, or a specific group of ancestors, believed to have possessed very similar serpentine features? Did they represent these divine ancestors as snake-headed figurines of the type found in Ubaid graves?

More pertinently, were these human serpents the Watchers of the book of Enoch, who were believed to have had long, serpentlike faces—*visages like vipers,* as the Testament of Amram so aptly puts it? Was their memory confused with the envisaged Fall in the terrestrial Paradise, through the serpent's temptation of Adam and Eve? Remember, the book of Enoch tells us that the Watcher named Gâdreêl was the serpent that "led astray Eve."[15]

ELITE RITUAL CENTER

No further information is available concerning the genetic background of the skulls found at Tell Arpachiyah, which is now thought to have been an "elite ritual center."[16] Yet it is worth considering whether the elite family group or caste that deformed the heads of their children among the Halaf and later Ubaid peoples might not have been descendants of Swiderian groups who entered eastern Anatolia from the north some four thousand to five thousand years before the foundation of Tell Arpachiyah around 5200 BC.

Intriguingly, overwhelming evidence indicates that the Halaf culture controlled the Lake Van and Bingöl obsidian trade,[17] distributing the black volcanic glass throughout the Near East from a series of centers in eastern Turkey, northern Syria, and northern Iraq, *including* Tell Arpachiyah.[18] In other words, the elite group here might have seen itself as the direct successors of the walking serpents that had controlled the obsidian trade in the distant past. Perhaps the Halaf even saw themselves as their lineal descendants, the reason they chose to accentuate their cranial features to make their children look more serpentlike in appearance. If this is true, then clearly by this time the European hunters' connections with totems such as the wolf and reindeer had long since been superseded by those of the serpent and vulture, two of the most familiar creatures associated with the beliefs and practices of the Pre-Pottery Neolithic world (it is interesting to note that in Aztec mythology, the serpent is linked directly with obsidian, and obsidian knives in particular).

The strange dark garments or cloaks of feathers worn by the Watchers were most likely the ritual paraphernalia of a shaman, arguably one associated with the vulture. This probably led eventually to claims that these individuals were bird people[19] or that they bore wings, something that was added to the description of angels as late as the fourth century AD.

Not only were the book of Enoch's Watchers seen as walking serpents, but the Anunnaki also were said to have had distinct serpentine qualities. For instance, Christian O'Brien points out that Ninkharsag, the wife of Enlil in the Nippur foundation cylinder, bears the epithet "Serpent Lady," while Enlil himself is described as the "Splendid Serpent of the shining eyes."[20] Remember, it is the Anunnaki that Klaus Schmidt proposes are perhaps represented by the T-shaped pillars at Göbekli Tepe. So are these anthropomorphic pillars representations of the Watchers as well?

CITY OF ENOCH

It would be wrong to identify the long-headed, hood-wearing anthromorphs represented by the stone pillars at Göbekli Tepe as *actual* Watchers, or indeed Anunnaki, simply because both derive from quite separate branches of human development that reached their zenith many thousands of years after the world that emerged in the *triangle d'or* sometime around the end of the Younger Dryas mini ice age, ca. 9600 BC. Having said this, the indirect connections between Göbekli Tepe and these human angels cannot be ignored. For instance, one Syrian chronicler wrote that the city of Şanlıurfa, ancient Edessa, was founded by "Orhay son of Hewya," the "Serpent,"[21] a clear allusion to the Watchers of the book of Enoch. Remember, Göbekli Tepe is just 8 miles (13 kilometers) away from the center of Şanlıurfa, where a Pre-Pottery Neolithic settlement dating to 9000 BC was investigated in 1997 following the discovery in Yeni Yol Street of a life-size human statue with obsidian disks for eyes (see chapter 4).[22] This was discovered in the same area of the city where Nimrod is said to have built his fortress and Abraham was born in a cave, the latter being the reason the whole area is considered sacred in Muslim tradition.

Strengthening the link between Enoch and Şanlıurfa still further is the fact that Bar Hebraeus (1226–1286), a historical chronicler and bishop of the Syrian Church, wrote that the prophet Enoch founded the city of Edessa, that is, Urfa or Orfa (even though, in fairness, he attributes the same role to Nimrod elsewhere in his writings).[23] This is interesting, as Enoch was said to have been visited in his dream-vision by two Watchers, who took him on a tour of the Seven Heavens, one of which contained the abode of the angels, while in another was the Garden of Righteousness. As we have seen, the geographical setting for the patriarch's amazing journey would appear to have been the Eastern Taurus Mountains and Armenian Highlands. So was Enoch's place of departure on this great adventure Şanlıurfa?

THE PERI AND CIN

We should also not forget that the Kurds of eastern Turkey preserve stories and traditions regarding mythical beings that inhabited this region in prehistoric times. They are the Peri—tall, strong, beautiful, "super human beings," whose fay-looking descendants were still thought to inhabit remote mountain villages as late as the twentieth century. As with the relationship between the Anunnaki and the Igigi, the Peri are said to have worked in concert with other beings of mythical origin called in Kurdish the Cin; that is, the Jinn of Persian folklore; the expression "Cin u Peri" being used to express the dual powers of these mythical creatures.

It was believed that King Solomon made the Cin go to work for him and that they "did what an ordinary human being could not do."[24] Both the Peri and Cin were able to carry heavy objects, build great monuments, and perform other grand feats, and it was put to me by my Kurdish contact, Hakan Dalkus, who was brought up in a small village in the foothills of the Eastern Taurus Mountains, that "maybe Göbekli Tepe was built by them. Or some people then or later believed so. It makes such a place sacred too. While for us Genies, [that is, Cin] mostly stand for bad characters to be feared, Peri is the opposite."[25]

In his book *The Fairy Mythology* (revised edition, 1850), celebrated Irish mythologist and historian Thomas Keightley (1789–1872) states that the Jinn, the Persian name for the Cin, "were created and occupied the earth several thousand years before Adam,"[26] whose death is usually said to have occurred five thousand, five years before the time of Christ (see chapter 35). So if the Cin or Jinn are in some cases the memory of a human culture that thrived in the Armenian Highlands in prehistoric times, then it suggests they entered the scene around the same time that Swiderian groups might well have arrived in the same territories during the Younger Dryas mini ice age, ca. 10,900–9600 BC. One of the leaders of the Jinn was Azâzêl,[27] a fallen angel, who was also a leader of the rebel Watchers, according to the book of Enoch, showing that traditions regarding the Watchers probably derive from the same origins as those of the Peri and Cin.[28]

Clearly, it was not Peri or Cin who built Göbekli Tepe, but human beings. However, there is an outside chance that, in their archaic stories about the Peri and Cin, the Kurds may have preserved the memory of incoming peoples of strange appearance who inspired the building of monuments and sacred places. The manner in which the Peri were able to cohabit with mortal kind is also reminiscent of the way the Watchers took mortal wives, who gave birth to giant offspring that resembled their Watcher fathers in appearance, being large bodied with pale and ruddied skin, just like the faylike descendants of the Peri.[29]

EGYPTIAN INFLUENCE?

So were the Nephilim and Sons of God of Genesis 6, along with the Watchers of the book of Enoch, really the memory of a Swiderian elite whose original homeland included the Carpathian Mountains of Central Europe? It is a persuasive theory, although we cannot dismiss the possibility that the Hooded Ones were made up of individuals from more than one ethnological background, with some reaching southeast Anatolia from other parts of the ancient world. We have already seen how the post-Zarzian peoples of the Eastern Taurus Mountains and Zagros Mountains might have provided the expertise to help create cult centers such as Hallan Çemi and even Göbekli Tepe, suggesting that the structures themselves were in fact the product of indigenous cultures, under the control of a power elite of Swiderian origin.

Yet other cultures from farther afield might also have been involved in the creation process. For instance, if Nilotic peoples from Egypt, Sudan, and even the Sahara were trading with the Natufian peoples, as seems likely from a number of disparate pieces of evidence now emerging from Epipaleolithic sites in the Levant corridor,* then it remains distinctly possible that groups or

---

*The Natufians probably imported figs from Egypt (see Kislev, Hartmann, and Bar-Yosef, "Early Domesticated Fig in the Jordan Valley," 1372–74), while the presence of cultivated grain seeds in early Natufian settlements argues for a connection with the peoples of the Nile Valley during this time. In addition to this, shellfish from the Nile Valley were found at the Natufian site of Ain Mallaha in the Jordan Valley.

individuals from the Nile Valley might have had a hand in the emergence of Göbekli Tepe.

These are possibilities that cannot be ruled out at this time. Yet what seems more certain is that the Swiderians, who would have reached eastern Anatolia during the Younger Dryas period, carried with them some semblance of the beliefs, practices, and ideologies that had earlier thrived among the Solutrean peoples of southwest and central Europe. They were also, very likely, carriers of magical traditions derived from the Kostenki-Streletskaya culture, whose descendants they would have encountered as they crossed the Russian steppes on their way to the Caucasus Mountains and Armenian Highlands. The Kostenki-Streletskaya peoples' own successors most probably included the Zarzians, who had followed a very similar route as the Swiderians, southward from the Russian steppes to eastern Anatolia, as much as ten thousand years earlier. All of these influences are interconnected and came to bear, eventually, on the construction of Göbekli Tepe, ca. 9500–8000 BC.

Our journey is almost over. Yet I still needed to make the link between Göbekli Tepe and the presence some two hundred miles (320 kilometers) away of the Garden of Eden. How did one affect the other when they existed in separate millennia, many thousands of years apart? Those living either in biblical times or much later during the formative years of Christianity cannot have known of Göbekli Tepe, even if they *did* recognize Armenia as the genesis point of human civilization. So what linked all these disparate elements together? The answer for me came with the confirmation of a dream.

PART SIX

Completion

35

A QUIET CORNER
OF EDEN

Thursday, March 1, 2012. Finally, after nearly eleven months of searching, I had found the monastery of my dream, the one in which the monks were celebrating life itself through the elevation of a holy relic thought to be a fragment of the Tree of Life. Called Yeghrdut (or Yeghrduti), the monastery was located 13.5 miles (21.5 kilometers) west of the town of Mush, in the foothills of the Eastern Taurus Mountains, overlooking the plain of Mush and the Murad Şu, or Eastern Euphrates.

EDEN-LIKE WOODLAND

Evidence of the existence of this monastery, destroyed during the Armenian Genocide of 1915, had utterly eluded me until now, even though I had consulted ample books on the history of Taron, the ancient Armenian kingdom that embraced the plain of Mush. Yet of all places, it was on Wikipedia that I first found reference to Yeghrdut. It had its own entry, and under the subheading "Legends," the following lines almost jumped off the page at me:

> According to popular belief, the Kingdom of Armenia has an Eden-like
> woodland named Yeghrdut in the Taron district, west of the Muş Valley. It is

believed that old men who come there from Muş valley and spend some time in that corner of unearthly beauty would become twenty years younger.[1]

This "Eden-like" woodland called Yeghrdut, where local men would come to be rejuvenated, sounded very much like the claims attached to the Fountain of Life (Ma'ul Hayat) or Waters of Life (Ab'i Hayat), identified in Kurdish folklore as being in the vicinity of Bingöl Mountain, 35 miles (56 kilometers) north of this area. Was this Armenian account simply an echo of these same legends, or could Yeghrdut relate to the presence in the region of the terrestrial Paradise? Clearly, Eden-*like* did not mean Eden itself, although I had a hunch there was far more going on here.

THE DISCIPLE THADDEUS

That day I searched online and found two webpages on Yeghrdut's history and legendary background written in Russian-Armenian.[2] What they contained simply stunned me and changed everything I thought I knew about Armenia's place in the story of the Garden of Eden. Apparently, the fourth-century Armenian churchman Zenob Glak, who wrote a history of Taron, recorded a quite fantastic story regarding the origins of the Yeghrdut monastery. It begins with the well-established account of how in AD 29 Thaddeus, one of the seventy (or seventy-two) disciples of Christ, traveled to the city of Edessa (modern Şanlıurfa) in Northern Mesopotamia at the behest of its king, Abgar, who wished to be cured of a serious skin malady.

According to early Christian legend, the king, having heard of miracles being performed by Jesus, sent out a request for this wonder worker to cure him of his illness. In response, the disciple Thomas dispatched Thaddeus of Edessa, who had earlier traveled from his homeland in Northern Mesopotamia to Judea, where he'd been baptized by John the Baptist in the River Jordan, and then, following the Baptist's death at the hands of King Herod, had become a follower of Jesus.

So when Jesus was still alive, according to the story, Thaddeus (also known as Addai) arrived in Edessa, his native city, carrying with him a handkerchief that Jesus is alleged to have wiped across his face, leaving behind a facelike impression. It was the power of this holy relic, known as the Image of Edessa, or the Mandylion, that is said to have cured Abgar of his malady.

The account goes on to state that Thaddeus afterward baptized King Abgar, who thus became the first monarch to adopt the Christian faith. As for Thaddeus, he apparently remained in Northern Mesopotamia preaching the word of God, and then in either AD 43 or AD 45 entered the neighboring kingdom of Armenia. Here he came upon a "woodland" called Yeghrdut, where he deposited a number of highly significant holy relics brought out of the Holy Land. Other variations of this tradition have Thaddeus being accompanied on his journey by the apostle Bartholomew.[3]

Fast forward to the fourth century, and the writer Zenob Glak now has the celebrated Armenian churchman Gregory the Illuminator being led by God to retrieve the holy relics left behind by Thaddeus three centuries earlier. Thereafter a monastery is founded on the spot in order to house them.[4]

The relics found by Gregory at Yeghrdut apparently included a small finger of Mary Magdalene, items belonging to Joseph of Arimathea, and bones from the right arm of John the Baptist,[5] hence the monastery's dedication to the saint.[6] Gregory also discovered a bottle, or container (Armenian *shish*), in which was preserved a remnant of the perfumed oil (known as the Myron, Muron, or Chrism) that had anointed "prophets and apostles"[7] and had been used by Thaddeus to help restore King Abgar's health and vitality following his miracle cure after coming into contact with the Image of Edessa. For this reason the monastery bore the alternative name of Shishyugho, which means "of the oil bottle,"[8] or Shuyugho, "young branch of the (oil) tree."[9]

EDEN
AND THE TREE OF LIFE

In Christian tradition such relics, if considered "genuine," would be deemed highly significant. However, for me they paled into insignificance when compared with what else Thaddeus supposedly deposited at Yeghrdut, for according to Armenian tradition he came bearing a fragment of the "Tree of Life" (Armenian Կենաց ծառի), which after its discovery became a key focus of veneration at the monastery.[10]

More incredibly, I discovered that Yeghrdut was believed to have been located not just in an "Eden-like woodland," but in "a corner" or "one corner" of "Eden" (Armenian եղեմային), which can also mean the "Garden of Eden." This, the Armenian source states, "was in Taron Province, south of the Mush plain (Armenian դաւոիզ)." It goes on to say that "The place was called Yeghrdut, and here the elderly man would travel to become younger by twenty years."[11]

As soon as I read these words, my stomach churned, and I knew inside that this was the monastery I had glimpsed in dream the previous year. Both the reference to the presence there of a piece of the Tree of Life and the monks' belief that their monastery stood in some quiet corner of the Garden of Eden seemed to confirm this fact. It was the same place I'd seen, smelt, and experienced, both in sleep and then afterward when recording my thoughts in diary form.

Yet double-checking what exactly a fragment of the Tree of Life actually means in Armenian Church tradition made me realize that the holy relic at Yeghrdut was slightly more complicated than I had first imagined, for it is also described as the "Stick of Life" (Armenian կենաց փայտով),[12] or a "piece of the Wood or Timber of (the Tree of) Life (Armenian Կենաց փայտի մի մասնիկը).""[13] It is a term that derives from a gradually evolving legend that has its inception in the first century AD and revolves around what happened to Adam and Eve following their expulsion from Paradise.

After departing the Garden of Eden, the couple settle down somewhere on its fringes, and here they raise two sons, Cain, a crop grower, and Abel, a shepherd. As the book of Genesis tells us, Cain kills Abel, creating the first murder and death in human history. As a consequence, Cain is cast out and lives the rest of his life in the enigmatically named land of Nod, while Adam and Eve's third son, Seth, is born. He becomes Adam's rightful successor and the inheritor of his heavenly wisdom and knowledge.

THE OIL OF MERCY

So far, this is the basic story in the book of Genesis. However, Jewish and later Christian works compiled between the third century AD and medieval times—containing what scholars refer to as Primary Adam Literature—continue where the Bible account leaves off. The most well-known of these are the Latin *Vita Adae et Evae* ("Life of Adam and Eve") and the Greek *Apocalypsis Mosis* ("Apocalypse or Revelation of Moses"). Both these texts, and others like them, relate the story of how when Adam was on his deathbed he asks his son Seth to approach the gates of Paradise and beseech God to part with a little of the "Oil of Mercy" that flows from the Tree of Life, in order that this might sustain his life. Obeying his father, Seth departs for Paradise in the company of Eve and implores God to give him some of the oil from the "tree of his mercy" in order that he might anoint his sick father (see figure 35.1).

After some time, an angel appears (usually this is Michael, although not always). He refuses their request, saying that the Oil of Mercy is reserved for the final days, adding that in five and a half thousand years a savior will come who will be baptized in the River Jordan. Thereafter he will "anoint from the oil of mercy all that believe in Him. And the oil of mercy shall be for generation to generation for those who are ready to be born again of water and the Holy Spirit to life eternal. Then the most beloved Son of God, Christ, descending on earth shall lead thy father Adam to Paradise to the tree of mercy"[14]; that is, the Tree of Life (see figure 35.2 on page 308).

HOLY ANOINTING OIL

In other words, the text prophesized that, following his baptism in the River Jordan at the hands of John the Baptist, Jesus would somehow become the vessel of the Oil of Mercy, which would be spread by the Holy Spirit. The Armenian Church believes that this power was given originally to Moses, who was instructed by God to make something called the holy anointing oil (Ex. 30:22–33). This was afterward used to anoint many generations of Old Testament prophets, and eventually it found its way into the hands of John the Baptist. Following his death it was given to Mary Magdalene, who used it to anoint Jesus's feet before his entry into Jerusalem prior to his arrest and crucifixion. He is said to have blessed it, after which time the oil was used to anoint apostles. Thaddeus of Edessa then carried the oil's container to Edessa, where the anointing oil was used to restore King Abgar's health and vitality. Thereafter the disciple continued his journey and buried the shish bottle "in Daron under an evergreen tree."[15]

The "Daron" mentioned here is an alternative rendering of "Taron," the plain of Mush, with the location of the "evergreen tree" being Yeghrdut (the

Figure 35.1. Section of the Death of Adam by Italian artist
Piero Della Francesca (1416–1492), from a painted fresco in the
Basilica of San Francesco in Arezzo, Italy. It shows Adam, on
his death bed, telling Eve and Seth, who stands to her right, to
go and ask the angel that guards the entrance to the Garden
of Eden for some of the Oil of Mercy that oozes from the
Tree of Life. In the background Seth is seen making this
request to the angel Michael.

Tree of Life was anciently considered to be an olive tree, which is an ever-green[16]). There is nothing about Jesus anointing the apostles in the New Testament—this is considered to have been bestowed on all 120 disciples of Christ by the Holy Spirit on the Day of Pentecost in Jerusalem.[17] However, the

Figure 35.2. American lithograph of the Tree of Life in
the terrestrial Paradise by the Currier and
Ives company (1857–1907).

Yeghrdut legend states that the holy anointing oil deposited there by Thaddeus had been used to anoint "prophets and apostles."[18]

THE ANGEL'S GIFT

In the story contained in the Latin *Vita Adae et Evae,* composed sometime between the third and seventh century using earlier source material, Seth and Eve depart from the Garden empty-handed. However, in alternative, and arguably later, accounts the angel gives Seth seeds or saplings from the Tree of Life to take away with him.[19] He and Eve then return to Adam, revealing what the angel said and what has been given to them. Thereafter Adam dies, and his body is laid to rest with the help of angels.

Prior to Adam's final interment, Eve and Seth place the seeds from the Tree of Life in his mouth, or alternatively, they plant the saplings over the position of Adam's skull (the accounts vary). These grow into either a single tree or three trees that wrap around each other to become one. Eventually the tree is cut down and the timber utilized for a number of quite fantastic purposes. It is used to fashion the rod of Moses. It becomes a beam in King Solomon's Temple, or it is used to make a bridge, over which the Queen of Sheba passes. As this happens, she realizes the sanctity of the wood and demands that it be taken up and placed inside Solomon's Temple as a sacred relic.

THE TRUE AND LIVING CROSS

Afterward, the Holy Wood, or Holy Timber, of Life, as it is called in the Western Church, finds its way into a carpenter's shop, where it is used to fashion the Cross of Calvary, known in medieval tradition as the Holy Rood. After Christ's crucifixion on Golgotha, the cross is buried nearby. Here also is Adam's skull, concealed during a much earlier age either by Shem, Noah's son and heir, and/or by Melchizedek, the first king of Salem; that is, Jerusalem. The blood trickling down the cross from Christ's body reaches Adam's skull, finally bringing redemption to Adam for causing the original sin. The symbolism between the burial of Adam's skull and Golgotha, which means the Place of the Skull, is purposeful. It is for this reason that we see a skull at the foot of the cross in Crucifixion scenes, and also on crucifixes.

Accordingly, the elderly Empress Helena, mother of Constantine the Great, the first Roman emperor to adopt and legalize Christianity, visits Jerusalem in AD 327 or AD 328 and is led by miraculous means to discover the remains of the Cross of Calvary beneath a Roman temple of Venus now occupying Golgotha Hill. As fragments of the holy cross are found to constantly sprout forth new green shoots (due to the wood originating from the earthly Tree of Life), it becomes known as the True and Living Cross. It is because of this regenerative power that fragments of the True Cross are thought to have the power to restore life in a sickly person.

Clearly, the fragment of the Tree of Life possessed by the Yeghrdut monastery must have come from a separate branch to the one used to create the Cross of Calvary, as this piece is said to have reached Armenia in either AD 43 or AD 45, a mere decade after the Crucifixion and nearly three centuries before the Empress Helena discovered the Cross of Calvary. The only other thing I could discover was that Yeghrdut's precious holy relic was kept in a reliquary box (see chapter 39) and, I could only assume, was brought out and elevated during special ceremonies in the absolute conviction that here was a true fragment of the Tree of Life in the Garden of Eden.

Yet there was more to this story than simply the existence at Yeghrdut of the Tree of Life fragment and the vessel containing the holy anointing oil, for after the foundation of the monastery in the fourth century, the monks would manufacture their own Myron, or holy anointing oil, always mixing it in the bottle that had contained the original oil created by Moses. This was done so that the new anointing oil would forever contain the essence of the original holy anointing oil used to bless "prophets and apostles." Apparently, Yeghrdut's sacred oil would be transported to the Mother See of Holy Echmiadzin in Vagharshapat, Armenia, where it was used in the inauguration of the Catholicos, the head of the Armenian Church.[20]

Naturally, I wanted to know more about Yeghrdut and its monks who, I felt sure, played heavily on their illustrious heritage and location on the edge of Eden itself. It was incredible to think that this monastery had thrived in the foothills of the Eastern Taurus Mountains just 170 miles (274 kilometers) away from Göbekli Tepe, a true site of the genesis of civilization.

Yet what was Yeghrdut's connection with Göbekli Tepe, and, more pressingly, where was this monastery? It did not appear on any detailed maps of Taron, and unless its location was found, there could be no absolute confirmation that this was the place of my dream.

36

THE RED CHURCH

I needed to know where exactly the Yeghrdut monastery was located, so I attempted to use the geographic coordinates provided by Wikipedia to find the site. Yet wherever engineer Rodney Hale and I looked on Google Earth, nothing could be seen (the coordinates were later found to be wrong). All I knew was that Yeghrdut lay somewhere in the vicinity of a village called Kızılağaç (or Kızılhaç, pronounced *kiz-a-large*), a part Turkish, part Kurdish name meaning "red cross," a sure sign that a Christian edifice lay nearby.

The break came at the end of March 2012, when I learned from my Kurdish contact, Hakan Dalkus, who had managed to contact the person running the Kızılağaç Facebook page, that in nearby mountains were Armenian ruins called Dera Sor, Kurdish for "Red Church." It took further three-way correspondence to pin down the geographical location of Dera Sor. Then on Friday, April 6, 2012, appropriately Good Friday in the Western calendar, I saw for the first time on Google Earth an enormous rectilinear structure on a forested mountain ledge 2.25 miles (3.6 kilometers) south-southeast of Kızılağaç and 1.5 miles (2.5 kilometers) west-southwest of the village of Suluca (located at the coordinates of 38°45'1.37"N, 41°20'24.69"E).

The ruins appeared to consist of an outer shell around 70 yards (64 meters) in length and just over 40 yards (37 meters) in width. From what I could make out from the shadows cast by the remaining sections of the wall, they remained

Figure 36.1. Google Earth image of Dera Sor, located on the northern slopes of the Eastern Taurus Mountains, overlooking the Mush Plain. Does it mark the site of the Garden of Eden? Courtesy of DigitalGlobe 2013.

fairly high in places. The foundation of a second structure in the southeast quadrant of the perimeter wall was also just visible, its axis skewed slightly more toward north (see figure 36.1).

Immediately outside Dera Sor's exterior walls were traces of other rectilinear features, showing that this had to have been a monastery of some considerable size, situated in the northern foothills of the Eastern Taurus Mountains, overlooking the plain of Mush and Murad Şu or Eastern Euphrates River. Looking at the site, I got a strong sense of seclusion, isolation, and deliberate remoteness. Unlike monasteries such as Surb Karapet and Surb Arakelots elsewhere in the Mush district, this one cannot have received many visitors, unless it was for a very good reason indeed.

Although I was able to confirm that the Google Earth ruins were those of Dera Sor, the Red Church, I had no way of knowing whether they belonged to the Yeghrdut monastery. Further correspondence between my Kurdish contact and the man from Kızılağaç drew a complete blank. No one seemed to know anything about Yeghrdut or its history.

I tried synching the geographical position of the Red Church with some old maps of Armenia, one of which had the word "Arkhavank," meaning "King's Monastery" (probably a reference to Jesus as King of the Jews), in the approximate same position, while another actually had a small diamond marking the position of Yeghrdut. They correlated pretty well, suggesting that Dera Sor, Arkhavank, and Yeghrdut were all one and the same.

STRANGE DECREE

Something else pretty curious was then discovered about Yeghrdut by a researcher colleague named Janet Morris. On my behalf, she had been studying and, where necessary, translating accounts of European travelers who had crossed the plain of Mush over the past four hundred years. One such person, she found, was the French geographer Vital-Casimir Cuinet (1833–1896), who was sent to eastern Turkey to survey and count the Ottoman Armenian population. He made a very curious statement following a visit to the Yeghrdut monastery:

> On the opposite side of the plain, at the summit of a picturesque hill, covered with a thick wood and whose view extends a long way over an agreeable country, is found a convent under the decollation of St John the Baptist. Its construction as that of Mar-Johanna goes back to high antiquity. Amongst other precious titles, this convent holds a firman of the fourth Caliph Rachedi, Ali, son-in-law and first cousin of Mohammed, who accorded certain autonomous privileges falling into disuse over the course of time.[1]

That Ali (AD 601–661), the son-in-law and cousin of the Prophet Muhammad, seen as the first imam in the Shia Muslim faith, signed a firman, or religious decree, on behalf of Yeghrdut begs the question of what might have been behind this decision. Clearly, Ali cannot have spent his time issuing and signing religious decrees for every Christian edifice the Arab armies came across as they conquered large parts of Asia, Africa, and Europe, so why was this monastery singled out for special attention?

In the year 15 AH (*anno Hegirae;* i.e., after the foundation point of the

Islamic faith, thus AD 637), the Commander of the Faithful, Caliph Umar ibn al-Khattab, issued a written decree acknowledging the due rights of all non-Muslim sects, including Christians. This was done to protect churches and monasteries in general. Yet the one issued for Yeghrdut seems entirely different and suggests that, like Saint Catherine's Monastery in the Sinai, which was issued a firman by Muhammad himself, it was believed to contain important holy relics. Somebody wanted whatever it contained preserved and not destroyed by the first marauders who came along looking for the spoils of battle. It hinted that Yeghrdut's claim to house holy relics belonging to Jesus, Mary Magdalene, John the Baptist, and Joseph of Arimathea was known at the time of the Arab-Muslim invasion of Armenia in the seventh century. (Much later I discovered a second reference to Yeghrdut's firman, which states that it was signed not just by Ali, but also by the Prophet Muhammad himself.[2] If nothing else, it tells us that Yeghrdut once held a religious status equal to that of Saint Catherine's monastery in the Sinai, which makes it a highly important place indeed.)

ONLINE APPEAL

I was getting frustrated. I really needed to know whether Dera Sor, the Red Church, was Yeghrdut, the Eden monastery of my dream, so I posted a message on an online forum called AniOnline that addresses matters relating to Armenian architecture in the Lake Van area. I asked for confirmation of the monastery's exact geographical coordinates and anything else anyone might come up with, citing exactly what I knew already.[3]

As I waited for a response, my Kurdish correspondent, Hakan, returned with more information on Dera Sor from the Facebook contact in Kızılağaç:

> It is easy to reach the Red Church from Suluca and Kızılağaç. Walls and two arches stand. . . . They say Red Church was a monastery. Monks, priests and sisters etc. were educated there. It was a very rich monastery. Farmers of the surrounding lands were giving 50 percent of their crops to the monastery. No other info.[4]

A few days later, Raffi Kojian, the mediator of the AniOnline forum, posted a few lines on the Yeghrdut monastery paraphrased from a Russian-Armenian dictionary of Armenian architecture:

From the monastery the following were visible: Aradzani and Meghraget [both rivers], S. Karapet Monastery, a few villages [and mountains, viz.], Byurakn [Bingöl], Nemrut [Dağ], Gurgur, Sipan [Suphan Dağ], and in the further distance, the gray top of Massis [Mount Ararat]. That last one seems like a stretch, but that's what it says.[5]

Rodney Hale used Google Earth to check whether each mountain peak—Bingöl Dağ, Nemrut Dağ, Suphan Dağ, and Agri Dağ (Mount Ararat or Mount Massis)—was indeed visible from Dera Sor. Sure enough, if one were to stand on the mountain ridge immediately above the monastery ruins, all the peaks mentioned would have been visible on a particularly fine day.

Two days later, Raffi Kojian again posted on his forum. He said he now had in his possession a lengthy entry on Yeghrdut taken from a Russian-Armenian encyclopedia on the churches and monasteries of the Taron Province, published in 1953. He had uploaded the opening lines to the Yeghrdut webpage on Armeniapedia, the online database for Armenian church architecture, which were now available to read.[6] Clicking the link, I found the following:

Located four to five hours west of Mush, in front of S. Garabed/Karapet Monastery, in "Yegherits" region (*yergir*), on Sim Mountain (*Sim ler*) or on Black Mountain (*Sev sar*), on the south side of Yeprad/Yeprat River [i.e., the Murad Şu or Eastern Euphrates]. The location of the monastery is unmatched. On four sides are cold springs and forest. The air is pure, but cold. The view is indescribable. Almost all of Mush's plain is flat like a floor, its green worked fields open up before your eyes.[7]

This place sounded incredible, situated at a near perfect location to perpetuate the belief that it was founded in some quiet corner of Eden itself. I later discovered that four springs surrounded the monastery, one on each side, beyond which lay forests containing oak, hazel, and cedar trees.[8]

HOLY TREE AND SACRED SPRING

The contact at Kızılağaç was shown this entry on Yeghrdut and confirmed that this was indeed the topographical description of Dera Sor, adding that one spring in particular flowed from beneath the shade of an ancient walnut tree.

Indeed, there was no other tree quite like it in the whole of Mush Province (walnut trees are considered sacred in Kurdish tradition). People came here from all over the district to drink the waters of the spring in the belief that it could cure ailments and maladies, and rejuvenate the body by as much as twenty years.[9] This was, it seemed, the latest incarnation of the "evergreen tree" beneath which Thaddeus supposedly deposited the various holy relics in the first century AD.

Clearly this was an important holy shrine and one that was venerated extensively in the past by Christians and Muslim Kurds alike. It almost seemed as if, with the presence at Yeghrdut of a piece of the Tree of Life, together with the bottle that contained the sacred Myron, or holy anointing oil, the monks might have seen this evergreen tree and sacred spring as earthly representations of the Tree of Life with its spring that watered the Garden of Eden. Indeed, the stream that takes its rise from the spring beneath the monastery's holy tree, which bears the name Kilise Şu, "Church Stream," flows into the Eastern Euphrates, making it a source of one of the four rivers of Paradise.

DERA SOR IS YEGHRDUT!

That same day, Thursday, April 12, 2012, a member of the AniOnline forum posted the geographical coordinates of Yeghrdut, which were those of Dera Sor, the Red Church. The two were the same. The person in question said he had walked the hills from Mush to the location and could confirm that it is identical to the topographical description of Yeghrdut. In response, Raffi, the mediator of the forum, added a Google Earth link to Yeghrdut's entry on Armeniapedia, which now clicked through to the site of Dera Sor.[10]

There could no longer be any doubt—Dera Sor was Yeghrdut, which for me now became the absolute site of the Eden monastery first glimpsed in dream almost exactly one year earlier. To say I was elated is an understatement, for it almost seemed as if something I had created in my mind had now taken root in reality. Yeghrdut was certainly real, and with its fragment of the Tree of Life, the bottle containing the holy Myron, the "evergreen tree" with its sacred spring, and, of course, its "indescribable" setting, it was everything one could hope for in a monastery located in Paradise itself. Yet still more research was required to truly understand the site's greater importance to this gradually emerging picture.

SIM MOUNTAIN

Something in the opening lines of the Yeghrdut entry in the Russian-Armenian encyclopedia on churches and monasteries of the Taron Province then caught my attention. It was the statement regarding the monastery being located on Sim Mountain (*Sim ler*) or Black Mountain (*Sev sar*). The latter is a quite common name for hills and mountains in the region, usually under the Turkish word for black, which is *kara*. However, Sim Mountain needed further investigation, as it seemed somehow familiar. So I checked the history and topography of Taron and found something very interesting indeed.

Movses Khorenatsi, the father of Armenian history, who lived in the fifth century AD, wrote extensively on the region's mythological past, in particular the life and exploits of Armenian cultural heroes thought to be descended from Noah (Armenians themselves believe they are descended from Noah[11]). For instance, Hayk, the conqueror of King Bel, or Nimrod, is said to have been the great-great-great grandson of Japheth, the son of Noah. Shem, Noah's chosen heir, is also connected with Armenia's legends, and according to Movses, after the ark came to rest, Shem departed with his sons and came upon a mountain, which he afterward named Sim (or Simsar, which means Mount Sim).[12]

According to Movses, Noah, having departed from the ark, established a dwelling for himself and his family (afterward named Thamanin, the modern Cizre in southeast Turkey), while Shem continued northwestward with his sons, and that

> coming to a plain in the high mountains, he stopped by a river and named the mountain Sim after his own name. He gave this region to his youngest son Tarpan [the Armenian word for ark is *Tapan*]. . . . Tarpan remained with his sons and daughters in the region given to him by his father and called it Taron and later Taruperan after his own name.[13]

Taron, or Taruperan, was, as we have already seen, the name of an ancient Armenian kingdom embracing the plain of Mush, implying, quite clearly, that Mount Sim overlooked the plain, which, of course, it does. Thus Yeghrdut was founded either on or very close to the spot where Shem and his sons are supposed to have set up camp after leaving the ark. As Movses Khorenatsi's home village was nearby Chorene, immediately south of Yeghrdut, it seems unlikely that the monks of the monastery would *not* have been aware of this clearly local tradition featuring Shem, the son of Noah.

Movses Khorenatsi's geographical positioning of Mount Sim and the wanderings of Noah and his family also make it clear that Mount Ararat is *not* the Place of Descent, the site where Noah's ark came to rest after the Flood. Shem is said to have traveled "northwest" to reach Sim Mountain in the kingdom of Taron (see figure 36.2), which fits perfectly with the ancient belief that the ark went aground on Mount al-Judi, the modern Cudi Dağ in southeast Turkey. In other words, the story as preserved in Movses's fifth-century history of Armenia was written with Mount al-Judi in mind as the Place of Descent, and *not* Mount Ararat, which lies some distance to the east-northeast of Sim Mountain.

Figure 36.2. Map of eastern Turkey showing the candidates for the Place of Descent in Noahic tradition. Note also the route taken by Noah's son Shem from the Place of Descent to Sim Mountain, said to overlook the kingdom of Taron, that is, the plain of Mush.

All these Armenian traditions indicate that the plain of Mush and the surrounding mountain ranges were seen as important to the events portrayed in the generations between Adam and Abraham, although what they did not do was give credence to the belief that here also was the terrestrial Paradise. What I needed was better confirmation that Armenia, and in particular the area under discussion, was once believed to have been the site of Eden, something that Movses Khorenatsi worryingly makes no mention of in his history of Armenia.

As we see next, that confirmation is provided by the Reverend Marmaduke Carver, who in his fabulous work *A Discourse of the Terrestrial Paradise,* published in 1666, did so much to show that the area between Thospites Lake (Lake Van), the Tigris Tunnel in Sophene, and Bingöl Mountain in the Armenian Highlands was the true site of the terrestrial Paradise.

THE SECRETS OF ADAM

The Reverend Marmaduke Carver wished also to find absolute confirmation that the southern part of Armenia Major, modern eastern Turkey, was the authentic site of the Garden of Eden. Writing in *A Discourse of the Terrestrial Paradise,* he notes: "Tradition successfully continued in these parts [i.e., after the Flood], that hereabout was the place of Adam's Paradise,"[1] adding:

The Author that affirms this is Methodius. . . . Now this ancient Author *(in lib. Revel.)* speaking of the death of Seth, and the secession of his posterity from the posterity of Cain, hath among other things this remarkable passage: *Mortuo* Seth *separavit se Cognatio ejus à sobole* Caini, *redierúntque ad natale solum. Nam & Pater corum vivens prohibuerat nè miscerentur. Et habitavit Cognatio* Seth *in* Cordan *monte, Paradiso terrestri proximo.*[2]

The Latin text translates as: "[After the death of Adam] Seth separated from the issue of Cain and returned to his native country, for his father had forbidden their lives to mix. And Seth lived with his kin on Mount Cordan, next to the terrestrial Paradise."

Having cited Methodius's words, Carver notes: "If the terrestrial paradise were near the Mount Cordan, and that Mount Cordan or Gordiæus stood in the same place where Ptolemy hath set it; then we may rest secured, that the happy seat of our First Parents Habitation was at or about the very place that we have described."[3]

THE REVELATIONS OF METHODIUS

Very pertinent words indeed, so who was Methodius and where was Mount Cordan, or Gordiæus? Methodius of Olympus was a theologian and prolific writer of the early fourth century (he died ca. AD 311). The quotation cited by Carver, or variations of it, is from a work accredited to Methodius entitled the *Apocalypse* or *Revelations* (*Revelatio*). It contains a commentary on the book of Genesis and an account of the coming of the Antichrist and the inevitable end of the world. However, there is a problem, as there is no record of Methodius ever having written such a book. Moreover, it is quite clear from its contents that the *Apocalypse* was written in response to the Arab invasion of Asia Minor in the second half of the seventh century AD, three hundred years after Methodius's death. In other words, its author was most likely a Christian writer of the seventh century who wanted to bolster the tract's value by accrediting it to Methodius.

Exactly who penned this pseudepigraphical, or falsely attributed, work is unclear (the author is now referred to as Pseudo-Methodius), although what *is* important is that it was written originally in Syriac, the language of Northern Mesopotamia, meaning that it could well have originated from somewhere close to the city of Edessa, modern Şanlıurfa. This seems certain, as just a year or two after its initial circulation, modified versions, known today as the *Edessene Apocalypse,* were being produced in the area, quite possibly in one of the monasteries locally.[4]

WHERE IS *CORDAN MONTE?*

Which version of the *Apocalypse* the Reverend Marmaduke Carver consulted for his book is not cited. Most likely it was a volume in the York Minster Library, where the churchman did much of his research for *A Discourse of the Terrestrial Paradise.* Yet if we accept Carver's translation as authentic (and I have certainly found a Latin version of the *Apocalypse* with a date of 1593 that contains these exact same lines[5]), it implies that in the late seventh century an accomplished theological writer, living close to Edessa and the site of Göbekli

Tepe, possessed knowledge implying that Seth, his father Adam, his mother Eve, and their extended family group inhabited "Cordan monte," or Mount Cordan. Even more significant is his conviction that this mountain was situated *proximo,* or "next," to the terrestrial Paradise; that is, the Garden of Eden.

Carver assumed that "Cordan monte" was a reference to the Gordiæus Mountains (also written Gordyene or Corduene), which, he says, the Greco-Roman geographer Ptolemy (AD 90–168) located in the district of Armenia Major. Apparently, Ptolemy saw them as at "the same latitude with the springs of the Tigris: Strabo joins them with Mount Taurus."[6] Today, this mountain range is identified with the Kardu Mountains, which are farther south and include Mount al-Judi, the traditional resting place of the ark. Yet the classical writers located the Gordiæus Mountains north of here, in the Eastern Taurus range, which borders the plain of Mush on its southern side.

So this fixed the mythical world of Adam, Eve, Seth, and their extended family firmly within reach not just of the source of the Tigris, but also Sim Mountain, where Shem and his sons settled, and the Yeghrdut monastery was founded in the fourth century AD. Is this where Adam and Eve came to rest after being expelled from the Garden of Righteousness, somewhere in the vicinity of Yeghrdut, where afterward Shem established his own home? Interestingly, it was Shem who Noah sent to retrieve Adam's skull from its place of burial in order that it might be brought on to the ark,[7] even though the bodies of Eve, Seth, and all the other early patriarchs were left in situ. Apparently, the site of Adam's burial was the "Cave of Treasures," located on a "Holy Mountain"[8] that was said to overlook the site of the original Garden of Eden.[9] Did this cave exist somewhere near Yeghrdut, and could it be found today?

Of course, the historical validity of any such material is at best questionable, and yet there is no denying that the power of belief in a fictional mythos can be just as real as if not more real than, a tangible, mundane reality. Moreover, mythical data can encode within it kernels of truth that can manifest in the real world, and so nothing should be ignored or dismissed out of hand without due consideration.

THE SEED OF SETH

So to suddenly find that Adam and Eve's homeland after their expulsion from the Garden of Eden was somewhere in the vicinity of the Eastern Taurus

Mountains was very compelling indeed. Moreover, the introduction of Seth to the story was also highly significant, as it was the "seed of Seth," or Seth's descendants, who were to inherit God's kingdom after the death of Adam. This belief is derived from a passage in Genesis 4:25, which reads:

> And Adam again knoweth his wife, and she beareth a son, and calleth his name Seth, "for God hath appointed for me another seed instead of Abel:" for Cain had slain him.

The words "another seed" is interpreted as meaning that through Seth, the third son of Adam, God created a new branch of humanity that some Jews and early Christians believed was the only truly righteous tribe of God. Everybody else was descended of Cain, Seth's evil brother, and was thus wicked by descent.

Many Gnostic sects that thrived in the first five centuries of the Christian era saw Seth as the first of three manifestations of Christ himself. The others would seem to have been Shem, the son of Noah, and Jesus Christ himself. Indeed, the heavenly Seth was seen to have manifested in this world through the incarnation of Jesus, the two being synonymous with each other.

THE NAG HAMMADI LIBRARY

Gnostic followers of Seth, or Sethites as they were known, flourished among religious sects and secret groups that thrived in regions such as Palestine, Syria, Asia Minor, Egypt, and Armenia. They had their own gospels, or scriptures, many of which were found together inside a cave near Nag Hammadi in Middle Egypt in 1945. What became known as the Nag Hammadi library is the most important collection of Gnostic and Sethite texts ever studied. One theory is that the codices may have belonged to a local Coptic monastery and were buried following Bishop Athanasius's condemnation of the use of non-canonical holy books, that is, those not officially recognized by the Roman Church, in AD 367.

Among the Sethian titles in the Nag Hammadi collection are the *Three Steles of Seth, Zostrianos* (some see Zostrianos as a manifestation of Zoroaster, the divine leader of the Zoroastrians), the *Second Treatise of the Great Seth,* the *Paraphrase of Shem* (or Seth), *Allogenes,* the *Trimorphic Prottenoia,* and *Melchizedek.* These Gnostic gospels have some very interesting things to say about Seth, who is occasionally confused or identified with Shem,[10] the son of Noah. For instance, it is suggested that before his death, Adam transmitted to Seth certain matters concerning everything from the divine or angelic nature of humankind to the movement of the stars and heavenly bodies, and the knowledge of a coming catastrophe involving fire and water. These "secrets of Adam" are said to have been recorded before being hidden away until humanity was ready to receive them. Some of these secrets were to be revealed, periodically, through the appearance of four Phosters, that is, revealers or illuminators, who would incarnate for this express purpose,[11] while others would remain hidden until the right time for their discovery.

THE PILLARS OF SETH

What intrigued me most about this tradition is that Seth apparently inscribed the secrets of Adam on pillars or wrote them down on stone tablets, called steles, which were then deposited somewhere in the ancient world, usually either on or within a mountain cave of some description. For instance, the Jewish writer Flavius Josephus (AD 37–100), in his book *The Antiquities of the Jews,* talks about Seth leaving behind children, who "inhabited the same country without dissensions, and in a happy condition." They were "the inventors of that peculiar sort of wisdom which is concerned with the heavenly bodies, and their order." He goes on to write:

> And that their inventions might not be lost before they were sufficiently known, upon Adam's prediction that the world was to be destroyed at one time by the force of fire, and at another time by the violence and quantity of water, they made two pillars, the one of brick, the other of stone: they inscribed their discoveries on them both, that in case the pillar of brick should be destroyed by the flood, the pillar of stone might remain, and exhibit those discoveries to mankind; and also inform them that there was another pillar of brick erected by them. Now this remains in the land of Siriad to this day.[12]

Here the secrets of Adam are inscribed on pillars, one of brick, the other of stone, which are erected to preserve this knowledge beyond the coming cataclysm involving both a conflagration and deluge. So where exactly is Siriad (also written Seiris or Sirian), the named location of the inscribed pillars?

THE LAND OF SIRIAD

Because of the confusion between Seth, the son of Adam, and Seth, the brother of Osiris in Egyptian mythology, it has long been assumed that Siriad means Egypt. Here the inhabitants venerated the bright star Sirius, a similar sounding name to Siriad, while the pillars of Seth themselves were identified with the Great Pyramid and its neighbor, the Second Pyramid. This was a surmise assumed by the scholarly world following the publication in 1737 of a very popular translation of Josephus's works by English theologian, historian, and mathematician William Whiston (1667–1752).[13] Although Whiston did not believe that the pillars of Seth could have survived the conflagration and Flood, he did identify the land of Siriad as Egypt.[14]

Yet this connection with Egypt is a misnomer, for even if Seth *did* somehow become associated with the Great Pyramid, we know that Adam's son "lived," as Pseudo-Methodius tells us, somewhere in Armenia, which, following the carving up of the Greek Empire after the death of Alexander the Great in 323 BC, came under the control of the Syrian Seleucid Empire. Even with the dissolution of the empire in 190 BC, two Seleucid satraps, or governors, revolted and assumed control of Armenia Major and Armenia Minor (or Lesser Armenia), located west of the Euphrates River, and proclaimed themselves kings. Hellenic Greek practices and customs continued to thrive in Armenia and Northern Mesopotamia with all its Syrian influences. What is more, Edessa's kings, who were mostly called Abgar or Manu, kept their links with Syriac culture and tradition, and retained Syrian as the main written language.

There is really nothing to link the pillars of Seth with Egypt, and all the indications are that Siriad is a straightforward reference to Syria. In fact, before William Whiston's translation of Josephus's works, earlier translators did not hesitate to link Siriad with Syria. D. Eduardi Bernardi, for instance, in a translation of Josephus published at Oxford in 1687, discusses whether Siriad means Syriac in origin or belonging to Syria.[15]

Elsewhere there is additional evidence that Seth was depositing the "secrets of Adam" closer to home. For instance, at the end of the Latin *Vita Adae et Evae*, the "Life of Adam and Eve," following Adam's death Eve instructs their children to write on tablets of stone and clay everything they have learned both from her and their father. During the coming cataclysm, that which is written on stone will survive the Flood, while that which is written on clay will survive the conflagration. The implication is that Seth then conceals the tablets in the same vicinity; in other words, somewhere close to the terrestrial Paradise.[16]

THE ROCK OF TRUTH

The *Apocalypse of Adam,* one of the Gnostic texts included in the Nag Hammadi library, contains the revelation that "Adam taught his son Seth in the seven hundredth year." Here Adam tells Seth to record all of his and Eve's experiences in the Garden of Paradise (see figure 37.1). This is to include the revelations conveyed to them by three angelic informants regarding the future adventures of the elect, that is, the seed of Seth, along with knowledge of the imminent cataclysm of fire and flood, and details of the coming savior, who is Seth himself. Collectively, this wisdom is described as the "hidden knowledge of Adam." The reader is told also that a special revelation is to be written "on a high mountain, upon a rock of truth."[17]

Figure 37.1. *Eve at the Fountain,* by English visionary painter John Martin (1789–1854), one of twenty illustrations done in mezzotint for the 1827 edition of John Milton's *Paradise Lost.*

Even though the whereabouts of the land of Siriad, or Seiris, is nowhere given in the Gnostic gospels, Adam's secret writings are repeatedly said to be hidden in a holy mountain. The work known as the *Allogenes,* for instance, proclaims: "Write down [the things that I Allogenes, a name of Seth] shall [tell] you and of which I shall remind you for the sake of those who will be worthy after you. And you will leave this book upon a mountain and you will adjure the guardian 'Come, O Dreadful One.'"[18]

THE GOSPEL OF THE EGYPTIANS

Then in *The Gospel of the Egyptians,* also from the Nag Hammadi library, we read:

> This is the book which the great Seth wrote, and placed in high mountains on which the sun has not risen, nor is it possible. And since the days of the prophets, and the apostles, and the preachers, the name has not at all risen upon their hearts, nor is it possible. And ear has not heard it.
>
> The great Seth wrote this book with letters in one hundred and thirty years. He placed it in the mountain that is called Charaxio, in order that, at the end of the times and the eras . . . it may come forth and reveal this incorruptible, holy race of the great savior, and those who dwell with them in love.[19]

These words are greatly enigmatic, for they speak of a book concealed "in" a mountain, the location of which, and even the name thereof, has not been uttered since the time of Seth. Yet then, as if pronounced as part of some magical spell, the name of the mountain is finally revealed: *Charaxio.* But where is Charaxio? Was this the true hiding place of the secrets of Adam?

THE SEARCH FOR CHARAXIO

Charaxio is said to be located "where the sun has not risen, nor is it possible," a clear allusion to the Land of Darkness, the otherworldly realm in the extreme north associated with Alexander the Great's quest to find the Fountain of Life and Gilgamesh's search to find the plant of immortality. It was here too that the god El had his abode and the two hundred rebel Watchers made the decision to descend to the plains below and take mortal wives. As Belgium-based

Near Eastern scholar Edward Lipinski determined, the Land of Darkness existed beyond the virtually impenetrable barrier created by the Eastern Taurus Mountains in Armenia Major.

Guy G. Stroumsa, a Gnostic scholar with the Hebrew University, Jerusalem, and Oxford University, England, has made a study of the mysterious mountain called Charaxio. He says that various attempts have been made to find its location. However, because Charaxio appears under this name only in *The Gospel of the Egyptians,* it has proved near impossible to trace. This said, the abbreviated form, Charax, *does* appear in antiquity.[20] John Lemprière's *Bibliotheca Classica: A Classical Dictionary,* published in 1788, reveals just one entry under this name, which is "a town in Armenia."[21]

That Charaxio might have been situated in Armenia makes sense of the fact that it was said to exist where the sun doesn't shine; that is, in the Land of Darkness, in the far north. Stroumsa himself took note of this, comparing Charaxio's description with "the dark regions mentioned in 1 *Enoch* 78:3"[22]; that is, the book of Enoch, which, as we have seen, can be linked with the Land of Darkness beyond the Tigris Tunnel. Realizing this, Stroumsa alludes to traditions regarding the prophet Enoch being handed books from his forefathers Adam and Seth, which he says were concealed on Mount Ararat in Armenia, so that they might remain safe during the coming deluge.[23]

MOUNT SIR

Pushing the matter still further, Stroumsa notes that "the link between Seiris (the land of the sons of Seth and the place of the Steles) and Mount Ararat" finds expression in another Gnostic text called *The Hypostatis of the Archons,* which is also found in the Nag Hammadi library. He continues: "Noah is asked by the demiurge (the creator of the physical world) to set the ark upon Mount Sir. . . . In some milieus, the mountain could have been given the name of the land in which the books were written Σειρ(ις)"[24]; that is, Seir(is).

So Guy Stroumsa proposes that Charaxio, Seiris, and Mount Sir (Seir) are all one and the same or that they are conflated forms of an original mountain of Seth, which he identifies as Mount Ararat, since this would have been the safest place for something to have been hidden with foresight of the coming conflagration and deluge. This is, in my opinion, smart thinking, yet once again we are back to Mount Ararat sucking up every legend and tradition that comes along, simply because of the Christian fixation with its being the Place of Descent of Noah's ark. Just one Gnostic work actually mentions Mount Ararat by name, this being the *Pistis Sophia* contained in the Askew Codex, a fifth-century parchment manuscript of Coptic origin now in the British Library. Yet it speaks only of Jesus in his spiritual form causing the patriarch Enoch to write the so-called Books of Yeu (or Jeu) when in Paradise, and then getting him to deposit them for safekeeping "in the rock Ararad," where a heavenly ruler is appointed to watch over them during the coming flood.[25] It does not mention Adam or Seth, and certainly makes no direct reference to Charaxio, Seiris, or Mount Sir.

So I looked again for any elucidation on the place-name Charaxio and found something very interesting indeed. I discovered that the Araxes River, which was also known by the abbreviated form of Arax, was itself once called the Charax,[26] making sense of John Lemprière's entry in his *Bibliotheca Classica* regarding a town called Charax in Armenia. Since we know that the Araxes takes its rise on Bingöl Mountain, the Abus Mons of antiquity, there has to be a good chance that it is also Charaxio, which with the *–io* suffix gives it the meaning "belonging to Charax"; that is, the Araxes River.

Charaxio's identification with Bingöl Mountain is strengthened by the words of Stroumsa himself, who concludes for perfectly good reasons that Charaxio, Seiris, and Mount Sir are all synonymous with Bingöl's main rival, Mount Ararat. Take Mount Ararat out of the picture and you are still left with his firm conviction that somewhere in Armenia Major is the real Charaxio. So was Bingöl Mountain really where Seth concealed the secrets of Adam on pillars or steles in order that they might be revealed in the final days? It is interesting that John Lemprière's entry for Abus Mons reads "a mountain in Syria, where the Euphrates rises."[27] It confirms that in classical times this region of Armenia Major was still classed as Syria, the ancient land of Siriad or Seiris, where Josephus tells us that Seth concealed his pillars of knowledge and his descendants continued to live after this time. Yet what about Mount Sir—where was that located?

MONS VICTORIALIS

A tract entitled *Opus Imperfectum in Matthaeum,* a commentary on the Gospel of Matthew, which circulated among a Christian sect known as the Arians during the fifth century, alludes to a lost book or books of Seth. It states that once a year a group of twelve scholars would climb a mountain called Mons

Victorialis, the "Victorious Mountain" or "Mountain of Victory," on which were abundant "fountains" and beautiful trees, and here they would enter a cave and examine an original work written by Seth.[28]

An eighth-century Syriac text known as the "Revelation of the Magi"[29] contains the same basic story, although here the twelve scholars are twelve Magi, who are both kings and "wise men,"[30] descendants of Seth,[31] who live in the land of Shir (i.e., Sir or Seiris).[32] The book takes the form of commandments given by Adam to Seth, who records them in written form. It speaks of a sign that will herald the birth of a god in human form, with that sign being a star in the likeness of a small child.[33]

Every year the Magi would purify themselves in a spring and then ascend the Mountain of Victory and pray in silence before entering the cave, which is identified as the Cave of Treasures of the Hidden Mysteries.[34] (See figure 37.2.) Here Adam and Eve had lived, just beyond the Garden of Eden, and after their deaths it had become the home of Seth, his family, and their descendants.

This same settlement of the antediluvian patriarchs, as we have already seen, was said by Pseudo-Methodius to have been located near Mount Cordan, in the Eastern Taurus range, close to the Yeghrdut monastery and the plain of Mush.

Inside the cave the Magi consulted the books of Seth containing the secrets of Adam and watched for the prophesied sign before returning to their kingdoms to instruct those of their people who wished to learn of the "hidden mysteries." The whole process was repeated across many generations, and when one of the twelve died, either a son or a close relative would replace him.[35]

The text alludes also to a book of revelations written by Seth, which states that Adam had originally seen the sign, the original star child, hanging over the Tree of Life in the Garden of Eden, but that it had disappeared when he committed the first sin.[36] The "Revelation of the Magi" then reveals how a star appears in the sky, before entering the cave, inviting the Magi to do the same. Inside they find not a star, but the likeness of a small child, who introduces himself as the Son of God. The wise men are instructed to follow the star so that they might worship him in human form. They are then led in a quite fantastic manner first to Jerusalem and then to Bethlehem, where the star enters a cave and becomes the infant Jesus, at which point the story reverts to the account of the Nativity as told in the gospel of Matthew

The Secrets of Adam   331

Figure 37.2. Twelfth-century representation of Adam and Eve inside the Cave of Treasures, located within Mons Victorialis, the Mountain of Victory. Here lived the "children of Seth" until the time of the Flood. Its discovery will reveal the books of Seth containing the secrets of Adam.

(2:1–12). Eventually, the Magi return to the land of Shir, and in time the apostle Judas Thomas arrives to convert the people through "mighty deeds"[37]; and here he now baptizes and anoints the Magi.

Although there have been attempts to identify the land of Shir with locations as far away as northeast Iran and even China,[38] it was likely located in the vicinity of the Cave of Treasures and, of course, the Garden of Eden. What is more, the Mountain of Victory, or Mons Victorialis, features in the sixth century Syriac text entitled the book of the Cave of Treasures as a name of the "Mountain of God" on which Adam, Eve, and their extended family—the "children of Seth"—live prior to the time of the Flood. These "children" constitute the entire line of early patriarchs and their families, from Seth right down to Noah.[39] Enoch is there also, ministering unto God inside the cave and burying his father, Jared, all this coming before his celebrated translation to Paradise in the company of angels (see figure 37.3). According to the book of the Cave of Treasures, at the time of the Flood, Shem, the son of Noah, returns to the cave to retrieve the body of Adam, which is then taken aboard the ark—the bodies of the other patriarchs being left behind in the cave.[40]

So was the land of Shir to be found somewhere in the vicinity of the plain of Mush, the most obvious site of the Garden of Eden? Was it to be identified with Sim Mountain, where Shem is said to have established a settlement after leaving the ark and where Thaddeus deposited the holy relics beneath Yeghrdut's evergreen tree in the first century AD? Remember, the alternative form of the Sumerian word for *snake,* muš, which might well be the root behind the Mush place-name, is šir, pronounced *shir* in the Akkadian language. Was the ancient Armenian kingdom of Taron, which included the plain of Mush, once known as the land of Šir, or Shir; that is, the land of the snake? This has to remain a very distinct possibility indeed.

If not in the vicinity of Yeghrdut, was the Mountain of Victory synonymous with Bingöl Mountain and Abus Mons, the best candidate by far for Charaxio, the mountain where *The Gospel of the Egyptians* tells us Seth hid his holy book, or books, containing the secrets of Adam? Is this where the Cave of Treasures will be found? Both sites, Yeghrdut and Bingöl, which are visible from each other, might easily have played some dual role in the construction of the Jewish, Gnostic, and later Christian myths concerning the true location not only of the original Garden of Eden but also where Adam and Eve's descendants, the "children of Seth," are said to have lived on the "holy mountain" of God. No other geographical region makes sense of all of these disparate stories, showing us quite clearly that in Judeo-Christian tradition this was where the events of the book of Genesis were played out, no more than a couple of hundred miles away from Göbekli Tepe.

So what exactly are the secrets of Adam? Can we go on to determine what Seth actually recorded, either in book form or in stone? As we see next, Adam's secrets might well turn out to contain forbidden knowledge regarding the angelic origins of humankind.

Figure 37.3. The patriarch Enoch is translated to Paradise after being anointed by the angel Michael and becoming like an angel himself.

38

AS ANGELS OURSELVES

W hat exactly are the secrets of Adam? What might they pertain to, and what relevance has any of this to Göbekli Tepe and the Yeghrdut monastery located in some quiet corner of the terrestrial Paradise? The first clue is *The Gospel of the Egyptians,* which tells of the creation of the Sethians. They, we are told, constitute "earthly counterparts of a heavenly church of angelic beings, the prototypical Sethians."[1] Moreover, we learn that when the book or stele that Seth placed in the mountain Charaxio is found, "it will identify the true race of Seth."[2]

There is little question that this "true race of Seth" is to be seen as the incarnated souls of the aforementioned "angelic beings, the prototypical Sethians," meaning that the secrets of Adam supposedly reveal the angelic nature of humankind.

LIKE THE ANGELS

What exactly does this mean? How can humans become like angels, especially if the rebel Watchers of the book of Enoch represent, arguably, a memory of the real prime movers behind the genesis of civilization? The key is that the angels were said to have inhabited Paradise itself and so benefited, like Adam and Eve before the Fall, from the presence of the Tree of Life, which conveys eternal life to whoever or whatever is in its presence.

Before the Fall, according to Gnostic tradition, Adam and Eve had spiritual bodies, "like the angels,"[3] but after their expulsion, their bodies grew more and more dense and languid until they were no more than "coats of skin."[4] Only with the "sweet odour of light," the perfumed oil from the Tree of Life, would they ever be able to regain their original divine body.[5]

Not only does any fragment from the Tree of Life remain "true and living," a concept reflected in Yeghrdut's holy tree being "evergreen," but the Oil of Mercy from the Tree of Life is said to bestow eternal light and life through the sacred process of anointing. Indeed, early Christian tradition asserted that Jesus was himself anointed with oil from the Holy Wood of the Tree of Life before incarnation in order that he might become Christ,[6] a word taken from the Greek Χριστός (Christos), meaning "the Anointed One."

As I already knew, the Tree of Life was anciently believed to have been an olive tree,[7] an evergreen that gave forth a fragrance or perfume,[8] a belief connected with the story contained in the book of Enoch in which Enoch, on his visit to Paradise in the company of two angels, is anointed with an oil fragranced by myrrh:

> And God said to Michael: "Approach and remove Enoch's earthly garments! Anoint him with My blessed oil and dress him with garments of My glory! Michael did what God told him; he anointed me and dressed me. The appearance of the oil was greater than a great light and its lubricant was like blessed dew, and its fragrance was like myrrh shining like the sun's rays. I looked at myself and saw that I was like one of His glorious ones and there was no obvious difference.[9]

So the removal of Enoch's physical garments and his anointing with perfumed oil have the purpose of taking away the patriarch's earthly skin and replacing it with divine garments that are symbolic of his transformation from a mortal person into an angelic being. This is the prerequisite for his permanent translation to Paradise, the story told in the book of Genesis.[10] Yet it is also a reference to the spiritual bodies, or "garments of light," that Adam bore before the Fall. So through this anointing process Enoch becomes as Adam was in Paradise, a person restored to his original state of divine glory, no different from the angels themselves.

THE HOLY MYRON

The perfumed oil used by the angel or Watcher named Michael to anoint Enoch can be compared with the Myron (or Muron), also known as the Chrism, used even today to anoint the Catholicos during his inauguration as spiritual head of the Armenian Church. It is obtained by mixing together pure olive oil with some forty or so herbs and spices, including myrrh, which is then exposed to the surviving essence of the original holy anointing oil made by Moses under Yahweh's instruction and brought to Yeghrdut in Taron by Thaddeus in the first century.

The Myron is considered to convey wisdom through the Holy Spirit or divine light of God since it bore the similitude of the heavenly Oil of Mercy from the Tree of Life. This is brought out in teachings attributed to Saint Peter, the founder of the Church of Rome, which state that one day Christians will be able to receive oil that comes directly from the Tree of Life and not simply from some created imitation: "If the oil blended by men had such power, think how great is the oil that was extracted by God himself from a branch of the tree of life."[11]

Very similar ideas are behind the anointing not just of church leaders worldwide but also of kings and queens. At a coronation, it is the anointing of the candidate that conveys kingship, *not* the crowning; the placement of the crown is merely a visible sign of the monarch's authority to rule in the eyes of God and of his or her newfound divinity.

From this it might be assumed that the secrets of Adam, written down by Seth, contain the manner in which we, as mortal humans, are able to regain our spiritual bodies of light lost at the time of the Fall. To do this and become as angels ourselves, we have to be anointed by the perfumed oil that bears the similitude of the Oil of Mercy from the Tree of Life. Within the influence of this divinely prescribed substitute for the Oil of Mercy, immortality is assured.

Clearly, this is a religious concept, utilized today by Jewish and Christian nations around the world. It might seem also to have little, if anything, to do with the discovery 170 miles (274 kilometers) from Yeghrdut of Göbekli Tepe. Yet empowerment and otherworldly transformation through the use of specific types of wood, and the oils and resins extracted from them, is something that might well have had its origins in the early Neolithic world of southeast Anatolia.

The discovery at Göbekli Tepe of burnt almond wood and spent almond shells[12] among the fill covering its sanctuaries indicates that almond oil was almost certainly known here. Its use could easily have been the origin behind much later anointing traditions that existed among the civilizations of ancient Mesopotamia and the Semitic peoples of the Levant (hence its association with biblical tradition). Interestingly, the rod of Aaron, Moses's brother, is said to have "bloomed blossoms, which spreading the leaves, were formed into almonds" (Num. 17:8), while the seven-branched candle of the Jews known as the menorah represents both an almond tree and the Tree of Life. The two are synonymous,[13] even though elsewhere the Tree of Life, as we have seen, is said to be an olive tree.

LINKS TO YEGHRDUT

In view of all this, the fact that Thaddeus travels all the way from Judea via Edessa to Yeghrdut to deposit both a fragment of the Tree of Life and the bottle containing the essence of the perfumed oil that Yahweh had instructed Moses to make has incredible implications. It suggests that the disciple was taking them to somewhere already connected with traditions associated with the Oil of Mercy and Tree of Life. This he recognized through the presence there of an earthly representation of the Tree of Life in the form of Yeghrdut's own evergreen tree, from beneath which flowed a source of the Euphrates, one of the four rivers of Paradise. It tells us also that Yeghrdut was considered the true foundation point of the Armenian Church, the Myron bottle and fragment of the Tree of Life being its symbols of divine authority over counter claims of supremacy from rival monastic foundations.

Of course, it might easily be argued that the Armenian Church made up the entire story of Thaddeus's visit to Yeghrdut and his concealment there of the holy relics. Yet if this were the case, why connect the legend with Yeghrdut and not Surb Karapet, Taron's showcase monastery on the opposite side of the plain of Mush? Why attribute this extraordinary tradition to Yeghrdut when Surb Karapet would have been a much better option, especially as it was founded around important relics of John the Baptist? Alternatively, why not connect the story to the Mother See of Holy Echmiadzin at Vagharshapat, Armenia's great spiritual center located within sight of Mount Ararat, where eventually Yeghrdut's sacred container was moved so that the holy Myron might continue to be manufactured there?

Everything points toward a long-held tradition suggesting that Yeghrdut's evergreen tree was seen to mark the site of the terrestrial Tree of Life, planted by Seth either within or upon the skull of Adam, the first man. If correct, then close by was the Cave of Treasures, where Adam and the early patriarchs lived and were buried after the time of the Fall, and the book or books containing the secrets of Adam lay hidden within the Mountain of Victory, located in the land of Shir, or Seir.

In Gnostic tradition, Seth incarnates to save his "seed" on three occasions: first as Seth, the man; second as Shem, the son of Noah; and finally as Jesus Christ (his lives as Seth and Jesus both linking him with traditions concerning the Oil of Mercy). A. F. J. Klijn in his important work *Seth in Jewish, Christian and Gnostic Literature* (1977) says that the "race of Seth" may have been a historical phenomena "which existed until the flood or [they were] a group which was to be saved at the end of time."[14] Yet as much as these ideas regarding the books, steles, or pillars of Seth are bound up in Jewish, Christian, and Gnostic millennialism, can they really be linked to the discoveries being made today at Göbekli Tepe?

THE CHILDREN OF SETH

An ancient Jewish religious work known as the book of Jubilees, which, like the book of Enoch, has been found among the Dead Sea Scrolls, talks about Cainan, the son of Arphaxad, or Arpachshad, who found "a writing which the ancestors engraved on stone," reminding us of the pillars or steles on which Seth wrote the secrets of Adam. These writings contained "the teaching of the Watchers by which they used to observe the omens of the sun and moon and stars within all the signs of heaven."[15]

It was this same starry wisdom that became the foundation of the beliefs of the Chaldeans; that is, the Sabaean star-worshippers of Harran, the ten-thousand-year-old city located on the plain beneath the gaze of Göbekli Tepe (see the Prologue for the full story). Arphaxad, Cainan's father, is said to have been the progenitor of the Chaldeans of Harran.[16] His name, Arphaxad, is a conflation of the place-name "Ur of the Chaldees,"[17] Abraham's birthplace in nearby Şanlıurfa, showing the firm connection between these early biblical characters and the *triangle d'or,* the birthplace of the Neolithic revolution. Completing the picture is the fact that Arphaxad's father was Shem, the son of Noah, whose settlement at Simsar, or Sim Mountain, in the Eastern Taurus range overlooking the plain of Mush, is today occupied by the Yeghrdut monastery.

Interestingly, the Sabaeans, the pagan inhabitants of Harran, were said to have been "worshippers of fire called Magi" and claimed to be keepers of the mysterious "book of Seth," because their founder was one "Sabius, a son of Seth."[18] Moreover, they asserted that "we acknowledge the religion of Seth, Idris (Enoch) and Noah."[19] So could the original book or books of Seth have been carved stone pillars, like those being uncovered today at nearby Göbekli Tepe? Were the twelve Magi that perpetually guarded the book or books of Seth an echo, however slight, of the rings of twelve anthropomorphic pillars erected at Göbekli Tepe some 11,500 years ago? Could these rings of stone reflect much later traditions regarding the "children of Seth" preserving the secrets of Adam in written form? If so, then who or what might the twin central pillars have come to represent in Jewish, Christian, and Gnostic tradition?

Too much speculation here would be foolish, although the fact that Gnostic writings emphasize that Cain and Abel, the twin sons of Adam, each had twin sisters is intriguing and reminds us of the belief that twins always grew inside the womb during pregnancy. Moreover, that Seth was born as Abel's replacement sets up a twinlike relationship between Cain and Seth, reflected in the stories regarding our descendancy either from the "sons of Cain" or the "seed of Seth"; that is, the Sethites. The central pillars at Göbekli Tepe are perhaps allusions to this twin tradition, although whether they can be seen in terms of the twin offspring of Adam, the first man, who in Gnostic teachings was overshadowed by his own celestial twin, is another matter altogether.

So in addition to revealing humanity's dual origins, angelic and mortal, do Göbekli Tepe's T-shaped pillars reflect an understanding of Adam's "astrological knowledge" which might have included information regarding the appearance of short-period comets? One brilliant-minded person once wrote that the secrets of Adam, handed down to Seth and Enoch, might have been "the knowledge of months, years and periods of comets that the remote generations had acquired—and the hope grew into faith that no such or similar destruction would come any more to decimate mankind."[20]

That person was Russian-Jewish psychiatrist Immanuel Velikovsky (1895–

1979), one of the greatest catastrophe theorists of the twentieth century. He realized that, in all likelihood, any such secret information *had* to relate not just to the conflagration and deluge itself but also to how to ensure that such catastrophes never again trouble our world.

Out there somewhere, in some lonely spot on Bingöl Mountain (in its likely role as Charaxio), or maybe in the vicinity of the Yeghrdut monastery (as a potential location of the Cave of Treasures), are perhaps the true secrets of Adam. Inscribed on standing pillars or on steles, similar to those seen today at Göbekli Tepe, they await discovery and interpretation. They might reveal how we, as mortal humans, can restore our bodies of light, lost at the time of the Fall, and be as angels ourselves; in other words, become as one with our incorporeal selves left behind during the process of incarnation on this earthly plane. They might also provide confirmation that the world was once brought to its knees by a comet impact and that only afterward did the genesis of civilization begin here in eastern Anatolia, the true location of the Garden of Eden.

A TRIP TO TURKEY

There was only one thing left for me to do, and this was to go to Turkey, where I would visit the ruins of the Yeghrdut monastery and get out to Bingöl Mountain somehow. I needed to find out what I could about these places and inquire locally into any folklore, myths, and legends that might help bring alive their geomythic reality. From there I would journey to Göbekli Tepe, where I hoped to interview Professor Klaus Schmidt.

I knew the region pretty well from my years of research, having visited Göbekli Tepe, Çayönü, Harran, and Karahan Tepe back in 2004. However, I saw one slight problem looming on the horizon like a dark cloud, and this was the fact that the mountains around Mush, including Bingöl Dağ and the Eastern Taurus Mountains beyond Yeghrdut, were currently the front line for the Kurdish uprising headed by the PKK, the Kurdistan Workers Party. They have been fighting for Kurdish independent rule and an autonomous Turkish Kurdistan for the past thirty-five years. Although most of the offensives against them by the Turkish army and secret police are today concentrated in the mountainous region close to the border with Iraqi Kurdistan, I was shocked to find that there had been recent military operations against the PKK in the area of Zengok (modern Yörecik), a village just 7 miles (11 kilometers) from the Yeghrdut monastery ruins, and even on a mountain named Kozma Dağ, immediately to the south of Dera Sor.

As the date of my departure for Turkey grew nearer, the matter did begin to worry me, yet there was very little I could do. Nothing, not even my better judgment, was going to stop me from getting out to Yeghrdut, which, however you look at it, was first introduced to my world though a simple, though quite profound dream.

39

THE RETURN TO EDEN

Monday, September 10, 2012. After a night spent in a dismal hotel on the outskirts of Istanbul, I journeyed on to eastern Turkey. From the small airport at Mush, a taxi took me to the hotel, which lay on the edge of town. Close by was the road out to the villages of Kızılağaç and Suluca, near to which I would find Dera Sor, the ruins of the Yeghrdut monastery.

The next morning, over breakfast, I was able to appreciate exactly where I was for the first time. Through the hotel's panoramic windows I could see the plain of Mush stretching away in every direction, beyond which was a seemingly impenetrable wall of mountains, reminding me of the seven mountains that encircle the Garden of Righteousness, according to the book of Enoch.[1] Only toward the east did they seem to lower slightly, and here I thought I could make out the summit of Nemrut Dağ, the extinct volcano on the western shores of Lake Van.

THE TAXI RIDE

With breakfast over I waited in the lobby as the hotel owner made various phone calls. These resulted in a taxi driver arriving just after ten, although the guide-interpreter situation was not good, apparently. For two hours I drank sweet black tea and waited, until finally two guys turned up, both

342

quite young, one of whom said he was usually paid the going rate as an interpreter for the European Union, which worried me slightly due to the potential expense. The other was his friend, who also spoke good English. Very quickly we were in the taxi on our way out to Suluca.

No one had heard of Dera Sor, or Yeghrdut, which seemed bizarre. I was telling them about a sacred site, an ancient ruin of substantial size with a fascinating history spanning nearly two thousand years, yet nobody knew a thing about it. If it had not been for the images I had brought along that showed Dera Sor on Google Earth, my new friends might not have believed it even existed.

As the taxi left the outskirts of town, I followed the route closely to ensure we were going in the right direction, but the driver knew Suluca, and very soon we were on a side road leading toward the foothills of the Eastern Taurus Mountains and a cluster of prefabricated buildings. We stopped to ask the way to Dera Sor, and an old man pointed immediately toward the heavily forested mountain slope behind him. So at least the ruins still existed and were known to the villagers of Suluca.

The elderly man climbed into the taxi and guided us to the start of an unmade track that marked the beginning of a very bumpy ride in a vehicle that was scarcely suitable for such a journey. As we climbed higher and higher, generally with the steep hillside to our left, we rose above the surrounding landscape, which stretched away to the north, and for the first time I got a glimpse of the Murad Şu, or Eastern Euphrates, winding its way across the plain of Mush.

PKK SITUATION

I did inquire about the situation with the PKK locally and was informed that the mountains were under rebel control, so much so that Turkish forces did not even venture into the area unless it was part of an official military offensive. I asked also about the chances of getting to Bingöl Mountain and was told that this area was currently an active front line and thus a no-go zone to visitors like me. This was a massive disappointment, but for the moment my principal goal was to get to Yeghrdut.

After driving for around fifteen to twenty minutes, we leveled out but still faced the prospect of an even higher climb to the east of our position. The taxi driver seemed lost, the guide and his friend didn't know what to do, and no one was around to ask for directions. My map seemed useless, so the only option left was to stand on a high spot and just look for any sign of ruins.

It was the guide's friend who first spotted Dera Sor. Over on a ridge, about half a mile away, was what appeared to be a long, red wall on a flat ridge. That had to be it, and without further ado we were back in the taxi trying to reach the spot. The path seemed strewn with potholes, so we left the vehicle in the capable hands of the guide's friend and continued on foot in the baking hot sun.

The track lifted up over an incline, beyond which on the left was a ridge of pine trees. I was struck immediately by the extreme redness of the earth, created no doubt by sandstone with a heavy iron oxide content that had long since crumbled to dust. To the right the ground sloped away toward the plain below. Scrub and a few clumps of trees grew here and there, but generally the land seemed parched and dry.

THE DERA SOR COMMUNITY

Coming into view now was a group of large, wigwamlike tents, some covered with white tarpaulin, others with tree branches. There were also circular pens full of turkeys and plenty of goats running loose around the whole camp. People were already emerging to see what all the commotion was about. I felt that the sight of an Englishman in desert suit, straw trilby hat, and black-framed glasses was not the norm for these people. Coming out to meet us were women wearing brightly colored hijab headscarves, several small children, three young men in their late teens, and a tall, thin, elderly gentleman with large moustache, gray jacket, and traditional Turkish fez, a black one that had seen better days. He was quite clearly the leader of the small community, which numbered fifteen to twenty individuals.

These people were seasonal pastoralists, who live out on the mountainside during the summer months, then retire to more urban environments when the cold weather sets in around November. From then on until March or April, the whole region can be covered from top to bottom in thick snow, making life very difficult indeed.

Our guide greeted the fez-wearing man and his family, and conversations ensued regarding the purpose of our visit. The subject of the ruins was discussed, and from the nods and points toward a large earthen ridge of debris immediately west of the settlement, above which I could see the tops of red-stone walls, I realized that there was no obvious problem with our being here. Yet before going any further I asked the elderly man about the monastery's sacred tree and holy spring. Did he know where these were?

A VISIT TO THE SPRING

Exchanges between the guide and the leader resulted in our moving out into parched scrubland between the camp and the ruins. Not 40 yards (37 meters) from where we had stood was the spring, close to the base of the north-facing hill slope. From its sunken entrance, marked by an arch of large, flat stones, the leader removed a mesh of tree branches bound together with nails, and put there to prevent animals from contaminating the water. With this I sought permission to climb inside the cramped space, created by a rounded roof of stonework overlaid with earth.

I wanted to get some pictures and drink a little water, which I now saw came up into a small pool before trickling away beneath the earth. Farther down the hill the water flow reemerged from a metal pipe, creating the beginnings of the Kilise Şu stream, which flows into the Eastern Euphrates. I was now at a source of one of the four rivers of Paradise.

Despite Yeghrdut's location on the edge of Paradise, I was dismayed to see plastic cups and containers, as well as cooking utensils and half-buried dustbin liners, strewn about inside the hollow. It was clear that the spring was no longer seen as sacred, a fact confirmed through conversations with the fez-wearing man.

THE HOLY TREE

I asked next to see the old walnut tree, which had been renowned throughout the entire province as a place of healing (see figure 39.1 on p. 346). Our hosts nodded, ushering us on another 20 yards (18 meters) to a dusty patch of ground. Here they pointed toward the remains of an old tree stump still in situ, with a girth of around 5 feet (1.5 meters). Clearly, this was not the original evergreen tree that had stood on the spot in Thaddeus's day, but it was certainly a potent symbol of its former presence here.

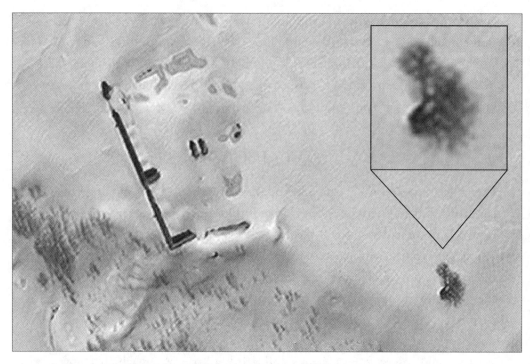

Figure 39.1. Dera Sor, the ruins of the Yeghrdut monastery, in snow, from a Google Earth image taken on April 1, 2009. Note the walnut tree, the final incarnation of the "evergreen tree," under which the disciple Thaddeus apparently deposited a piece of the Tree of Life and the container that held the essence of holy oil used to anoint "prophets and apostles." Courtesy of DigitalGlobe 2013.

When I inquired about what had happened to the tree, I was told that it had fallen down around two years earlier, and that two trucks were needed to carry away all the timber. Hearing this made me incredibly sad and a little annoyed that the tree had not been better preserved, especially given that it reflected nearly two thousand years of history at the site.

According to what I had found out over the past few months,[2] the evergreen tree under which Thaddeus had concealed the holy relics was said to have survived to the present day, an unlikely claim particularly after examining the pitiful remains of the walnut tree. According to tradition, an eagle had nested at the summit of the original tree. A flowing stream emerged from beneath its trunk, and a stone wall, with an altar at one end, had protected its roots. Women and young ladies in particular would come here not just to rest beneath its shade but also to take water from the stream to cure ailments. They would take away any small part of the tree they could find—leaves, bark, twigs, and so forth, which would be placed inside their clothes, against the body, to relieve pain. Apparently, any greenery removed from the tree was the ultimate healing aid, with the ability to retain its healing potency forever.[3]

I learned also that the fragment of the Tree of Life deposited at Yeghrdut by Thaddeus was the subject of a quite extraordinary legend.[4] One day a shepherd visiting the monastery saw the simple box containing the relic and decided to steal it, thinking that its contents might be worth money. He got home and decided to take a look at what was inside. Yet on seeing that it contained a piece of wood, the man panicked and threw the box on the fire. No sooner had he done this than flames burst forth from the hearth and consumed the entire house, sending the shepherd running for his life.

Prompted by the fire, the great eagle that guarded the holy tree then swooped down and snatched up the box with its precious contents, neither of which had been damaged in any way. The bird took them back to its nest and thereafter became their constant guardian, never letting anyone with ill intent near them.

EAGLE ON THE WORLD TREE

This legend, which seems like something out of a book of Turkish folktales, was believed fervently by the monks of the monastery and is included in the entry for Yeghrdut in the aforementioned encyclopedia of monasteries and churches of the Taron Province.[5] Whatever its reality, the story oozes mythological symbolism. The eagle sitting atop the tree guarding a piece of the Tree of Life is suggestive of the world tree Yggdrasil in Norse tradition, which also has an eagle nesting on its summit.

The similarity between the name Yeghrdut and Yggdrasil is probably coincidental, although it has not stopped people from drawing comparisons between *yggdr,* one possible root behind the name Yeghrdut, and Yggdrasil, and also between Hızır, or al-Khidr, a guardian of the Waters of Life, and Odin, the god who hangs on the Norse world tree to gain the knowledge of the runic alphabet.[6] Interestingly, compelling evidence indicates that the origins of some Norse mythology, and perhaps even the roots of the Scandinavian people, are to be looked for in the region around Lake Van. World-renowned explorer Thor Heyerdahl (1914–2002) was working on these theories shortly before his death.[7] The exact derivation of the word *Yeghrdut* still remains unclear, as it is not a proper Armenian word, although it does seem to relate to Armenian word roots meaning "king," "flower," and "willow,"[8] or, as I had already established, *shuyugho,* the "young branch of the (oil tree)."[9]

The eagle itself was the symbol of the ancient kingdom of Taron, which was established in the fourth century AD by an Armenian dynasty of kings called the Mamikonians, whose emblem was the double-headed eagle. This connection between Taron and the eagle might easily have stemmed from the existence of a pagan god in the form of an eagle that was venerated in Armenia Major during former ages. The association between the eagle of Yeghrdut and the holy tree, however, might well stem from a source much closer to the root of the mystery.

THE WOOD THAT CUTS

There are many different variations of the story of how the Holy Wood or Holy Timber of Life used to create the Cross of Calvary, which originated in some manner from the Tree of Life. One version has Adam being given a branch upon his departure from the Garden of Eden; in another it is handed to Seth in the form of seeds or saplings; and in still another a bird known as the roc, a gigantic, mythical eagle of Arabic tradition, picks up "a piece of wood from one of the trees in the garden."[10] This mythical bird carries the branch to Jerusalem and there drops it onto a huge, upside-down copper cauldron, beneath which is the bird's young. They are being held captive by King Solomon, who has snatched them away from their mother after searching for guidance from God as to how he might go about finishing the temple begun by his father, David.

The weight of the wood smashes the cauldron, releasing the bird's young. Thereafter, Solomon realizes that the wood left by the roc can miraculously cut stone blocks, enabling the king to complete the temple. Following a long story involving King Solomon and the Queen of Sheba, the Holy Wood finds its way to the carpenter's shop, where, as in the more traditional story, it is fashioned into the cross on which Christ is crucified.[11]

The important part of this story is that this piece of wood taken from "one of the trees in the garden," an allusion unquestionably to the Tree of Life, is linked with an eaglelike bird, just as it is in the Yeghrdut legend. This lends support to the belief that the monastery had in its possession a fragment of the Holy Wood of Life thought to derive from the Tree of Life itself.

THE RUINS EXPLORED

After asking for and getting a few small fragments of the remaining tree trunk (as well as a walnut shell, confirming it as the holy tree mentioned in the correspondence with the contact from Kızılağaç), we now moved on to the goal of the expedition—the monastery itself. Walking about 40 yards (37 meters) we now climbed a huge pile of rubble and debris and saw spread out before us the ruins in all their glory. The raised mound marked the position of the structure's eastern wall, while similar piles of rubble marked the location of the north and south walls. However, in the west, the remaining wall, made up of a thick base of rust-red bricks and an upper level of lighter-colored gray stone, was substantial, being as much as 15 feet (4.5 meters) in height, with a large breach toward its northern end.

In all, the west wall was around 70 yards (64 meters) in length, with a returning wall at its southern end, which quickly reduces down to ground level. Walking up to the remaining wall, I noticed a series of linear foundations jutting out at right angles, which I suspected marked the position of small cells, most likely living quarters for the monks. It is incredible to think that this immense structure was, apparently, two stories high and almost equal in size to the more famous monastery of Surb Karapet, located in the foothills of the Armenian Highlands on the opposite side of the plain of Mush (indeed, the monasteries, both dedicated to Saint John the Baptist, would each have been visible to the other).

FINDING THE CHURCHES

The only other architectural features that remain standing at the monastery site are two beautiful stones arches, around 12 feet (3.7 meters) high, one positioned directly in front of the other (see figure 39.2 on p. 350). These are oriented east-northeast (at approximately 20 degrees north of east) and once formed the northern entrance into a large building located in the southeast quadrant of the monastery. All around the arches are piles of rubble and debris, reducing their interior height, although it is still possible to pass beneath them fairly comfortably.

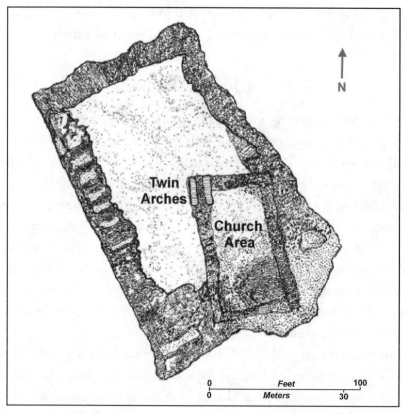

Figure 39.2. Plan of Dera Sor, the ruins of the Yeghrdut monastery, drawn by the author following his return from the site in September 2012. Note the different alignment of the building structure contained within the southeast quadrant of the perimeter wall, suggesting that it might belong to a different age.

The identity of the ruins attached to the twin arches has been impossible to establish with any degree of certainty, as no surviving photographs or plans of the monastery have been found.[12] Present somewhere in the monastery's southeast quadrant was a large, domed church dedicated to the Mother of God. Attached to it was a chapel of Saint John the Baptist in which was a martyrium where the saint's relics were kept. Here too was another chapel dedicated to Gregory the Illuminator, located beyond the church's northwest corner. Its position was marked by an imposing bell tower, under which was a walkway into the main church, the walls of which were constructed of stone in three different colors—black, yellow, and reddish brown. Apparently, the bell tower collapsed during an earthquake in 1866, a portent perhaps of the imminent destruction of the monastery and the disappearance of its monks at the time of the Armenian Genocide of 1915. Exactly what happened here at Yeghrdut may never be known, but it is unlikely to have been pleasant, and as for the fate of the monastery's precious relics, no one can say. Those Armenians who remain today in Mush have adopted a radical form of Islam, so it is unlikely that any real answers will be forthcoming any time soon.

I was pretty sure that the bell tower was located somewhere in the vicinity of the stone arches; indeed, they might easily have formed its support columns, under which one passed to enter the main church. In my dream the monks had conducted the strange ritual involving the elevation of the fragment of the Tree of Life at the center of the church. So I now stood the closest I was going to get to that very spot, which was a strange sensation, especially after traveling nearly 2,200 miles (3,500 kilometers) to be there.

SPECTACULAR VIEWS

As I moved across to the piles of debris marking the north wall, I realized just how spectacular the view was from this elevated position; to say it was impressive would be an understatement. The monastery, as I knew only too well, looked out across the plain of Mush and the Eastern Euphrates, beyond which were the foothills and peaks of the Armenian Highlands. Yet the monastery itself is sheltered beneath hilly slopes to the southeast, south, and west, which would have afforded it some degree of protection from the elements during the long, harsh winters.

For an hour or so, I followed the course of the perimeter wall, obtaining photos, getting video footage, and taking in the ambience, always with one of our hosts by my side. Scattered everywhere were potsherds of all shapes and sizes, which I could see embraced a time frame from medieval times right down to the modern day. However, I was not concerned with ceramics on this occasion. I wanted to find evidence that the site had been occupied prior to the arrival of Christianity in the fourth century. Yet, in all honesty, I found nothing of interest, even though there was every possibility that a settlement from a former age could have occupied a position higher up the hill, closer to its summit perhaps.

One legend fervently believed by the monks of Yeghrdut tells how near "a small workshop" somewhere beyond the monastery, a concealed copy of the "Old Testament" was found. It was apparently seen as a gift of the eagle, presumably the one that lived in the holy evergreen tree.[13] The implication of this chance discovery is that the book belonged to an age that antedated the monastery, implying that the site was important even before the arrival of Gregory the Illuminator in the fourth century.

IS THIS EDEN?

It was very difficult to take in the setting during this one brief visit. My sense, however, was that the monastery had been deliberately left to fall into decay. The site had been neglected, this was clear, and no one really seemed interested in its history or preservation. It was difficult to come to terms with the fact that until 1915 Yeghrdut had been a thriving monastery, as well as a tranquil place of healing for Armenians and Kurds alike. Men and women came here not just to cure ailments but also to rejuvenate both body and soul. There was a natural vitality about this site, which people believed was channeled through the holy tree and spring, the reason they took away leaves, twigs, and bark, not to mention the holy water itself.

All that is now gone. All that remains is the tranquillity of the site and its extraordinary setting, which is simply outstanding. This was the sight the monks of Yeghrdut woke up to every morning, making it easy to understand why they might have believed this was some quiet corner on the edge of Eden itself.

THE RED EARTH OF ADAM

The monks also cannot have failed to notice the absolute redness of the earth, especially the hill slope to the southeast of the monastery. It would have reminded them that the first-century Jewish scholar Flavius Josephus wrote that Adam was created out of red clay:

> That God took dust from the ground, and formed man, and inserted in him a spirit and a soul. This man was called Adam, which in the Hebrew tongue signifies one that is red, because he was formed out of red earth, compounded together; for of that kind is virgin and true earth.[14]

Another tradition said that after Adam's death, he was buried by angels "in the spot where God found the dust" to fashion his body.[15] So if the monks did see the red earth surrounding the monastery as significant (and it is rarely glimpsed anywhere else in the area), then it might well have strengthened the conviction that their monastery existed close to the site where Adam and Eve lived after their expulsion from Paradise, and where afterward their son Seth and his descendants continued to live right down to the time of the flood.

A RESPITE

After completing our visit to the ruins, the elderly man and his wife opened up their home to us. Inside the large, conical tent, its opening directed toward the plain below, we sat down on a bed of brightly patterned kilim rugs that overlaid a bed of flat stone slabs. Placed in front of us was an enormous silver platter containing glasses of sweet tea and bowls of local food, including yogurt, Turkish flat bread, and salad. The kindness of these people was overwhelming, particularly as they did not know me, our guide, or the taxi driver, who were all afforded the same degree of hospitality.

I then learned something important from the fez-wearing man. He told me that somewhere on the hill slope, immediately behind the monastery's west wall, there was once a large cave opening. Yet it had vanished after the "rich" Armenian monks had stuffed it full of "gold" prior to their rapid departure. Local people had attempted to find the cave entrance in order to reach the "gold," but so far all efforts had come to nothing.

I found the story difficult to believe, first, because there was no sign of any cave existing today (I checked afterward), and, second, the fervent belief that Armenian monks were so rich that they simply could not carry away all their cumbersome gold treasure was quite simply fantasy. The only thing it did do was remind me of the legends regarding the Cave of Treasures, where Adam, Eve, Seth, and their family had lived and where they were supposedly buried upon their deaths. Was the role model for the Cave of Treasures around here somewhere, if not close to the monastery, then in the foothills of the mountains immediately to the south of Yeghrdut? Was it there that the secrets of Adam, inscribed either on steles or pillars, would one day be found? Or was it north of the plain of Mush, somewhere in the vicinity of Bingöl Mountain? There were no hard and fast answers, and for now the matter would have to rest there.

One other piece of information I picked up was that around fifteen years before, workmen had arrived one day and broken down whole sections of the monastery's remaining walls, with the resulting piles of rubble being carried away in waiting trucks. Hearing this instantly made me concerned about the fate of the remaining ruins, which are not protected in any manner, and so could, presumably, be destroyed at any time.

Shortly after that it was time to leave. A thunderstorm was close by, and once it hit, any resulting flash floods could make driving back down the mountainside treacherous. So as the taxi now began to make its descent, I watched awestruck as a rolling gray cloud came in from the west and seemed to follow the course of the Euphrates, sending out lightning flashes that struck the plain of Mush and even the waters of the river itself. No wonder the Semitic peoples of Syria and Canaan came to believe that the abode of the god El was to be found in this otherworldly Land of Darkness.

AN UNEXPECTED JOURNEY

That night and the next day I recorded my thoughts and impressions about the trip to the monastery. There was a sense that I had achieved what I had come here to do, but I wanted to go back one more time, and this I managed to do on Wednesday, September 12, with the same taxi driver, although this time with a new guide, a social worker named Idris, who spoke perfect English. He knew every village, large and small, on the plain of Mush, as he visits them as part of his day-to-day job. We shared a mutual passion for keeping alive the rich cultural heritage of the region and so very quickly became friends.

The following day Idris asked if I would like to accompany him the next day to a village called Muska, not far from Bingöl Mountain. He had friends there who were Alevi and thought this might be an ideal opportunity for me to speak with them about their beliefs and practices. Even though I was due to leave Mush early the morning after that, this was too good an opportunity to miss, so I said yes.

I asked Idris about the situation regarding access to Bingöl Mountain, as I understood it was a virtual no-go area because of the recent army offensives. He said we would be fine and that if we did encounter any PKK units in the hills, he knew what to say (Kurdish sympathy among the local population runs very high indeed). With that, I accepted finally that I might get to glimpse Bingöl Mountain, at least from a distance, which is something I had almost abandoned any thought of achieving on this journey of discovery.

40

A TRIP TO PARADISE

Friday, September 14, 2012. The drive by *dolmus* (a Turkish minibus) from Mush to the Alevi town of Varto, in the foothills of the Armenian Highlands, was breathtaking. After leaving the great plain, the road follows the course of the Eastern Euphrates, which runs alongside the road for part of the way. Once that had veered away toward the east, the vehicle climbed ever higher until, finally, we entered Varto itself. The town is a bustling hive of activity even in the baking hot sun, and having left behind the dolmus, we journeyed on foot until we reached a local hospital, where Idris picked up a car for us to complete the journey (it belonged to a work colleague).

After departing Varto, we moved into a beautiful green landscape, utterly different from the dusty, volcanic earth that proliferates on the plain of Mush, and very soon my eyes became focused on something I never expected to see on this journey—the summit of Bingöl Mountain looming up ahead. Seeing it as a single mountain is in fact inaccurate, for Bingöl is in reality a north-south oriented ridge, or massif, with two separate peaks, linked by a saddleback indentation.

MOUNTAIN LION

Unbelievably, the car journey took us right alongside the mountain, which was on our right-hand side at a distance of no more than 4–5 miles (6.5–8 kilometers). What I saw transfixed me, for the twin peaks give the mountain's elevated summit the likeness of a large feline, most obviously a lion, its protruding head, shoulders, and forelegs made up of the northern peak, with the saddleback indentation and southern peak creating the creature's body, hind legs, and tail (see plate 31). The whole thing looks as if it is emerging from the mountain's rocky surface in order to rise into the sky. The form is unmistakable and cannot have been missed by those who inhabited the region in the past. Of course, not everyone is going to interpret this rock simulacrum as a lion, although the likeness is striking enough for it to have impressed some people along the way, including perhaps the Armenians who would come here each spring to venerate Anahita, the goddess of fertility and the waters of life. She is depicted in Persian religious art as a shining being standing on a lion.

PEOPLE OF TRUTH

A lion sitting astride a world mountain, guarding the axis mundi or world pillar as Bingöl Mountain appears to do in Armenian myth and legend, reminded me also of a similar leonine beast featured in the creation myth of a Kurdish religion named Ahl-e Haqq, which means "People of Truth." Although this ethnoreligious group, known also as the Yâresân, exists mostly in Iraqi Kurdistan and northwest Iran, some still remain in remote parts of eastern Turkey. According to them, a charismatic leader named Sultan Sahak founded the Ahl-e Haqq religion during the fourteenth century, although beyond that their origins remain obscure.

As part of the Yâresân creation myth, the divine essence, called Khavankar, brings into existence the seven Haftan, or archangels, and two of them, Ruchiyar and Ayvat (or Yar), become a cow and lion, respectively. The divine essence then creates a fish in the primordial waters and places a large white stone on its back. The cow then steps on the white stone, and the lion stands on the back of the cow. The divine essence places the earth on the horn of the cow, and on the head of the lion he places the "Supreme Sphere"; that is, the vault of heaven.[1]

The relationship of the fish, cow, and lion expresses a three-tiered universe, with a watery abyss in the lower world, a material existence in the middle world, and a cosmic realm in the upper world, all of them linked via an imaginary line of ascent.

COSMIC LION

Elsewhere in Yâresân myth the lion is the avatar of Ali, the son-in-law and cousin of Muhammad,[2] just as he is in the beliefs of the Alevi, who probably share similar traditions. The Alevi see Ali as the first of the twelve imams, or spiritual leaders, and depict him as a lion surrounded by twelve stars. This echoes the lion-headed figure named Zurvan Akarana featured in the religion of Zurvanism, a form of Zoroastrianism once practiced in Armenia. He is the *kosmokrator*, or controller of the revolution of time, symbolized by the seven planets and the twelve signs of the zodiac. Clearly, throughout the region the lion was seen as some kind of cosmic being associated with the stability of the world pillar that links the world mountain with the celestial pole, the turning point of the heavens.

The significance of the lion to the Alevi faith was brought home to me later that day when, on leaving Muska, I saw a large feline carved in relief on the wall of a single-story house. Is it possible that the lion simulacrum is linked with Bingöl's role as Katar Erkri, the "Summit of the Earth"?[3] In China, a peak called Kulkun (in the modern Bayan Kat Mountains) was known as "King of Mountains, the summit of the earth, the supporter of heaven and the axis which touches the pole."[4] Similar legends, I suspect, were once attached to Bingöl Mountain.

ARRIVAL AT MUSKA

What I had learned the night before about our destination seemed almost unbelievable. Muska, where Idris's friends live, is the site of Hızır Çeşmesi, the Fountain of Hızır (the Alevi form of al-Khidr), with its accompanying dream incubation house. Although Muska is the generally used name of the village, which has a population of around 120 people, its modern Turkish name is Beşikkaya Köyü. However, this name is rarely used by the local population, since it was imposed on the village by Turkish authorities as part of a concerted attempt to rid the region of any kind of unwanted cultural ethnicity. I was hoping we could visit the fountain, which from the few pictures I had managed to view online, looked absolutely idyllic, with the spring water emerging from the base of an old gnarled tree.

The very last of the scattering of houses making up the village ceased as we now entered a small enclosed valley, beyond which to the east and north were mountain slopes, part of a northern extension of the Bingöl massif. I looked out on the landscape below, which seemed abundantly rich in green trees, lush meadows, and beautiful mountain streams. It was unimaginable the difference between here and the more arid conditions on the plain of Mush.

Getting out of the car, I saw instantly several pieces of obsidian just lying about on the track. I picked up a few examples as we began a walk across what appeared to be an extended garden area. Here we navigated the outpouring of a mountain brook that ran down from a plush green environment up ahead. No one was about as, with the sound of trickling water all around us, we entered a sheltered canopy of trees at the base of the mountain valley. I recognized it immediately as the Fountain of Hızır, which seemed absolutely bizarre, as our actual destination was a property immediately beyond it on slightly higher ground. This all seemed a little weird—Idris's friends just happening to live next to one of the most holy sites in Alevi tradition.

FOUNTAIN OF HIZIR

Before me now stood an eight-sided column, painted canary yellow, with a spout on each facade, from which came mountain water of the purest kind. This really was a fountain and not a well, with the water somehow being projected through the column by the action of gravity. The structure was not old—fifty to seventy years at the most—although the site was as old as the hills themselves. There were inscriptions in black on the column, but none offered any real words of wisdom. One read "Hızır Çeşmesi hepimizindir cevreyi temiz tutalim," which means "Fountain of Khidr is for everyone, let's keep the environment clean"! It was advice clearly taken, because the entire site was still as nature intended, although the childish graffiti scrawled into the fountain seemed unnecessary.

The source of the spring was beneath an overhanging tree close by. Off to our left some 20 feet (6 meters) away, and sheltered by overhanging branches, was the building used for dream incubation. It was simple and unassuming, and for some reason it reminded me of a waiting room on a railway station (sans the bad smells, of course).

At the fountain, Idris and I sampled the water, which tasted good. It was much needed, and just maybe it would have some beneficial effect on our health. I took time to take in the ambience of the place, realizing that I had been led, almost by chance, to somewhere quite special indeed.

To say that this site was scenic would be to do it an injustice, for the sunlight glinting off the sparkling waters seemed almost to bring alive the sheer abundance of life that prospered here. Trees, plants, and flowers seemed to grow with an almost enchanting beauty. It was as if this place was imbibed with the spirit of life itself, making me wonder whether this really was the Ma'ul Hayat, the Fountain of Life, where al-Khidr, the genius loci of the site, was given immortality, or the Ab'i Hayat, the Waters of Life, where Alexander the Great achieved immortality himself following a quest that had brought him right here to Bingöl Mountain.

FISH FARM

Just beyond the Fountain of Hızır is, rather surprisingly, a prefabricated factory unit, which, it must be pointed out, blends in pretty well with the environment. Between it and the Fountain of Hızır is a cluster of industrial-sized pools, for I learned that Idris's friends run a commercial fish farm, a strange site perpetuation echoing the manner in which al-Khidr achieves immortality by catching and eating a fish swimming about in the Fountain of Immortality.

Slightly uphill of both the factory unit and the Fountain of Hızır was our final destination—an unassuming cottage, in the garden of which introductions were quickly made. Welcoming us was the owner of the house, a tall, thin, bearded man in his sixties, who at this point I had no idea was a renowned Alevi poet and musician named Hıdır Çelik. Youths also were present, apprentices at the fish farm and relatives perhaps of Hıdır. A couple of men from the community greeted us, as did Hıdır's daughter, Gülüzar, who seemed to be in her twenties.

She and a female friend started to prepare salad for a meal, as black tea was served, and one of the youths now reappeared with a whole bag of fresh fish and started cooking them on a grill supported above an open fire. Gülüzar washed cutlery and glasses in the mountain brook, which actually ran through the garden, making it clear that this was their main source of water. Neither Hıdır, his daughter, nor anyone else present other than Idris spoke English, so all conversations were in Turkish or Kurdish. At suitable moments, I took my leave to gaze down at the Fountain of Hızır not 50 yards (46 meters) away. I watched a shepherd herding his flock of sheep along the edge of the mountain slope and went across to the outdoor bathroom positioned on a nearby hill ridge, providing me with an opportunity to refine my collection of obsidian pieces, disgorged by Bingöl Mountain when it was still an active volcano.

Were pieces of obsidian like this instrumental in instigating the construction of places like Göbekli Tepe, and through it initiating the Neolithic revolution? The earliest known mirrors are highly polished disks of obsidian found at Çatal Höyük in southern-central Anatolia, and also at Aşıklı Höyük, a ten-thousand-year-old town complex discovered in the 1960s near Aksaray in central Turkey. I thought it fitting therefore that among the forbidden arts of heaven that Azâzêl, one of the leaders of the Watchers, is said to have revealed to humankind was "the fabrication of mirrors, and the workmanship of bracelets and ornaments."[5]

An obsidian bracelet, more than nine thousand years old, discovered at Aşıklı Höyük during the 1990s, is deemed so unique that it was given special attention by researchers from the Institut Français d'Etudes Anatoliennes in Istanbul and the Laboratoire de Tribologie et Dynamique des Systèmes in Lyon, France.[6] They determined that it was made using highly specialized manufacturing techniques and is almost perfectly regular in shape. Additionally, they found that the symmetry of the central annular ridge is within a degree of accuracy, while the mirrorlike surface of the bracelet would have required "the use of complex polishing techniques capable of obtaining a nanometer-scale surface quality worthy of today's telescope lenses."[7]

Could the technique of producing finely polished obsidian mirrors and bracelets have been introduced to the early Neolithic world of central and eastern Anatolia by Swiderian master craftsmen, remembered in myth and legend as the Watchers and Anunnaki, as well as the Peri of Persian and Kurdish folklore? Were some of these individuals in fact Neanderthal human-hybrids of striking appearance, whose original homeland was the Russian Plain, or even the Carpathian Mountains of Central Europe? It did seem possible.

POETRY READING

Following food and a tour of the fish farm, Idris and I were given copies of the Alevi poet's book of poems, written partly in Turkish and partly in Zâzâ, the native language of the Alevi, who are mostly Dimli Kurds.[8] There were calls for Hıdır to read a poem or two, which he did in his native tongue. His words sounded emotive and meaningful.

After more tea, it was time to leave, and with the car dropped off safely in Varto, there were just moments to spare before the final dolmus departed for Mush. We never did encounter the PKK on our travels, and no one seemed in any way concerned that elsewhere in Bingöl Province, as well as in other parts of eastern Turkey, a very real war was being waged every day, with it rarely even getting a mention in the international media.

The following morning I left Mush for Göbekli Tepe, traveling purposely by coach in order to experience the nail-biting journey through the Eastern Taurus Mountains on the old obsidian route, first to Diyarbakır and then on to Şanlıurfa, where I planned to stay for the final three days of the trip. We passed close to the source of the Tigris River, as well as the site of Çayönü, and also Nevalı Çori, submerged by the floodwaters caused by the opening of the Atatürk Dam in 1992. We also passed within reach of Karaca Dağ, the source of so many strains of modern wheat, pinpointing this region—the heart of the *triangle d'or*—as the true foundation point for the emergence of agriculture in the Near East. All of these important marks on the pages of history are just a stone's throw away from the road between Mush and Göbekli Tepe.

41

GÖBEKLI TEPE
REVISITED

I first visited Göbekli Tepe back in 2004. Back then many of the enclosures were either only partially excavated or they were enclosed in temporary structures with corrugated roofs. At the time, I had the whole place to myself and encountered only the man who owns the pastureland thereabouts, and who is acknowledged as the "discoverer" of the site. His name is Şeymus Yıldız, and in the 1980s he kept coming across fragments of carved stone when tilling the fields, which he simply picked up and placed on boundary walls. He did report these finds to the archaeological museum in Şanlıurfa, but no one ever came to inspect them until the German archaeologist Dr. Klaus Schmidt turned up at the site in 1994.

Today, nearly all the pillars in the large enclosures are fully exposed, while new structures are being unearthed to the west and northwest of the main group of sanctuaries. There are too many mysteries oozing from every corner of this enigmatic archaeological site to do it justice in one book, although I knew this was what I would be attempting to do upon my return to the United Kingdom.

After hanging around the site long enough, I did finally manage to get an impromptu interview with Klaus Schmidt, who was very forthcoming on a number of different subjects. He told me, for instance, that he does not discount the possibility that some of the enclosures might have been built with celestial or astronomical considerations in mind. Yet he admits it is not his "favorite theory" regarding the purpose of the sanctuaries.

UNFINISHED MONOLITH

On the second day, I was able to walk out to the unfinished monolith, located on a northwest extension of the mountain ridge, a quarter of a mile (400 meters) away from the main enclosures. For the journey I was accompanied by one of Klaus Schmidt's archaeological colleagues (name withheld at his request), with whom I was able to discuss many aspects of the discoveries at the site.

The partly hewn pillar—bigger than anything seen in the enclosures so far—has major fracture lines across its surface, suggesting that the Göbekli builders broke it even before they had a chance to remove it from the bedrock. Most probably they moved on to another site elsewhere on the plateau and began carving out a new stone there. When a finished pillar *was* finally freed from the bedrock it would leave behind a gaping hole. Within this, my archaeological friend informed me, a fierce fire would be kindled to burn the thousands of limestone chips that would inevitably result from fashioning a pillar of this size. These would then be pulverized to make the fill necessary to create the beautifully finished terrazzo floors seen in some of the sanctuaries.

The bigger question left in my mind, however, was why supersize everything at the site, especially when no one before had even attempted to create stone sanctuaries on this scale. Only the great stone wall and tower at Jericho *might* be contemporaneous with the earliest building phases of Göbekli Tepe. Further back in time we have only the carved stone blocks fashioned by the Solutrean peoples to create rock friezes within the caves of southwest Europe.

So why the sudden change in policy at places like Göbekli Tepe in southeast Anatolia during the tenth millennium BC? My archaeological friend suggested that Göbekli Tepe was the culmination of a natural evolution in building construction across a period of thousands of years, which was also the opinion of his mentor, Klaus Schmidt. I thought differently, citing fear as the greatest motivation—fear that something bad would happen if you *didn't* do it. He did consider the possibility before deciding to differ with me on this point.

JUTTING HEADLAND

After the archaeologist's departure, I spent some time in the baking heat walking out to the tip of a narrow headland that juts toward the northeast of the main east-west aligned mountain ridge. Although purely natural, I had a sense that this promontory might have played some role in the beliefs and practices of the Göbekli builders.

The closer I got to the end of the headland, the more the flint tools that litter the bellylike tepe almost disappear. Either this place was completely left unoccupied or it was reserved for special occasions. Large, rectilinear blocks that had fractured away from the limestone bedrock had clearly been removed to leave a flat, rectangular enclosure that faced roughly north toward the direction of Karaca Dağ and, of course, the stars of the northern night sky. Here the Göbekli builders could have watched Cygnus rise and set and the Milky Way's Great Rift form an entrance to the sky world. There was little question that this place possessed an ancient sanctity even more primeval than the large enclosures on the top of the ridge, which, as the crow flies, are about a third of a mile (550 meters) away from this location.

The only other evidence of human activity I saw was what appeared to be a small fragment of a stone bowl, most likely from the Pre-Pottery Neolithic age. It would remain undisturbed until such time as the archaeologists turned their attention to this strange place, which, I sensed, was not going to be any time soon. It would take decades to excavate the many enclosures still to be uncovered beneath the artificial mound, and that was always going to be their primary focus of attention.

NEW LION PILLAR

As I returned to the occupational mound, I passed the square grid of 30-foot (9 meter) trenches opened to the northwest of the main enclosures and caught sight of a new discovery sticking out of the ground. It was another major pillar that, even with its T-shaped termination missing, stands an impressive 7 feet (2 meters) in height. On its western face is the carved relief of a leaping lion (see plate 20), occupying the same position as the foxes on the central pillars in the enclosures forming part of the main group. Next to nothing is known about the enclosure that once surrounded the pillar, although presumably this great monolith stood proud as part of a pair at the center of the structure. That the carved lion appears on its western face, directed toward the entrant approaching from the south, implies that this is the eastern pillar, its western neighbor probably still awaiting discovery somewhere beneath the compact soil and rock debris forming the surface of the mound.

MIGHTY LION

Seeing this mighty lion, which was just about to be encased in wood to protect it against potential vandalism and the harsh winter ahead, made me recall the lion simulacrum crowning the summit of Bingöl Mountain and the lion of Ali, sacred to the Alevi and Yâresân. Did this carved lion on the side of a Göbekli pillar symbolize the kosmokrator, the guardian of the world pillar and keeper of cosmic time, like the lion-headed cosmic being called Zurvan Akarana in the branch of Zoroastrianism known as Zurvanism? Or was it yet another form of the cosmic trickster, a creature of Ahriman, the dark principle in Zoroastrianism, just like the wolf and fox? In ancient Egypt, the goddess Hathor, in her guise as the lioness-headed Sekhmet, rained down fire on the earth and nearly destroyed humankind when the sun god Re deemed that humankind had become "too old," a memory perhaps of the terrifying destruction that accompanied the Younger Dryas comet impact of 10,900 BC. Was this same leonine destructress depicted on the newly uncovered pillar at Göbekli Tepe, or was it simply a creature encountered upon entering the sky world, perhaps a proto-form of the Mesopotamian sky panther [MUL]UD. KA.DUH.A, made up of stars belonging to Cygnus and the neighboring constellation of Cepheus (as described in chapter 8)? It is too early to say, especially since each new pillar or porthole stone uncovered raises even more questions about this extraordinary place.

To confirm that the carving on the newly uncovered pillar was really a lion and not some other species of quadruped, I pointed to the stone and called out, "azlan?" The two men, who were probably about 30 yards (27 meters) away, stopped what they were doing, waved, and shouted back, "azlan," which is Turkish for "lion."

I felt I was done at Göbekli Tepe. I could do no more here for the time being. Yet before leaving I vowed to come back to this place whenever time and money would permit, for it was clear that discoveries were being made all the time and that I could always expect to learn something new whenever I returned to this sanctuary on the edge of Eden itself.

42

A LOSS OF INNOCENCE

The following afternoon I departed for London, reaching home some twenty-four hours later. The world for me soon returned to normal, but I could not get out of my mind one persisting image no matter what I did, even at the local gym that week. As I lay on a bench, using a chest machine, the hardest possible rap music was pumping out of the speakers, alienating me from the activities taking place in the room and somehow allowing my mind to escape this unnerving madness.

I was back in Hıdır Çelik's garden in Muska, the noise of the nearby Fountain of Hızır and the network of tiny brooks that passed through this paradise still audible in my ear. Golden sunlight sparkled off the running water as it trickled gently over a trail of pebbles, some of them undoubtedly pieces of polished obsidian ejected in some former age by Bingöl Mountain itself.

We had finished eating the fresh fish, cooked by the youth on an open fire, and Hıdır's daughter, Gülüzar, now gathered water from the mountain stream running through the garden. These people, all Alevi by birth, seemed completely at peace living their lives on a mountainside, only rarely coming into contact with the pressures and tensions of the outside world. They are relatively free of the stresses and strains that come with a modern, urban existence like the one most of us are doomed to suffer during our lives.

Without even trying, these people experience a harmony with nature that allows them a purity of heart, and a certain sense of grace, that almost seems reflected in the fecundity of everything that grows in and around the garden. From the trees overhanging the sacred Fountain of Hızır to the bright green fields and meadows that fill the local landscape, and even the abundance of fish that thrive here in the thousands, everything appears utterly awash with life and vitality.

A SENSE OF GUILT

I imagined that this was the same innocence, the same purity of heart, that must have prevailed in the Garden of Eden before the serpent beguiled Adam and Eve into partaking of the fruit of the Tree of Knowledge of God and Evil. Instantly, their innocence vanished as their eyes were opened to the fact that they were naked. I am sure they must have noticed before that they wore no clothes, the difference being that now they felt a sense of shame and guilt over this innocent act, and so covered themselves up. This was something they did, according to some accounts, by using fig leaves picked from the same tree that the couple had eaten from, implying that the Tree of Knowledge of Good and Evil was a fig tree,[1] just like the one that graces the summit of Göbekli Tepe today.

DEATH OF AN IDYLLIC WORLD

Adam and Eve, as our First Parents, are merely metaphors for humanity as it existed before we woke up to our "nakedness." Before this time we had lived in a state of innocence and grace that was taken away from us, and ever since that time we have been made to suffer and toil, not only in body, but also in spirit. The eternal golden age of hunting and foraging, when people were free to experience life on their own terms, would appear to have been halted by a cataclysm, arguably the proposed comet impact of 10,900 BC, and this changed everything. From these ashes arose people who wanted to tell us that thinking for ourselves and making decisions based on our own vision of life were essentially wrong, immoral even, and that whenever we have such thoughts we should feel guilt and shame, exactly what happened to Adam and Eve in the Garden of Eden. It was a form of social conditioning imposed on our ancestors by those who assumed control over the way the future would now be shaped in the wake of the Neolithic revolution.

The greatest clue in this transition from a state of innocence to one of mental entrapment is in the fact that after being expelled from Paradise, Adam and Eve are condemned to forever till the land, for as Yahweh makes clear to Adam:

> *Cursed is the ground for your sake;*
> *In toil you shall eat of it*
> *All the days of your life . . .*
> *In the sweat of your face you shall eat bread*
> *Till you return to the ground.*[2]

In other words, humankind began to live by the process of subsistence agriculture, something that could only be done if everyone worked side by side with a more-or-less hive mentality under the control of taskmasters. No longer could we have the free lives of hunters, to do exactly what we wanted, when we wanted. People had now to exist day in, day out under regulated, and often confined, working environments. From such communities, which must have supplied the quarry men, stone masons, knappers, carvers, butchers, and construction workers for the creation of places like Göbekli Tepe, came much larger agricultural centers, leading eventually to Neolithic town complexes such as Çatal Höyük and Aşıklı Höyük in central Turkey. Founded around the same time that Göbekli Tepe was finally abandoned, ca. 8000 BC, Aşıklı Höyük was made up of a tight network of residential dwellings, workshops, and claustrophobic streets, no wider than alleyways, where beautiful obsidian mirrors, bracelets, and necklaces were manufactured.

TRAUMA AND INJURIES

Exactly what the work ethics might have been at Aşıklı Höyük is quite another matter. Skeletal remains show that men lived until they were fifty-five to fifty-seven years of age, while women lived only to the age of twenty to twenty-five years.[3] Severe trauma and injuries to the shoulders and spine indicate that these women carried heavy loads during their lives or were bending over or kneeling constantly, perhaps in front of a saddle quern used to make cereal grain. The skeletal remains of the men, on the other hand, show signs of joint disease and trauma of the type that might be expected from constant heavy labor, such as wood logging, construction work, and tilling the land.

Clearly, living in the first industrial age, where everyone had to have a home and be fed equally, took its toll on the population in a manner that might raise the question of who exactly was in charge at Aşıklı Höyük. Curiously, one ancient tradition asserts that the forbidden fruit consumed by Adam and Eve that brought about the misery of the original sin was "an ear of wheat,"[4] emphasizing once again that the introduction of widescale sedentary farming was at the root of humanity's loss of innocence.

> *In the sweat of your face you shall eat bread*
> *Till you return to the ground.*

No longer were we now just individuals, thinking and making decisions for ourselves on behalf of our families and friends. Others now told us how to think, what to do, when to get up, when to eat, and when we could go to sleep. Since that time, we have been unable to break free from the fear that something bad will happen if we deviate from this path, and ultimately there is very little we can do to escape this torment. Those who do try to break free of their psychological shackles are often vilified or persecuted as blasphemers, heretics, dropouts, or just plain lunatics.

BACK TO EDEN

Various religious groups and communities throughout history have realized that the return to Paradise, and the freedom of thought that it brings, is through a simple innocence and purity of heart, just as it was with our First Parents before the time of the Fall. It is actually a good philosophy, and the strange thing is that some of the most successful of these communities had their inception in the same geographical region as that identified in this book as the true site of the Garden of Eden. They include the Cathars, or Albigensians, who in the twelfth and thirteenth centuries advocated a return to a simple purity in places such as Italy and France. That was, of course, until they were annihilated in the Albigensian Crusade, a mass genocide of atrocious proportions orchestrated by the Church of Rome.

The doctrine of the Cathars derived from the Bogomils, who thrived in Eastern Europe during the tenth and eleventh centuries AD. Their communities grew from exiled Christians of a semi-Gnostic nature who arrived here from the foothills of the Armenian Highlands, north of Lake Van. Known as the Paulicians, they owed at least some of their ideas to the Arevordi, the Children of the Sun, who, although broadly classed as Armenian Zoroastrians, followed a simple faith in complete harmony with nature.[5] Unbelievably, surviving elements of all these faiths, whether Christian, Zoroastrian, or pagan, were absorbed into the indigenous religions of the Kurds, most notably the Alevi.[6]

A RETURN TO THE SOURCE

So even though I was unable to communicate directly with the Alevi I met, their message got through loud and clear. Finding Eden, ultimately, is not about putting pins in maps and saying, "This is it—I have found Paradise." It is about an inner journey—it is about returning to the source of human experience and understanding exactly who we were before someone, somewhere, conditioned us to feel guilt and shame for the first time—shame about who we are as individuals, how we should act and behave, and what we should do with our lives. This is not a declaration of anarchy or a license to do what you want. It is a call for us to try to regain some small sense of the innocence and purity of heart that prevailed in the past, and I glimpsed just for a moment among the Alevi people who still occupy the Garden of Eden today, for their world seems a happier place than ours.

USEFUL DATES

The following is a list of useful dates relating to topics discussed in this book. Many of the dates are generalizations and should not be seen as absolute.

41,000 BC	Cro-Magnons arrive in Europe
40,000 BC	Earliest known settlement sites at Kostenki, Central Russia
30,000 BC	Kostenki-Streletskaya culture established at sites on the Russian steppes and plain, including Kostenki and Sungir
30,000 BC	The Venus and the Sorcerer panel created at Chauvet, France
30,000 BC	Sungir burials take place
23,000 BC	Brünn type appears in Central Europe
23,000 BC	Solutrean tradition established in Europe
20,000 BC	Last Glacial Maximum (LGM)
19,000 BC	Kostenki-Streletskaya culture culminates
19,000 BC	Zarzian culture appears in the Caucasus and Zagros regions
18,000 BC	Solutreans arrive in North America?
17,000 BC	Solutrean rock frieze created at the Roc-de-Sers shelter, France
16,500 BC	Deneb in Cygnus becomes Pole Star
16,500 BC	Shaft Scene created at Lascaux, France (radiocarbon date)

14,500 BC	Delta Cygni becomes Pole Star
14,500 BC	Solutrean tradition disappears
13,000 BC	Vega in Lyra becomes Pole Star
13,000 BC	End of the last Ice Age
11,300 BC	Clovis culture appears in North America
11,000 BC	Vega ceases to be Pole Star
11,000 BC	Swiderian culture appears in Central Europe
10,900 BC	Younger Dryas Boundary impact event (proposed date)
10,900 BC	Younger Dryas mini ice age begins
10,500 BC	Swiderian culture enters eastern Anatolia?
10,500 BC	Zarzian culture disappears
10,500 BC	Gobustan rock art, Azerbaijan (earliest possible date)
10,250 BC	Hallan Çemi founded in Eastern Taurus Mountains
9600 BC	Younger Dryas period ends
9500 BC	Age of oldest known enclosures at Göbekli Tepe
8630 BC	Çayönü founded in southeast Anatolia
8500 BC	Nevalı Çori founded in southeast Anatolia
8000 BC	Göbekli Tepe abandoned
8000 BC	Aşıklı Höyük founded in central Anatolia
7500 BC	Çatal Höyük founded in southern central Anatolia
6000 BC	Halaf culture appears
5000 BC	Ubaid culture appears
2900 BC	Sumerian civilization founded
2600 BC	Foundation cylinder deposited at Nippur in southern Iraq containing the story of the Anunnaki and their Kharsag/Eden settlement
2300 BC	Assyrian civilization founded
2150 BC	Abraham departs from Harran, according to biblical chronology
1894 BC	Babylonian civilization founded
200 BC	Book of Enoch/Dead Sea Scrolls constructed

ca. AD 29	The disciple Thaddeus journeys to Edessa to cure King Abgar
ca. AD 43/45	Thaddeus conceals relics at Yeghrdut in the Armenian kingdom of Taron (the modern plain of Mush)
3rd century	"Life of Adam and Eve" appears, based on much older material of Jewish origin
4th century	Yeghrdut monastery founded
post 367	Gnostic library concealed at Nag Hammadi, Egypt, containing various Sethian texts
5th century	Cave of Treasures stories begin circulation
5th century	Mount Ararat elevated as official resting place of Noah's ark by the Armenian Church
1666	The Reverend Marmaduke Carver *A Discourse of the Terrestrial Paradise* published, demonstrating that the terrestrial Paradise was in Armenia Major
1821	First English translation of the book of Enoch published
1883	Ignatius Donnelly's *Ragnarök: The Age of Fire and Gravel* published, demonstrating that a comet impacted with the earth toward the end of the glacial age
1891	Skulls of the Brünn type discovered at Brünn, Czech Republic
1894	More evidence of the Brünn type discovered at Předmost, Czech Republic
1918	Nippur foundation cylinder published, with English translation by George A. Barton
1940	Lascaux Caves discovered
1945	Nag Hammadi library discovered
1947	Dead Sea Scrolls discovered
1948	Swiderian cranium found at Kebeliai, near Priekulė in Lithuania, identified as belonging to Neanderthal-human hybrid
1956	Sungir burials discovered in Vladimir, Russia

1963	Peter Benedict of the University of Chicago surveys Göbekli Tepe, cataloguing it as site V52/1
1985	Christian and Barbara Joy O'Brien's *The Genius of the Few* published, containing a new interpretation of the Nippur foundation cylinder, and suggesting that Eden and Kharsag were one and the same
1994	Chauvet Cave discovered
1994	Professor Klaus Schmidt visits Göbekli Tepe for the first time
1995	First digging campaign begins at Göbekli Tepe
1996	The author's book *From the Ashes of Angels* published, proposing that the stories of the Watchers and Anunnaki are a memory of the shamanic elite responsible for the Neolithic revolution in southeast Anatolia
2000	Göbekli Tepe's discovery announced to the world

NOTES

PROLOGUE. IN QUEST OF ANGELS

1. Green, *The City of the Moon God,* 13, quoting Muhammad Ibn Abd Allah al-Kisa'i, *The Tales of the Prophets of Al-Kisa'i.*
2. Lloyd and Brice, "Harran," 90–91.
3. Budge, *The Chronography of Gregory Abû'l Faraj, the Son of Aaron, the Hebrew Physician, Commonly Known as Bar Hebraeus,* vol. I, 7.
4. See Lloyd and Brice, "Harran," 77–111. They report on surface finds at Harran, including distinctive ceramic ware belonging to the Halaf culture.
5. Yardimci, *Mezopotamya'ya açilan kapi Harran,* 362–64.
6. Book of Jubilees, 8:1–4.
7. Josephus, "The Antiquities of the Jews," bk. I, ch. vi, verse 4.
8. Hommel, *The Ancient Hebrew Tradition,* 292–97.
9. Segal, *Edessa,* p. 2 n. 2.
10. Ibid., p. 2 n. 4, 106.

CHAPTER 1. A LIFETIME'S WORK

1. Hony and Fahir, *A Turkish-English Dictionary,* s.v. "göbek."
2. Schmidt, "The 2003 Campaign at Göbekli Tepe (Southeastern Turkey)," 5.
3. Benedict, "Survey Work in Southeastern Anatolia," 150–91.
4. Schirmer, "Some Aspects of Building at the 'Aceramic-neolithic' Settlement of Çayönü Tepesi," 378.
5. Cauvin, *The Birth of the Gods and the Origins of Agriculture,* 172–73.
6. Schirmer, "Some Aspects of Building at the 'Aceramic-neolithic' Settlement of Çayönü Tepesi," 382.
7. Dates for the PPNA and PPNB taken from Cauvin, *Birth of the Gods,* 76.
8. Schmidt, "Göbekli Tepe, Southeastern Turkey," 46.

9. Ibid.

10. Cauvin, *Birth of the Gods,* 91.

11. See Lewis-Williams and Pearce, *Inside the Neolithic Mind;* Hancock, *Supernatural.*

12. Schmidt, "Göbekli Tepe, Southeastern Turkey," 46.

13. Ibid.

14. Ibid.

15. Schmidt, "Göbekli Tepe—the Stone Age Sanctuaries," p. 241, n. 1.

CHAPTER 2. MONUMENTAL ARCHITECTURE

1. Schmidt, *Göbekli Tepe,* 216. This is the 2012 English language edition of the book *Sie bauten die ersten Tempel: Das rätselhafte Heiligtum der Steinzeitjäger,* published in 2006. All references will be taken from the English edition. See also Collins, *The Cygnus Mystery,* 209–14, which explores the possibility of psychoactive substances, mushrooms in particular, being used at Göbekli Tepe.

2. Harner, "Common Themes in South American Indian Yagé Experiences," 160–64.

3. Ibid., 162, 164.

4. Mann, "The Birth of Religion," 48.

5. Schmidt, "Göbekli Tepe, Southeastern Turkey," 51.

6. Ibid.

7. Schmidt, "Göbekli Tepe—the Stone Age Sanctuaries," 242.

8. Schmidt, "Göbekli Tepe, Southeastern Turkey," 51.

9. Mann, "The Birth of Religion," 57.

10. Waverly Fitzgerald, "Transformation Mysteries of Grain and Grapes," School of the Seasons, www.schooloftheseasons.com/pdfdocs/harvestsample.pdf (accessed January 15, 2014).

11. Peters and Schmidt, "Animals in the Symbolic World of Pre-Pottery Neolithic Göbekli Tepe, South-eastern Turkey," 214.

12. Karapetyan and Kanetsyan, "Pre-Urartian Armavir," 52.

13. Schmidt, "Göbekli Tepe, Southeastern Turkey," 48.

14. Ibid.

15. Peters and Schmidt, "Animals in the Symbolic World," 179–218.

16. Schmidt, "Göbekli Tepe, Southeastern Turkey," 48.

17. Heun, Schäfer-Pregl, Klawan, et al., "Site of Einkorn Wheat Domestication Identified by DNA Fingerprinting," 1312–14.

18. Schmidt, "Göbekli Tepe, Southeastern Turkey," 48.

CHAPTER 3. FROZEN IN STONE

1. Schmidt, *Göbekli Tepe,* 140–1.

2. Banning, "So Fair a House," 619–60.

3. Schmidt, *Göbekli Tepe,* 148.

4. Dietrich, Köksal-Schmidt, Kürkcüoglu, et al., "Göbekli Tepe," 30–31.

5. Çelik, "A New Early Neolithic Settlement in Southeastern Turkey," 3–5; Çelik, "Hamzan Tepe in the Light of New Finds," 257–68.

6. Çelik, "Sefer Tepe," 23–25.

7. Çelik, Güler, and Güler, "Türkiye'nin Güneydoğusunda Yeni Bir Çanak Çömleksiz Neolitik Yerleşim" 225–36.

8. Çelik, "A New Early-Neolithic Settlement: Karahan Tepe," 6–8.

9. Verhoeven, "Person or Penis? Interpreting a 'New' PPNB Anthropomorphic Statue from the Taurus Foothills," 8–9.

10. Aurenche and Kozlowski, *La naissance du néolithique au Proche Orient ou le paradis perdu,* figure 13.

11. Izady, *The Kurds,* 23.

12. Schmidt, *Göbekli Tepe,* 235.

CHAPTER 4. STRANGE GLYPHS AND IDEOGRAMS

1. Reichel-Dolmatoff, *Basketry as Metaphor,* 33.

2. Personal communication with Kelly Delaney Stacy and Amadeus Diamond in March 2013.

3. Ibid.

4. Baldwin Spencer, *Across Australia,* 402–3.

5. Ibid., 401.

6. Ibid., figure 278 opp. p. 403.

7. Çelik, "An Early Neolithic Settlement in the Center of Şanlıurfa, Turkey," 4–6.

8. Cauvin, *The Birth of the Gods and the Origins of Agriculture,* 123–25.

CHAPTER 5. GATEWAY TO HEAVEN

1. Schmidt, "Göbekli Tepe Excavations 2005," 100.

2. David Frawley, "Vedic Origins of the Zodiac: The Hymns of Dirghatamas in the Rig Veda," American Institute of Vedic Studies, www.vedanet.com/2012/06/vedic-origins-of-the-zodiac-the-hymns-of-dirghatamas-in-the-rig-veda/ (accessed January 15, 2014).

3. Rao, *Lothal,* 40–41.

4. Callataÿ, *Annus Platonicus.*

5. John A. Halloran, "Sumerian Lexicon: Version 3.0," Sumerian.org, www.sumerian.org/sumerian.pdf (accessed January 15, 2014), see "ùš" (placenta), "úš" (blood, death, etc.), "uš" (foundation place, base).

6. King, *African Cosmos,* 53.

7. Williams, *Spirit Tree,* 147–48.

8. Roscoe, *The Baganda,* 235.

9. Ibid., 236.

10. Ibid., 236; Frazer, *The Magic Art and the Evolution of Kings,* vol. 1, 196.

11. Rice, *Egypt's Making*, 108–9. See also Long, "The Placenta in Lore and Legend," 233–41.

12. King, *African Cosmos*, 53.

13. Griaule and Dieterlen, *The Pale Fox*, 153–59.

14. Frazer, *Magic Art and the Evolution of Kings*, vol. 1, 195.

CHAPTER 6. WINDOW ON ANOTHER WORLD

1. Belmonte, "Finding Our Place in the Cosmos," 2052–62.

2. Rappenglück, *Eine Himmelskarte aus der Eiszeit?*

3. Ibid. See also Belmonte, "Finding Our Place in the Cosmos."

4. See Collins, *The Cygnus Mystery*.

5. Mellaart, *Çatalhöyük*, 178.

6. Dietrich, *The Origins of Greek Religion*, 106–7.

CHAPTER 7. TURNED TOWARD THE STARS

1. See Schoch, *Forgotten Civilization*, 53–57.

2. Magli, Giulio, "Possible Astronomical References in the Project of the Megalithic Enclosures of Göbekli Tepe," Cornell University Library online, http://arxiv.org/abs/1307.8397 (accessed March 20, 2014).

3. Ibid.

4. Collins and Hale, "Göbekli Tepe and the Rising of Sirius," 2013, www.andrewcollins.com/page/articles/G%F6bekli_Sirius.htm (accessed January 15, 2014).

5. Ibid.

6. See Collins, *The Cygnus Mystery*, and the references therein, for a full exegesis of this topic.

7. Ibid.

8. Schmidt and Dietrich, "A Radiocarbon Date from the Wall Plaster of Enclosure D of Göbekli Tepe," 82–83.

9. Ibid.

10. Oliver Dietrich, "PPND—The Platform for Neolithic Radiocarbon Dates," Ex Oriente, www.exoriente.org/associated_projects/ppnd_site.php?s=25 (accessed January 15, 2014).

11. Ibid.

12. The mean azimuths of individual buildings are based on Özdoğan and Özdoğan, "Çayönü," 65–74, using an extinction altitude for Deneb of 2 degrees including refraction.

13. Yakar, "Anatolian Chronology and Terminology," 67, summarizing Damien Bischoff, "CANeW 14C Databases and 14C Tables: Upper Mesopotamia (SE Turkey, N Syria and N Iraq 10,000–5000 cal BC)," 2006, www.canew.org; and Damien Bischoff, "CANeW Material Culture Stratigraphic Tables: Upper Mesopotamia (SE Turkey, N Syria and N Iraq 10,000–5000 cal BC)," 2007, www.canew.org.

14. Schmidt, *Göbekli Tepe,* 141–42.

15. Schmidt, *Göbekli Tepe,* 99.

16. For an examination of this subject, see Koster, *The Late Roman Cemeteries of Nijmegen: Stray Finds and Excavations 1947–1983.*

17. See Avetisian, "Urartian Ceramics from the Ararat Valley as a Cultural Phenomenon," 293–314.

18. A house with a seelenloch in the Tyrolean village of Serfaus in the Landeck district of Austria can be viewed here with a description: *Serfaus Intern* 4/2011, www.serfaus.gv.at/gemeindeamt/download/222301657_1.pdf (accessed January 15, 2014).

19. For an overview of Caucasian dolmens and their dating, see Trifonov et al., "The Dolmen Kolikho, Western Caucasus," 761–69.

20. For a good introduction to holes used by shaman to reach the lower and upper world, see Harner, *The Way of the Shaman,* 31–35. See also Eliade, *Shamanism,* 259–60.

21. For an examination of the celestial symbolism of bi and pi disks see Shu-P'Ing, "The Original Significance of Bi Disks," 165–94.

22. Czaplicka, *Aboriginal Siberia,* 211–22; Walter and Fridman, *Shamanism,* vol. 1, p. 611. See also Lombard, "Bored Stones, Lithic Rings and the Concept of Holes in San Shamanism," 25.

CHAPTER 8. THE PATH OF SOULS

1. Tedlock, *Popol Vuh,* 356; also Jenkins, *Maya Cosmogenesis 2012.*

2. Hatch, "An Hypothesis on Olmec Astronomy, with Special Reference to the La Venta Site," 1–38.

3. John Major Jenkins, "Commentary on Stuart and Houston's Study of Mayan Place Names in 'Studies in Pre-Columbian Art and Archaeology 33, 1994,'" Edj.net, http://edj.net/mc2012/fap11.html (accessed January 15, 2014).

4. For a full review of these Native American star myths, see Greg Little, "Can the Alignments of the Giza Pyramids be Explained from Moundville, Alabama Artifacts?—Part 2" Archaeotrek, Alternative Perceptions Magazine, http://apmagazine.info/index.php?option=com_content&view=article&id=273 (accessed January 15, 2014). See also the various internal texts of Reilly III and Garber, *Ancient Objects and Sacred Realms,* for a fuller account of this subject, especially Lankford, "The 'Path of Souls': Some Death Imagery in the Southeastern Ceremonial Complex," 174–212.

5. White, *Babylonian Star-lore,* 159–60.

6. See "MUL.APIN 1.2: The 33 Stars on the Path of Enlil, within the Ellipse of the Milky Way," MUL.APIN Tablet No. 86378, British Museum, column 1, line 28, Lexiline: A Renaissance in Learning, www.lexiline.com/lexiline/lexi173.htm (accessed January 15, 2014).

CHAPTER 9. CULT OF THE VULTURE

1. Schmidt, *Göbekli Tepe*, 131–32.
2. Mellaart, *Çatalhöyük*, 104.
3. Allen, *Star Names and Their Meaning*, s.v. "Cygnus."
4. Hodder, *Çatalhöyük*, 196.
5. Uyanik, *Petroglyphs of South-eastern Anatolia*, 12.
6. Ibid.
7. Klaus Schmidt, television interview by Dr. Graham Phillip, "Death Cult Temple and Bog Bodies of Ireland," *Ancient X-Files*, National Geographic Channel, 2012.
8. Solecki and Solecki, "The Zagros Proto-Neolithic and Cultural Developments in the Near East," 120.
9. See Solecki, "Predatory Bird Rituals at Zawi Chemi Shanidar," 42–47.
10. Solecki and Solecki, "Zagros Proto-Neolithic and Cultural Developments," 120.
11. Solecki, "Predatory Bird Rituals at Zawi Chemi Shanidar," 42–47.
12. Solecki and Solecki, "Zagros Proto-Neolithic and Cultural Developments," 117.
13. Belmonte, "Finding Our Place in the Cosmos," 2052–62.
14. Horowitz, *Mesopotamian Cosmic Geography*, 156, 180–81, 259; White, *Babylonian Star-lore*, 177–81.
15. Bricker and Bricker, "Zodiacal References in the Maya Codices," 148–83.
16. See Vachagan Vahradyan and Marine Vahradyan, "About the Astronomical Role of 'Qarahunge' Monument," Anunner.com, www.anunner.com/vachagan.vahradyan/About_the_Astronomical_Role_of__"Qarahunge"_Monument_by_Vachagan_Vahradyan,_Marine_Vahradyan (accessed January 15, 2014).

CHAPTER 10. COSMIC BIRTH STONE

1. Verhoeven, "Person or Penis?" 8–9.
2. Gimbutas, *The Language of the Goddess*, 185, 265.
3. See Collins, *The Cygnus Mystery*.
4. Silva, *Archaeology of Intangible Heritage*, 125.
5. Kay, *Bird Gods*, 197.
6. Róheim, *Hungarian and Vogul Mythology*, 63.
7. Lüling, *A Challenge to Islam for Reformation*, 207.

CHAPTER 11. THE HOODED ONES

1. Schmidt, *Göbekli Tepe*, 238.
2. Klaus Schmidt, television interview by Dr. Graham Phillip, "Death Cult Temple and Bog Bodies of Ireland," *Ancient X-Files*, National Geographic Channel, 2012.

CHAPTER 12. FEAR OF THE FOX'S TAIL

1. Peters and Schmidt, "Animals in the Symbolic World of Pre-Pottery Neolithic Göbekli Tepe, South-eastern Turkey," 209.
2. Ibid.
3. Sagan and Druyan, *Comet,* 19.
4. John and Caitlin Matthews, "The Element Encyclopedia of Magical Creatures," Otakuyume, http://otakuyume.angelfire.com/magic1.html (accessed January 15, 2014).
5. Ribas, *History of the Triumphs of Our Holy Faith amongst the Most Barbarous and Fierce Peoples of the New World,* 676.
6. "Halley's Comet," Wikipedia, http://en.wikipedia.org/wiki/Halley's_Comet (accessed January 15, 2014).

CHAPTER 13. COSMIC TRICKSTER

1. Santillana and von Dechend, *Hamlet's Mill,* 385.
2. Ibid.
3. White, *Babylonian Star-lore,* 86.
4. Pseudo-Hyginus, *Astronomica,* part 2, trans. by Mary Grant, s.v. "The Bull," Theoi Greek Mythology, www.theoi.com/Text/HyginusAstronomica2.html#21 (accessed January 15, 2014).
5. Schmidt, *Göbekli Tepe,* 184.
6. Ibid., 185.
7. Alastair McBeath and Andrei Dorian Gheorghe, "Romanian Astrohumanism (III): Sky Myth and Great Sky Dragon," Romanian Society for Meteors and Astronomy (SARM), www.cosmopoetry.ro/ashuman/ (accessed January 15, 2014).
8. Ibid.
9. Ibid.
10. Ibid.
11. Ibid.

CHAPTER 14. FROM A FOX TO A WOLF

1. Kuperjanov, "Estonian Sky," 151–52.
2. Ibid., 152.
3. See Collins, *The Cygnus Mystery.*

CHAPTER 15. TWILIGHT OF THE GODS

1. Zoega, *A Concise Dictionary of Old Icelandic,* s.v. "ragna-."
2. Ibid.
3. Anderson, *Norse Mythology.*

4. Donnelly, *Ragnarök*, 142.

5. Byock, *The Prose Edda*, 164.

6. Anderson, *Norse Mythology*, 417.

7. Donnelly, *Ragnarök*, 142.

8. Ibid., 143.

9. Anderson, *Norse Mythology*, 417.

10. Donnelly, *Ragnarök*, 143.

11. Anderson, *Norse Mythology*, 418.

12. Donnelly, *Ragnarök*, 144.

13. Anderson, *Norse Mythology*, 418.

14. Donnelly, *Ragnarök*, 144.

15. Anderson, *Norse Mythology*, 418.

16. Donnelly, *Ragnarök*, 146.

17. Anderson, *Norse Mythology*, 418.

18. Ibid., 419.

19. Donnelly, *Ragnarök*, 147.

20. Lindow, *Norse Mythology*, s.v. "Fenrir."

21. Anderson, *Norse Mythology*, 419.

22. Ibid., 416.

23. Ibid., 429.

24. Donnelly, *Ragnarök*, 403–4.

25. Ibid., 152.

26. Ibid.

CHAPTER 16. THE WOLF PROGENY

1. Otto S. Reuter, "Skylore of the North," trans. by Michael Behrend, Website by Michael Behrend, www.cantab.net/users/michael.behrend/repubs/reuter_himmel/pages/index.html (accessed January 15, 2014).

2. Thorsson, *Futhark*, 53.

3. Ibid., 54.

4. "Týr," Wikipedia, http://en.wikipedia.org/wiki/Týr (accessed January 15, 2014).

5. Lubotsky, *Leiden Indo-European Etymological Dictionary Series*, 167.

6. Reuter, "Skylore of the North."

7. Grimes, *The Norse Myths*, s.v. "Fenris."

8. Afanasyev, *The Life Tree*, 168, quoted in Vladimir V. Rubtsov, "Tracking the Alien Astroengineers," *RIAP Bulletin* 4, no. 4 (October–December 1998), www.biblio tecapleyades.net/universo/esp_sirio06.htm (accessed January 15, 2014).

9. Rubtsov, "Tracking the Alien Astroengineers," *RIAP Bulletin* 4, no. 4 (October–December 1998), www.bibliotecapleyades.net/universo/esp_sirio06.htm (accessed January 15, 2014).

10. Ivanov, "Ancient Balkan and All-Indo-European Text." In Rubtsov, "Tracking the Alien Astroengineers."

11. Grumeza, *Dacia,* 76.

12. Grimm, *Teutonic Mythology,* vol. 1, 244.

13. Ibid., 244–45.

14. Ibid., 245.

15. Ibid.

16. Bundahishn, quoted in Charles Francis Horne, *The Sacred Books and Early Literature of the East: Ancient Persia,* vol. 7, 1900, ch. xxx, verse 18, p. 182, Forgotten Books, www.forgottenbooks.org.

17. Ibid., p. 182, n. 7.

18. Massey, *The Natural Genesis,* vol. 2, 103.

19. Bundahishn, quoted in Horne, *Sacred Books and Early Literature of the East,* vol. 7, ch. xxx, verse 19, p. 182.

20. Ibid., verse 31, p. 183.

21. Ibid., verse 25, p. 183.

22. Clow, *Catastrophobia.*

CHAPTER 17. A DARK DAY IN SYRIA

1. Bruce Fellman, "Finding the First Farmers," *Yale Alumni Magazine* (October 1994), http://archives.yalealumnimagazine.com/issues/94_10/agriculture.html (accessed January 15, 2014).

2. Ted E. Bunch, Robert E. Hermes, Andrew M. T. Moore, et al., "Very High-temperature Impact Melt Products as Evidence for Cosmic Airbursts and Impacts 12,900 Years Ago," PNAS Online, June 18, 2012, www.pnas.org/content/early/2012/06/14/1204453109.full.pdf (accessed January 15, 2014).

3. Ibid.

4. Ibid.

5. Ibid.

6. Ibid.

7. Kloosterman, "The Usselo Horizon, a Worldwide Charcoal-rich Layer of Allerod Age."

8. Hoesel, Hoek, Braadbaart, et al., "Nanodiamonds and Wildfire Evidence in the Usselo Horizon," 7648–53.

9. Bunch, Hermes, Moore, et al., "Very High-temperature Impact Melt Products."

10. For a full examination of the effect of the Younger Dryas Boundary impact event on the Clovis culture, see Firestone, West, and Warwick-Smith, *The Cycle of Cosmic Catastrophies,* especially pages 132–47.

11. Ibid. Although see objections from Surovell, Holliday, Gingerich, et al., "An Independent Evaluation of the Younger Dryas Extraterrestrial Impact Hypothesis," 18155–58, and Boslough, Nicoll, Holliday, et al., "Arguments and Evidence against

a Younger Dryas Impact Event," 13–26. Counterarguments come from Malcolm A. LeCompte, Albert C. Goodyear, Mark N. Demitroff, et al., "Independent Evaluation of Conflicting Microspherule Results from Different Investigations of the Younger Dryas Impact Hypothesis," PNAS Online, www.pnas.org/content/early/2012/09/12/1208603109.abstract (accessed January 15, 2014), as well as Wittke, Weaver, Bunch, et al., "Evidence for Deposition of 10 Million Tonnes of Impact Spherules across Four Continents 12,800 Y Ago," who have identified the date of the Younger Dryas impact event as 12.8 kya (± 0.15 ka); that is, 12,800 years ago.

CHAPTER 18. AFTERMATH

1. See Andrew Collins, "One Week in Kurdistan," Andrewcollins.com, www .andrew collins.com/page/articles/kurdistan.htm (accessed January 15, 2014).
2. Mackrel, *Halley's Comet over New Zealand*, 95.
3. Bunch, Hermes, Moore, et al., "Very High-temperature Impact Melt Products."
4. Firestone, West, and Warwick-Smith, *The Cycle of Cosmic Catastrophes*, 304. See also Legrand and De Angelis, "Origins and Variations of Light Carboxylic Acids in Polar Precipitation," 1445–62, and Firestone, West, Kennett, et al., "Evidence for an Extraterrestrial Impact 12,900 Years Ago That Contributed to the Megafaunal Extinctions and the Younger Dryas Cooling," 16016–21.
5. Firestone, West, and Warwick-Smith, *Cycle of Cosmic Catastrophes*, 304.
6. Ibid., 304–5.
7. Ibid., 305.
8. Ibid.

CHAPTER 19. THE REINDEER HUNTERS

1. Roberts, *The Incredible Human Journey*, 276.
2. Ibid.
3. Ibid.
4. Ibid.
5. Settegast, *Plato Preshistorian*.
6. Ibid., 55–57.
7. Ibid., 104–5, figure 62.
8. Ibid., 55–57.
9. Bailey and Spikins, *Mesolithic Europe*, 294.
10. Clark, *World Prehistory*, 54.

CHAPTER 20. SWIDERIAN DAWN

1. A date of 12.94 kya is given. See Haynes, "Geochronology of Paleoenvironmental Change, Clovis Type Site, Blackwater Draw, New Mexico," 317–88, and Haynes, "Appendix B: Nature and Origin of the Black Mat," in Haynes and Huckell, 2007, 240–49.

2. Vogel and Waterbolk, "Groningen Radiocarbon Dates V," 354.

3. Ibid.

4. Ibid.

5. Jażdżewski, *Ancient Peoples and Places*, 45–46.

6. Ibid., 46.

7. V. O. Manko, "To the Question about the Chronology of Crimean Swiderian and Its Origin," *Stone Age Times in Ukraine* 14 (2011): 162–71, www.nbuv.gov.ua/portal/soc_gum/kdu/2011_14/162-171.pdf (accessed January 15, 2014).

8. Bailey and Spikins, *Mesolithic Europe*, 289.

9. Nikolaeva and Safronov, *Istoki slavianskoi i evraziiskoi mifologii*, as translated into English on Yahoo Groups in message from "jdcroft" to "nostratic@yahoogroups.com" dated April 02, 2002, retrieved November 28, 2013, http://groups.yahoo.com/neo/groups/nostratic/conversations/topics/534. Full quotation: "The existence of a site like Suren' 2 in the Crimea is estimated as spreading cultural influences from the side of the Swiderian culture from more Northern regions of East Europe. The possibility of the direct migration of a group of Swiderian population in the Crimea is not excluded."

10. Formozov, "Etnokulturnîie oblasti na terrotorii evropeiskoi ciasti SSSR v kamennom veke," 59, 68, 71. For a good review of Formozov's hypothesis, see Valentyn Stetsyuk, "Primary Settling of Europe and Caucasus," Valentyn Stetsyuk (Lviv) Personal Site, www.v-stetsyuk.name/en/NorthCauc.html (accessed January 15, 2014).

11. See Earth's International Research Society, "Göbekli Tepe Report," Academia.edu, www.academia.edu/1960727/Gobekli_Tepe_Report (accessed January 15, 2014). Here you'll find stone blades found at Göbekli Tepe that are strikingly similar to Swiderian points.

12. Hartz, Terberger, and Zhilin, "New AMS-dates for the Upper Volga Mesolithic and the Origin of Microblade Technology in Europe," 155–69.

13. Balkan-Atli and Cauvin, "Das Schwarz Gold der Steinzeit," 202–7; Chabot and Pelegrin, "Two Examples of Pressure Blade Production with a Lever," 181–98.

14. See, for instance, Takala, *The Ristola Site in Lahti and the Earliest Postglacial Settlement of South Finland*.

15. Hartz, Terberger, and Zhilin, "New AMS-dates for the Upper Volga Mesolithic."

16. Ibid. See also Olofsson, *Pioneer Settlement in the Mesolithic of Northern Sweden*.

17. Valentyn Stetsyuk, "Introduction to the Study of Prehistoric Ethnogenic Processes in Eastern Europe and Asia: The Anthropological Type of Autochthon Europeans and Their Language," Valentyn Stetsyuk (Lviv), http://alterling2.narod.ru/English/AO21ab.doc (accessed January 15, 2014).

18. Gimbutas, *The Prehistory of Eastern Europe*, 28.

19. Ibid.

20. Ibid., 31–32.

21. Peake and Fleure, *Corridors of Time*, 67, 73–74; Osborn, *Men of the Old Stone Age*, 334–37. For the original discovery of the Brno skulls, see Makowsky, "Der diluviale Mensch im Loss von Brünn," 73–84, and for recent radiocarbon dating of the Brno 2 skull to 23,680 +/- 200 years BP, see Pettitt and Trinkaus, "Direct Radiocarbon Dating of the Brno 2 Gravettian Human Remains," 149–50. Although the skull is said to be Gravettian in age, Pettitt and Trinkaus say that the dating would make it exceptionally late for this period, suggesting that it could be related to the Szeletian culture; that is, the proto-Solutreans of Central Europe.

22. Osborn, *Men of the Old Stone Age*, 334.

23. Peake and Fleure, *Corridors of Time*, 71–73, 74; Osborn, *Men of the Old Stone Age*, 334–37.

24. Osborn, *Men of the Old Stone Age*, 337.

25. Peake and Fleure, *Corridors of Time*, 67–68.

26. Coon, *The Races of Europe*, 36–39.

27. Shtrunov, "The Origin of Haplogroup I1-M253 in Eastern Europe," 7, 9.

CHAPTER 21. THE SOLUTREAN CONNECTION

1. McKern and McKern, *Tracking Fossil Man*, 147.

2. Šatavičius, "Brommian (Lyngby) Finds in Lithuania," 17–45.

3. Ibid.

4. Montelius, "Palaeolithic Implements Found in Sweden."

5. For further information, see Stanford and Bradley, *Across Atlantic Ice*.

6. Oakley, *Frameworks for Dating Fossil Man*, 163–65; Burkitt, *Prehistory*, 129–30. The culture is known as the Szeletian, and for a full discussion on the subject see Adams, "The Bükk Mountain Szeletian," 427–40, particularly page 433. Here the author argues against the Szeletian culture being either Neanderthal or the product of a Neanderthal-AMH (anatomically modern human) interaction.

7. Osborn, *Men of the Old Stone Age*, 337. See also page 345.

8. Peake and Fleure, *Corridors of Time*, 67.

9. Bradley, Anikovitch, and Giria, "Early Upper Paleolithic in the Russian Plain," 989–98. See also Stanford and Bradley, *Across Atlantic Ice*, 144.

10. Maron et al, "Single Amino Acid Radiocarbon Dating of Upper Paleolithic Modern Humans," 6878–81.

11. Zubov, *Sungir*, 144–62.

12. Childe, *The Prehistory of European Society*, 21–2.

13. Jochim, "Upper Palaeolithic," 88.

14. Aujoulat, *Lascaux*. The author speaks of a radiocarbon date of 18,600 ± 190 BP being obtained in 1998 from a fragment of reindeer antler baton found at the foot of the panel of the Shaft Scene. It places the art at the boundary between the Upper Solutrean and the Badegoulian age.

15. Mannermaa, Panteleyev, and Sablin, "Birds in Late Mesolithic Burials at Yuzhniy Oleniy Ostrove," 19–20.

16. Grumeza, *Dacia,* 75.

17. Ibid.

18. Eliade, "The Dacians and Wolves," 1–20. See also Eliade, *De la Zalmoxis la Genghis-Han,* 11–13.

19. Grumeza, *Dacia,* 76.

20. Eriksen, "Resource Exploitation Subsistence Strategies and Adaptiveness in Late Pleistocene Early Holocene Northwest Europe," 119, 125.

21. See Laurentiu Puicin, "Historical Considerations regarding the Shepherd and the Origins of the Romanian Carpathian Shepherd Dog Breed Text," trans. by Daniel Milea, http://carpatini.cabanova.ro/Consideration.html (accessed January 15, 2014; to retrieve download in text format only).

CHAPTER 22. OBSIDIAN OBSESSION

1. See Stanford and Bradley, *Across Atlantic Ice,* 134.

2. Viola T. Dobosi, "Obsidian Use in the Palaeolithic in Hungary and Adjoining Areas," *Natural Resource Environment and Humans* 1 (March 2011): 83–95, www.meiji.ac .jp/cols/english/research/6t5h7p00000de6rx-att/06.pdf (accessed January 15, 2014).

3. Ibid.

4. O'Hanlon, Larry, "Volcanic Artifacts Imply Ice-age Mariners in Prehistoric Greece," Phys Org, August 29, 2011, http://phys.org/news/2011-08-volcanic-artifacts-imply -ice-age-mariners.html (accessed January 15, 2014).

5. Perlès, "L'outillage de pierre taillée néolithique en Grèce," 1–42.

6. Tripković, Milić, and Shackley, "Obsidian in the Central Balkans," 163–79.

7. Kozlowski, "West Carpathians and Sudeten at the End of the Upper Palaeolithic," 127–37.

8. Ibid. See also Dobosi, "Obsidian Use in the Palaeolithic."

9. Osipowicz and Szeliga, "Functional Analysis of a Late-Palaeolithic Obsidian Tanged Point from Wolodz, District Brzozów, Podkarpacie Voivodship," 153–60.

10. Buck, "Ancient Technology in Contemporary Surgery," 265–69.

11. Dobosi, "Obsidian Use in the Palaeolithic," and Rómer, *Műrégészeti Kalauz különös tekintettel Magyarországra,* as paraphased by László Szathmáry, http://jam .nyirbone.hu/konyvtar/evkonyv/97-98/Szathmar.htm (accessed January 15, 2014).

12. Ibid.

13. Rómer, *Műrégészeti Kalauz különös tekintettel Magyarországra.*

14. Spence, *The Magic and Mysteries of Mexico,* 81.

CHAPTER 23. THE BINGÖL MASTERS

1. F.-X. Le Bourdonnec, "Towards a Materiality of Pilgrimage? Characterizing

Obsidian from Neolithic Göbekli Tepe (Urfa Region, SE Turkey)," *Rapport Sur Le Projet Eu-Artech* 7 (April 2008), www.yumpu.com/en/document/view/19543365/ user-report-eu-artech (accessed January 15, 2014).

2. Owen Jarus, "'World's Oldest Temple' May Have Been Cosmopolitan Center," *LiveScience,* March 15, 2012, www.livescience.com/19085-world-oldest-temple -tools-pilgrimage.html (accessed January 15, 2014).

3. Ibid.

4. Clark, *World Prehistory,* 58.

5. Mellaart, *Earliest Civilizations of the Near East,* 16.

6. Settegast, *Plato Preshistorian,* 61.

7. Ibid., 59–61.

CHAPTER 24. WOLF STONE MOUNTAIN

1. Forrest and Skjaervo, *Witches, Whores and Sorcerers,* 104.

2. Zaehner, *Zurvan,* ix.

3. Hrach Martirosyan, "Studies in Armenian Etymology" (dissertation, University of Leiden, 2008), 3.5.2.4, 632, www.vahagnakanch.files.wordpress.com/2011/04/ armenian-etymologies.pdf (accessed January 15, 2014).

4. Ibid., 4.3, 641, 649.

5. Ibid., 3.5.2.4, 631.

6. Ibid., "Studies in Armenian Etymology," 4.3, 649–51.

7. Ibid., 4.3, 652; 4.5, 653.

8. Ibid., 3.5.2.4, 631–32.

9. Ibid., 3.5.2.4, 633.

10. Ibid., 4.3, 649.

11. Ibid., 4.3, 649.

12. Ibid., 4.3, 650.

13. Ibid., 4.3, 649. Martirosyan takes this information from Hübschmann, *Die altarmenischen Ortsnamen,* vol. 2, 287, where he proposes that Gaylaxaz-ut is Baghir Dağ and that the village of Xač is Khach Dağ. However, Hübschmann adds that he cannot decide which mountain range is being indicated and that it could be somewhere else altogether.

14. Hübschmann, *Die altarmenischen Ortsnamen,* vol. 2, 371.

15. Pliny, *Historiarum naturae,* vol. 2, translated by Pierre Danès, bk. 37, ch. 24.

16. "Peri," Dictionary.com, http://m.dictionary.com/d/?q=PERIS (accessed January 15, 2014).

17. Hübschmann, *Die altarmenischen Ortsnamen,* s.v. "Gail."

18. Strecker and Kiepert, *Beiträge zur geographischen erklärung des rückzuges der zehntausend durch das armenische hochland,* 8.

19. Personal communication between Hakan Dalkus and the author.

20. Personal communication between Hakan Dalkus and the author on February 28, 2012.
21. Personal communication between Hakan Dalkus and the author in March 2013.

CHAPTER 25. SAVIORS OF THE WORLD

1. Czaplicka, *Aboriginal Siberia*, 296, cf. Jochelson, *The Koryak*, 89.
2. Ibid.
3. Czaplicka, *Aboriginal Siberia*, 295, cf. Jochelson, *The Koryak*, 89–90.
4. Ibid., 261.
5. Thorsson, *Futhark*, 53.
6. Ibid., 54.
7. Hultkrantz, "A New Look at the World Pillar in Arctic and Sub-Arctic Religions," 32.
8. Ibid.
9. Ibid.
10. Ibid.
11. Zaliznyak, "The Archaeology of the Occupation of the East European Taiga Zone at the Turn of the Palaeolithic-Mesolithic," 95, 104–6.
12. Peters and Schmidt, "Animals in the Symbolic World of Pre-Pottery Neolithic Göbekli Tepe, South-eastern Turkey," 179–218.
13. Yeshurun, Bar-Oz, and Weinstein-Evron, "The Role of Foxes in the Natufian Economy," 1–15.

CHAPTER 26. STRANGE-LOOKING PEOPLE

1. Burney, *From Village to Empire*, quoted in Settegast, *Plato Prehistorian*, 63.
2. Roberts, *The Incredible Human Journey*, 2010, 276.
3. Ibid.
4. Schmidt, "Göbekli Tepe and the Early Sites of the Urfa Region," 9–11.
5. Ibid., 10.
6. Ibid.
7. See Schoch, *Forgotten Civilization*, 101.

CHAPTER 27. IN THE GARDEN OF EDEN

1. Tom Knox, "Do These Mysterious Stones Mark the Site of the Garden of Eden?" *Daily Mail Online*, March 5, 2009, www.dailymail.co.uk/sciencetech/article-1157784/Do-mysterious-stones-mark-site-Garden-Eden.html#ixzz2Jglfu1fT (accessed January 15, 2014).
2. Ibid.
3. For a full account of theories on the whereabouts of the Garden of Eden, or terrestrial Paradise, see Delumeau, *History of Paradise*.
4. Biblical quotation from *Young's Literal Translation of the Bible*, 1898.

5. Rohl, *Legend,* 47.

6. Johns, *An Assyrian Doomsday Book,* 38.

7. "Togarmah," Bible History Online, www.bible-history.com/isbe/T/TOGARMAH/ (accessed January 15, 2014).

8. Smith, *The Chaldean Account of Genesis,* 175.

9. Strabo, *Geography,* bk. 11, ch. 13. v. 7.

10. Ibid., bk. 11, ch. 14, v. 9.

11. Ibid., bk. 11, ch. 14, v. 14.

12. Rohl, *Legend,* 52.

13. Walker, "The Real Land of Eden."

14. McClintock and Strong, *Cyclopaedia of Biblical, Theological, and Ecclesiastical Literature,* s.v. "Gihon."

15. Clarke, *The Holy Bible,* 41–42.

16. Strabo, *Geography,* bk. 11, ch. 14, v. 9.

17. Forbes, *Metallurgy in Antiquity,* 151.

18. Strabo, *Geography,* bk. 11, ch. 14, v. 12.

19. Carver, *A Discourse of the Terrestrial Paradise,* 155.

20. Ibid.

21. Ibid.

22. Wigram and Wigram, *The Cradle of Mankind,* 264; Nichols, *Rome and the Eastern Churches,* 2010, 59.

23. See, for instance, "History of the Nestorian Church," Nestorian.org, www .nestorian.org/history_of_the_nestorian_churc.html (accessed January 15, 2014).

24. Isin, *Sherbet and Spice,* 39.

25. *Encyclopedia Britannica,* 1911, s.v. "Bitlis."

26. Issawi, *The Fertile Crescent, 1800–1914.*

27. See, for instance, "Astragalus," Biogeociencias.com, www.biogeociencias.com/ Webimpacts/2009/WorksofTurkishSchool/PLANT%20&%20ANIMALS%20 htmls/geven.html (accessed January 15, 2014), where the distribution of the genus is cited as "Turkey (Anatolian), Hakkari."

28. Clarke, *The Holy Bible,* 41–42.

CHAPTER 28. THE FOUNTAIN OF PARADISE

1. *Encyclopedia Britannica,* 1911, s.v. "Mush."

2. Garsoïan, "Taron as an Early Christian Armenian Center," 63–65.

3. Sauer, "The River Runs Dry," 52–54, 57, 64.

4. Ibid.

5. See, for instance, Wayne Blank, "Where Was the Garden of Eden?" Daily Bible Study, www.keyway.ca/htm2002/eden.htm (accessed January 15, 2014).

6. See, for instance, Lawrence E. Stager, "Jerusalem as Eden," *Biblical Archaeological*

Review 26, no. 3 (May–June 2000), http://cojs.org/cojswiki/Jerusalem_as_Eden,_Lawrence_E._Stager,_BAR_26:03,_May/Jun_2000 (accessed January 15, 2014).

7. See Movsisyan, *The Sacred Highlands,* and the references therein.

8. Taken from Burke, *A Genealogical and Heraldic History of the Commoners of Great Britain and Ireland,* 634.

9. Drake, *An Accurate Description and History of the Cathedral and Metropolitical Church of St. Peter, York,* 102.

10. Carver, *A Discourse of the Terrestrial Paradise,* Dedication.

11. Ibid., 1.

12. Ibid., 42.

13. Ibid., 45.

14. Ibid., 43, 45, 47.

15. Ibid., 43.

16. Strabo, *Geography,* bk. 11, ch. 14, v. 8.

17. Pliny, *The Natural History,* bk. 6, ch. 31. Ed. by John Bostock and H. T. Riley, Perseus Digital Library, www.perseus.tufts.edu/hopper/text?doc=Perseus%3Atext%3A1999.02.0137%3Abook%3D6%3Achapter%3D31 (accessed January 15, 2014).

18. Carver, *A Discourse of the Terrestrial Paradise,* 152.

19. Ibid., 152–53.

20. Kinneir, *Journey through Asia Minor, Armenia, and Koordistan in the Years 1813 and 1814,* 384.

21. Carver, *A Discourse of the Terrestrial Paradise,* 153.

22. Gaidzakian, *Illustrated Armenia and the Armenians,* 21, quoting *The Dix Neuwine Sircle,* Paris, May 17, 1891.

23. Wigram and Wigram, *Cradle of Mankind,* 26.

24. Massey, *The Natural Genesis,* vol. 2, 231.

25. Speiser, *Genesis,* 16, 19.

26. Millard, "The Etymology of Eden," 103–6.

27. Herbert, *Some Yeares Travels into Divers Parts of Asia and Afrique,* vol. 2, p. 221. See also Houtsma, *Encyclopedia of Islam, 1913–1936,* s.v. "Bingöldagh."

28. Pliny, *Historiarum naturae,* vol. 2, bk. 37, ch. 24. Translation by Pierre Danès.

29. Ibid.

30. Strabo, *Geography,* bk. 11, ch. 14, v. 2.

31. W. B. Fisher and C. E. Bosworth, *Encyclopaedia Iranica,* s.v. "Araxes River," www.iranicaonline.org/articles/araxes-river (accessed January 15, 2014).

32. Houtsma, *Encyclopedia of Islam, 1913–1936,* s.v. "Bingöldagh."

33. One tradition holds that the true source of the Tigris is Lake Nazook, which lies on the southern slopes of the Armenian Highlands, near the town of Bulanık. See Williams, *Two Essays on the Geography of Ancient Asia, etc.,* 273.

CHAPTER 29. THE WORLD'S SUMMIT

1. Hübschmann, *Die altarmenischen Ortsnamen,* vol. 2, 370.

2. Hewsen and Shirakats'i, *The Geography of Ananias of Širak,* 59, 63.

3. Movsisyan, *The Sacred Highlands,* 29–30.

4. Ibid., 29.

5. Ibid.

6. Houtsma, *Encyclopedia of Islam, 1913–1936,* s.v. "Bingöldagh."

7. Strecker and Kiepert, *Beiträge zur geographischen erklärung des rückzuges der zehntausend durch das armenische hochland.*

8. Xenophon, *Anabasis,* ed. by Carleton L. Brownson, Perseus Digital Library, www.perseus .tufts.edu/hopper/text?doc=Perseus:text:1999.01.0202 (accessed January 15, 2014).

9. Strecker and Kiepert, *Beiträge zur geographischen erklärung,* 8.

10. Ibid., 8, n. 1.

11. See Rohl, *Legend,* 53, 54, 56, 62, 66, 68, etc.

12. Budge, *The Life and Exploits of Alexander.*

13. Coomaraswamy, "Khwaja Khadir and the Fountain of Life in the Tradition of Persian and Mughal Art," 157–67.

14. See, for instance, "Bingöl Evlilik," eCift, www.ecift.com/evlilik/bingoel-evlilik .html (accessed January 15, 2014).

15. Qur'an 18: 60–65.

16. Anderson, *Green Man,* 29, 75.

17. Leeming, *Creation Myths of the World,* vol. 1, 248.

18. Archi, "The God Hay(y)a (Ea-Enki) at Ebla," 15–36.

19. Movsisyan, *Sacred Highlands,* 47–49.

20. Ibid., 69.

21. "Byurakn," HyeForum, http://hyeforum.com/index.php?showtopic=6497 (accessed January 15, 2014).

22. Heinberg, *Memories and Visions of Paradise,* 42.

23. Roux, *Ancient Iraq,* 1980, 106.

24. Ibid.

25. Tabakow, "Reflections on a Fulbright Year in Bahrain."

26. Kramer, *Sumerian Mythology,* 1998, 81.

27. Izady, *The Kurds,* 19.

28. Ibid., 67.

29. Ibid., 44.

30. Ibid.

31. Bruinessen, "Aslini Inkar Eden Haramzadedir! The Debate on the Ethnic Identity of the Kurdish Alevis," 5.

32. See Russell, *Zoroastrianism in Armenia,* 515–27.

33. Ibid.

CHAPTER 30. RISE OF THE ANUNNAKI

1. Schmidt, *Göbekli Tepe,* 206–7.
2. Black, "The Sumerians in Their Landscape," 41–62.
3. Ibid.
4. Horowitz, *Mesopotamian Cosmic Geography,* 316 (K. 2873:3–4). See also Katz, *The Image of the Netherworld in the Sumerian Sources,* for a full review of this topic.
5. Hennerbichler, "The Origin of Kurds," 64–79.
6. Horowitz, *Mesopotamian Cosmic Geography,* 316 (K. 2873:3–4).
7. Jastrow, *The Religion of Babylonia and Assyria,* 558.
8. Sayce, "Two Accadian Hymns," 130.
9. Warren, *Paradise Found,* 127, 166, 170.
10. Barton, *Miscellaneous Babylonian Inscriptions,* 5.
11. See, for example, Miller, *Har-Moad,* 2, 179, 194.
12. Sale, *The Koran,* 1833, vol. 2, 15, note a.
13. Ibid.
14. Ibid.
15. Ibid.
16. Garsoïan, "Taron as an Early Christian Armenian Center," 65.
17. Ibid.
18. Miller, *Har-Moad,* 20, 179, 194.
19. Jastrow, *Religion of Babylonia and Assyria,* 558.
20. Sayce, "Two Accadian Hymns," 130.
21. See Wiggermann, "Mythological Foundations of Nature," 279–306.
22. Ibid.
23. O'Brien with O'Brien, *The Genius of the Few,* 37.
24. Ibid., 43.
25. Barton, *Miscellaneous Babylonian Inscriptions,* 4.
26. Ibid., 16.
27. Ibid.
28. O'Brien with O'Brien, *Genius of the Few,* 46.
29. For a full account of Zenob Glak's story, see Seth, *Armenians in India,* and Avdall, "A Hindoo Colony in Ancient Armenia," 181–86.
30. O'Brien with O'Brien, *Genius of the Few,* 48–49.
31. Izady, *The Kurds,* 18–19.

CHAPTER 31. THE MAKING OF HUMANKIND

1. Leick, *Göbekli Tepe,* s.v. "Igigi," 85.
2. Ibid. For the full story see "Atrahasis 1," in Dalley, *Myths from Mesopotamia,* 9–17. See also Brown, *The Ethos of the Cosmos,* 140.
3. "Atrahasis 1," in Dalley, *Myths from Mesopotamia,* 9.

4. Ibid., 10.

5. Ibid., 14–15.

6. Ibid., 15.

7. Ibid., 15–16.

8. Josephus, "The Antiquities of the Jews," vol. 1, 1, 2.

9. Barton, *Miscellaneous Babylonian Inscriptions*, 16.

10. Olyan, *Asherah and the Cult of Yahweh in Israel*, 70–71.

CHAPTER 32. THE COMING OF THE WATCHERS

1. Movsisyan, *The Sacred Highlands*, 29–30. See also Houtsma, *Encyclopedia of Islam, 1913–1936*, s.v. "Bingöldagh."

2. "Bingöl Dagları," Wikipedia, http://ca.wikipedia.org/wiki/Bing%C3%B6l_Da%C4%9Flar%C4%B1 (accessed January 15, 2014).

3. E-mail communication between Jonathan Bright and the author dated October 20, 2012.

4. Charles, trans., *The Book of Enoch or 1 Enoch*, 1 En. 8:1, 3.

5. Various references in 1 En. For a full examination of the Watchers' physical traits see Collins, *From the Ashes of Angels*, 46–56, and the references therein.

6. Eisenman and Wise, *The Dead Sea Scrolls Uncovered*, 153–56, see 4Q543, Manuscript B, Fragment 1.

7. Graves and Patai, *Hebrew Myths*, 106.

8. Charles, trans., *The Book of Enoch or 1 Enoch*, 1 En. 69:12.

9. Ibid., 1 En. 69:6.

10. Milik, *The Books of Enoch*, 306, 307, 313, quoting extracts from the "Book of Giants."

11. Eisenman and Wise, *The Dead Sea Scrolls Uncovered*, 153–56, see 4Q543, Manuscript B, Fragment 1.

12. Charles, trans., *The Book of Enoch or 1 Enoch*, 2 En. 1:4–5.

13. "Human Figures, Wild Animal Reliefs Unearthed in 11,000-year-old Gobeklitepe Tumulus," Hurriyet Daily News, November 10, 2006, www.hurriyetdailynews.com/default.aspx?pageid=438&n=human-figures-wild-animal-reliefs-unearthed-in-11000-year-old-gobeklitepe-tumulus-2006-10-11 (accessed January 15, 2014).

14. Schodde, trans., *The Book of Enoch*, 1 En. 13:10.

15. O'Brien with O'Brien, *The Genius of the Few*, 48–49, 108–9.

CHAPTER 33. MOUNTAIN OF THE WATCHERS

1. Baty, trans., *Enoch the Prophet*, 1 En. 2:7–8.

2. Baty, *Enoch the Prophet*, xv.

3. Ibid.

4. Ibid.

5. Hewitt, *Primitive Traditional History*, 25.

6. Baty, trans., *Enoch the Prophet*, xv; 1 En. 2:21.

7. Bochart, *Geographia sacra*, vol. 1, ch. III, p. 23, who states that Jerome (347–420 AD) used the place-name Armon in connection with Armenia. No citation is given.

8. Ibid. The author writes that Aquila and Symmachus, second century translators of the Old Testament, both used the place-name Armona in connection with Armenia. No citation is given.

9. Ibid., vol. I, ch. III, p. 22.

10. Jer. 51:27.

11. Smith, *Smith's Bible Dictionary*, s.v. "Armenia," www.ccel.org/ccel/smith_w/ bibledict.txt (accessed January 15, 2014).

12. Christian Abraham Wahl as quoted in Rosenmüller, *Biblical Geography*, 149. Unfortunately, Rosenmüller fails to provide a full citation for Wahl's statement, recording only that it derives from "*Asien*, p. 807, note."

13. Tavernier, *Viaggi nella Turchia, nella Persia, e nell' Indie*, vol. 1, 16. See also Carari, "A Voyage round the World (1699)," 350–51.

14. Tavernier, *Viaggi nella Turchia, nella Persia, e nell' Indie*, vol. 1, 16.

15. Shea and Troyer, *The Dabistán*, vol. 1, 150; vol. 3, index.

16. Yates, *Hindustání and English*, s.v. "Míná," 518a.

17. Ibid., s.v. "Mínú," 518b.

18. Ibid., s.v. "Jhil," 194b. See also Gilchrist, *The Hindee Moral Preceptor*, s.v. "jul," 163.

19. Lipinski, "El's Abode," 43, and all references therein.

20. Ibid.

21. Ibid.

22. Ibid., 44.

23. Ibid., 46.

24. Coomaraswamy, "Khwaja Khadir and the Fountain of Life in the Tradition of Persian and Mughal Art," 157–67.

25. Lipinski, "El's Abode," 46.

26. Ibid., 46.

27. Ibid., 47, quoting 1 En. 17:2.

28. Ibid., quoting 1 En 17:7–8.

29. Ibid., 48, quoting 1 En 32:2–3.

30. Ibid., 48.

31. Charles, ed., *Apocrypha and Pseudepigrapha*, "Apocalypse of Moses."

32. Lipinski, "El's Abode," 48.

33. Ibid., 49–55.

34. Ibid., 55–56.

35. Ibid., 57.

36. Peiser, "Eine babylonische Landkarte," 361–70. For a full description and account of the clay tablet, see Horowitz, *Mesopotamian Cosmic Geography*, 20–42.

37. Horowitz, *Mesopotamian Cosmic Geography*, 22.

38. Ibid., 33.

39. Private communication between Gagik Avagyan and the author dated June 10, 2013.

40. Private communication between Gagik Avagyan and the author dated June 8, 2013.

CHAPTER 34. WALKING WITH SERPENTS

1. Valentyn Stetsyuk, "Introduction to the Study of Prehistoric Ethnogenic Processes in Eastern Europe and Asia: The Anthropological Type of Autochthon Europeans and Their Language," Alternative Historical Linguistics, http://alterling2.narod.ru/English/AO21ab.doc (accessed January 15, 2014).

2. Shtrunov, "The Origin of Haplogroup I1-M253 in Eastern Europe," 7, 9.

3. Gimbutas, *The Prehistory of Eastern Europe*, 28, 31–32.

4. Graves and Patai, *Hebrew Myths*, 106.

5. Mallowan and Rose, "Excavations at Tell Arpachiyah 1933," 1–178.

6. Molleson and Campbell, "Deformed Skulls at Tell Arpachiyah," 45–55.

7. Mallowan and Linford, "Rediscovered Skulls from Arpachiyah," 52.

8. Molleson and Campbell, "Deformed Skulls at Tell Arpachiyah," 49–50.

9. Ibid., 50.

10. Ibid.

11. Ibid.

12. Ibid., 51–52.

13. Ibid., 52.

14. Gilbert and Cotterell, *The Mayan Prophecies*, 118–25, quoting José Diaz Bolio, *The Rattlesnake School* and *Why the Rattlesnake in Mayan Civilization*.

15. Charles, trans., *The Book of Enoch or 1 Enoch*, 1 En. 69:6.

16. Peregrine, *Encyclopedia of Prehistory*, s.v. "Arpachiyah (Tepe Reshwa)."

17. Bressy, Poupeau, and Yener, "Cultural Interactions during the Ubaid and Halaf Periods," 1560–65.

18. Charvát, *Mesopotamia before History*, 51.

19. Milik, *The Books of Enoch*, 306, 307, 313, quoting extracts from the "Book of Giants."

20. O'Brien with O'Brien, *The Genius of the Few*, 48–9, 62–3.

21. Segal, *Edessa*, p. 2 n. 4, 106.

22. Çelik, "An Early Neolithic Settlement in the Center of Şanlıurfa, Turkey," 4–6.

23. Segal, *Edessa*, p. 2 n. 2.

24. Personal communication between Hakan Dalkus and the author dated February 7, 2012.

25. Ibid.

26. Keightley, *The Fairy Mythology*, 25.

27. Ibid.

28. The relationship between the Watchers and the Persian Peri and Jinn is a matter discussed at length in the author's book *From the Ashes of Angels*. See, for example, pages 100–101, 198–201, 271–72.

29. See, for example, the account of the birth of Noah in Avigad and Yadin, *A Genesis Apocryphon*.

CHAPTER 35. A QUIET CORNER OF EDEN

1. "Yeghrdut," Wikipedia, http://en.wikipedia.org/wiki/Yeghrdut_monastery (accessed January 16, 2014).

2. Murad Hasratyan, *Christian Armenia Encyclopedia*, s.v. "Yeghrduti Monastery," 313–14.

3. Oskian, *Die Klöster von Taron-Turuberan*, s.v. "Yeghrduti."

4. Madatyan, "Srbaluys myuron," http://araratian-tem.am/media/Myuron.doc. If you're unable to access this link, go to "Wayback Machine" at http://archive.org/web/ and type in "http://araratian-tem.am/media/Myuron.doc" and press enter. The document will automatically download.

5. Ibid.

6. Ibid.

7. Ibid. See also Armeniapedia, s.v. "Yeghrtud Monastery," www.armeniapedia.org/index.php?title=Yeghrtud_Monastery, cf. *Dictionary of Armenian Place Names*.

8. "Yeghrduti Monastery," Hasratyan, http://archive.is/0TQs (accessed January 16, 2014).

9. I want to thank Gagik Avagyan for the interpretation of this word.

10. Ayvazyan, *Armenia Christian Encyclopedia*, s.v. "Yeghrdut"; "Yeghrduti Monastery," Hasratyan, http://archive.is/0TQs (accessed January 16, 2014).

11. "Yeghrduti Monastery," Hasratyan, http://archive.is/0TQs (accessed January 16, 2014).

12. Thanks go out to Gagik Avagyan for this information.

13. Madatyan, "Srbaluys myuron."

14. "Books of Adam and Eve," 40:3–5, in *Apocrypha and Pseudepigrapha of the Old Testament*, ed. by Charles. See also Johnson, "The Life of Adam and Eve," 249–96.

15. "Holy Anointing Oil," Wikipedia, http://en.wikipedia.org/wiki/Holy_anointing_oil (accessed January 16, 2014).

16. See Isenberg, trans., "Gospel of Philip," 153, which alludes to the Chrism or anointing oil coming from the olive tree. For a full account of this subject see Margaret Barker, "The Holy Anointing Oil," www.margaretbarker.com/Papers/TheHolyAnointingOil.pdf (accessed January 16, 2014).

17. This tradition is inferred in the Western Church by the words of Acts 1:12–17.

18. Madatyan, "Srbaluys myuron." See also "Yeghrtud Monastery," Armeniapedia, www.armeniapedia.org/index.php?title=Yeghrtud_Monastery (accessed January 17, 2014).

19. For all the different variations of the story see Quinn, *The Quest of Seth for the Oil of Life*, and Rappoport, *Mediæval Legends of Christ*, 210–34.

20. Hasratyan, "Yeghrduti Monastery," http://archive.is/0TQs (accessed January 16, 2014).

CHAPTER 36. THE RED CHURCH

1. Cuinet, *Turquie d'Asie Géographie Administrative,* 584.
2. Oskian, *Die Klöster von Taron-Turuberan,* s.v. "Yeghrduti," 91–129.
3. See my post on VirtualAni dated April 4, 2012, and all responses, under the main heading "Yeghrdut monastery," www.network54.com/Forum/146256/message/1333496514/Yeghrdut+monastery (accessed January 16, 2014).
4. Personal communication between Hakan Dalkus and the author dated April 8, 2012.
5. Raffi Kojian, "The Info I Have," VirtualAni, April 10, 2012, www.network54.com/Forum/146256/message/1334065482/The+info+I+have (accessed January 16, 2014).
6. "Yeghrtud Monastery," Armeniapedia, www.armeniapedia.org/index.php?title=Yeghrtud_Monastery (accessed January 16, 2014).
7. Oskian, *Die Klöster von Taron-Turuberan,* s.v. "Yeghrduti."
8. Ibid.
9. Murad Hasratyan, *Christian Armenia Encyclopedia,* s.v. "Yeghrduti Monastery," Yerevan, http://archive.is/0TQs (accessed January 16, 2014).
10. "Yeghrtud Monastery," Armeniapedia, www.armeniapedia.org/index.php?title=Yeghrtud_Monastery (accessed January 16, 2014).
11. The Armenians claim descent from Togarmah, the third son of Gomer, and grandson of Japheth, one of the sons of Noah. See "Togarmah," Wikipedia, http://en.wikipedia.org/wiki/Togarmah (accessed January 16, 2014).
12. Khorenatsi, *History of the Armenians,* 80.
13. Ibid. See also "Haik," TourArmenia, www.tacentral.com/mythology.asp?story_no=6 (accessed January 17, 2014).

CHAPTER 37. THE SECRETS OF ADAM

1. Carver, *A Discourse of the Terrestrial Paradise,* 165.
2. Ibid., 166.
3. Ibid., 167.
4. Reinink, "East Assyrian Historiography in Response to the Rise in Islam," 88.
5. Pererii Valentini, *Commentariorvm et Disputationum in Genesim,* 6.
6. MacBean and Johnson, *Dictionary of Ancient Geography,* s.v. "Gordene" and "Gordiaei Montes," cf. Ptolemy, London, 1773.
7. Malan, *The Book of Adam and Eve,* III, 5–6, 147–51.
8. Budge, *Book of the Cave of Treasures;* Ri, *La Caverne des Trésors;* and Malan, *Book of Adam and Eve,* III, iv, 146–47.

9. Malan, *Book of Adam and Eve*, III, vii, 151–53.

10. Klijn, *Seth in Jewish, Christian and Gnostic Literature*, 88.

11. Logan, *Gnostic Truth and Christian Heresy*, 90.

12. Josephus, "The Antiquities of the Jews," I, ii, 3.

13. Whiston, *The Works of Flavius Josephus*.

14. See footnote accompanying Josephus, "Antiquities," I, ii, 3.

15. Josephus, *Historiarum de Bello Judaico, Liber Primus, et Pars Secondi, Quibus, Ea summatim continentur quæ Josephus susius prosequitur postremis novem Antiquitatum libris*, 13.

16. Charles, ed., *Apocrypha and Pseudepigrapha of the Old Testament*, vol. 2, "Vita Adae et Evae," 51:1–3.

17. MacRae, trans., "Apocalypse of Adam."

18. Turner and Wintermute, trans., "Allogenes."

19. Böhlig and Wisse, trans., "Gospel of the Egyptians."

20. Stroumsa, *Another Seed*, 115.

21. Lemprière, *Bibliotheca Classica*, s.v. "Charax," 143a.

22. Stroumsa, *Another Seed*, 116.

23. Ibid.

24. Ibid., cf. Layton, trans., "The Hypostasis of the Archons," 92.

25. Mead, *Pistis Sophia*, ch. 134, p. 292. For the dating of the Askew MS (BL Additional 5114) containing the *Pistis Sophia* text see Ibid., xxvi, and Legge, *Forerunners and Rivals of Christianity*, vol. 2, 134, 194.

26. Gürtler and Pearson, *Criticorum Sacrorum sive Lectissimarum in Sacro-Sancta Biblia Utriusque Foederis Annotationum atrus Tractatuum Theologico-Philologicorum Supplementum*, 175–76. See also Josephus, *Historiarum de Bello Judaico*, IV, 31.

27. Lemprière, *Bibliotheca Classica*, s.v. "Abas."

28. Widengren, *Die Religionen Irans*, cf. *Opus imperfectum in Matthaeum*, Hom. bk. II, ch. 56.

29. The text for the "Revelation of the Magi," otherwise known as the "Chronicle of Zuqnin," is taken from "The Sages and the Star-child," trans. by Landau.

30. "Revelation of the Magi," 2:3.

31. Ibid., 3:3–4.

32. Ibid., 2:4.

33. Ibid., 4:2–10.

34. Ibid., 5:8.

35. Ibid., 5:9–10.

36. Ibid., 6:2–3.

37. Ibid., 29:1.

38. For a good summary, see Landau, "The Sages and the Star-child," 83.

39. Ri, trans., *La Caverne des Trésors*, "Book of the Cave of Treasures," 14:1.

40. Budge, *Book of the Cave of Treasures*, and Ri, *La Caverne des Trésors*, various references.

CHAPTER 38. AS ANGELS OURSELVES

1. Mills, *Mercer Dictionary of the Bible,* s.v. "Gospel of the Egyptians."
2. Ibid.
3. Mead, "An Anonymous System from Irenæus," in *Fragments of a Forgotten Faith,* 189.
4. Ibid.
5. Ibid.
6. *Clementine Recognitions,* 1.45, quoted in Margaret Barker, "The Holy Anointing Oil," www.margaretbarker.com/Papers/TheHolyAnointingOil.pdf (accessed January 16, 2014).
7. Isenberg, trans. "Gospel of Philip," ch. 71, 73. For a fuller account of the subject see Barker, "Holy Anointing Oil."
8. 4 Ezra 2:12.
9. 2 En. 22:8–10, in Florentina Badalanova Geller, *2 (Slavonic Apocalypse of) Enoch: Text and Context,* Max Planck Institute for the History of Science, www.mpiwg-berlin.mpg.de/Preprints/P410.PDF (accessed January 16, 2014).
10. Gen. 5:24. See also Heb. 11:5.
11. *Clementine Recognitions* 1.46, quoted in Barker, "Holy Anointing Oil."
12. Neef, "Overlooking the Steppe-Forest," 13–15.
13. Yardin, *Tree of Light,* 40.
14. Klijn, *Seth in Jewish, Christian and Gnostic Literature,* 106.
15. Wintermute, trans., *Old Testament Pseudepigrapha,* "Book of Jubilees," 8, 1.4.
16. Josephus, "The Antiquities of the Jews," bk. 1, ch. vi, verse 4.
17. Hommel, *The Ancient Hebrew Tradition,* 292–97.
18. Heckford, *A Succinct Account of All the Religions,* 316.
19. al-Kisa'i, quoted in Green, *The City of the Moon God,* 13.
20. Immanuel Velikovsky, "A Hebrew Cosmogony," Immanuel Velikovsky Archive, www.varchive.org/ce/hebcos.htm (accessed January 16, 2014).

CHAPTER 39. THE RETURN TO EDEN

1. Charles, trans., *The Book of Enoch or 1 Enoch,* 1 En. 32:1–2.
2. Oskian, *Die Klöster von Taron-Turuberan,* s.v. "Yeghrduti."
3. Ibid.
4. Ibid.
5. Ibid.
6. See "The Sage's Guild: Historical Discussion" and the post dated March 17, 2011, from "Ancalimon," http://forums.taleworlds.com/index.php?topic=147199.340;wap2 (accessed January 16, 2014).
7. The theory was outlined in two books—Heyerdahl, *Ingen grenser,* and Heyerdahl and Lilliestrøm, *Jakten på Odin*—and criticized at the time by Norwegian

academics. See "Jakten på Odin," Wikipedia, http://en.wikipedia.org/wiki/Jakten_
på_Odin (accessed January 16, 2014).

8. Personal communication between the author and Raffi Kojian of AniOnline on
January 29, 2012. See also Armenian Dictionary of Roots at http://nayiri.com/
imagedDictionaryBrowser.jsp?dictionaryId=7&query=%D4%B5%D5%B2%D6%8
0%D5%A4%D5%B8%D6%82%D5%BF (accessed January 16, 2014).

9. I want to thank Gagik Avagyan for the interpretation of this word.

10. Rappoport, *Mediæval Legends of Christ*, 230.

11. Ibid., 231.

12. Oskian, *Die Klöster von Taron-Turuberan*, cites various Armenian and Soviet-
Armenian references to Yeghrdut. Should anyone wish to track these down, I would
be happy to supply details.

13. Oskian, *Die Klöster von Taron-Turuberan*, s.v. "Yeghrduti."

14. Josephus, "Antiquities," bk 1, ch. 1, verse 2.

15. Charles, ed., *Apocrypha and Pseudepigrapha*, 40:6.

CHAPTER 40. A TRIP TO PARADISE

1. Hamzeh'ee, *The Yaresan*, 263.

2. Ibid., 268.

3. Hewsen and Shirakats'i, *The Geography of Ananias of Širak*, 59, 63.

4. Nuttall, *The Fundamental Principles of Old and New World Civilizations*, 287–88.

5. Laurence, trans., *Book of Enoch the Prophet*, 1 En. 8:1.

6. "Turkey: Oldest Obsidian Bracelet Reveals Amazing Craftsmen's Skills in the
Eighth Millennium BC," CNRS News Release, Paris, December 6, 2012, www2
.cnrs.fr/en/1941.htm (accessed January 16, 2014).

7. Ibid.

8. See Başi, *Gula Xizirî*.

CHAPTER 42. A LOSS OF INNOCENCE

1. Charles, ed., *Apocrypha and Pseudepigrapha*, "Apocalypse of Moses," 20: 4–5.

2. Genesis 3:17, 19, New King James Version.

3. Esin and Harmankaya, "Aşıklı," 115–32.

4. Sale, *The Koran*, p. 7. n. c, cf.

5. See Conybeare, *The Key of Truth*, and Russell, *Zoroastrianism in Armenia*, 516–27.

6. See, for instance, "Ishikism" for the relationship between the Paulicians, the
Bogomils, and the Alevi, Wikipedia, http://en.wikipedia.org/wiki/Ishikism
(accessed January 16, 2014).

BIBLIOGRAPHY

Abusch, Tzvi, ed. *Riches Hidden in Secret Places: Ancient Near Eastern Studies in Memory of Thorkild Jacobsen.* Winona Lake, Ind: Eisenbrauns, 2002.

Adams, Brian. "The Bükk Mountain Szeletian: Old and New Views on 'Transitional' Material from the Eponymous Site of the Szeletian." In *Sourcebook of Paleolithic Transitions: Methods, Theories, and Interpretations,* edited by M. Camps Calbet and P. R. Chauhan. New York: Springer, 2009.

Afanasyev, A. N. *The Life Tree.* Moscow: Sovre-mennik, 1983. Quoted in Rubtsov 1998.

Allen, Richard Hinckley. *Star Names and Their Meaning.* New York: Dover, 1963.

Anderson, Rasmus Björn. *Norse Mythology.* Chicago: Griggs, 1875; London: Trubner, 1879.

Anderson, William. *Green Man.* London and San Francisco: HarperCollins, 1990.

Ansart, Cyrante F. *Caii Plinii Secundi Historia naturalis ex recensione I. Harduini et recentiorum adnotationibus.* Vol. 2. Turin: Augustae Taurinorum, 1831.

Archi, Alfonso. "The God Hay(y)a (Ea-Enki) at Ebla." *Culture and History of the Ancient Near East* 42 (2010): 15–36.

Aujoulat, Norbert. *Lascaux: Movement, Space and Time.* New York: Harry N. Abrams, Inc., 2005.

Aurenche, O., and S. K. Kozlowski. *La naissance du néolithique au Proche Orient ou le paradis perdu.* Paris: Errance, 1999.

Avdall, Johannes. "A Hindoo Colony in Ancient Armenia." *Asiatic Journal* 22 (January–April 1837): 181–86.

Aveni, Anthony F., ed. *The Sky in Mayan Literature.* New York: Oxford University Press, 1992.

Avetisian, Haik. "Urartian Ceramics from the Ararat Valley as a Cultural Phenomenon (A Tentative Representation)." *Iran and the Caucasus* 3 (1999/2000): 293–314.

Avigad, Nahman, and Yigael Yadin. *A Genesis Apocryphon.* Jerusalem: Hebrew University, 1956.

403

Ayvazyan, Hovannes. *Armenia Christian Encyclopedia*. Yereven: Haykakan Hanragitaran, 2002.

Bailey, Geoff, and Penny Spikins, eds. *Mesolithic Europe*. Cambridge and New York: Cambridge University Press, 2008.

Baldwin Spencer, Sir Walter, and F. J. Gillen. *Across Australia*. London: Macmillan, 1912.

Balkan-Atli, N., and M. C. Cauvin. "Das Schwarz Gold der Steinzeit: Obsidian in Anatolien." In *Vor 12.000 Jahren in Anatolien: Die ältesten Monumente der Menschheit*, edited by Lichter Clemens. Karlsruhe, Germany: Badisches Landesmuseum, 2007.

Banning, E. B. "So Fair a House: Göbekli Tepe and the Identification of Temples in the Pre-Pottery Neolithic of the Near East." *Current Anthropology* 52, no. 5 (October 2011): 619–60.

Barton, George A. *Miscellaneous Babylonian Inscriptions*. New Haven, Conn.: Yale University Press, 1918.

Başi, Xidirê. *Gula Xizirî*. Istanbul, Turkey: Weşanxaneyê Vateyî/Vate Yayınevi, 2012.

Baty, John, trans. *Enoch the Prophet: Translated from the German of Andrew Gottlier Hoffman*. London: Samuel Jefferson, 1836.

Belmonte, J. A. "Finding Our Place in the Cosmos: The Role of Astronomy in Ancient Cultures." *Journal of Cosmology* 9 (2010): 2052–62.

Benedict, Peter. "Survey Work in Southeastern Anatolia." In *Prehistoric Research in Southeastern Anatolia*, edited by H. Çambel and R. J. Braidwood. Istanbul, Turkey: Edebiyat Fakiiltesi, 1980.

Birch, Samuel, ed. *Records of the Past*. Vol. 11, *Assyrian Texts*. London: Samuel Bagster, 1878.

Black, Jeremy, "The Sumerians in Their Landscape." In *Riches Hidden in Secret Places: ancient Near Eastern studies in memory of Thorkild Jacobsen*, edited by Tzvi Abusch. Winona Lake, IN: Eisenbrauns, 2002.

Bochart, Samuel. *Geographia sacra seu Phaleg et Chanaan*. Cadomi (Caen), France: Petri Cardonelli, 1646.

Böhlig, Alexander, and Frederik Wisse, trans. "Gospel of the Egyptians." In *The Nag Hammadi Library*, edited by James M. Robinson. 3rd edition. Leiden, Netherlands: E. J. Brill, 1996.

Bolio, José Diaz. *The Rattlesnake School*. Merida, Mexico: Area Maya, Mayan Area, n.d (ca. 1982).

———. *Why the Rattlesnake in Mayan Civilization*. Merida, Mexico: Area Maya, Mayan Area, 1988.

Boslough, M., K. Nicoll, V. Holliday, et al. "Arguments and Evidence against a Younger Dryas Impact Event." In *Climates, Landscapes, and Civilizations*, Geophysical Monograph Series 198, edited by L. Giosan, D. Q. Fuller, K. Nicoll, R. K. Flad, and P. D. Clift. Washington, D.C.: American Geophysical Union, 2012.

Bradley, Bruce A., M. Anikovitch, and E. Giria. "Early Upper Paleolithic in the Russian Plain: Streletskayan Flaked Stone, Artefacts and Technology." *Antiquity* 69, no. 266 (1995): 989–98.

Bressy, C., G. Poupeau, and K. A. Yener. "Cultural Interactions during the Ubaid and Halaf Periods: Tell Kurdu (Amuq Valley, Turkey) Obsidian Sourcing." *Journal of Archaeological Science* 32 (2005): 1560–65.

Bricker, Harvey M., and Victoria R. Bricker. "Zodiacal References in the Maya Codices." In *The Sky in Mayan Literature*, edited by A. F. Aveni, 148–83. New York: Oxford University Press, 1992.

Brown, William P. *The Ethos of the Cosmos: The Genesis of Moral Imagination in the Bible.* Grand Rapids, Mich.: Wm. B. Eerdmans, 1999.

Bruinessen, "Aslini Inkar Eden Haramzadedir! The Debate on the Ethnic Identity of the Kurdish Alevis." In *Syncretistic Religious Communities in the Near East*, edited by Krisztina Kehl-Bodrogi, Barbara Kellner-Heinkele, and Anke Otter Otter-Beaujean. Leiden, Netherlands: E. J. Brill, 1997.

Buck, B. A. "Ancient Technology in Contemporary Surgery." *The Western Journal of Medicine* 136, no. 3 (1982): 265–69.

Budge, E. A. Wallis. *The Book of the Cave of Treasures.* London: Religious Tract Society, 1927.

———, trans. *The Chronography of Gregory Abû'l Faraj, the Son of Aaron, the Hebrew Physician, Commonly Known as Bar Hebraeus 1.* London: Oxford University Press, 1932.

———. *The Life and Exploits of Alexander.* London: C. J. Clay, 1896.

Burke, John. *A Genealogical and Heraldic History of the Commoners of Great Britain and Ireland, Enjoying Territorial Possessions or High Official Rank, etc.* Vol. 2. London: Henry Colburn, 1835.

Burkitt, M. C. *Prehistory.* Cambridge: Cambridge University Press, 1921.

Burney, Charles. *From Village to Empire.* London: Phaidon Press, 1977.

Byock, Jesse, trans. *The Prose Edda.* London: Penguin, 2006.

Cahill, Michael A. *Paradise Rediscovered: The Roots of Civilisation.* Carindale, Queensland, Australia: Glass House Books, 2012.

Callataÿ, Godefroid de. *Annus Platonicus.* Louvain-la-Neuve, France: Université Catholique De Louvain, Institut Orientaliste, 1996.

Çambel, Halet, and R. J. Braidwood, eds. *Prehistoric Research in Southeastern Anatolia.* Istanbul, Turkey: Edebiyat Fakiiltesi, 1980.

Campbell, S., and A. Green, ed. *The Archaeology of Death in the Ancient Near East.* Oxford: Oxbow, 1995.

Camps Calbet, Marta, and Parth R. Chauhan. *Sourcebook of Paleolithic Transitions: Methods, Theories, and Interpretations: Humanities, Social Science and Law.* New York: Springer, 2009.

Carari, John Francis Gemelli. "A Voyage round the World (1699)." Books 1–7. In *A Collection of Voyages and Travels,* vol. 4, edited by A. Churchill and J. Churchill. London: Churchill, 1704. Reprint, 1732.

Carver, Marmaduke. *A Discourse of the Terrestrial Paradise, Aiming at a More Probable Discovery of the True Situation of That Happy Place of Our First Parents Habitation.* London: James Flesher, 1666.

Cauvin, Jacques. *The Birth of the Gods and the Origins of Agriculture.* Translated by Trevor Watkins. Cambridge: Cambridge University Press, 2000. Reprint, 2007.

Çelik, Bahattin. "An Early Neolithic Settlement in the Center of Şanlıurfa, Turkey." *Neo-Lithics* 2–3/00 (2000a): 4–6.

———. "Hamzan Tepe in the Light of New Finds." *Documenta Praehistorica* 37 (2010): 257–68.

———. "A New Early Neolithic Settlement in Southeastern Turkey." *Neo-Lithics* 2/04 (2004): 3–5.

———. "A New Early-Neolithic Settlement: Karahan Tepe." *Neo-Lithics* 2–3/00 (2000b): 6–8.

———. "Sefer Tepe: A New Pre-Pottery Neolithic Site in Southeastern Turkey." *Neo-Lithics* 1/06 (2006): 23–25.

Çelik, Bahattin, Mustafa Güler, and Gül Güler. "Türkiye'nin Güneydoğusunda Yeni Bir Çanak Çömleksiz Neolitik Yerleşim: Taşlı Tepe." *Anadolu (Anatolia)* 27 (2011): 225–36.

Chabot, Jacques, and Jacques Pelegrin. "Two Examples of Pressure Blade Production with a Lever: Recent Research from the Southern Caucasus (Armenia) and Northern Mesopotamia (Syria, Iraq)." In *The Emergence of Pressure Blade Making,* edited by P. Desrosiers. New York: Springer, 2012.

Charles, R. H., ed. *The Apocrypha and Pseudepigrapha of the Old Testament.* Oxford: Oxford University Press, 2 vols., 1913.

———, trans. *The Book of Enoch or 1 Enoch.* Oxford: Oxford University Press, 1912.

Charlesworth, James H. *The Old Testament Pseudepigrapha.* Vol. 2. London: Darton, Longman and Todd, 1985.

Charvát, Petr. *Mesopotamia before History.* Hove, East Sussex, UK: Psychology Press, 2013.

Childe, V. Gordon. *The Prehistory of European Society.* London: Cassell, London, 1958. Revised edition 1962.

Churchill, A., and J. Churchill, eds. *A Collection of Voyages and Travels.* Vol. 4. London: Churchill, 1704. Reprint, 1732.

Clark, Grahame. *World Prehistory: In New Perspective.* Cambridge: Cambridge University Press, 1969.

Clarke, Adam. *The Holy Bible . . . A Commentary and Critical Notes.* Vol. 1, *Genesis to Deuteronomy.* New York: T. Mason and G. Lane, 1837.

Clemens, Lichter. *Vor 12.000 Jahren in Anatolien: Die ältesten Monumente der Menschheit.* Karlsruhe, Germany: Badisches Landesmuseum, 2007.

Clow, Barbara Hand. *Catastrophobia: The Truth behind Earth Changes in the Coming Age of Light.* Rochester, Vt.: Bear & Co., 2001.

Collins, Andrew. *The Cygnus Mystery.* London: Watkins, 2007.

———. *From the Ashes of Angels.* Rochester, Vt.: Bear & Co., 1996.

Conybeare, Fred C. *The Key of Truth: A Manual of the Paulician Church of Armenia.* Oxford: Oxford University Press, 1898.

Coomaraswamy, Ananda K. "Khwaja Khadir and the Fountain of Life in the Tradition of Persian and Mughal Art." Chap. 17 in *What Is Civilisation? And Other Essays,* 157–67. Cambridge, UK: Golgosova Press, 1989.

———. *What Is Civilisation? And Other Essays.* Cambridge, UK: Golgosova Press, 1989.

Coon, Carleton Stevens. *The Races of Europe.* New York: Macmillan, 1939.

Cuinet, Vital. *Turquie d'Asie Géographie Administrative.* Paris: Ernest Leroux, 1892.

Czaplicka, M. A. *Aboriginal Siberia: A Study in Social Anthropology.* Oxford: Oxford University Press, 1914.

Dalley, Stephanie. *Myths from Mesopotamia: Creation, the Flood, Gilgamesh, and Others.* New York: Oxford University Press, 1989.

Delumeau, Jean. *History of Paradise: The Garden of Eden in Myth and Tradition.* Urbana and Chicago: University of Illinois Press, 1992. Reprint, New York: Continuum, 2000.

Desrosiers, Pierre, ed. *The Emergence of Pressure Blade Making: From Origin to Modern Experimentation.* New York: Springer, 2012.

Dietrich, B. C. *The Origins of Greek Religion.* New York: Walter de Gruyter, 1973.

Dietrich, Oliver, Çiğdem Köksal-Schmidt, Cihat Kürkcüoglu, et al. "Göbekli Tepe: A Stairway to the Circle of Boars." *Actual Archaeology* 5 (Spring 2013): 30–31.

Donnelly, Ignatius. *Ragnarök: The Age of Fire and Gravel.* London: Sampson Low, Marston, Searle and Rivington, 1883.

Drake, Francis. *An Accurate Description and History of the Cathedral and Metropolitical Church of St. Peter, York.* York, UK: T. Wilson, C. Etherington, W. Tesseyman, J. Todd, H. Sotheran, and D. Peck, 1768.

Eisenman, Robert, and Michael Wise. *The Dead Sea Scrolls Uncovered.* Shaftesbury, Dorset, UK: Element, 1992.

Eliade, Mircea. "The Dacians and Wolves." In *Zalmoxis: The Vanishing God,* 1–20. Chicago: Chicago University Press, 1973.

———. *De la Zalmoxis la Genghis-Han.* Paris: Humanitas, 1970.

———. *Shamanism: Archaic Techniques of Ecstacy.* Princeton, 1970: Princeton University Press.

———. *Zalmoxis: The Vanishing God (Comparative Studies in the Religions and Folklore of Dacia and Eastern Europe).* Chicago: Chicago University Press, 1973.

Encyclopedia Britannica. Vol. IV, CUP, New York, N.Y., 1911.

Encyclopedia Britannica. Vol. XIX, CUP, New York, N.Y., 1911.

Eriksen, Berit Valentin. "Resource Exploitation Subsistence Strategies and Adaptiveness in Late Pleistocene Early Holocene Northwest Europe." In *Humans at the End of the Ice Age,* edited by L. G. Straus, B. V. Eriksen, J. M. Erlandson, and D. R. Yesner. New York: Springer, 1996.

Esin, U. M, and S. Harmankaya. "Aşıklı." In *Neolithic in Turkey,* edited by M. Özdoğan and N. Başgelen. Istanbul, Turkey: Arkeoloji ve Sanat Yayınları, 1999.

Firestone, R. B., A. West, J. P. Kennett, et al. "Evidence for an Extraterrestrial Impact 12,900 Years Ago That Contributed to the Megafaunal Extinctions and the Younger Dryas Cooling." *PNAS* 104 (2007): 16016–21.

Firestone, Richard, Allen West, and Simon Warwick-Smith. *The Cycle of Cosmic Catastrophes.* Rochester, Vt.: Bear & Co, 2006.

Forbes, Robert James. *Metallurgy in Antiquity: A Notebook for Archaeologists and Technologists.* Leiden, Netherlands: E. J. Brill, 1950.

Formozov, A. A. "Etnokulturnîie oblasti na terrotorii evropeiskoi ciasti SSSR v kamennom veke." *Ethnokulturgebiete der Steinzeit im europäischen Teil de Sowjetunion.* Moscow, 1959.

Forrest, S. K. Mendoza, and Prods Oktor Skjaervo. *Witches, Whores and Sorcerers.* Austin: University of Texas Press, 2012.

Frazer, James George. *The Magic Art and the Evolution of Kings.* 2 vols. London: Macmillan, 1920.

Gaidzakian, Ohan. *Illustrated Armenia and the Armenians.* Boston: Privately printed, 1898.

Garsoïan, Nina G. "Taron as an Early Christian Armenian Center." In *Armenian Baghesh/Bitlis and Taron/Mush,* edited by R. G. Hovannisian, 59–69. Costa Mesa, Calif.: Mazda, 2001.

Gilbert, Adrian, and Maurice Cotterell. *The Mayan Prophecies.* Shaftesbury, Dorset, UK: Element, 1995.

Gilchrist, John Borthwick. *The Hindee Moral Preceptor; or, Rudimental Principles of Persian Grammar.* Part 1. London: Black, Kingsbury, Parbury, and Allen, 1821.

Gimbutas, Marija. *The Language of the Goddess.* London: Thames and Hudson, 1989.

———. *The Prehistory of Eastern Europe: Part 1—Mesolithic, Neolithic and Copper Age Cultures in Russia and the Baltic Area.* Cambridge, Mass.: Peabody Museum, 1956.

Ginkel, Jan J. Van, H. L. Murre-Van den Berg, and T. M. Van Lint. *Redefining Interaction in the Middle East Since the Rise of Islam.* Louvain, Belgium: Peeters, 2005.

Giosan, L., D. Q. Fuller, K. Nicoll, R. K. Flad, and P. D. Clift, eds. *Climates, Landscapes, and Civilizations.* Geophysical Monograph Series 198. Washington, D.C.: American Geophysical Union, 2012.

Graves, Robert, and Raphael Patai. *Hebrew Myths: The Book of Genesis.* London: Cassell, 1964.

Green, Tamara. *The City of the Moon God: Religious Traditions of Harran, Religions in the Graeco-Roman World 114.* Leiden, Netherlands: E. J. Brill, 1992.

Griaule, M., and G. Dieterlen. *The Pale Fox.* Chino Valley, Ariz.: Continuum Foundation, 1965.

Grimes, Heilan Yvette. *The Norse Myths.* Boston: Hollow Earth, 2010.

Grimm, Jacob. *Teutonic Mythology.* 4 vols. London: Geo. Bell, 1883–1888.

Grumeza, Ion. *Dacia: Land of Transylvania, Cornerstone of Ancient Eastern Europe.* Lanham, MA: Hamilton; Devon, UK: Plymouth, 2009.

Gürtler, Nicolaus, and John Pearson. *Criticorum Sacrorum sive Lectissimarum in Sacro-Sancta Biblia Utriusque Foederis Annotationum atrus Tractatuum Theologico-Philologicorum Supplementum.* Tomus Primus, Vol. 8. Frankfurt, Germany: Johannis Philippi Andreæ and Joh. Nicolai Andreæ, Herborna-Nassovici, 1700.

Hamzeh'ee, M. Reza. *The Yaresan.* Berlin: Klaus Schwarz, 1990.

Hancock, Graham. *Fingerprints of the Gods.* London: Heinemann, 1995.

———. *Supernatural: Meetings with the Ancient Teachers of Mankind.* London: Century, 2005.

Hancock, Graham, and Santha Faiia. *Heaven's Mirror.* London: Michael Joseph, 1998.

Harner, Michael J., "Common Themes in South American Indian Yagé Experiences," In *Hallucinogens and Shamanism,* edited by Michael J. Harner. London/New York: OUP, 1973.

———, ed. *Hallucinogens and Shamanism,* London/New York: OUP, 1973.

———. *The Way of the Shaman.* New York: HarperOne, 1990.

Hartz, Sönke, Thomas Terberger, and Mikhail Zhilin. "New AMS-dates for the Upper Volga Mesolithic and the Origin of Microblade Technology in Europe." *Quartär* 57 (2010): 155–69.

Hatch, Mary Popenoe. "An Hypothesis on Olmec Astronomy, with Special Reference to the La Venta Site." *Contributions of the University of California Archaeological Research Facility: Papers on Olmec and Maya Archaeology* 13 (1971): 1–38.

Haynes C. V., Jr. "Appendix B: Nature and Origin of the Black Mat, Stratum F2." In Haynes and Huckell, 2007.

———. "Geochronology of Paleoenvironmental Change, Clovis Type Site, Blackwater Draw, New Mexico." *Geoarchaeology* 10, no. 5 (1995): 317–88.

Haynes Jr., C.V., and B. B. Huckell. *Murray Springs: a Clovis Site with Multiple Activity Areas in the San Pedro Valley, Arizona.* Tucson: The University of Arizona Press, 2007.

Heckford, William. *A Succinct Account of All the Religions, and Various Sects in Religion etc.* London: William Lane, 1741.

Heinberg, Richard. *Memories and Visions of Paradise.* Wellingborough, Northamptonshire, UK: Aquarian Press, 1989. Reprint, 1990.

Hennerbichler, F. "The Origin of Kurds." *Advances in Anthropology* 2, no. 2 (2012): 64–79.

Herbert, Sir Thomas. *Some Yeares Travels into Divers Parts of Asia and Afrique*. 2 vols. London: Jacob Blome and Richard Bishop, 1638.

Heun, Manfred, Ralf Schäfer-Pregl, Dieter Klawan, et al. "Site of Einkorn Wheat Domestication Identified by DNA Fingerprinting." *Science* 278, no. 5341 (November 14, 1997): 1312–14.

Hewitt, J. F. *Primitive Traditional History: History and Chronology of the Myth-making Age*. 2 vols. London: James Parker, 1907.

Hewsen, Robert H., and Anania Shirakats'i. *The Geography of Ananias of Širak: Ašxarhacoyc,' the Long and the Short Recensions*. Wiesbaden, Germany: Ludwig Reichert, 1992.

Heyerdahl, Thor. *Ingen grenser*. Oslo, Norway: Stenersens, 1999.

Heyerdahl, Thor, and Per Lilliestrøm. *Jakten på Odin*. Oslo, Norway: Stenersens, 2001.

Hodder, Ian. *Çatalhöyük: The Leopard's Tale*. London: Thames and Hudson, 2006.

Hoesel, Annelies van, Wim Z. Hoek, Freek Braadbaart, et al. "Nanodiamonds and Wildfire Evidence in the Usselo Horizon Postdate the Allerød-Younger Dryas Boundary." *PNAS* 109 (April 30, 2012): 7648–53.

Hommel, Dr. Fritz. *The Ancient Hebrew Tradition*. New York: E. & J. B. Young; London: Soc. for Promoting Christian Knowledge, 1897.

Hony, H. C., and Iz Fahir. *A Turkish-English Dictionary*. 2 vols. Oxford: Oxford University Press, 1957.

Horowitz, Wayne. *Mesopotamian Cosmic Geography*. Winona Lake, Ind.: Eisenbrauns, 1998.

Houtsma, Martijn Theodoor. *Encyclopedia of Islam, 1913–1936*. Leiden, Netherlands: E. J. Brill, 1993.

Hovannisian, Richard G., ed. *Armenian Baghesh/Bitlis and Taron/Mush*. Costa Mesa, Calif.: Mazda, 2001.

Hübschmann, H. *Die altarmenischen Ortsnamen*. Vol. 2. Strasbourg, France: Karl Trübner, 1904.

Hultkrantz, Åke. "A New Look at the World Pillar in Arctic and Sub-Arctic Religions." In *Shamanism and Northern Ecology*, edited by J. Pentikäinen. Berlin: Walter de Gruyter, 1996.

Isenberg, Wesley W., trans. "Gospel of Philip." In *The Nag Hammadi Library*, edited by James M. Robinson. 3rd edition. Leiden, Netherlands: E. J. Brill, 1996.

Isin, Mary. *Sherbet and Spice: The Complete Story of Turkish Sweets and Desserts*. London and New York: I. B. Tauris, 2013.

Issawi, Charles, ed. *The Fertile Crescent, 1800–1914: A Documentary Economic History*. New York: Oxford University Press, 1988.

Ivanov, V. V. "The Ancient Balkan and All-Indo-European Text of the Myth of the Hero-killer of the Dog and Some Eurasian Parallels." In *Slavyanskoye I Balkanskoye Yazykoznaniye*. Moscow: Nauka, 1977. Quoted in Rubtsov 1998.

Izady, Mehrdad R. *The Kurds: A Concise Handbook.* London: Crane Russak, 1992.

Jastrow, Morris. *The Religion of Babylonia and Assyria.* Boston: Ginn, 1898.

Jażdżewski, Konrad. *Ancient Peoples and Places: Poland.* London: Thames and Hudson, 1965.

Jenkins, John Major. *Maya Cosmogenesis 2012.* Rochester, Vt.: Bear & Co., 1998.

Jochim, Michael A. "The Upper Palaeolithic." In *European Prehistory: A Survey,* edited by Sarunas Milisauskas. New York: Springer, 2002.

Johns, C. H. W. *An Assyrian Doomsday Book; or, Liber Censealis.* Leipzig, Germany: J. C. Hinrichs'sche Buchhanglung, 1901.

Johnson, M. D. "The Life of Adam and Eve." In *The Old Testament Pseudepigrapha,* vol. 2, edited by J. H. Charlesworth. London: Darton, Longman and Todd, 1985.

Josephus, Flavius. "The Antiquities of the Jews." In *The Works of Flavius Josephus,* edited by W. Whiston. London and New York: George Routledge, 1873.

———. *Historiarum de Bello Judaico, Liber Primus, et Pars Secondi, Quibus, Ea summatim continentur quæ Josephus susius prosequitur postremis novem Antiquitatum libris.* Translated by D. Eduardi Bernardi. Oxford: Theatro Sheldoniano, 1687.

Karapetyan, Inessa, and Amina Kanetsyan. "Pre-Urartian Armavir." *Revista sobre Oriente Próximo y Egipto en la antigüedad* 7 (2004): 48–62.

Katz, Dina, *The Image of the Netherworld in the Sumerian Sources.* Potomac, Md.: Capital Decisions, 2003.

Kay, Charles de. *Bird Gods.* New York: A. S. Barnes, 1898.

Kehl-Bodrogi, Krisztina, Barbara Kellner-Heinkele, and Anke Otter-Beaujean, eds. *Syncretistic Religious Communities in the Near East.* Leiden, Netherlands: E. J. Brill, 1997.

Keightley, Thomas. *The Fairy Mythology.* London: H. G. Bohn, 1850.

Kephalides, August Wilhelm. *De historia maris Caspii.* Göttingen, Germany: Vandenhoek et Riprecht, 1814.

Khorenatsi, Movses. *History of the Armenians.* Translated by Robert W. Thomson. Cambridge, Mass.: Harvard University Press, 1978.

King, Noel Q. *African Cosmos: An Introduction to Religion in Africa.* Belmont, Calif.: Wadsworth Publishing, 1986.

Kinneir, Sir John Macdonald. *Journey through Asia Minor, Armenia, and Koordistan in the Years 1813 and 1814: With Remarks on the Marches of Alexander and Retreat of the Ten Thousand.* London: John Murray, 1818.

al-Kisa'i, Muhammad Ibn Abd Allah, *The Tales of the Prophets of Al- Kisa'i.* Translation by W. M. Thrackston. Boston: G. K. Hall, 1978.

Kislev, M. E., A. Hartmann, and O. Bar-Yosef. "Early Domesticated Fig in the Jordan Valley." *Nature* 312 (2006): 1372–74.

Klijn, A. F. J. *Seth in Jewish, Christian and Gnostic Literature.* Leiden, Netherlands: E. J. Brill, 1977.

Kloosterman, J. B. "The Usselo Horizon, a Worldwide Charcoal-rich Layer of Allerod Age." Unpublished paper, 1999.

Koster, Annelies. *The Late Roman Cemeteries of Nijmegen: Stray Finds and Excavations 1947–1983*. Steures D.C., Netherlands: Museum Het Valkhof, 2013.

Kozlowski, S. K. "The West Carpathians and Sudeten at the End of the Upper Palaeolithic." *Preistoria Alpina* 28 (1994): 127–37.

Kramer, Samuel Noah. *Sumerian Mythology*. Philadelphia: University of Pennsylvania Press, 1961. Reprint, 1998.

Kuperjanov, Andres. "Estonian Sky: Constellations and Starlore." *Bulgarian Astronomical Journal* 9 (2007): 149–54.

Landau, Brent Christopher. "The Sages and the Star-child." PhD dissertation, Harvard, 2008.

Lankford, George E. "The 'Path of Souls': Some Death Imagery in the Southeastern Ceremonial Complex." In *Ancient Objects and Sacred Realms: Interpretations of Mississippian Iconography*, edited by F. Kent Reilly III and James F. Garber. Austin, Texas: University of Texas Press, 2007.

Laurence, Richard, trans. *The Book of Enoch the Prophet*. Oxford: John Henry Parker, 1821. Reprint, 1838.

Layton, Bentley, trans. "The Hypostasis of the Archons." In *The Nag Hammadi Library*, edited by James M. Robinson. 3rd edition. Leiden, Netherlands: E. J. Brill, 1996

Leeming, David Adams. *Creation Myths of the World: An Encyclopedia*. Vol. 1. Santa Barbara, Calif.: ABC-Clio, 2010.

Legge, F. *Forerunners and Rivals of Christianity Being Studies in Religious History From 330 B.C. to 330 A.D.*, 2 vols. Cambridge: Cambridge University Press, 1915.

Legrand, M. R., and M. De Angelis. "Origins and Variations of Light Carboxylic Acids in Polar Precipitation." *Journal of Geophysical Research* 100, no. D1 (1995): 1445–62.

Leick, Gwendolyn. *A Dictionary of Ancient Near Eastern Mythology*. New York: Routledge, 1998.

Lemprière, John. *Bibliotheca Classica: A Classical Dictionary*. London: T. Cadell, 1788.

Lewis-Williams, David, and David Pearce. *Inside the Neolithic Mind*. London: Thames and Hudson, 2005.

Lindow, John. *Norse Mythology: A Guide to Gods, Heroes, Rituals, and Beliefs*. New York: Oxford University Press, 2002.

Lipinski, Edward. "El's Abode: Mythological Traditions Related to Mount Hermon and to the Mountains of Armenia." *Orientalia Lovaniensa Periodica* 2 (1971): 13–69.

Lloyd, Seton, and William Brice. "Harran," *Anatolian Studies* 1 (1951): 77–111.

Logan, A. H. B. *Gnostic Truth and Christian Heresy*. London and New York: Continuum, 1996.

Lombard, M. "Bored Stones, Lithic Rings and the Concept of Holes in San Shamanism." *Anthropology Southern Africa* 25: 1 and 2 (2002): 17–27.

Long, E. Croft. "The Placenta in Lore and Legend." *Bulletin of the Medical Library Association* 51, no. 2 (April 1963): 233–41.

Lubotsky, Alexander. *Leiden Indo-European Etymological Dictionary Series: Etymological Dictionary of Latin and the Other Italic Languages.* Vol. 7. Leiden, Netherlands, and Boston: E. J. Brill, 2008.

Lüling, Günter. *A Challenge to Islam for Reformation: The Rediscovery and Reliable Reconstruction of a Comprehensive Pre-Islamic Christian Hymnal Hidden in the Koran Under Earliest Islamic Reinterpretations.* New Delhi, India: Motilal Banarsidass Publisher, 2003.

MacBean, Alexander, and Samuel Johnson. *A Dictionary of Ancient Geography.* London: G. Robinson, 1773.

Mackrel, Brian. *Halley's Comet over New Zealand.* Willington, New Zealand: Reed Methuen, 1985.

MacRae, George W., trans. "Apocalypse of Adam." In *The Nag Hammadi Library,* edited by James M. Robinson. 3rd edition. Leiden, Netherlands: E. J. Brill, 1996.

Makowsky, Alexander. "Der diluviale Mensch im Loss von Brünn." *Mitt. Anthropol. Gesell. Wien* 22 (1892): 73–84.

Malan, the Reverend S. C. *The Book of Adam and Eve.* Montmartre, France: Charles Carrington, 1882.

Mallowan, Max E. L., and Hilda Linford, "Rediscovered Skulls from Arpachiyah: Introductory Discussion." *Iraq* 31 (1969): 49–58.

Mallowan, Max E. L., and J. C. Rose. "Excavations at Tell Arpachiyah 1933." *Iraq* 2 (1935): 1–178.

Mann, Charles C. "The Birth of Religion: The World's First Temple." *National Geographic Magazine* 219, no. 6 (June 2011): 34–59.

Mannermaa, Kristiina, Andrei Panteleyev, and Mikhail Sablin. "Birds in Late Mesolithic Burials at Yuzhniy Oleniy Ostrov (Lake Onega, Western Russia)—What Do They Tell About Humans and the Environment?" *Fennoscandia archaeologica* XXV (2008): 3–25.

Maron, Anat, James S. O. McCullagh, Thomas F. G. Higham, et al. "Single Amino Acid Radiocarbon Dating of Upper Paleolithic Modern Humans." *Proceedings of the National Academy of Sciences* 109, no. 18 (2012): 6878–81.

Massey, Gerald. *The Natural Genesis.* Vol. 2. London: Williams and Norgate, 1883.

McClintock, John, and James Strong. *Cyclopaedia of Biblical, Theological, and Ecclesiastical Literature.* Vol. 3. New York: Harper, 1894.

McKern, Sharon, and Thomas McKern, *Tracking Fossil Man: An Adventure in Evolution.* London: Wayland, 1970. Reprint, 1972.

Mead, George Robert Stow. *Fragments of a Faith Forgotten.* London: Theosophical Publishing, 1900. Reprint, 1906.

———. *Pistis Sophia.* London: Watkins, 1921.

Meijer, D. J. W., ed. *Natural Phenomena: Their Meaning, Depiction and Description in the Ancient Near East.* Amsterdam, The Netherlands: Verhandelingen/Koninklijke Nederlandse Akademie van Wetenschappen. Afdeling Letterkund, n.s., 152, 1992.

Mellaart, James. *Çatalhöyük: A Neolithic Town in Anatolia.* London: Thames and Hudson, 1967.

———. *Earliest Civilizations of the Near East.* London: Thames and Hudson, 1965.

Milik, J. T. *The Books of Enoch: Aramaic Fragments of Qumrân Cave 4.* Oxford: Oxford University Press, 1976.

Milisauskas, Sarunas. *European Prehistory: A Survey.* New York: Springer, 2002.

Millard, A. R. "The Etymology of Eden." *Vetus Testamentum* 34 (1984): 103–6.

Miller, O. D. *Har-Moad; or The Mountain of the Assembly.* North Adams, Mass.: Stephen M. Whipple, 1892.

Mills, Watson E., ed. *Mercer Dictionary of the Bible.* Macon, Ga.: Mercer University Press, 1990.

Molleson, Theya, and S. Campbell. "Deformed Skulls at Tell Arpachiyah: The Social Context." In *The Archaeology of Death in the Ancient Near East,* edited by S. Campbell and A. Green. Oxford: Oxbow, 1995.

Montelius, Oscar. "Palaeolithic Implements Found in Sweden." *The Antiquaries Journal* 1, no. 2 (April 1921): 98–104.

Movsisyan, Artak. *The Sacred Highlands.* Yerevan, Republic of Armenia: Yerevan University Publishers, 2004.

Murdin, Paul, and Lesley Murdin. *New Astronomy.* Cambridge: Cambridge University Press, 1978. Reprint, 1985.

Neef, Reinder. "Overlooking the Steppe-Forest: A Preliminary Report on the Botanical Remains from Early Neolithic Göbekli Tepe (Southeastern Turkey)." *Neo-Lithics* 2, no. 3 (2003): 13–15.

Nichols, Aidan. *Rome and the Eastern Churches: A Study in Schism.* Edinburgh: T. & T. Clark, 1992. Reprint, San Francisco: Ignatius Press, 2010.

Nikolaeva, N. A., and V. A. Safronov. *Istoki slavianskoi i evraziiskoi mifologii.* Moscow: Belyi Volk, 1999.

Nuttall, Zelia. *The Fundamental Principles of Old and New World Civilizations . . .* Archaeological and Ethnological Papers of the Peabody Museum, Harvard University, vol. 2. Cambridge, Mass.: Peabody Museum of American Archaeology and Ethnology, 1901.

Oakley, Kenneth. *Frameworks for Dating Fossil Man.* London: Weidenfeld and Nicolson, 1964. Reprint, Piscataway, N.J.: Aldine, 2002.

O'Brien, Christian, with Barbara Joy O'Brien. *The Genius of the Few.* Wellingborough, Northamptonshire, UK: Turnstone Press, 1985.

Olofsson, Anders. *Pioneer Settlement in the Mesolithic of Northern Sweden.* Archaeology and Environment 16. Umeå, Sweden: Umeå University, 2003.

Olyan, Saul M. *Asherah and the Cult of Yahweh in Israel.* Society of Biblical Literature Monograph Series 34. Atlanta, Ga.: Scholars Press, 1988.

Osborn, Henry Fairfield. *Men of the Old Stone Age.* New York: Scribner, 1916.

Osipowicz, G., and M. Szeliga. "Functional Analysis of a Late-Palaeolithic Obsidian Tanged Point from Wolodz, District Brzozów, Podkarpacie Voivodship." *Acta Archaeologica Carpathica* 39 (2004): 153–60.

Oskian, Hamazasp. *Die Klöster von Taron-Turuberan.* Vienna: Mechitaristen, 1953.

Özdoğan, M., and A. Özdoğan. "Çayönü: A Conspectus of Recent Work." *Paleorient* 15, no. 1 (1989): 65–74.

Özdoğan, Mehmet, and Nezih Başgelen, eds. *Neolithic in Turkey: The Cradle of Civilization.* Istanbul, Turkey: Arkeoloji ve Sanat Yayınları, 1999.

Peake, Harold, and Herbert John Fleure. *The Corridors of Time.* Vol. 2, *Hunters and Artists.* Oxford: Oxford University Press, 1927.

Peiser, F. E. "Eine babylonische Landkarte." *Zeitschrift für Assyriologie und verwandte Gebiete* 4 (1889): 361–70.

Pentikäinen, Juha, ed. *Shamanism and Northern Ecology.* Berlin: Walter de Gruyter, 1996.

Peregrine, Peter Neal. *Encyclopedia of Prehistory: South and Southwest Asia.* New York: Springer, 2001.

Pererii Valentini, Benedicti. *Commentariorvm et Disputationum in Genesim.* Lugduni (Leiden, Netherlands): Ex officina Iuntarum, 1593.

Perlès, Catherine. "L'outillage de pierre taillée néolithique en Grèce: approvisionnement et exploitation des matières premières." *Bulletin de Correspondance Hellénique* 114, no. 1 (1990): 1–42.

Peters, J., and K. Schmidt. "Animals in the Symbolic World of Pre-Pottery Neolithic Göbekli Tepe, South-eastern Turkey: A Preliminary Assessment." *Anthropozoologica* 39, no. 1 (2004): 179–218.

Pettitt, Paul B., and Erik Trinkaus. "Direct Radiocarbon Dating of the Brno 2 Gravettian Human Remains." *Anthropologie* 38, no. 2 (2000): 149–50.

Pliny, *Historiarum naturae*, vol. 2, translated by Pierre Danès. Paris: Ioanem Paruum, 1532.

Quinn, Esther Casier. *The Quest of Seth for the Oil of Life.* Chicago: University of Chicago Press, 1962.

Rao, S. R. *Lothal.* New Delhi, India: Director General, Archaeological Survey of India, Janpath, 1985.

Rappenglück, Michael A. *Eine Himmelskarte aus der Eiszeit?* Frankfurt am Main, Germany: Peter Lang, 1999.

Rappoport, A. S. *Mediæval Legends of Christ.* London: Ivor Nicholson and Watson, 1934.

Reichel-Dolmatoff, Gerardo. *Basketry as Metaphor: Arts and Crafts of the Desana Indians of the Northwest Amazon.* Occasional Papers of the Museum of Cultural History 5. Los Angeles: University of California, 1985.

Reilly III, F. Kent, and James F. Garber, eds. *Ancient Objects and Sacred Realms: Interpretations of Mississippian Iconography.* Austin: University of Texas Press, 2007.

Reinink, G. J. "East Assyrian Historiography in Response to the Rise in Islam: The Case of John Bar. In *Redefining Interaction in the Middle East Since the Rise of Islam,* edited by J. J. Van Ginkel, H. L. Murre-Van den Berg, and T. M. Van Lint. Louvain, Belgium: Peeters, 2005.

Ri, A. Su-Min. *La Caverne des Trésors: Les Deux Recensions Syriaques.* 2 vols. Louvain, Belgium: Peeters, 1987.

Rìbas, Andrés Pérez de. *History of the Triumphs of Our Holy Faith amongst the Most Barbarous and Fierce Peoples of the New World.* Tucson: University of Arizona Press, 1999. First published in 1645.

Rice, Michael. *Egypt's Making.* London: Routledge, 2003.

Roberts, Alice. *The Incredible Human Journey.* London: Bloomsbury, 2009. Reprint, 2010.

Robinson, James M., ed. *The Nag Hammadi Library.* 3rd edition. Leiden, Netherlands: E. J. Brill, 1996.

Róheim, Géza. *Hungarian and Vogul Mythology.* Monographs of the American Ethnological Society 23. Locust Valley, N.Y.: J. J. Augustin, 1954.

Rohl, David. *Legend: The Genesis of Civilization.* London: Century, 1998.

Rómer, Dr. Flóris. *Műrégészeti Kalauz különös tekintettel Magyarországra.* Pest, Hungary: Nyomatott Emich Gusztáv Magy. Akad. Nyomdásznál, 1866.

Roscoe, the Reverend John. *The Baganda: An Account of Their Native Customs and Beliefs.* London: Macmillan, 1911.

Rosenmüller, E. F. C. *The Biblical Geography of Central Asia.* Translated by Rev. N. Morren. Edinburgh: Thomas Clark, 1836.

Roux, Georges. *Ancient Iraq.* Harmondsworth, Middlesex, UK: Penguin, 1966. Reprint, 1980.

Rubtsov, Vladimir V. "Tracking the Alien Astroengineers." *RIAP Bulletin* 4, no. 4 (October–December 1998).

Russell, James R. *Zoroastrianism in Armenia.* Cambridge, Mass.: Harvard University Press, 1987.

Sagan, Carl, and Ann Druyan. *Comet.* London: Michael Joseph, 1985.

Sale, George. *The Koran, Commonly Called the Alcoran of Mohammed.* 2 vols. London: C. Ackers for J. Wilcox, 1734. Editions consulted: vol. I—London: J. Walker, 1812; vol. 2—Philadelphia: Thomas Wardle, 1833.

Santillana, Giorgio de, and Hertha von Dechend. *Hamlet's Mill: An Essay on Myth and the Frame of Time.* Boston: Gambit, 1969. Reprint, Jaffrey, N.H.: David R. Godine, 1977.

Šatavičius, Egidijus. "Brommian (Lyngby) Finds in Lithuania." *Lietuvos archeologija* 25 (2004): 17–45.

Sauer, James A. "The River Runs Dry." *Biblical Archaeology Review* 22, no. 4 (July– August 1996): 52–54, 57, 64.

Sayce, A. E. "Two Accadian Hymns." In *Records of the Past,* vol. 11, *Assyrian Texts,* edited by S. Birch, 130–32. London: Samuel Bagster, 1878.

Schirmer, Wulf. "Some Aspects of Building at the 'Aceramic-neolithic' Settlement of Çayönü Tepesi." *World Archaeology* 21, no. 3 (1990): 363–87.

Schmidt, Klaus. "Boars, Ducks, and Foxes: The Urfa Project 99." *Neo-Lithics* 3, no. 99 (2002): 12–15.

———. "Death Cult Temple and Bog Bodies of Ireland." Television interview by Dr. Graham Phillip. *Ancient X-Files,* National Geographic Channel, 2012.

———. *Göbekli Tepe: A Stone Age Sanctuary in South-eastern Anatolia,* Berlin, Germany: ex oriente e.V., 2012.

———. "Göbekli Tepe and the Early Sites of the Urfa Region: A Synopsis of New Results and Current Views." *Neo-Lithics* 1, no. 1 (2002): 9–11.

———. "Göbekli Tepe Excavations 2005." In *Kazı sonuçları toplantısı 2 cilt, Canakkale 2006,* 97–110. Ankara, Turkey: Kültür ve Turizm Bakanlığı Dösim Basımevi, 2007.

———. "Göbekli Tepe, Southeastern Turkey. A Preliminary Report on the 1995–1999 Excavations." *Paléorient* 26, no. 1 (2000): 45–54.

———. "Göbekli Tepe—the Stone Age Sanctuaries: New Results of Ongoing Excavations with a Special Focus on Sculptures and High Reliefs." *Documenta Praehistorica* 37 (2010): 239–56.

———. *Sie bauten die ersten Tempel: Das rätselhafte Heiligtum der Steinzeitjäger.* Munich, Germany: C. H. Beck, 2006.

———. "The 2003 Campaign at Göbekli Tepe (Southeastern Turkey)." *Neo-Lithics* 2/03 (2003): 2–8.

Schmidt, Klaus, and Oliver Dietrich. "A Radiocarbon Date from the Wall Plaster of Enclosure D of Göbekli Tepe." *Neo-Lithics* 2, no. 10 (2010): 82–83.

Schoch, Robert. *Forgotten Civilization: The Role of Solar Outbursts in Our Past and Future.* Rochester, Vt.: Inner Traditions, 2012.

Schodde, the Reverend George H. *The Book of Enoch.* Andover, Hampshire, UK: Warren F. Drapper, 1882.

Segal, J. B. *Edessa: "The Blessed City."* Oxford: Oxford University Press, 1970.

Seth, Dr. Mesrob Jacob. *Armenians in India ("Hindoos in Armenia").* Calcutta, India: Armenian Church Committee of Calcutta, 1982.

Settegast, Mary. *Plato Prehistorian.* Cambridge, Mass.: Rotenberg Press, 1986. Reprint, Hudson, N.Y.: Lindisfarne Press, 1990.

Shea, David, and Anthony Troyer. *The Dabistán; or, School of Manners: Translated from the Original Persian.* Vols. 1 & 3. Paris: Benjamin Duprat; London: Allen and Co., 1843.

Shtrunov, Alexander, "The Origin of Haplogroup I1-M253 in Eastern Europe." *Russian Journal of Genetic Genealogy* 1, no. 2 (2010): 1–11.

Shu-P'Ing, Teng. "The Original Significance of Bi Disks: Insights Based on Liangzhu Jade Bi with Incised Symbolic Motifs." *Journal of East Asian Archeology* 2, no. 1–2 (2000): 165–94.

Silva, Francisco vaz da. *Archaeology of Intangible Heritage.* New York: Peter Lang, 2008.

Smith, George. *The Chaldean Account of Genesis.* New York: Scribner, Armstrong, 1876.

Smith, William. *Smith's Bible Dictionary.* Philadelphia: John C. Winston, 1884.

Solecki, Ralph S., Rose L. Solecki, and Anagnostis P. Agelarakis. *Proto-Neolithic Cemetery in Shanidar Cave.* College Station: Texas A&M University, 2004.

Solecki, Rose. "Predatory Bird Rituals at Zawi Chemi Shanidar." *Sumer* 33 (1977): 42–47.

Solecki, Rose L., and Ralph S. Solecki. "The Zagros Proto-Neolithic and Cultural Developments in the Near East." In *Proto-Neolithic Cemetery in Shanidar Cave.* Austin: Texas A&M University, 2004.

Speiser, E. A. *Genesis.* 2nd edition. New York: Doubleday, 1978.

Spence, Lewis. *The Magic and Mysteries of Mexico.* London: Rider, 1922.

Stanford, Dennis J., and Bruce A. Bradley. *Across Atlantic Ice: The Origins of America's Clovis Culture.* Berkeley: University of California Press, 2012.

Steadman, Sharon R., and Gregory McMahon, eds. *The Oxford Handbook of Ancient Anatolia: 10,000–323 BCE.* New York: Oxford University Press, 2011.

Strabo. *Geography.* Translated by H. L. Jones. Cambridge, Mass.: Harvard University Press; London: Wm. Heinemann, 1917–1932.

Straus, Lawrence Guy, Berit Valentin Eriksen, Jon M. Erlandson, and David R. Yesner, eds. *Humans at the End of the Ice Age.* New York: Springer, 1996.

Strecker, W., and H. Kiepert. *Beiträge zur geographischen erklärung des rückzuges der zehntausend durch das armenische hochland.* Berlin: Dietrich Reimer, 1870.

Stroumsa, Guy G. *Another Seed: Studies in Gnostic Mythology.* Leiden, Netherlands: E. J. Brill, 1984.

Surovell, Todd A., Vance T. Holliday, Joseph A. M. Gingerich, et al. "An Independent Evaluation of the Younger Dryas Extraterrestrial Impact Hypothesis." *PNAS* 106, no. 43 (2009): 18155–58.

Tabakow, Philip. "Reflections on a Fulbright Year in Bahrain." *Bridgewater Review* 25, no. 1, (June 2006): Article 7.

Takala, H. *The Ristola Site in Lahti and the Earliest Postglacial Settlement of South Finland.* Lahti, Finland: Lahti City Museum, 2004.

Tavernier, Giovanni Battista. *Viaggi nella Turchia, nella Persia, e nell' Indie.* Rome: Giuseppe Corvo, 1688.

Tedlock, Dennis. *Popol Vuh: The Mayan Book of the Dawn of Life.* New York: Touchstone/Simon & Schuster, 1985, 1996.

Thorsson, Edred. *Futhark: A Handbook of Rune Magic.* New York: Weiser, 1984.

Trifonov, V. A., et al. "The Dolmen Kolikho, Western Caucasus: Isotopic Investigation of Funeral Practice and Human Mobility." *Proceedings of the 6th International Radiocarbon and Archaeology Symposium* 54, no. 3–4 (2012): 761–69.

Tripković, B., M. Milić, and S. Shackley. "Obsidian in the Central Balkans." *Abstracts Book of 13th Annual Meeting of the European Association of Archaeologists,* 163–79, September 18–23, 2007, Zadar, Croatia.

Turner, John D., and Orval S. Wintermute, trans. "Allogenes." In *The Nag Hammadi Library,* edited by J. M. Robinson. 3rd edition. Leiden, Netherlands: E. J. Brill, 1996.

Uyanik, Muvaffak. *Petroglyphs of South-eastern Anatolia.* Graz, Austria: Akademishe Druck- u. Verlagsanstalt, 1974.

Verhoeven, Marc. "Person or Penis? Interpreting a 'New' PPNB Anthropomorphic Statue from the Taurus Foothills." *Neo-Lithics* 1, no. 1 (2001): 8–9.

Vita Adae et Evae, see "The Books of Adam and Eve." Charles, 1913.

Vogel, J. C., and H. T. Waterbolk. "Groningen Radiocarbon Dates V." *Radiocarbon* 6 (1964): 349–69.

Walker, R. A., "The Real Land of Eden." *Still Trowelling: Newsletter of the Ancient and Medieval History Book Club* 11 (ca. 1986).

Walter, Mariko Namba, and Eva Jane Neumann Fridman. *Shamanism: An Encyclopedia of World Beliefs, Practices, and Culture,* vol. 1. Google e-book: ABC-CLIO, 2004.

Warren, William. *Paradise Found.* London: Sampson Row, Marston, Searle, and Rivington, 1885.

Whiston, William. *The Works of Flavius Josephus.* London and New York: George Routledge, 1873.

White, Gavin. *Babylonian Star-lore.* London: Solaria, 2007.

Widengren, George. *Die Religionen Irans.* Stuttgart: Kohlhammer, 1965.

Wiggermann, F. A. M. "Mythological Foundations of Nature." In *Natural Phenomena: Their Meaning, Depiction and Description in the Ancient Near East,* edited by D. J. W. Meijer. Amsterdam: Royal Netherlands Academy, 1992.

Wigram, W. A., and Edgar T. A. Wigram. *The Cradle of Mankind.* London: Adam and Charles Black, 1914.

Williams, E. Leslie. *Spirit Tree: Origins of Cosmology in Shintô Ritual at Hakozaki.* Landham, Md.: University Press of America, 2007.

Williams, John. *Two Essays on the Geography of Ancient Asia, etc.* London: John Murray, 1829.

Wintermute, O. S., trans. "Book of Jubilees." In *The Old Testament Pseudepigrapha,* vol. 2, edited by J. H. Charlesworth. London: Darton, Longman and Todd, 1985.

Wittke, James H., James C. Weaver, Ted E. Bunch, et al. "Evidence for Deposition of 10 Million Tonnes of Impact Spherules across Four Continents 12,800 Y Ago." *PNAS* 110, no. 23 (May 20, 2013): E2088–97.

Yakar, Jak. "Anatolian Chronology and Terminology." In *The Oxford Handbook of Ancient Anatolia,* edited by S. R. Steadman and G. McMahon. New York: Oxford University Press, 2011.

Yardimci, Nurettin. *Mezopotamya'ya açilan kapi Harran.* Istanbul, Turkey: Ege Yayın Yılı, 2008.

Yardin, Leon. *The Tree of Light: A Study of the Menorah, the Seven-branched Lampstand.* Vol. 1. London: East and West Library, 1971.

Yates, W. *Hindustání and English.* Calcutta, India: Baptist Mission Press, 1847.

Yeshurun R., G. Bar-Oz, and M. Weinstein-Evron. "The Role of Foxes in the Natufian Economy: A View from Mount Carmel, Israel." *Before Farming: The Archaeology and Anthropology of Hunter-gatherers* 3 (2009): 1–15.

Young, Robert. *Young's Literal Translation of the Bible.* UK: Greater Truth Publishers, 2005. (Originally published in 1898.)

Zaehner, Robert Charles. *Zurvan: A Zoroastrian Dilemma.* Oxford: Clarendon Press, 1955. Reprint, New York: Biblo and Tannen, 1972.

Zaliznyak, Leonid. "The Archaeology of the Occupation of the East European Taiga Zone at the Turn of the Palaeolithic-Mesolithic." *Archaeologia Baltica* 7 (2006): 94–108.

Zick, Michael. "Der älteste Tempel der Welt." *bild der wissenschaft* 8 (2000): 60–66.

Zoega, Geir T. *A Concise Dictionary of Old Icelandic.* Oxford: Oxford University Press, 1910.

Zubov, Aleksandr. *Sungir: antropologicheskoe issledovanie.* Moscow: Izdat. Nauka, 1984.

ABOUT THE AUTHOR

Andrew Collins is a historical writer and explorer living in the United Kingdom. He is the author of more than a dozen books that challenge the way we perceive the past. They include *From the Ashes of Angels* (1996), which establishes that the Watchers of the book of Enoch and the Anunnaki of the Sumerian texts are the memory of a shamanic elite that catalyzed the Neolithic revolution in the Near East at the end of the last ice age; *Gateway to Atlantis* (2000), which pins down the source of Plato's Atlantis to the Caribbean island of Cuba and the Bahamian archipelago; *Tutankhamun: The Exodus Conspiracy* (coauthored with Chris Ogilvie Herald, 2002), which reveals the truth behind the discovery of Tutankhamun's famous tomb; and *The Cygnus Mystery* (2007), which shows that the constellation of Cygnus has been universally venerated as the place of first creation and the entrance to the sky world since Paleolithic times.

In 2008 Andrew and colleague Nigel Skinner Simpson discovered a previously unrecorded cave complex beneath the pyramids of Giza, which has brought him worldwide acclaim. It is a story told in his book *Beneath the Pyramids* (2009).

For more information, go to **www.andrewcollins.com**.

INDEX

Page numbers in *italics* indicate illustrations.